Critical Perspectives on Canadian Theatre in English
volume nine

Space and the
Geographies
of Theatre

Edited by Michael McKinnie

Playwrights Canada Press
Toronto • Canada

Playwrights Canada Press
215 Spadina Avenue, Suite 230, Toronto, Ontario CANADA M5T 2C7
416-703-0013   fax 416-408-3402
orders@playwrightscanada.com • www.playwrightscanada.com

Financial support provided by the taxpayers of Canada and Ontario through the Canada Council for the Arts and the Department of Canadian Heritage through the Book Publishing Industry Development Programme, and the Ontario Arts Council.

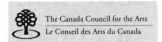

Cover image: Jin-me Yoon, between departure and arrival, 1996/1997. Partial installation view, Art Gallery of Ontario. Video projection, video montage on monitor, photographic mylar scroll, clocks with 3-D lettering, audio. Dimensions variable. Courtesy of the artist and Catriona Jeffries Gallery, Vancouver.
Production Editor/Cover Design: JLArt

Library and Archives Canada Cataloguing in Publication

Space and the geographies of theatre / edited by Michael McKinnie.

(Critical perspectives on Canadian theatre in English ; v 9)
Includes bibliographical references.
ISBN 978-0-88754-808-6

1. Canadian drama (English)--20th century--History and criticism.
2. Geography in literature. 3. Setting (Literature). 4. Canada in literature. I. McKinnie, Michael II. Series.

PS8169.G4S63 2007   C812'.540932   C2007-902791-1

First edition: May 2007
Printed and bound by Hignell Printing at Winnipeg, Canada.

To Harry

Table of Contents

General Editor's Preface

Critical Perspectives on Canadian Theatre in English sets out to make the best critical and scholarly work in the field readily available to teachers, students, and scholars of Canadian drama and theatre. In volumes organized by playwright, region, genre, theme, and cultural community, the series publishes the work of scholars and critics who have, since the so-called renaissance of Canadian theatre in the late 1960s and early 1970s, traced the coming-into-prominence of a vibrant theatrical community in English Canada.

Each volume in the series is edited and introduced by an expert in the field who has selected a representative sampling of the most important critical work on her or his subject since circa 1970, ordered chronologically according to the original dates of publication. Where appropriate, the volume editors have also commissioned new essays on their subjects. Each volume also provides a list of suggested further readings, and an introduction by the volume's editor.

It is my hope that this series, working together with complementary anthologies of plays published by Playwrights Canada Press, Talonbooks, and other Canadian drama publishers, will facilitate the teaching of Canadian drama and theatre in schools, colleges, and universities across the country for years to come. It is for this reason that the titles so far selected for the series—*Aboriginal Drama and Theatre, African-Canadian Theatre, Judith Thompson, Feminist Theatre and Performance, George F. Walker, Theatre in British Columbia, Queer Theatre, Environmental and Site Specific Theatre,* and *Space and the Geographies of Theatre*—are designed to work as companion volumes to a range of Canadian drama anthologies recently published or forthcoming from the country's major drama publishers that complement them: *Staging Coyote's Dream: An Anthology of First Nations Drama in English* (Playwrights Canada, 2003); the two volumes of *Testifyin': Contemporary African Canadian Drama* (Playwrights Canada, 2000, 2003); *Judith Thompson: Late 20ᵗʰ Century Plays* (Playwrights Canada, 2002); the various collections of plays by George F. Walker published by Talonbooks; *Playing the Pacific Province: An Anthology of British Columbia Plays, 1967-2000* (Playwrights Canada, 2001); and other projected volumes. I hope that with the combined availability of these anthologies and the volumes in this series, courses on a variety of aspects of Canadian drama and theatre will flourish in schools and universities within Canada and beyond its borders, and scholars new to the field will find accessible and comprehensive introductions to some of the field's most provocative and intriguing figures and issues.

Finally, the titles selected for *Critical Perspectives on Canadian Theatre in English* are designed to carve out both familiar and new areas of work. It is my intention that the series at once recognize the important critical heritage of scholarly work in the field and attempt to fill in its most significant gaps by highlighting important work from and about marginalized communities, work that has too often been neglected in courses on and criticism of Canadian drama and theatre. In its nationalist phase in the late 1960s and 70s, English-Canadian theatre criticism tended to neglect work by women, by First Nations peoples and people of colour, by Gay, Lesbian, Bi- or Trans-sexual artists, and by those working in politically, geographically, or aesthetically alter-native spaces. While respecting, honouring, and representing important landmarks in Canadian postcolonial theatrical nationalism, *Critical Perspectives on Canadian Theatre in English* also sets out to serve as a corrective to its historical exclusions.

Ric Knowles

Acknowledgements

Perhaps most importantly, I would like to thank those—authors, journals, and presses—who agreed to allow the work collected in this volume to be reprinted, or, in one case, published for the first time. I would also like to thank Ric Knowles and the editors at Playwrights Canada Press for their work on this volume, and on the Critical Perspectives on Canadian Theatre series as a whole. My colleagues in the School of English and Drama at Queen Mary, University of London (especially Bridget Escolme, Jen Harvie, and Nicholas Ridout) provided a welcome combination of intellectual challenge and collegiality that smoothed the production of this collection. Louisa Pearson, an MA student at Queen Mary, particularly deserves my gratitude for her excellent work in helping to prepare the collection. Finally, I would like to thank Ruth Fletcher for her part in making this book possible.

All of the essays included in this volume are published with permission of the copyright holder. Bessai, Diane. "The Regionalism of Canadian Drama." *Canadian Literature* 87 (1980): 7–20; Leggatt, Alexander M. "Playwrights in a Landscape: The Changing Image of Rural Ontario." *Theatre History in Canada/L'Histoire théâtrale au Canada* 1.2 (1980): 135–48; Wagner, Anton. "'A Country of the Soul': Herman Voaden, Lowrie Warrener and the Writing of *Symphony.*" *Canadian Drama/L'Art dramatique canadien* 9.2 (1983): 203–19; Filewod, Alan. "Between Empires: Post-Imperialism and Canadian Theatre." *Essays in Theatre/Études théâtrales* 11.1 (1992): 3–15; Knowles, Ric. "Reading Material: Transfers, Remounts, and the Production of Meaning in Contemporary Toronto Drama and Theatre." *Essays on Canadian Writing* 51–52 (1993–1994): 258–95; Gómez, Mayte. "Healing the Border Wound: *Fronteras Americanas* and the Future of Canadian Multiculturalism." *Theatre Research in Canada/Recherches théâtrales au Canada* 16.1–2 (1995): 26–39; Wallace, Robert. "Theorizing a Queer Theatre: Buddies in Bad Times." In *Contemporary Issues in Canadian Drama.* Ed. Per Brask. Winnipeg: Blizzard, 1995. 136–59; Grace, Sherrill. "Degrees of North: An Introduction." *Staging the North: Twelve Canadian Plays.* Ed. Grace, Sherrill, Eve D'Aeth and Lisa Chalykoff. Toronto: Playwrights Canada 1999. ix–xxv; McKinnie, Michael. "Urban National, Suburban Transnational: Civic Theatres and the Urban Development of Toronto's Downtowns." *Theatre Journal* 53.2 (2001): 253–276; Appleford, Rob. "'No, the Centre Should be Invisible': Radical Revisioning of Chekhov in Floyd Favel Starr's *House of Sonya.*" *Modern Drama* 45.2 (2002): 246–58; Hurley, Erin. "Theatre as National Export: On Being and Passing in the United States." *Performing National Identities: International Perspectives on Contemporary Canadian Theatre.* Ed. Sherrill Grace and Albert-Reiner Glaap. Vancouver: Talonbooks, 2003.

160–80. Verdecchia, Guillermo. "In the MT Space." *Canadian Theatre Review* 125 (2006): 107–10; Levin, Laura. "TO Live with Culture: Torontopia and the Urban Creativity Script." Commissioned for this volume, 2007.

Appleford is reprinted by permission of the author, *Modern Drama*, the Graduate Centre for the Study of Drama at the University of Toronto, and University of Toronto Press Incorporated (www.utpjournals.com).

Leggatt and Gómez are reprinted by permission of the authors and *Theatre Research in Canada/Recherches théâtrales au Canada*, c/o: the Graduate Centre for the Study of Drama, University of Toronto, 214 College Street, 3rd floor, Toronto, Ontario, M5T 2Z9. Tel: 416-978-7984, fax: 416-971-1378. Email: tric.rtac@utoronto.ca, web: http://www.lib.unb.ca/Texts/TRIC/.

McKinnie is reprinted by permission of *Theatre Journal* and Johns Hopkins University Press.

Michael McKinnie

Introduction. Theatrical Geographies, Geographies of Theatre

by Michael McKinnie

Geography is too important to be left to geographers. (Harvey 116)

For many readers of this volume, geography may prompt memories of sitting at a desk in elementary school, shading in maps of Canada with coloured pencils, each province and territory given its particular hue. When completed, the multi-coloured map (with each provincial capital recorded and Ottawa marked) visually symbolized the way in which the nation wanted to see itself: vivid, diverse, vast in scale yet comprehensible, and, perhaps above all else, unified. Such memories, however, almost certainly fail to do justice to the complexity of Canadian geography—whether now or in the past. It is also too easy to dismiss the symbolism of the multi-coloured map as naively appealing but ultimately inconsequential. Geography in Canada is a complex issue, and is too important to be left only to geographers.

As even a brief encounter with geographical research illustrates, the term "geography" can encompass a diversity of concerns and critical practices. But one thing it has not tended to address is theatre. This volume attempts, at least in part, to fill that gap. During the past three decades, English-language Canadian theatre scholarship has become increasingly concerned with the spaces of performance in Canada. This concern has been reflected in two key ways: first, in a critical interest in theatre practices that appear to engage the geography (however defined) of Canada itself; second, in the way in which individual instances of contemporary Canadian theatre scholarship, when read together over time, coalesce into distinct geographies of the many social practices (some theatrical and some not) that mutually constitute Canadian performance. As a way of introducing the contributions that elaborate these concerns, then, it is worth asking several key questions. Why geography? What kinds of geographies? And what might these geographies reveal?

Why Geography?

It is important to distinguish between geography as academic discipline and geography as critical practice. The essays in this collection are better placed in the latter context. Geographical research may emerge from a variety of disciplines beyond that explicitly named "geography," including history, sociology, political studies, and even theatre studies. At the simplest level, geographical research seeks to analyze the spatiality of human and non-human phenomena over time. Within this very broad critical remit, a host of different lineages have emerged. The tradition that most accords with popular conceptions of geography is, perhaps, physical geography, which attempts to account for the physical features of the earth through such fields as landscape ecology, oceanography, and climatology. Human geography, in turn, includes a great range of enterprises that attempt to understand the spatio-temporality of human practices (often in relation to non-human elements of the environment). These fields include economic geography, historical geography, environmental geography, political geography, and cultural geography, to name but a minority (see Livingstone for more information on the history of geography as a research endeavour).

As even the brief list above indicates, two of the more salutary features of modern geographical research are its diversity and its potential utility across academic disciplines. Indeed, a number of the essays in this collection reflect the extent to which theatre studies writ large has increasingly drawn upon geography in order to engage the places of performance (examples of this interest within theatre studies internationally include Chaudhuri and Fuchs, Kobialka, Kruger, McAuley, Tompkins, Wiles). Most of the spatial literature engaged by theatre scholars betrays no explicit interest in performance, yet, as a result of its (often innovative and occasionally ham-fisted) critical appropriation by theatre scholars, the purchase of geographical research within theatre studies has never been greater. But the extent to which the essays in this collection exemplify, and contribute to, trends in international performance scholarship is not the only reason for framing them as geographical—the relevance of geography also arises from the distinct development of English-language Canadian theatre itself, and the particular interests of the contemporary critics who have analyzed it.

While the explicit use of geographical scholarship within Canadian theatre research is a relatively recent phenomenon, the presence of geographical concerns in Canadian theatre practice and criticism is more longstanding. For example, Marc Lescarbot's *The Theatre of Neptune in New France* (1606), the first European performance in what would become Canada, might be described as an environmental pageant, having been staged on the water and shore of the Bay of Fundy for an audience of French and Aboriginal spectators. As Alan Filewod observes, the performance was "a symbolic ritual that enacted the incorporation of this vast and (to the European eye) savage wilderness into the template of the French cultural imaginary" (*Performing Canada*, xii). Filewod notes that this performance was subsequently recuperated by English-language Canadian theatre scholars during the 1970s and 1980s as a founding event of Canadian theatre, and it is arguable that part of its appeal lies in the way in which *The Theatre of Neptune in New France* chimed with an emerging critical interest in Canadian theatre's relationship with the natural environment (an interest that also led to renewed attention to the work of early twentieth century stage artists like Merrill Denison, Gwen Pharis Ringwood, and Herman Voaden). Critics often employed a geographical calculus as they sought to define Canadian theatre's national distinctiveness vis-à-vis the United States and the United Kingdom and to highlight the regional diversity of theatre practice within Canada. While interest in the natural landscapes of Canadian theatre waned during the 1980s, for both practitioners and critics, it would be a mistake to assume that this implied a decline in critical interest in the spaces of Canadian theatre. Instead, it signalled the way in which the geographies of Canadian theatre had begun to multiply.

Geographies of Canadian Theatre

I want to suggest that the geographies of Canadian theatre offered by the essays in this collection are best grouped into three areas: environmental geography, political geography, and cultural geography. This is not to deny the possibility that these contributions may also offer other geographies, or that they may only be confined to one category (there is undoubtedly crossover between all three areas, and particularly between political geography and cultural geography). But as a way of accounting for changes in the spaces of Canadian theatre practice and criticism over time, these three areas predominate, and they are productive ways to organize the dominant critical practices that feature in this volume.

Environmental Geographies

Environmental geography is primarily concerned with the spatial organization of human activity and the relationship between this activity and the ecology of the physical environment. If, as Filewod argues in his essay in this volume "[t]he search for 'true Canadianism' has always been an imperative project of Canadian theatre"—for practitioners, policy-makers, and critics—it is not surprising to find an interest in the element of Canada that is impossible to replicate elsewhere, and which, therefore, might be considered a marker of national distinctiveness: the physical environment. Both Alexander Leggatt's "Playwrights in a Landscape: The Changing Image of Rural Ontario" (1980) and Anton Wagner's "'A Country of the Soul': Herman Voaden, Lowrie Warrener and the Writing of *Symphony*," (1983) are concerned with the way in which the natural landscape (as opposed to the built environment) served as source material for a number of Canadian theatre practitioners during the twentieth century. For Leggatt, writing in only the second volume of the journal *Theatre History in Canada* (which would later become *Theatre Research in Canada*), Canadian theatre's preoccupation with the rural landscape constitutes a defining feature of the national drama, and is the geographical criterion that allows the construction of a dramatic heritage that can link artists like Denison, writing in the 1920s, with Voaden (1930s), Robertson Davies (1940s and 1950s), James Reaney (1960s and 1970s), and collective creations such as Theatre Passe Muraille's *The Farm Show* (1970s). For Wagner, Voaden and Warrener's attempt to refine stage practices (which became known as "symphonic expressionism") that adequately represented the physical and mythical elements of the Canadian landscape is emblematic of Canadian theatre's use of the natural environment to mark out its indigeneity. Sherrill Grace's "Degrees of North," (1999) which introduces the collection of plays she edited with Eve D'Aeth and Lisa Chalykoff entitled *Staging the North: Twelve Canadian Plays*, picks up this environmental theme nearly two decades later. Grace shares Leggatt's and Wagner's interest in the ways in which Canadian theatre has represented the country as a northern nation, and, at least to some extent, rooted the distinctiveness of both the country and its drama in this nordicity. But Grace also reflects the emphasis on representational plurality that grew within Canadian theatre criticism during the 1980s and 1990s. She is concerned not with the singular "North" but with plural "Norths," the production of which may occur anywhere in Canada, and which, she argues, offer an inclusive geography that can register but still bridge the diversity of the nation.

Political Geographies

Political geography is primarily concerned with the relationship between political units, institutions, and groups. Two issues arising from political geography are particularly relevant within the context of this collection. First: how the political territories that circumscribe Canadian performance might be understood. Second: how social agents (who may include both theatre practitioners and state policy-makers) attempt, often anxiously, to exercise cultural sovereignty within and across these political territories.

It is in the first context that Diane Bessai's "The Regionalism of Canadian Drama" (1980) is particularly significant. While the environmental strand of Canadian theatre criticism has undoubtedly been concerned with definite localities or landscapes, the value of analyzing these environments has often been transposed to a national level: one looked at representations of rural Ontario, for example, because it revealed something greater about the nation as a whole. Bessai breaks with this national calculus of theatrical value by redefining the political geography of the theatre she examines. She advocates a regional analysis of Canadian theatre that, in her view, can best account for the geographical and post-colonial conditions from which it emerged, and the decentralized industrial structure it assumed. Bessai prompts challenging questions about the territoriality of Canadian theatre that continue today (ones that are engaged in a number of pieces in this volume). How do we define the political geography of English-language Canadian theatre? Is it national? Is it regional? Is it local? Is it rural? Is it urban? Is it northern or southern, eastern or western? Is it imperial, post-imperial, colonial, post-colonial, multinational or transnational? While it is possible to territorialize Canadian theatre in any of these ways—and in combinations of them—the critical consequences of doing so are different, and a number of the essays in this collection illustrate this fact.

Alan Filewod's "Between Empires: Post-Imperialism and Canadian Theatre" (1989) links post-World War II cultural policy and theatrical practice in Canada to a longstanding anxiety over Canada's perception of itself as caught between two political and cultural empires: the United States and the United Kingdom. Filewod argues that "[t]he evolutionary patterns of Canadian theatre and drama in the twentieth century can be read as the expression of a post-colonial impulse that failed to transcend the contradictions of colonialism," with the consequence that the desire to locate a "true Canadianism" can never be fulfilled.

My own "Urban National, Suburban Transnational: Civic Theatres and the Urban Development of Toronto's Downtowns" (2001) is concerned with Canadian theatre's negotiation of economic transnationalism and urban political economy. The changing terms of this negotiation, I argue, can be measured in civic theatres like Toronto's St. Lawrence Centre (built in the late 1960s) and North York's Ford Centre for the Performing Arts (built in the early 1990s, and now known as the Toronto Centre for the Performing Arts). The dominant civic ideology of Toronto in the late 1960s was different from that of today, and theatre has been implicated in this change. Put simply, at the time of the Centennial in 1967, Toronto saw itself primarily as part of the nation. Today, Toronto sees itself primarily as part of the globe and its civic self-fashioning has changed to reflect this fact. Civic theatres in Toronto are effective indices of the city's attempts to adapt geographically and ideologically to economic forces over which it has had decreasing influence, while attempting to construct a plausible, if not always consistent, civic narrative (for an extended treatment of these issues, see my *City Stages: Theatre and Urban Space in a Global City*).

Erin Hurley, in "Theatre as National Export: On Being and Passing in the United States" (2003), also considers the geography of Canadian theatre in the context of economic and cultural globalization. She focuses, however, on the way in which the Canadian state enlists Canadian theatre as part of the country's self-promotion around the world. What counts as Canadian theatre, she asks, when the category of nation is no longer dominant or determinant? Hurley argues that globalization has intensified the extent to which Canadian policy-makers have emphasized Canadian theatre's "representative function" outside Canada (what it tells other countries about being Canadian). This, she suggests, has come at the expense of its "actantial function" (its potential to act with material effect within a transnational political economy).

Cultural Geographies

Cultural geography focuses on the relationship between place, subjectivity, representation, and power. It is the branch of academic geography that has seen the greatest growth during the past four decades, and it is perhaps not surprising that the largest group of essays in this collection fits within a cultural remit. The importance of cultural geography should not only be measured through its growth as a research field, however, but also through the extent to which it indicates a concern within Canadian theatre scholarship about how the complexities of theatrical production, reception, and circulation may be spatialized.

This collection's first example of a cultural geography of Canadian theatre is Ric Knowles' "Reading Material: Transfers, Remounts, and the Production of Meaning in Contemporary Toronto Drama and Theatre" (1993–94). Through an analysis of several larger-scale remounts of (at least initially) transgressive productions during the 1980s and early 1990s, Knowles invites consideration of how the sites of performance—and the way audiences are invited to engage those sites—condition the production of meaning within theatre events. Knowles examines the ways in which both semantic and performative efficacy are geographically contingent: change the site of performance, change the meaning and politics of that performance (both within the theatre and within the broader public sphere through which that theatre circulates).

Mayte Gómez shares a similar concern with the way in which the site of performance becomes a nexus for the negotiation of dramaturgy and cultural politics in "Healing the Border Wound: *Fronteras Americanas* and the Future of Canadian Multiculturalism" (1995). She also introduces an important concern with spaces of subjectivity and cultural difference (a concern that arises again, albeit in different ways, in essays by Robert Wallace, Rob Appleford, and Guillermo Verdecchia that are discussed below). Gómez argues that Canada is constituted through continental and individual borders, and that the material effects of borders can be found both in the lived experience of its people and in its psychogeography. When performed at Toronto's Tarragon Theatre, where affluent white audiences have tended to predominate, Verdecchia's *Fronteras Americanas* (whose ambiguous opening line, it is worth recalling, is "Here we are" [*Fronteras* 19]) performs an intercultural geography in which the theatre space becomes the site through which issues of migration, diaspora, language, identity, and race can not only be engaged, but a new intercultural, transcontinental geography of Canada might begin to be imagined.

In "Theorizing a Queer Theatre: Buddies in Bad Times" (1995), Robert Wallace suggests that performance sites can come to embody the subjectivity of the theatre companies that occupy them—in this case Toronto's major queer theatre company, Buddies in Bad Times. Wallace explores the implications of Buddies' move to larger, newly renovated premises at 12 Alexander Street in the mid-1990s (the site had previously been occupied by the now-defunct Toronto Workshop Productions). Although the move brought the theatre into closer physical proximity to the heart of Toronto's gay and lesbian community at Church and Wellesley streets, Wallace argues that the symbolic geography of the move actually distanced the company from the dominant subjectivites of gender and sexuality it primarily negotiated: the move to 12 Alexander Street amplified the company's distance from Toronto's politically and theatrically dominant straight community, but it also consolidated Buddies' shift away from the city's gay and lesbian mainstream to a more emphatically queer sexual and theatrical politics.

Rob Appleford examines the circulation of dramaturgical models across cultures, (First) Nations, and territories in "'No, the Centre Should be Invisible': Radical Revisioning of Chekhov in Floyd Favel Starr's *House of Sonya*" (2002). Appleford argues that Floyd Favel Starr's appropriation of Anton Chekhov's *Uncle Vanya* complicates and blurs the familiar cultural-geographical axes through which Aboriginal theatre is often defined: as either traditional/local or contemporary/international. Favel Starr's *House of Sonya* played in a Regina venue sympathetic to Aboriginal artists and cross-cultural experimentation, and the performance mixed Aboriginal, English, and Russian vernacular and stage objects. Appleford suggests that Favel Starr's production elaborated a vision of cultural circulation as a kind of radical transplantation, resulting in a hybrid theatrical practice rooted in multiple times and places of cultural production and reception.

"In the MT Space" (2006), Guillermo Verdecchia's contribution to this collection, shares with other contributors (particularly Laura Levin, below, and McKinnie) a concern for the demands placed by the urban environment on theatrical production. Unlike other contributors, however, Verdecchia focuses on the ways in which Canadian cities accommodate an intensity of cultural difference and intercultural negotiation that the theatre practised in those cities frequently does not. Verdecchia argues that there is a disjuncture between Canada's urban publics and its theatrical publics: if Canadian theatre is to be a space for healthy public encounter (here Verdecchia intriguingly echoes the thinking of urban theorist Richard Sennett), then it cannot foreclose the cultural diversity of the urban public in which it resides. Furthermore, when it makes diverse urban citizenship visible in performance, it needs to do so in ways that expand upon the familiar—and verging on the hoary— dramaturgy of the "ethnic family drama."

Finally, Laura Levin's "TO Live with Culture: Torontopia and the Urban Creativity Script" (2007), which was commissioned for this volume, focuses on the way that the city of Toronto has increasingly mobilized urban performances that were largely created outside dominant cultural institutions (and outside dominant theatrical forms) as part of civic policy-making and self-promotion. In recent years Toronto has perceived itself as a city in decline, and, Levin argues, the arts have become appealing markers of a "creative city" that might attract the high-status tourists and businesspeople that are desirable within a transnational economy. Levin also illustrates the fact that undertaking an urban cultural geography encourages the consideration of more performance practices than theatre alone. Theatre is an important part of the contemporary urban performance ecology, but it is only one element.

Critical Efficacy

What do these geographies of Canadian theatre actually reveal, then? The three broad geographies outlined above emerge from a synchronic consideration of the essays in this volume, extracting themes that cross the historical scope of the collection. But it is worth considering them diachronically as well, according to the chronology in which the essays were originally published (this is, after all, the way the book is organized, and organizing it in this way reveals things about the development of Canadian theatre criticism). Furthermore, it is worth considering briefly what gaps appear in this collection, and what the significance of these might be.

Considering the essays in this collection both chronologically and cumulatively, a number of critical trajectories become clear. I do not want to suggest that the shifts identified here indicate a move to an ever-better critical practice. Quite the opposite, in fact: one of the benefits of a collection like this is the ability to understand how work that was relevant in its own time and place might be generative, albeit in different ways, today. Nonetheless, it is worth outlining how some of the geographical concerns of Canadian theatre criticism have changed over time:

> • There has been a shift in emphasis from Canadian theatre's negotiation of the natural environment to its negotiation of the built environment. This has been accompanied by a change in focus from rural landscapes to urban landscapes.

> • More recent criticism is less likely to focus on the representation of the environment in the work of individual practitioners or companies, and more likely to focus on the environment as a material condition of theatrical production and reception. As part of this, the way in which theatre intervenes in the environment as a political and economic enterprise has become increasingly important.

> • The political-geographical axes of analysis have changed to some degree. Whereas the dominant axes in the 1970s and early 1980s were often national and regional, there is a growing trend toward the local and transnational. Furthermore, critics regularly explore the ways in which these axes are mutually constitutive rather than oppositional, and highlight the extent to which the boundary between them is porous.

> • There has, undoubtedly, been an increasing concern with the geographies of subjectivity and cultural difference since the late 1980s. This often arises from a sense that the cultural composition of Canada has changed considerably during the past four decades (particularly in its cities), but that theatre practice and criticism has sometimes struggled to accommodate, and account for, this diversity. Geography becomes a way to redress this imbalance.

> • Arguably, the centrality of theatre itself within Canadian theatre studies has diminished as critics attempt to take on board issues with which theatre scholars have historically not been terribly concerned. Sometimes this involves placing Canadian theatre within a wider context of other, non-theatrical performance practices (both artistic and social). Other times this involves considering practices that are neither theatre nor performance. Geography, then, denotes an increasingly interdisciplinary form of critical practice.

It is also worth drawing attention to some gaps in this collection. There are at least two that arise immediately: the temporal gap in its chronology, and other work that might be relevant to the purview of the volume but that is not included here. Readers will notice that there is a nine-year gap between Wagner and Filewod. The simple explanation for this could be that nothing of geographical interest was published during this period. This justification, however, would be slightly misleading. In the first instance, Robert Wallace published "Writing the Land Alive: The Playwrights' Vision in English Canada" (1985) in *Contemporary Canadian Theatre: New World Visions*, a collection edited by Anton Wagner. [1] Although relevant to this book's remit it is not included because of the inclusion of a later piece by Wallace that introduced a new spatial concern (subjectivity and sexual politics) rather than extending an existing one (the land). The second explanation for the temporal gap is more interesting, if somewhat propositional. Those who either experienced, or have studied, the conditions under which Canadian theatre was produced in the 1980s will be aware of a growing attention, within the theatre industry at the time, paid to the conditions of the theatre sites in which practitioners were working, and the increasing scarcity of such sites as the scale of the industry grew. Discussion and advocacy related to this topic can be found in the pages of *Canadian Theatre Review* during the 1980s (see, for example: Czarnecki; Peel; Stuart), and there was a series of reports and plans attempting to respond to these concerns (with varying degrees of success) emerging from theatre organizations, bodies of inquiry, and government departments (see, for example: Gelber; Toronto). While many theatre academics participated in these debates, it is arguable that Canadian theatre criticism had not yet developed a critical apparatus that could deal with some of the intellectual implications of these and other spatial problems in a sustained way (as opposed to the practical imperatives involved, of which many working in both professional theatre and universities were all too aware). This is not to say that Canadian theatre criticism fully possesses this critical capacity now, or that any field ever could—but it is plausible that the interval between the spatial issues of the 1980s and their later theorization can be explained not only because of the frequent time lag between events and their analysis, but also because such analysis called for the acquisition and deployment of new, or at least unfamiliar, critical tools.

There is also criticism relevant to this collection that is not included here because it has been reprinted in other volumes in the Critical Perspectives on Canadian Theatre in English series. This work includes: Robert Nunn's "Spatial Metaphor in the Plays of Judith Thompson" (1989) and Laura Levin's "Environmental Affinities: Naturalism and the Porous Body" (2005), both of which appeared in the Judith Thompson volume edited by Ric Knowles; Marlene Moser's "Reconfiguring Home: Geopathology and Heterotopia in Margaret Hollingsworth's *The House that Jack Built* and *It's Only Hot for Two Months in Kapuskasing*" (2002), which was published in the Theatre in British Columbia volume edited by Ginny Ratsoy; and Rinaldo Walcott's "Dramatic Instabilities: Diasporic Aesthetics as a Question for and about Nation" (2004), which appeared in the African-Canadian Theatre volume edited by Maureen Moynagh. The interests of these essays—which include the spatiality of gender, race, stagecraft, diaspora, and dramaturgy, among other things—only amplify the concerns of those articles comprising this book. Their presence in other volumes in this series is also significant because it demonstrates that Canadian theatre scholarship may be effective in multiple critical contexts; that is, an essay like Nunn's not only provides an insight into the plays of Judith Thompson, the spatiality of its analysis is also productive within a geographical genealogy of Canadian theatre criticism.

The essays comprising this collection demonstrate a welcome diversity of critical interest and critical practice. For me, one of the rewards of editing the volume has been the way in which the theme of the collection allows connections to be drawn between work that otherwise might not be immediately visible. It also illustrates the ways that criticism of Canadian theatre has changed over time, both in terms of its objects of analysis and its methods of analysis. Finally, the contributions collected here demonstrate that Canadian theatre criticism has a healthy contribution to make to geographical investigations of theatre internationally. Geography is too important to be left to geographers, and Canadian theatre criticism shows why.

(2007)

Note

¹ Wallace has considerable expertise related to the development of Canadian theatre as an industry, and both his *Producing Marginality: Theatre and Criticism in Canada* (1990), and "Survival Tactics: Size, Space and Subjectivity in Recent Toronto Theatre" (1991) demonstrate an awareness of some of the spatial challenges that arose within professional theatre in Canada during the 1970s and 1980s. It is also no accident that such concerns registered in the pages of *Canadian Theatre Review* during Wallace's tenure as editor.

Works Cited

Chaudhuri, Una and Elinor Fuchs, eds. *Land/Scape/Theater.* Ann Arbor: U of Michigan P, 2002.

Czarnecki, Mark. "To Serve the Art." *Canadian Theatre Review* 45 (1985): 6–11.

Filewod, Alan. *Performing Canada: The Nation Enacted in the Imagined Theatre. Textual Studies in Canada* 15 (2002).

Gelber, Arthur. "A Personal Assessment of Capital Needs for Facilities Used by the Professional Performing and Visual Arts Community in Metropolitan Toronto and Surrounding Area and Shaw and Stratford Festival Theatres." Ontario Ministry of Citizenship and Culture, 1986.

Grace, Sherrill, Eve D'Aeth and Lisa Chalykoff. *Staging the North: Twelve Canadian Plays.* Toronto: Playwrights Canada, 1999.

Harvey, David. *Spaces of Capital: Towards a Critical Geography.* Edinburgh: Edinburgh UP, 2001.

Kobialka, Michal. "Theatre and Space: A Historiographic Preamble." *Modern Drama* 46.4 (2003): 558–79.

Kruger, Loren. "Theatre, Crime, and the Edgy City in Post-apartheid Johannesburg." *Theatre Journal* 53.2 (2001): 223–52.

Livingstone, David. *The Geographical Tradition: Episodes in the History of a Contested Enterprise.* Oxford: Blackwell, 1992.

McAuley, Gay. *Space in Performance: Making Meaning in the Theatre.* Ann Arbor: U of Michigan P, 1999.

McKinnie, Michael. *City Stages: Theatre and Urban Space in a Global City.* Toronto: U of Toronto P, 2007.

Peel, Bill. "Models for the Future: The Space Crisis in Toronto." *Canadian Theatre Review* 60 (1989): 81–89.

Sennett, Richard. *The Fall of Public Man.* New York: W.W. Norton, 1976.

Stuart, Ross. "A Circle Without a Centre: The Predicament of Toronto's Theatre Space." *Canadian Theatre Review* 38 (1983): 18–24.

Tompkins, Joanne. *Unsettling Space: Contestations in Contemporary Australian Theatre.* Basingstoke, UK: Palgrave Macmillan, 2006.

Toronto Theatre Alliance. Small Theatres Caucus. "Facilities for Small Theatres: The Other Housing Crisis; a Brief Submitted to Mr. Arthur Gelber, Special Advisor to the Minister of Citizenship and Culture to Review Demand for Toronto Arts Facilities." 1986. XZ1 MS A970006. Theatre Centre Archives, University of Guelph Library.

Verdecchia, Guillermo. *Fronteras Americanas.* Toronto: Coach House, 1993.

Wallace, Robert. *Producing Marginality: Theatre and Criticism in Canada.* Toronto: Coach House, 1990.

——. "Survival Tactics: Size, Space and Subjectivity in Recent Toronto Theatre." *Essays in Theatre/Études théâtrales* 10.1 (1991): 5–15.

——. "Writing the Land Alive: The Playwrights' Vision in English Canada." *Contemporary Canadian Theatre: New World Visions.* Ed. Anton Wagner. Toronto: Simon and Pierre, 1985: 69–81.

Wiles, David. *A Short History of Western Performance Space.* Cambridge: Cambridge UP, 2003.

The Regionalism of Canadian Drama [1]

by Diane Bessai

Neither modern Canadian theatre nor modern Canadian dramatic literature is so well-established that one can pronounce on them absolutely at this stage of development. However, for the present the term *regional* is the most descriptively useful: in the past decade, the period which has seen the definite rise of a native Canadian theatre at last, regional activity has made the most identifiable and creative contribution to the movement. Of recent playwrights, Reaney, Cook, Tremblay, Murrell and Glass are among those who write from specifically regional observation and experience. Among theatres and theatre companies such names come to mind as Alberta Theatre Projects, Theatre Passe Muraille, Open Circle, Mermaid, the Globe and the St. John's Mummers as examples of the varied regional voices in the Canadian theatre scene.

As a term, *regional* creates bad vibrations in the collective aesthetic psyche—perhaps second only to the term *provincial*. Certainly I do not use the words synonymously, in as much as the latter suggests subjugation to some central cultural influence or control. Nor need regionalism be regarded, as it often is, as narrow, limited, parochial, backward, out-dated or isolationist. In its positive sense regionalism means rooted, indigenous, shaped by a specific social, cultural and physical milieu. It reflects the past as well as the present and at its best absorbs innumerable influences from beyond its borders, particularly as these have bearing on the informing regional perspective.

Thus no denigration need be implied in the suggestion that the late-developing arts of the modern theatre in Canada have little dependence for their vitality on influences radiating from a particular centre. Canadian theatre in the present day exists in pockets, and while some pockets bulge more than others, there is still no *national* theatre movement per se—at least not one to which we can point as our own special equivalent to Broadway, the West End, or other such models of artistic or commercial success. We do have a National Arts Centre in Ottawa, but from the national point of view this functions only as a theatrical crossroads, insofar as it hosts successful productions mounted in Canadian theatres elsewhere. While the NAC's recently inaugurated policy of country-wide tours of its own permanent companies has been heralded by some as the long overdue beginning of a genuine national theatre, this is to ignore the real dynamic of theatre growth in this country. Another form of irrelevance to the essential reality of Canadian theatre activity is the equally spurious ambition for instant internationalism. This is a peculiarly inverted form of provincialism observable in theatre circles with an ambition to develop exportable productions; ironically the process as observed most recently involves preliminary importation. This happened most conspicuously in Edmonton in 1978 with the controversial hiring of Britisher Peter Coe as artistic director of the Citadel. Coe's avowed internationalism in his choice of programme and players in his first season is a simple sign of that theatre's archaic view of the Canadian scene. In one way this recalls that until the late 1940s professionals usually came from outside the country and that Canada's theatres were touring houses to accommodate them. By now, however, with the notable exceptions of Toronto's O'Keefe Centre and the Royal Alexandra, theatres are no longer committed to road-house policies. Touring comes from regions within the country rather than from outside, and normally the mandate of the regional theatres is not the international market (coming or going in either direction).

The tradition of regionalism in Canadian theatre of course originates in the peculiar geographical and cultural conditions of the colonial and post-colonial era. In the days of the predominance of foreign professionals, such native development of theatre as there was depended on the many dedicated groups of amateurs who developed their own community theatres—which they did virtually in every region of the country. Inevitably provincialism predominated in its most parochial terms. This became evident when the Earl Grey Musical and Dramatic Competitions (held between 1907 and 1911) attempted to provide the community groups with a sense of participation in a national theatrical adventure. Clearly from the participator's point of view such an enterprise appealed to regional rather than national pride, whatever the intentions of the organizers. For example, when the Edmonton Amateur Drama Club won the trophy in 1911 with *The Tyranny of Tears*, there was obvious local satisfaction in the triumph over companies from Toronto, Ottawa and London, because Ontario was then the colonial centre for Western Canada. Further, when Albert E. Nash, the lead in the play, also won the best acting award, there was relish in the adjudicator's comment that the part was played with "such intellectual distinction" that he almost suspected Mr. Nash a professional. From Edmonton's point of view this was no mean praise from Hector Charlesworth, a Toronto drama critic of distinction. The most dazzling compliment of all (quoted admiringly by A. B. Watt in a 1949 series of articles "Old Edmonton Theatre Days" in the Edmonton *Journal)* was that this production "coming from a town as far away as Edmonton [the location for the festival that year was Winnipeg's Walker Theatre], where opportunities for studying the best theatrical models are almost non-existent, came as a genuine surprise."

The question of when local boosterism in a given area turns into genuine and self-confident pride in local achievement would be difficult to answer, but as the community theatre movement grew stronger, particularly in the decade following World War I, the problem of non-existent theatrical models certainly became considerably less acute. Betty Lee, in *Love and Whiskey*, identifies the completion of Hart House at the University of Toronto in 1919 as "the first real sign of the coming amateur boom": its theatre offered over 100 plays between 1921 and 1925 alone. The Winnipeg Community Players, the Vancouver Little Theatre, the Ottawa Drama League and the Edmonton Little Theatre Association were among the many community groups founded in the 1920s. The organization of provincial festivals marked the next phase of development; thus the time was ripe for Lord Bessborough's 1932 invitation of country-wide representatives from the regional amateur groups to meet in Ottawa for discussion of the foundation of the Dominion Drama Festival.

The debate over this development as a positive detriment to the rise of a native Canadian professional theatre still goes on, but certainly, with the decline of the syndicated touring companies in the depression years, a theatre vacuum was filled. Nevertheless in 1933 B.K. Sandwell expressed telling reservations about the organization of a nationwide amateur movement. He thought that the "impelling motive" of "self-conscious patriotism" was a bad start for the serious development of the dramatic arts in Canada. He also feared that amateurism would not provide proper direction for either writers or performers; this "must be competent, original, experienced, creative," he wrote in *Saturday Night.* "It must also be continuous over a considerable period of time" (Lee 113). Hindsight makes it easy to second-guess the specific problems he had in mind: the "pointless socializing" which so disgusted Dora Mavor Moore even back at the time of the Earl Grey competitions, or perhaps the limited aspirations inevitably imposed by the boosterism inherent in competition which in theatre leads to safe choice of play. The failure of the Festival to accommodate itself to experimental theatre was early noted by Laurence Mason in the Toronto *Globe:* there was simply no marking system provided for the proper evaluation of a play such as Herman Voaden's *Rocks,* for example. Years later, in "Ten Years at Play" *(Canadian Literature,* 1969), James Reaney was to note to his dismay and astonishment that for amateur groups he worked with in London, Ontario, the most important rehearsal was the theatrical one—surely a carryover from the competition era.

On the positive side, E.G. Sterndale Bennett, who was a regional adjudicator for the first festival, postulated at the end of the first season that the Dominion Drama Festival could serve as the foundation stone from "which we might erect a glorious edifice of drama, a National Theatre." But this, he added, need not mean "a centralized plant with its difficulties of maintenance and management but, rather, a brotherhood of effort assisted, guided and encouraged by some parent body" (Lee 120). Indeed, the DDF can take a portion of the credit for its part in laying the foundation of certain professional companies within regions where the participating community theatres flourished. In Quebec, Father LeGault's Les Compagnons de St. Laurent was the seedbed of Jean Gascon's Théâtre du Nouveau Monde established in 1952; in the late 1960s two francophone professional groups unabashedly entered and won most of the D.D.F. awards (Gurik's Le Théâtre de la Mandragore and Pierre Voyer's Les Enfants de Voiture).

In English-speaking Canada, the most significant development of a professional theatre company from amateur roots was the Manitoba Theatre Centre; technically this was an amalgamation of the long-established Winnipeg Little Theatre and a new professional company of one season called Theatre 77 founded by John Hirsch and Tom Hendry. The latter were both Winnipeggers who had served their theatrical apprenticeship in the WLT. In his retrospective comments for *Canadian Theatre*

Review (Fall 1974), Hirsch spoke of "the excitement that can come from a theatre that grows out of a community" and Tom Hendry paid strong tribute to the role of the WLT in the new theatre centre development. The whole conception was summed up in Hirsch's account of an interview he had given to Ann Henry of the *Winnipeg Tribune* some four years previously:

> I outlined what I wanted to see happen, not only in Winnipeg but in Canada. I said that Winnipeg needs a theatre centre, a regional theatre with a children's theatre attached and a school which would tour regularly. I said that this Centre would be the first in a series of theatres across the country that would eventually be linked.

Interestingly, this is a professional version of Sterndale Bennett's conception of a decentralized national theatre among the amateur groups. It is extremely important also to note that at the outset MTC was linked to its specific community in several vital ways. As Christopher Dafoe points out in the same *CTR* issue, while production was expanded to make room for first class professionals from outside, the theatre school also expanded to take touring productions to local schools. Also Hirsch recalls how "we constantly went to the community to get extras and good young people for small parts." For several years there was a policy of bringing original material to the stage as well. [2]

Hirsch had a philosophy of community theatre as creating "an organic connection between the audience and what went on stage":

> Even the plays which were not about Winnipeg responded to something close to our audience. Repertoire was always chosen with the community in mind. I didn't mind doing *Arsenic and Old Lace* because I knew the next show would be *Mother Courage*. I knew *The Dybbuk* was not a Canadian play but I also knew that 60 percent of our audience were Jewish and that a lot of Ukrainians in the city would understand this play about peasants, the kind of background from which many of them came.

Unfortunately by the time of this 1974 interview Hirsch had to admit that many of these important connections between the MTC and its audience had begun to fade. He himself left the organization in 1966, although in subsequent years he was a frequent guest director. After the building of the new large theatre on Market Avenue in 1970, the school did not flourish, and it was closed in 1972; nor did regional touring and theatre workshop develop according to the initial hopes of the founders. In recent years the centre has concentrated more and more on traditional repertoire. Nor have smaller, alternative groups developed out of the MTC's initial creative energy as had been the hope in earlier days. Nevertheless, the foundation and the development of the whole idea of a regional centre here is of great importance in modern Canadian theatre history and in its initial conception could well stand as a model for newer regional developments elsewhere. [3] Nevertheless the example of MTC is instructive on the negative as well as the positive side: pride of space seems to encourage conservative tastes among many of the now established Canadian regional theatres, and perhaps, too, the ghosts of the old DDF regional boosterism still enforce conventional rather than experimental standards of theatre excellence. Fortunately, however, there are other forms of regional expression in the theatre, offering healthy signs of truly indigenous contemporary development in Canadian drama.

For a theatre movement to stay alive and develop, it is necessary to go beyond mere conformity, to initiate rather than to imitate. Therefore it is important to consider the process whereby provincial dependency develops into a genuine regional cultural maturity. Recently even Northrop Frye has given his consent to theories about regionalism: in his Henry Marshall Tory lecture at the University of Alberta, "Reflections of a Canadian Humanist" (October 1978), he spoke of a mature Canadian cultural direction as "a decentralizing movement," finding genuine unity the opposite of conformity, and he emphasized that the more specific the literary material, the more universal its application. The negative term for Frye, however, is "localism," for which he rather curiously chooses the contemporary cultural crisis in Quebec as his prime example. Certainly in the colonial phase of the Canadian theatre movement—the Earl Grey Competition phase, for example—the last thing a group wanted to be accused of was localism. But in modern times the term does have a certain positive thrust, Frye notwithstanding. Indeed one might argue that localism in its contemporary theatrical forms is a demonstrably important phase in the establishment of a mature, decentralized culture.

For example, it is not by accident that in the drama, localism is often firmly rooted in various forms of documentary. In many ways Canada is still, as Catharine Parr Traill termed it in 1836, "a matter of fact country." Carl Ballstadt, in his introduction to a collection of nineteenth- and early twentieth-century critical essays, *The Search for English-Canadian Literature,* notes that many of the early literary commentators saw great virtue in work which recognized the need to establish and clarify fact and immediate experience as the basis for literary development in a new country (where the temptation to borrow inappropriately from established traditions from elsewhere was all too strong). In the second half of the twentieth century, in a country with practically no native dramatic tradition of relevance to the modern day, one type of borrowing from European, British and American sources has lent itself both to assimilation and further inventiveness more than any other: European forms of political, epic, and documentary drama—in combination with the American "living newspaper" of the 1930s—have found fruitful soil in several Canadian regions in recent years. In fact, the need to develop such a type of drama in Canada has arisen from the similar cultural conditions which have made documentary theatre popular in regional theatres in Britain. In his book *Post-War British Theatre,* John Elsom has recently noted that

> For the growing regional repertory theatre movement in the 1960s, the local documentaries provided a means of establishing a theatre's identity as part of a town or region, without losing its function as a theatre. (102)

His prime example is Peter Cheeseman's Victoria Theatre at Stoke-on-Trent, where local documentaries have been developed through the careful research of the actors and writers in an effort to focus on working-class themes of this particular community. In regional Britain, local creativity in the theatre has been overshadowed because the transfer and touring systems to and from the West End are the inhibiting factors. The aim of Peter Cheeseman (and those who subsequently took their lead from him, as in Hull, Newcastle and Leeds) was to establish new local theatrical material for new local audiences who otherwise would seldom venture into a theatre at all. In this, of course, he had the model of Joan Littlewood, both in her pre-war Manchester days and the post-war establishment of Theatre Workshop in London's East End.

In Canada, the problem of establishing a theatre's local identity is also a key factor in its success, if, in part, for different reasons. The task is further complicated by the need to establish the identity of the locality itself in dramatic terms. James Reaney pointed to the problem succinctly in his article "Ten Years at Play" when he wrote:

> The tendency in the society in which I lived was to see drama as, first, something somebody else wrote thousands of miles away, and as something that you could evolve physically, as out of a can. (72)

Paul Thompson returned to Canada in 1967 after working with Planchon in France (eventually to become artistic director of Theatre Passe Muraille) with the conviction that imported Broadway and West End plays (or Canadian imitations thereof) were bad business in the typical community theatres which

> try to over-reach themselves with something like *There's a Girl in My Soup* or *The Entertainer* where they're trying to deal with people and problems (not to mention accents) that they've only encountered in other plays or movies, when there is such rich and satisfying and much more immediate material in the living community around them. (qtd. in Johns 31)

To make the living community yield its own material and to proffer a theatrical interpretation and analysis of this material has been the intent of a number of small theatre groups which came into existence in various regions during the 1970s.

Most groups of this type begin as localist and may choose to stay that way: this is particularly true of those that concentrate primarily on collective creations. The Mummers' Troupe of St. John's is a prime example of a company formed with the explicit intention of creating new audiences for theatre, to be drawn through mutual interest in original material of local appeal. In critical comments about the Mummers it has become almost commonplace to point out the flawed qualities of their plays and the inexperience of their actors. Certainly they eschew any obvious ideals of slick professionalism, are very much a company in process, and play for the audience they please most and in a manner they believe reaches that particular audience most effectively. In a July 9, 1975, *Toronto Star* interview, the artistic director Chris Brookes said:

Theatre in Newfoundland is moving away from art-as-art to specific social usefulness. We're very community-development oriented. It's living in Newfoundland, where you're always engaged in a social-cultural emergence. You have to be. You've got to show people themselves before they forget who they are.

The activist bias of the company first emerged in a public way in 1973 when they were soundly condemned on the front page of the Cornerbrook *Western Star* for their show *Gros Mourn*. In this they intruded both on provincial and federal governments during the inauguration of Gros Morne National Park by focussing attention (albeit too late) on the plight of the residents of Sally's Cove, one of the several small coastal communities sacrificed to the project. Breakdown or threats to community traditions have been strong motifs in the Mummers' repertory ever since. (This has been a characteristic form of Newfoundland *angst* since the resettlement projects of the late 1950s.) In 1974 the troupe was invited by the workers of the company town of Buchans to create a play which examined the continuing uncertainty of the community's very existence because of the depleting resources of the mines which are its life-line. In Toronto, *Star* critic Urjo Kareda found the play theatrically "unadventurous" in comparison to the socially-oriented collective creations of Passe Muraille. However, Brookes had already forestalled such an attitude (in the 1975 interview) with his remark that

> The people in Buchans thought it important to do ... because Buchans is symptomatic of a bigger system. At the same time, however, the show is made for Buchans: I'm not interested in saving anyone's soul in Toronto.

From the beginning, tours through both the outports and the interior of Newfoundland have been essential to the Mummers' mandate. Eventually they even managed to compete with perennial Newfoundland bingo fervour and are welcomed wherever they go as a voice of the people. In April 1976 Sandra Gwyn wrote in *Saturday Night* of the response in the logging town of Badger to the *I.W.A. Show,* a production which dealt with an important strike there in 1959:

> In the Town Hall, plastered with pink crepe-paper rosettes left over from the Kinsmen's Dance, I sit down by a pair of loggers and their wives. They're big, impressive people in their fifties, and for quite a while it's hard to tell how they're reacting. When the play gets to the sequences Donna [Butt] worked out, where she plays a striker's wife who changes gradually from a shy homebody to a fiery militant who takes her husband's place on the picket line when he goes to jail, the two women sit bolt upright. Almost before the scene ends, they jump to their feet and start clapping. Then they turn and put their arms around each other.

Still adhering to the philosophy that "Newfoundland frames and motivates us," the Mummers toured *They Club Seals Don't They?* across Canada in 1978; this was a show

designed as much for the road as the home audience, presenting as it did the controversial sealing question to the rest of the country from the Newfoundlander's point of
view. But even here they refused to compromise their home-based production techniques: even the three-ringed circus they made of the Greenpeace mission, while a
rather amateurish, farcical line of attack to those who have more sophisticated views
of satire, could be seen as the proper reflection of the situation for the audiences for
whom the production was initially intended. When the Mummers travel, they are simply inviting others to be an extended Newfoundland audience for an evening.

The Theatre Passe Muraille conception of touring shows is quite different and
with this difference can be seen the possibilities of the wider interest of grassroots or
"localist" theatres. This is to say that the collective creations this company began to
develop under the artistic directorship of Paul Thompson (appointed in 1971) are
intended for varieties of audiences from varieties of locations and walks of life. Their
strongest breakthrough in this direction was in September 1972 with their first
version of *The Farm Show*. That summer the company had been living and working
in the farm community of Clinton, Ontario, with the deliberate intention of creating
a play from their experience. The next year they tried a similar project, although of
urban orientation, in the decaying mining town of Cobalt; *Under the Greywacke* was
the result. In a *Performing Arts Magazine* interview (Winter 1973), Thompson said of
these productions:

> we went right to the people in Clinton and Cobalt and made our play
> out of those people, out of the texture of those people. I keep talking to
> the actors about texture work because one of the things that is missing
> in Canadian Theatre in general is an identifiable base for characters.
> Instead, there's a kind of general base and you see too much of what
> I call movie-acting where, for example, if you want to do a small town
> character, everybody's trying to be Paul Newman in *Hud* instead of
> going out to a small town and sitting around in the corner drugstore,
> finding out how people are there, catching their rhythms and building
> off that. Part of the problem is we're still … well, I guess "culturally
> imperialized" is the phrase the nationalists use.

The attempt "to bring back a kind of living community portrait or photograph"
in these various "essays" of dramatic journalism has stood this company in good stead
on the several occasions when they have gone outside their own region; for example,
they spent the summer of 1975 working in Saskatchewan to create *The West Show,*
consisting of another series of portraits, sketches, historical vignettes through which
they made a highly successful attempt to interpret Saskatchewan rural life. They
caught its radical spirit in politics and the sturdy independence of mind of its farm
people in the face of Saskatchewan's well publicized environmental obstacles. Their
work with Rudy Wiebe—specifically for their dramatic adaptation of Sam Reimer's
Vietnam call from *The Blue Mountains of China*, led to plans for a full scale play in
co-operation with that writer. In April 1977, they presented *Far As the Eye Can See* at
Theatre 3 in Edmonton: here they were able to combine their interpretive talents with

Wiebe's special knowledge of the Alberta political and social scene. The result was a script which examined specific energy issues of the time from both a localist and regional point of view.

During that first summer in Saskatchewan, Passe Muraille also established a fruitful contact with Andy Tahn's 25th Street Theatre House Players in Saskatoon. This company, too, was anxious to develop local material for performance. *If You're So Good Why are You in Saskatoon?* was the piquant title of their apprenticeship collective, a work which, with the help of Thompson's troupe, provided them with the essential experience for this kind of theatre—leading in 1977 to their more ambitious and widely toured *Paper Wheat,* a play about the formation of the wheat co-operatives in the West.

Since 1976 Theatre Network, based in Edmonton, has been developing similar collectives and touring them on a smaller scale; its first was *Two Miles Off,* based on the experience of living in Elnora, a small decaying community in the Red Deer area. Network's most successful and most widely toured show is drawn from observation of life in the burgeoning Tar Sands community of Fort McMurray. *Hard Hats and Broken Hearts* attempts to combine the techniques of the collective vignette format with a specific plot line dealing with some of the social problems brought about by the uprooting of people in a changing environment.

The collective has become increasingly popular in the West. In the fall of 1978, Regina's Globe Theatre toured *Number One Hard* in Saskatchewan, a play developed by the company in collaboration with playwright Rex Deverell. In some ways a challenge to *Paper Wheat,* this work subtitles itself "an investigative documentary on the grain industry" and is a satirical attack against the mismanagement of grain resources. The Globe's experience with this form, however, is of longer standing than that of the other Western companies referred to thus far, and more closely parallels Theatre Passe Muraille's development of the collective documentary play. In the spring of 1971 each theatre presented productions of this type: the Globe opened March 1 in Regina with *Next Year Country* (having first performed it in Prince Albert as a "homecoming" production), a collective compiled by the company in collaboration with writer Carol Bolt, while in April of that year Passe Muraille presented its company-researched play *Doukhobors* in Toronto.

The subsequent history of the Bolt-Globe *Next Year Country* makes an instructive comment on the way in which initial local and regional definitions can prompt broader dramatic patterns. In 1972 Bolt and Theatre Passe Muraille collaborated in a reworking of the script to create *Buffalo Jump* for Toronto performance. A large portion of the revised play deals with the inception of the work camp strike, the organization of the working men in Vancouver and the counter movement of the prime minister's Ottawa office. It also focuses on the human interest of the mass boxcar ride in its various stages before Regina—in the process offering a variety of comic and satiric views of several locales through which the unemployed passed. Caricatures, particularly of R.B. Bennett and Bible Bill Aberhart, are also prominent.

What the play lost in its specifically prairie flavour and historical detail, the new *Buffalo Jump* gained in dramatic shape, particularly through its form of cross-country coverage and its borrowings from agitprop tradition. At the time of the play's publication Carol Bolt said that she was more interested in "myth" than history in any case—here the romantic celebration of the heroic failure of those brought low by the machinations of an autocratic government. In this manner the play also gained something of the energy of the post-October Crisis era, particularly in the guerilla theatre technique of its last scene, as performed in Toronto: instead of staging a full-scale version of the Regina riot of the strikers and the RCMP, a brief scene of violence was quickly terminated by actor policemen who promptly began to hustle an astonished audience out of the theatre door. In 1977 Bolt worked with the Great Canadian Theatre Company in Ottawa to add additional Ottawa material to the script, providing for this audience a specifically local perspective by adding scenes which dealt with the large convergence on Ottawa at the time by eastern workers who planned to join the Westerners in their assault on the Bennett government. The expanded localism of the play during its successive performances was an interesting exercise in the dramatic analysis of an historic national issue from a variety of regional points of view.

Clearly then, localism and various forms of collective creativity are important in themselves to the initiation of indigenous theatre, exemplifying a dynamic relationship integrating actor, director, writer and audience. Yet inasmuch as this type of work energizes new and special interests in the theatre, so does it also provide a proper environment for a new dramatic literature whose chief strength also lies in its regional origins. The point may be illustrated well by reference to certain of the Western regional theatres which have done much to promote the writing of new plays. For example, in the first four years of its existence, Alberta Theatre Projects in Calgary, founded by Douglas Riske and Lucille Wagner in 1972, produced only Canadian plays, most of these commissioned from local writers. [4] The practice of engaging a playwright-in-residence has also been fruitful at ATP. For two years John Murrell worked in Calgary in this capacity, leading to the production of his *A Great Noise, A Great Light* in 1976, a fictional play of the Aberhart era, and *Waiting for the Parade,* 1977, a nostalgic recollection of the Calgary World War II home front.

Rex Deverell's similar association with the Globe has not only led to his development as one of the best writers of young peoples' plays in Canada (for example, *Next Town Nine Miles,* 1976, and *Superwheels,* 1977); he has also achieved some success with his adult play *Boiler Room Suite,* 1977. That the setting for this semi-Absurd work is the basement of an abandoned Regina hotel is certainly not the play's chief point, yet this does nevertheless indicate that regional roots provide the basis for dramatic exploration of contemporary human conditions in the urban world. [5]

There are also several Western playwrights who have responded more individually to the demands generated by regional theatres. Ken Mitchell, for example, combined his talents with Humphrey and the Dumptrucks for the 1975 premiere of *Cruel Tears* at Persephone Theatre, Saskatoon. This prairie folk opera version of the Othello story was performed the following year at the Habitat Festival in Vancouver and the Olympic festival in Montreal, later to be revived by the Vancouver Arts Club for a cross-Canada tour. Mitchell has also worked at the Globe: in 1972 he adapted Arnold Wesker's *Roots* to a Saskatchewan setting, and in 1978 his play *Davin: The Politician* was premiered there. This last is a lively chronicle of Nicholas Flood Davin, founder of the Regina *Leader* and volatile federal M.P. for the Northwest Territories in the post-Riel era.

Sharon Pollock's *Walsh,* a version of the Sitting Bull-in-Canada incident, was first developed at Theatre Calgary in 1973 under the direction of Harold Baldridge and performed at Stratford in revised form the following summer. Pollock has also worked considerably in Vancouver, there too responding to contemporary regional interests in her plays: *Out Goes You,* 1975, is a satire on BC provincial politics, performed at the Vancouver Playhouse. The following season saw the Playhouse production of *The Komagata Maru Incident,* a semi-documentary handling of an ugly World War I racist incident in Vancouver harbour concerning the admission of Sikh immigrants; the general as well as the regional appeal of the work has been demonstrated by subsequent productions elsewhere.

The important point to be made here is that the impetus for the writing of new plays has had to come from the theatres, and where the record for the prairies on the whole is not spectacular, there has been a steady flow of original work in the past ten years or so. MTC has made two important commissions, ten years apart. In Centennial year Ann Henry was asked for *Lulu Street;* and for MTC's twentieth anniversary in the 1977–78 season, Joanna Glass was requested to write *The Last Chalice.* These two cases are interesting in different ways. During the formative years of MTC, Henry (as theatre critic for the Winnipeg *Tribune*) was a sympathetic observer of the theatre's development. John Hirsch wanted a play about the 1919 Winnipeg general strike and turned to Henry because, in her words:

> My father was one of the platform people, one of the speakers, so I had grown up with stories about it; met people like Woodsworth and others.... I had many of my father's speeches. I think it's absolutely essential to know the truth about our history, and you can say things in a play that you can't say otherwise. I was fascinated by the effects on people, the stresses and the strike. It was a marvellous opportunity to write a play. (Yates 15)

The result was a happy example of the way local subject matter of deeply embedded interest can attract audiences. The report on the attendance at this play makes its own point about the value of the material: people came who had never been to a theatre before because they were deeply interested in how the strike would be handled. Thus a new playwright emerged out of specific local interest.

The instance of the Joanna Glass play is instructive from an opposite perspective. Glass is an expatriate Canadian (born in Saskatoon) who now lives in Connecticut.[6]

Her initial recognition as a playwright has come from the United States: the now well-known pair of one act plays *Canadian Gothic* and *American Modern* were presented first in workshop at the Manhattan Theatre Club in 1972. The premiere of *Artichoke* was at the Long Wharf Theatre in New Haven, 1975. Between these years and since, however, these plays have been given several performances in Canada. Their specific appeal (with the obvious exception of *American Modern*) is in their sensitive rendering of prairie experience. Yet the MTC invitation was the first time Glass was approached to write a play for a major staging in a Canadian theatre.

Clearly the regional theatres are not always as sensitive to the potential for new plays as they should be, nor are they always responsive to already established work. The instance of Herschel Hardin is illustrative in the West, with specific reference to his play *The Great Wave of Civilization*. Written in 1962, this quite powerful Epic theatre analysis of the winning of the West through the heartless abuse of the Indian peoples won a Centennial prize in Alberta five years later, but waited another nine years for its premiere performance at the Lennoxville Festival. It has never had a prairie performance, although Hardin's later play *Esker Mike and His Wife Agiluk*, premiered at Factory Lab Theatre, Toronto, in 1971, was mounted at MTC in the 1973–74 season. In the past two or three years some theatres are making concerted efforts to locate more plays and playwrights. In Edmonton, for example, The Playwrights Unit, jointly sponsored by Theatre 3 and Northern Light, provides a playreading service and offers professional workshops of half a dozen plays a year. Their efforts have led to several full scale productions in prairie theatres. [7]

It will be observed that much of the regional drama referred to in this discussion has either historical, political, or sociological bias. There is a view that such interests merely serve a playwright in his apprenticeship (and perhaps Canadian drama in *its* apprenticeship) rather than in his maturity. This would be to say that the inexperienced dramatist lacks the confidence to write out of the fullness of his personal experience and therefore must, at first, take refuge behind issues and fact. It is certainly true that a playwright's work in collectives (and these frequently fall into the category of documentary) can serve as an excellent training in writing for the theatre—although equally well an experienced playwright can help the actors and director better realize their intentions on the stage. But the truly important considerations about contemporary Canadian regional drama are that, first, regional drama establishes the validity of a specific milieu as the subject for dramatic interpretation; second that it draws its strength from the audience interest it thereby generates; and third and equally important, that it feels free to experiment in styles and stagings in order to communicate its particular vision in its own particular way. Indeed there is a positive advantage in the very lateness of the development of a Canadian dramatic literature. No Canadian playwright need feel the constraints of the well-made tradition and its modern sitcom variations.

Further, while the evolutionary theory of cultural development (that we move *from* history to individuality, for example, or *from* either nationalistic or regionalist self-consciousness to a more cosmopolitan artistic realization) may have its attractions, its desirability and even its validity are open to question. James Reaney, the best of the Canadian regional playwrights, and therefore quite possibly the best of all English-speaking playwrights in Canada up to now, has demonstrated in his Donnelly trilogy that regional historical detail can be animated by a gifted dramatic imagination. The universals of personality or individuality are surely best contained within the fabric of a specifically realized time and place. The imagination must soar if that is its gift, but the best chance for its success lies in its continuing reinforcement of that rootedness which makes flight possible.

(1980)

Notes

¹ The citation style of the original publication of this essay omitted much information that was required for conversion to the MLA style that is the one used in the Critical Perspectives series. Where such information was difficult to recover, we have retained some elements of the original style—Ed.

² Hendry lists *Desperate Journey,* by Mort Forer; *Look Ahead and All About Us* by Len Petersen; *A Very Close Family,* Bernard Slade; *Names and Nicknames,* James Reaney; and two Canadian adaptations by Betty Jane Wylie: *An Enemy of the People* and *Georges Dandin.*

³ While the country does now have theatres in almost every major centre, this does not constitute a true network which the term "decentralized national theatre" implies. Among such organizations as the Neptune, Theatre New Brunswick, Toronto Arts Productions or Vancouver Playhouse, one may see one or two of the early aims of MTC taking root, but none exemplifies all of them.

⁴ Playwright Paddy Campbell and composer William Skolnik have collaborated in several musical plays: *Hoarse Muse,* 1974; *Under the Arch,* 1975 (which evolved from the company's first production, *The History Show*); *Passengers,* 1978. Other playwrights who have provided regional material for this stage include Bonnie Le May, *Roundhouse,* 1975; Jan Truss, *A Very Small Rebellion,* 1974; and Claudia Gibson, *We Don't Need Another Widow McEachren,* 1973.

⁵ Rod Langley also worked as a writer with the Globe: *Tales of a Prairie Drifter,* 1973; *Bethune,* 1974, a joint commission with the Centaur, Montreal. The choice of subject as well as the co-sponsorship can be seen as another way in which regional interests work in Canada: Saskatchewan's political radicalism and Montreal's belated local pride in Bethune combined suitably to create a play of general interest but from a specifically regional impetus.

⁶ She studied acting with Betty Mitchell in Calgary in 1955 and obtained an Alberta Arts Council scholarship to work further at the Pasadena Playhouse.

⁷ These include Frank Moher's *Stage Falls;* Mary Baldridge's *The Mary Shelley Play;* and Gordon Pengilly's *Songs for Believers,* all in the 1978 season.

Works Cited

Elsom, John. *Post-War British Theatre.* London: Routledge and Kegan Paul, 1976.

Johns, Ted. "Interview with Paul Thompson." *Performing Arts Magazine* (Winter 1973): 30–32.

Lee, Betty. *Love and Whiskey: The Story of the Dominion Drama Festival.* Toronto: McClelland and Stewart, 1973.

Reaney, James. "Ten Years at Play." *Dramatists in Canada.* Ed. W.H. New. Vancouver: U of British Columbia P, 1972: 70–78.

Yates, Sarah. *Manitoba Theatre Centre: The First Twenty Years: Conversations with MTC People From 1958 to 1978.* Winnipeg: Manitoba Theatre Centre, 1978.

Playwrights in a Landscape:
The Changing Image of Rural Ontario

by Alexander M. Leggatt

The history of the theatre includes not only the facts that can be documented—productions, playhouses, sets and costumes—but a number of less tangible factors as well. One of particular importance to the Canadian theatre is the history of attitudes to the theatre itself. That is the history I would like to trace in this article. The fifty-year span the study covers shows a change in the handling of one particular theme—the theme of the land itself—that reflects a corresponding change, at a deeper level, in the attitude of the Canadian playwright to the theatre he works in.

Theatre has not always been taken for granted in this country, least of all by its practitioners. In 1928 Merrill Denison wrote, "I find writing about the Canadian theatre or drama depressingly like discussing the art of dinghy sailing among the bedouins … It is not at all surprising that there should be no Canadian drama. One's surprise comes from learning that anyone could have seriously believed that there ever could be a Canadian drama" (65). Denison was of course using his artist's prerogative of exaggerating to make a point. But we know enough of the struggles of that time to realize that beneath the bitter joke lay a real problem: Canadian drama and theatre existed, but without deep roots and with little continuity of achievement.

The main reason Denison gave for this problem was that we lacked a national cultural capital, a single city that could be for us the equivalent of London, Paris or New York: a place where the theatre could put down permanent roots and flourish. Denison did not anticipate the development of strong regional theatres in the 1960s, an international phenomenon in which Canada has shared, and which has had much to do with the flourishing of professional theatre in this country. But if his assumption that you need a single capital has proved wrong, there is a deeper idea behind it that is still valid, and that posed a more fundamental problem for the Canadian drama of his day. Whatever its origins in folk ritual, drama is traditionally an urban form. It breeds in cities. And, while one can think of many exceptions, it seems on the whole to take more naturally to city life as its subject matter—the busy traffic of man with man in a crowded world—than it does to the quieter life of the countryside. And until after the Second World War, Canada was predominantly a rural culture. I do not mean simply that the majority of the population lived outside the big cities; I am thinking not of statistics but of a state of mind. Canadians *thought* of themselves as a rural people. (There are still traces of this left. The peculiar Canadian academic year, with its exceptionally long summer vacation, reflects the assumption that when summer comes students are needed on the farm.) And

Canadians identified their country more easily with its landscape than with anything man had made. They saw the landscape as uninhabited, even alien. In literature, men against nature was a favourite theme.[1] Possibly the most important, and certainly the best known, expression of Canadian culture in the early years of the Twentieth Century was the Group of Seven school of landscape painting. It is a feature of these paintings that, unlike European landscapes, they contain no human figures.

But from the Second World War onwards there has been a gradual change in the way Canadians think of themselves. We can see the change outlined in the way James Reaney's *Colours in the Dark* traces, simultaneously, the growth of Reaney's own imagination and the history of his country. The central character begins as a child in a small Ontario town and then becomes a student in Toronto and a teacher in Winnipeg. The play's images go from church picnics, berry-picking and thunderstorms to railway stations, city streets and boarding-houses: from the rural to the urban. The historical period at which the central character becomes a city dweller is roughly equivalent to the period at which Canadians as a whole started moving to the cities in droves.

We now have our national drama. It has developed at a time when our culture has been moving away from the land that used to nourish the national imagination and made that imagination distinctive. Indeed, the move may be a vital factor in making our achievement in drama possible. In the argument that follows I would like to explore this paradox and its implications in a historical way, showing what Canadian playwrights from Denison onwards have thought of rural life, and how their image of rural life has been bound up, consciously or not, with their views of their own roles as playwrights and of the culture in which they worked. I am concentrating on the drama of Ontario because it is least complicated by other factors, such as memories of the Depression in Western Canada or the special political issues of Quebec. But what this drama shows us may have broader implications for the Canadian playwright's developing view of his art.

The first playwright who claims our attention is Merrill Denison himself. The title of his 1923 collection of plays, *The Unheroic North,* indicates his reaction against the popular, Romantic image of Canada as a land of tall pines and rugged mountains, peopled by a race of clean-cut young men with clear blue eyes. Denison presents his own view of backwoods Ontario, which he knew not from tourist posters but first hand. The best known of these plays is *Brothers in Arms,* a one-act farce about a big city businessman, J. Altrus Browne, who finds himself trapped in the backwoods trying to get back to town for an urgent appointment. His wife Dorothea is unperturbed by his problems, as she is delighted to be in the romantic wilderness, with its strong silent men she has seen in movies like "Land of the Summer Snows." Unfortunately the backwoodsmen her husband encounters are not so much strong and silent as talkative, evasive and stupid. Browne wants someone to drive him to the station to catch a train; the particular backwoods man he is dealing with would rather tell rambling stories about deer-hunting than deal with the business at hand. To any direct question his answer is always "It's kinda hard to say." The integrity of rural life in this play consists in its being slow-moving, stupid and impenetrably self-contained.

The most ambitious play in the collection is *Marsh Hay,* a full-length drama about the futility and despair of a farming family trying to eke out a living on the Canadian shield. The phrase that describes their farm, "fifty acres of grey stone," is repeated throughout the play almost to the point of self-parody; but the repetition is Denison's way of conveying the mind-numbing futility of his characters' existence. The central character is the father of the family, John Serang, who spends his time denouncing the land, the government, his wife and children—anything that will excuse his own failure as a farmer. There is some point to his diatribes, as when he attacks the "head lads" in Toronto for neglecting an area in which "They's townships that ain't got twenty voters if they got that many" (43); but there is also something self-destructive about Serang. He could leave his land and try his luck in the West, but he always finds some reason not to. At the start of the play, he comes back from cutting marsh hay with the complaint that there is not enough hay on the marshes "to winter a cat" (10); but we also know that he has left the cutting too late, as he does every year, and others have been there before him. He takes an extra job to bring in some money, but it doesn't last: "Got histed out'n my job. Some fellow from Hendale come along and offered to do the teamin for fifty cents a day less. I quit" (45). The ambiguity of the line is revealing: he was hoisted out of his job; he quit of his own volition. Serang is a put-upon man, the victim of other people, he is also a proud man, who will destroy himself rather than suffer a slight to his pride. Above all, he is the victim of his own despair. His bitterness is not that of a wounded idealist but that of a man who cannot accept that anything ever could go right. When one of his friends tells him "You're expectin too much," he replies, "I ain't expectin nothin, Andy. I ain't crazy" (43).

Serang's despair is mirrored in the action of the play as a whole. His daughter Sarilin becomes pregnant; Serang tries to handle the affair in the usual way by forcing the girl and her seducer into a shotgun wedding; but his wife Lena, who has got some unconventional ideas from a city woman, tries to treat Sarilin's pregnancy differently. She puts the girl to bed, tidies up the house, puts up new curtains and does everything she can to create a decent home for the baby to be born into. As part of this campaign she sets her face against any marriage between Sarilin and the worthless young lout who happens to be the baby's father. Under Lena's influence the Serang household, which we saw in the first act as a place of filth and misery, becomes clean, bright, and even dignified, much to Serang's own bewilderment. But Lena has reckoned without Sarilin. As Lena is making a big speech about how "that baby is goin to be born into the world with the best chancet I can give it" (39) there is a scream offstage; Sarilin has had, not a baby, but a self-induced abortion. In the last act the play's structure becomes circular: the household relapses into its former squalor, and Sarilin, recovered from her abortion, is out on the tiles again. In the dying moments of the play, Lena and Serang have a revealing dialogue that many another playwright would have used to create a moment of comfort or understanding in the gloom. Lena, after surveying the misery of their life together, says "We must've been kinda fond of each other to stick together all these years, John?" We listen for the violins—but Serang replies, "Fond? Fond be damned. We stuck together because we couldn't get away from each other…. We're chained here" (46). The sentimental moment is deliberately blocked; the play's vision of despair is uncompromising.

Marsh Hay was printed in 1923; there are unconfirmed rumours of a production in Kiev in the 20s; but the first performance we know of took place at Hart House Theatre in Toronto in the spring of 1974, nearly fifty years later. [2] Denison, then an old man but still full of fire, was in the audience. Discussing the play with the cast afterwards, he made an interesting confession: he thought, on reflection, that he had underestimated the people of the backwoods. They had, he declared, more gumption and more resilience than the despairing vision of *Marsh Hay* had credited them with. In particular, he called John Serang "a false character." Always a skeptic, Denison was finally skeptical about his own most ambitious play. But his view, if valid, simply means that the play is not a literally true account of life in Northern Ontario. It remains a true account of a certain state of mind, an examination of despair and futility that has its own validity, beyond its function as social reporting. But Denison's confession that he went beyond the facts leads us to speculate as to why he did so. And it may be fair to suggest that the answer lies in that 1928 essay in which he declared that discussing the theatre in Canada was like discussing dinghy sailing among the bedouins. In that bitter joke one hears the authentic voice of John Serang: "I ain't expectin nothing, Andy. I ain't crazy." The vision of rural life in *Marsh Hay* may be in the last analysis a vehicle for Denison's own sense of futility about his art. The plight of a dramatist trying to work without an established theatre may bear more than an accidental resemblance to the plight of a farmer trying to work fifty acres of grey stone. If *Marsh Hay* is an inaccurate picture of rural Ontario, that may be because it is a more personal play than it appears at first to be.

Denison's vision is deliberately unromantic, even antiromantic. A younger contemporary, Herman Voaden, took a very different view of the Canadian north. In his play *Murder Pattern*—which reversed the fate of *Marsh Hay*, being performed in 1936 but not printed till 1972—we see a brave but perilous attempt to deal with the theme of man and nature in a romantic, even mystical way, through the medium of drama. Voaden uses a peculiar form, for which his own term is "symphonic theatre"; it looks now like a branch of Expressionism, in its use of rhythm and light effects and above all in its deliberate abstraction. The play concerns a murder that took place in Northern Ontario: the central character, the murderer Jack Davis, is surrounded by choric figures with labels like First Earth Voice, Second Earth Voice, The Friendly One, The Accusing One. We piece together the story of the murder; we explore Davis's state of mind; but what really interests Voaden is the relation between Davis and the landscape around him. The choric voices are not simply a gimmick of the avant-garde theatre of Voaden's time, though they are that in part; they are also his way of bringing the countryside onto the stage, giving it a positive theatrical presence. There are descriptive, atmospheric passages—"Dark as death are the swamps and forests. The lone moon-disc whitens the farms, and silvers the quiet mirrors of the lakes" (48). As we are set up for the murder, the landscape seems bleak and menacing, the barrenness of *Marsh Hay* deepened into something destructive: "Shut off from the world to the south, life stood still. There was no fresh blood. Here and there, in the great solitude, life moved backwards, towards the animal, the grotesque, the warped and evil" (47). There are, later, psychological explanations for the murder; but it seems at first to be an emanation of the landscape itself: "With the darkness, comes the cold. Pity the isolate hill folk, fearful, estranged. They have no words to speak the terror of the gloom, and the silence, and the unending distances that wall in life from life" (48).

But once Davis has been imprisoned, the dark, menacing nature of the first part of the play is transformed. To the prisoner the countryside now seems like a lost home: "O prisoner, hill-bound to the end, forest-bound to the end. Born to the desolate, austere and eternal land, born to the fear of the wilderness, born to the lonely beauty of hill and water and forest valley ... even in dreams you see Clear Lake, and the beaver marsh, and the falls, and the little stream that flows out past your silent house to Long Lake" (57). In the process the nature of the landscape is changed; it becomes no longer menacing but vital and beautiful: "Come back to the dark woods and the shining waters, where the wind is warmth and strength ... Come back to the clear sunlight of the lake-land, to the rapture of the giant-lifted skies" (58–59). Finally, Davis is released on compassionate grounds, and returns to the lakes and hills to die. The final speech, from the First Earth Voice, reads, "You have entered the temple now at last, O lonely one. You are part of the mystery at last. Your body is one with the earth. Your dreams shall blow steadily in the eternal winds. In them your spirit shall brood and pass endlessly among the hills ... lonely and enduring as the hills" (60).

Time has not been kind to *Murder Pattern*. Its poetic language now seems stilted and overdecorated. Its theatrical devices of drumbeats and choric voices must have looked at the time like a vision of the drama of the future; and nothing dates so fast as visions of the future. But there is a more fundamental problem. Voaden himself called, quite explicitly, for the creation of a national drama inspired by the paintings of the Group of Seven (see Evans 37)—inspired, in other words, by paintings in which there are no human figures. Yet the fundamental medium of drama is the human being; without the actor, there is no theatre. There are ways of evoking nature as part of the human drama, as Shakespeare and Ibsen did, in their different ways. But Voaden wanted to bring nature onto the stage in its own right, to make it the subject of a play as much as it can be the subject of a painting or a poem. There may be a way of doing that, but Voaden has not found it. Neither, to my knowledge, has anyone else. Denison and Voaden both wrote in a culture in which the national imagination was dominated by landscape. Denison shows the helplessness of man, with the landscape in the background, bleak and ugly, as one of the causes of that helplessness; but he gives us primarily a human drama of futility. *Marsh Hay* now creaks in places, but it still works well enough to merit revival. *Murder Pattern* tries to depict the landscape directly and poetically; it is now a curiosity, a theatrical museum piece. To put it a bit unkindly, while Denison wrote about failure Voaden achieved it. The common factor is the frustration of being a playwright in a primarily rural culture.

That theme is not explicit in the plays I have been examining, and has to be teased out of them by implication, as I have been doing here. But in the early plays of Robertson Davies the theme is very close to the surface, and it does not take much critical ingenuity to uncover it. Davies' own early career is relevant here. Born in Ontario, he went to Oxford; he acted with the Old Vic; he returned to Canada in the early 1940s to edit *The Peterborough Examiner*. Through his early work runs the theme of cultural deprivation: Canada is a barren land for artists and for lovers of art; for imaginative nourishment they look wistfully to the old world and even (in moments of desperation) to the United States. The theme finds typical expression in the early one-act play, *Hope Deferred*, in which Frontenac, as Governor of Quebec, tries to organize a performance of *Tartuffe* and is blocked by the Church. He concludes bitterly, "There is no tyranny like that of organized virtue," (76) and sees behind this one failure a whole society with its priorities desperately wrong: "if trade and piety thrive, art can go to the devil: what a corrupt philosophy, what stupidity for a new country" (76).

Hope Deferred is a sad, angry play. A more farcical and more effective treatment of the same theme is found in Davies' *Overlaid* (1948) which is set in a farmhouse in rural Ontario. Here we find Pop, an old farmer, sitting in the kitchen dressed in a top hat and white working gloves, listening to the Metropolitan Opera broadcast from New York, applauding wildly, and emitting cries of "Yippee!" and "Hot Dog!" at appropriate moments. Meanwhile his daughter Ethel is trying to get on with the ironing, and deploring her father's loose conduct. The conflict of the play begins when Pop gets a windfall of $1200 from his insurance company: to Ethel's horror, he wants to spend it all on one glorious spree in New York:

> I'd get some stylish clothes, and I'd go into one o' these restrunts, and I'd
> order vittles you never heard of—better' n the burn truck Ethel calls
> food—and I'd get a bottle o' wine—cost a dollar, maybe two—and drink
> it all, and then I'd mosey along to the Metropolitan Opera House and I'd
> buy me a seat right down beside the trap-drummer, and there I'd sit an'
> listen, and holler and hoot and raise hell whenever I liked the music, an'
> throw bookies to the gals, an' wink at the chorus, and when it was over
> I'd go to one o' these here nightclubs an' eat some more, an' drink
> whisky, and watch the gals that take off their clothes—every last dud,
> kinda slow an' devilish till they're bare-naked—an' maybe I'd give one of
> 'em fifty bucks for her brazeer—. (98)

This produces, from Pop's hearers, cries of "Jeepers!" and "You carnal man!" But Pop is, in Davies' terms, a spiritual man—a representative of art, culture, and the imagi-nation. A literary critic would say that he represents the Dionysiac impulse; but Pop himself puts it more eloquently: "God likes music an' naked women an' I'm happy to follow his example" (99).

There is no doubt that Pop is, within the special terms of the play, Davies' hero and spokesman. The values he represents are values Davies has been preaching all through his career. But of course he represents those values in a caricatured form, though the caricature is a friendly one; and in the second half the play changes tone a little as Ethel warns him, "If you go to New York you'll just be a lost old man, and everybody will laugh at you and rob you" (102). We have to recognize the truth of that; and beneath the boisterous caricature of Pop there is an underlying sadness—this parody opera lover is the best that Smith Township can produce; his heart is in the right place, but if he ever tried to turn his fantasy into reality he would be sadly out of his depth. However, in the second half Pop himself becomes more serious, and makes some cogent attacks on the rural community that has left his imagination frustrated: "There was just one purty thing in sight o' this farm—row of elms along the road; they cut down the elms to widen the road an' then never widened it" (102). He has a quarrel with the church, too: "Last fifty bucks I gave 'em was for a bell, and what'd they do? Bought a new stove with it … there's always a gol-danged necessity to get in the way whenever you want somethin' purty" (102–03). This is the heart of Davies' attack on rural society: concerned with material necessities, it is blind to the deeper necessity of feeding the imagination, which it regards as a needless luxury.

In the end, Pop realizes that one reason Ethel is so upset at his plan to go to New York is that she has her own dream of what to do with the money. He manages to winkle it out of her: she wants a granite headstone for the family plot. Pop surrenders; the dark forces of respectability have won. But in his last speech Pop declares "I ain't overlaid for good" (109) and as the play ends he is whistling an air from *Lucia di Lammermoor*. Unlike *Hope Deferred*, *Overlaid* suggests that the Ethels of this world will not have it all their own way, and in a play that is shamelessly open about its symbolism it may be worth noting that Pop has switched off the broadcast from New York and is doing his own whistling.

Davies returns to the theme of *Overlaid* in a more sombre and enigmatic play, *At My Heart's Core*, first produced in 1950. This is set in Upper Canada during the rebellion of 1837, and is concerned with the frustration of three talented women living the pioneer life in the backwoods—Frances Stewart, Catherine Parr Traill, and Susanna Moodie. Mrs. Stewart is a lady of charm and beauty who could have married a lord and become a great society hostess; Mrs. Traill is a skilled naturalist; Mrs. Moodie has a literary gift. All three have their talents blocked and frustrated by the rigors of pioneer existence—including the necessity of subordinating themselves to their husbands. Their talents threaten to wither because there is no opportunity to exercise them. This view is put to each of them in turn by a sinister, Byronic tempter named Cantwell, who has himself given up on Canada and is returning to the Old Country. He claims that his view is widely shared: "I have watched some of those officers here in Upper Canada following the plough, and whenever they rest—which it must be said to their eternal credit is rarely—they always come to a halt facing east. I think that without knowing it they are looking toward England, as they wipe the sweat from their brows" (38). The play's central ambiguity lies in Davies' attitude to Cantwell. Up to a point he is, like Pop, a spokesman for ideas that are recognizably those of the playwright: the vital importance of art and culture, the crime of allowing talent to be neglected. But in tempting the women with these ideas, he has no positive end in mind; he is merely being cruel, revenging himself against an imagined social slight. He states his purpose as follows: "It is only the crude seducer who takes a woman's honour, and in order to do that he must have some liking for her. It is a more lasting and serious injury to rob her of her peace of mind. These ladies will never, I think, know perfect content again" (80).

With Mrs. Traill and Mrs. Moodie, Cantwell succeeds: they end the play in precisely the state of discontent that he wants, with no hope of escaping from it, though Davies may be counting on our knowledge that the historical equivalents of these characters actually became considerable figures in early Canadian literature. Davies himself has recently described At My Heart's Core as "a Women's Lib play," because of the sympathy it shows for the plight of the three women. And it may be remarked that the frustration of the artist in a pioneer society runs parallel to, and is involved with, the severe restraints on the role of women in a male-dominated society. The men of the play are allowed full public lives and a good deal of freedom; they belong to a kind of club from which the women are excluded. The women's role is domestic, and nothing else. Insofar as the play protests against this, Davies' description of it as "Women's Lib" is fair enough. But the ending is another matter. Frances Stewart, the only one of the women to find content, finds it in her role as Mr. Stewart's wife: that is enough for her. In 1950 domestic subordination could be presented as a happy ending for a woman much more easily than it can be now. But I suspect Davies was not just following conventional thinking, for he is still prepared to take this idea seriously long after it has become unfashionable. In his recent play, Question Time, the Prime Minister's wife sees her own role in these terms, and declares, "Many a one hath cast away her final worth when she hath cast away her servitude" (39).

In Davies' 1949 play Fortune, my Foe, the young university teacher who is the hero accepts the fact that while Canada is a frustrating place for men of his kind it is still his country and he has to stay. For one thing, if he and his kind leave, the country will never get any better. Mrs Stewart, accepting her role as a wife, is also accepting her role as a settler; and Mrs Traill tells us exactly what that means: "A new country brings new hope, and it also demands sacrifice. Have you ever walked in our graveyard? Many stones there mark the graves of children. One of those children was—is mine. A fair hope vanished, Mr Cantwell. And other hopes must be buried which may even be harder to give up. New countries mean not only hopes fulfilled but hopes relinquished" (47). For all their occasional wit and charm, these early plays of Robertson Davies present a bleak view of Canada. It is a barren wilderness; its rural life is the cultural equivalent of John Serang's fifty acres of grey stone. Art, culture, imagination—these are firmly identified with the old world, and in Pop's case with New York. There seems to be no way of closing the gap. You leave, and betray your country; or you stay and suffer. The main virtue is that of Frances Stewart or the hero of Fortune, my Foe—the virtue of submission. But just as there is a touch of hope at the end of Overlaid, so there is one hint in At My Heart's Core that imaginative nourishment can be drawn from the soil of Canada itself, and need not always be sought elsewhere. The comic Irish settler Phelim Brady, who sees himself as an artist because of his capacity for spinning tall stories, commiserates with Mrs. Traill: "We're the songbirds that aren't wanted in this bitter land, where the industrious robins, and the political crows get fat, and they with not a tuneful chirp among the lot of 'em." It sounds like a typical Davies complaint: but Mrs. Traill retorts, "How odd that poets are such bad naturalists! There are songbirds all about you, you foolish old man!" (41).

The promise implied in that line, "There are songbirds all about you," is not actually fulfilled in Davies' early plays; they remain poised between acceptance and frustration, with hope perpetually deferred. In that way they report the state of Canadian culture as Davies saw it around thirty years ago. But as the cities have grown and the theatres have at last flourished, new playwrights have turned again to the countryside to look at it with fresh eyes—to see in it not the spiritual wasteland of Davies and Denison but a place that has its own culture, its own integrity, a place that can in its own way nourish the imagination. We might suggest that this vision has become possible only because the writers are no longer bound themselves to a rural culture; they can see it with a certain artistic detachment that reveals in it a power and interest not always evident to those who live in it every day. A fascinating example is *The Farm Show*, a collective creation of Theatre Passe Muraille. The actors went to live in a farming community, and produced a series of scenes based on the lives of the people they met; they then toured the show around rural Ontario, presenting the farmers to themselves, before finally taking it to Toronto. It was printed in 1976, the written version being the responsibility of one of the actors, Ted Johns. In the production photos that accompany the text, there is a disconcerting contrast between the soft faces of the young actors from Toronto and the tough, weatherbeaten faces of their farm audiences. These people, one feels, are trying to make a play out of a life that is utterly alien to them. The odds against *The Farm Show* were great: it could have been condescending, or sentimental. It is neither: it presents an honest account of rural life, accepting the facts for what they are, with sympathy but without judgement. Early in the play one of the young actors is made a kind of sacrificial victim in order to establish the play's attitude: he greets the farmers with sentimental gush about "organic vegetables from your own garden and all, far out!" (24). He is then made to load bales for several hours on a blistering hot day. He concludes, "Why would any human being *choose*, for the better part of his life, *twice* a year, to put himself through that total and utter hell? I didn't understand it then—and I don't understand it now" (43). If he had claimed a new wisdom and insight from the experience; the moment would have been as sentimental as his earlier cooing over organic vegetables. Instead, he has simply learned one important fact, that farming is damnably hard work. And he reports that fact for its own sake. This is the attitude of the play throughout: it tells us what's there—the frustrations, the eccentricities, the occasional fun; the Orangemen's parades, the hot-gospel religion—above all, the farmer's dependence on machinery. In one scene, actors impersonate rival tractors in a contest of strength at a country fair; in another, a housewife describing a harrassing day stands symbolically inside her washing machine. But through the reporting an attitude emerges, one of respect for a demanding and frequently absurd way of life that has, in the end, an integrity of its own. In this play farm life is not, as it is for Davies, a vehicle for a larger commentary of Canadian culture. Pop, of *Overlaid*, would recognize this life and point out that it still has no glamour, no sophistication, and certainly no opera;

the difference is that the creators of *The Farm Show* do not care; for them, farm life has in itself sufficient material to feed the imagination. The gap between culture and farming has been sealed up.

But *The Farm Show* is still a documentary: its interest is in reporting the facts as they are; it is poetic only if one uses that term very loosely indeed. For a transformation of the rural past into poetry we have to turn to James Reaney's trilogy *The Donnellys: Sticks and Stones, St. Nicholas Hotel,* and *Handcuffs.* This story of a family of Irish settlers massacred by their neighbours was becoming one of our national myths even before Reaney got hold of it, but he has given it a particularly vivid—possibly definitive—form. In doing so he has used a special, idiosyncratic style of theatre that he developed during the 1960s, mostly in plays written for children. A company of actors not only plays an enormous cast of characters, doubling and sharing roles, but also impersonates landscapes, roads, animals, trains—anything the play needs. Time and space are telescoped, and the awareness of theatrical make-believe is constant. (In one of the early children's plays, *Geography Match*, a group of actors has to impersonate Niagara Falls.) This makes the plays hard to read, till one is used to the idiom; but they act brilliantly. And it gives Reaney, like the creators of *The Farm Show*, a freedom to bring documentary facts to the stage: the actors recite place names, railway timetables, entries from census reports. They impersonate roads by lining up in straight lines and calling out the names of the settlers who lived on those roads. In *Sticks and Stones* especially, there is a remarkable evocation of the maps of pioneer Canada, with the wilderness cut into straight lines and rectangles—man starting from scratch with the land, imposing on it a neat pattern that still exists today—"wild lands ... cut into concessions ... cut into farms" (47). We seem to be in at the birth of a society.

Reaney gives these facts an imaginative resonance. The straight lines of the roads, represented by ladders, become walls that hem the Donnellys in. The tollgates along a coach route become barriers the Donnellys must pass. The facts of the map acquire extra significance in lines like "Why is our father's farm so narrow?" As Mrs. Donnelly tramps the roads to collect signatures on a petition to save her husband from hanging, the names of the places she passes through are alternated with a recitation of the accounts for the building of the gallows: "Rope from W.E. Grace 24¢ Four long polls at $1 each ... One mask $12^1/_2$¢ One white cap for prisoner 50¢ (115). Swiftly and economically, documentary becomes drama. The objects that now clutter our pioneer museums, tools, barrels, ladders, become weapons charged with menace. The events of pioneer life, from logging bees to barn-burnings, become as ritualized as the ceremonies of the Catholic church, which Reaney also uses throughout the plays.

And the Donnellys themselves, whatever they may have been in history, become in Reaney's play figures with the stature of myth. Mr. Donnelly, the leader of clan, is a stubborn man who will not submit to the demands of the tribe. The root of the trouble between him and his neighbours comes from his refusal, back in Ireland, to join the secret terrorist society of the Whitefeet. He and his family are labelled Blackfeet, and the taunt follows them to the new world. The Donnellys are marked out as special: the first play begins with the crippled Will Donnelly being put through a catechism in the forest by his mother—"Baptism, Confirmation, and Holy Orders can be received only once because they imprint on the soul—a spiritual mark, called a character, which lasts forever" (37). Later his priest tells him, "your lameness is God's marking you for His own" (66). Finally we are told that "the sacraments that can be received only once" are not Baptism, Confirmation and Holy Orders but "Your mother, your father, your brothers" (143).

Throughout the plays the Donnellys are associated with the fertility of the land and of the crops, especially in the recurring Barleycorn ballad. The barley grain is, like the Donnellys, cut down—"But, when I got into the jug / I was the strongest man" (36). Mr. Donnelly taunts one of his enemies: "Having myself seven sons and a girl I ask you what children have you? What have you got between your legs, Cassleigh— a knife?" (152). They are hard to kill. In the ceremonies that follow the massacre, the bodies of the victims are represented by stones placed on the stage; but the characters themselves are represented by living actors who accompany the symbolic corpses—a device that allows the surviving daughter Jenny to have a last dance with the ghost of her mother. Finally, though their house is destroyed, a great wheat field grows around it, suggesting their immortality. The Donnelly house is also a centre of love, in a community full of hatred and prejudice. Besides the affection that binds them together, they provide a haven for children from the loveless homes of their neighbours. Most important, they have vital imaginations in a community that is often grimly material, as represented by one of their neighbours who uses an old sword as a turnip knife and does not notice there is writing on it. Like some of Davies' characters, they are poets in a hostile environment: the difference is that they embrace their fate with a kind of joy. A speech from the end of *Sticks and Stones* tells us what it means to be a Donnelly:

> Because from the courts of Heaven when you're there you will see that however the ladders and sticks and stones caught you and bruised you and smashed you, and the bakers and brewers forced you to work for them for nothing, from the eye of God in which you will someday walk you will see … that once, long before you were born, … you chose to be a Donnelly and laughed at what it would mean, the proud woman put to milking cows, the genius trotting around with a scallion, the old sword rusted into a turnip knife. You laughed and lay down with your fate like a bride, even the miserable fire of it. So that I am proud to be a Donnelly against all the contempt of the world. (154)

The conscious theatrical make-believe of the plays is connected with this vision of the Donnellys as immortal figures of myth; as characters in Reaney's play they can discuss their own lives and deaths with the detachment of those who are beyond life. As Mrs. Donnelly advises one of her sons to "look straight ahead past this stupid life and death they've fastened on you" (*St. Nicholas Hotel* 152) so Mr. Donnelly declares "I'm not in Hell for I'm in a play" (*Sticks and Stones* 49). Finally, like the hero of *Murder Pattern*, they are absorbed into the world around them: "look we are everywhere / In the clouds, in the treebranch, in the puddle, / There. Here. In your fork. In your minds. / Your lungs are filled with us, we are the air you breathe" (*Handcuffs* 133).

Reaney has taken the hard facts of rural pioneer life and turned them into poetry. For him they are sources not of frustration but of imaginative nourishment. He has also succeeded where Voaden failed in dramatizing man's involvement with nature. He succeeds because he never loses sight of the *human* drama, and his language is concrete and economical where Voaden's is simply overloaded. There are no disembodied Earth Voices here; nature wears a fully human face. The Donnellys acquire mythic dimensions—but like all good myths they are ultimately concrete and particular, and they have their roots in human reality. They also have their roots in the rural life of Canada. When that life was all we knew, we were unable to make any satisfactory drama out of it except a drama of frustration. Now that we are free of it artists like Reaney and the creators of *The Farm Show* can return to it with that balance of engagement and detachment that the artist needs in order to shape his material properly, The Donnelly trilogy takes the rural life that seemed for so many years to deny the possibility of drama, and succeeds in making drama not in spite of it, or in reaction against it, but through it, and of it. Reaney's achievement is a sign—one of many—that Canadian drama itself has come of age.

(1980)

Notes

[1]   Eugene Benson has discussed the place of this theme in Canadian drama in the introduction to his anthology *Encounter: Canadian Drama in Four Media* (3–4).

[2]   The production (in which the author of this article played a small part) was sponsored by the Graduate Centre for the Study of Drama and directed by Richard Plant.

Works Cited

Benson, Eugene. Introduction. *Encounter: Canadian Drama in Four Media.* Ed. Eugene Benson. Toronto: Methuen, 1973. 3–4.

Davies, Robertson. "*At My Heart's Core*" and "*Overlaid.*" Toronto: Clarke, Irwin, 1966.

———. "*Hope Deferred.*" "*Eros at Breakfast*" and Other Plays. Toronto: Clarke, Irwin, 1949.

————. *Question Time*. Toronto: Macmillan of Canada, 1975.

Denison, Merrill. *Marsh Hay*. Toronto: Simon and Pierre, n.d.

————. "Nationalism and Drama." *Dramatists in Canada: Selected Essays*. Vancouver: U of British Columbia P, 1972: 65–69.

Evans, Chad. "Herman Voaden and the Symphonic Theatre." *Canadian Theatre Review* 5 (1975): 37–43.

Reaney, James. *The Donnellys, Part One: Sticks and Stones*. Erin: Porcepic, 1976.

————. *The Donnellys, Part Three: Handcuffs*. Erin: Porcepic, 1977.

————. *The Donnellys, Part Two: St. Nicholas Hotel, Wm. Donnelly Prop*. Erin: Porcepic, 1976.

Theatre Passe Muraille. *The Farm Show*. Toronto: Coach House, 1976.

Voaden, Herman. *Murder Pattern. Canadian Theatre Review* 5 (1975). 44–60.

"A Country of the Soul": Herman Voaden, Lowrie Warrener and the Writing of *Symphony*

by Anton Wagner

English-Canadian theatre in this century is differentiated from theatre activity in earlier periods by the concerted attempt to create an indigenous national theatre reflecting a Canadian natural environment and society and the lives of its people in it. In his essay "Waiting for a Dramatist" published in the *Canadian Magazine* in 1914, Fred Jacob declared:

> Self-expression must be the outstanding sign of national consciousness just as it is the indication of growing consciousness in the individual. Canada is finding expression in the prose writers of the country, and the day has now arrived when they can secure a hearing in their own land without going abroad and sending their work back with the stamp of foreign approval upon it...

> But Canada still lacks a dramatist, and it will not be possible for us to claim that our self-expression is complete until some aspect of the life of the nation has been placed behind the foot-lights. (142)

Five years later Harcourt Farmer, in the *Canadian Bookman,* still calling for "our own plays in our own theatres" and "national interpretation in terms of individual expression through drama," asked, "Where are the Canadian playwrights?" "I mean persons of Canadian descent, or adoption, who have written plays the subject matter of which deals with some intrinsic part of Canadian life, past or present, and whose plays are directly artistic representations of Canadian life, or interpretations of Canadian temperament" (55).

Jacob and Farmer probably would never have suspected that the question of what constitutes a Canadian play might still be problematic six decades later. When Merrill Denison, at the 1974 "Canadian Theatre Before the Sixties" Conference asked, "will someone tell me, what is a Canadian play?" Herman Voaden quickly responded, "it is a play written by a Canadian ... a play that looks at the world through a particular identity related to the land in which it is written." Denison and Voaden had already debated the creation of a Canadian national drama four decades earlier. In his acerbic essay "Nationalism and Drama" published in Bertram Brooker's *Yearbook of the Arts in Canada* 1928–1929, Denison asserted that Canadian plays could be Canadian only in their locale because of the similarity of social and economic conditions in the United States and Canada. He maintained that "life in Cleveland and Toronto is iden-

tical" and that "anyone writing plays in Canada will have the London or, more probably, the New York theatre in mind." "Our culture is of two kinds," Denison declared,

> either it is colonial or American. In a discussion of the theatre, it does
> not seem to matter much which. In either case the possibilities of a
> native theatre are nil ... Search for a distinctive Canadian subject and
> you are confined to the life centering about the vice-regal establishment
> at Ottawa and around the gubernatorial mansions in the provincial
> capitals...
>
> Until the national intentions of Canada are greatly clarified the theatre
> would at best be an artificial graft supported with as great travail of the
> spirit and the purse as a native orange industry. (53–55)

In his introduction to *Six Canadian Plays*, published in 1930, Voaden conceded in
a veiled reference to Denison's caustic skepticism that "the road to a National Drama
and Theatre in Canada is not an easy one. The way is beset with pitfalls. Some think
it not to be accomplished in a score of generations; others proclaim the journey
fruitless, the goal an illusion." Voaden agreed with Denison that Canadian authorship
alone, or simply dramatizing a Canadian locale, would be insufficient to create a
uniquely Canadian drama. But he suggested that "an original relation to the universe"
could be derived from an aesthetic awareness of the austere beauty of Canadian nature
and from an artistic and philosophic idealism. "There must be dedication, a faith and
idealism to give unity and purpose to creation. Nothing supremely great was ever
created except in this spirit of dedication." Like the Irish Literary Renaissance, the
birth of a Canadian national theatre and drama could result, Voaden asserted, from
such a "spirit of dedication" combined with "keen observation, sympathetic study and
patient 'awareness' of a new environment" (xv).

Voaden and Denison's contrary critical views reflected not only their distinct
individual personalities and life philosophies but were derived directly from their own
theatre work. Supporting himself through his writing, Denison had become
disillusioned with the attempts to create a national theatre in Canada in the 1920s and
emigrated for a financially more rewarding career in the U.S. in 1931. In his survey
"A National Drama and a National Dramatist: The First Attempt," Terence Goldie
indicates of Denison's *Contract,* his last drama produced in Canada, that "it has all the
superficial faults and virtues of a successful domestic comedy from the contemporary
Broadway" (17). The March 30, 1929 Toronto *Star* indicated that Denison had, indeed,
"had his eye on New York" in writing the play (qtd. in Goldie, "Canadian" 221).

Voaden, by contrast, was just at the beginning of an exciting playwriting career.
His first drama, *The White Kingdom,* had been completed in the winter of 1927–1928
before the end of his tenure as the first artistic director of the Sarnia Drama League.
Northern Storm, his second drama, was written in August of 1929 for Glenn Hughes'
playwriting course at Mills College, Oakland, following a cross-continent automobile
trek through the United States with the painter Lowrie Warrener and Gordon
Alderson. *Northern Song,* written following a trip to the north shore of Lake Superior

in late December of 1929, dramatized a painting expedition by Warrener and the aesthetic philosophy of the Group of Seven. *Western Wolf,* a realistic folk play completed in May of 1930, won Voaden admission to George Pierce Baker's graduate playwriting course at Yale University. *Symphony: A Drama of Motion and Light For a New Theatre,* written with Lowrie Warrener during a trans-Canada train journey in the summer of 1930, pointed to the creation of the distinct "Canadian 'Art of the Theatre' and related Drama different from the accepted pattern of both realistic and romantic plays" called for by Voaden in his introduction to *Six Canadian Plays,* published in November of 1930. With its synthesis of a metaphysical theme and non-realistic multi-media form, *Symphony* is also a forerunner of the "symphonic expressionist" dramas written and produced by Voaden between 1932 and 1942.

Lowrie Warrener's artistic collaboration with Voaden dates to his winning Craig-inspired designs for a permanent stage setting at the Central High School of Commerce in April of 1929. He designed the sets for the three prize-winning plays of Voaden's 1929/1930 playwriting competition (requiring an exterior northern setting) published in *Six Canadian Plays:* J.E. Middleton's *Lake Doré,* Charles Edwin Carruther's *God-Forsaken* and Dora Smith Conover's *Winds of Life.* In his April 19, 1930 Toronto *Globe* review, Lawrence Mason praised the "originality, vigor and beauty of some of the designs and lighting effects" (by Warrener and Voaden respectively) and indicated of the Central High School of Commerce productions that

> the whole undertaking was of the utmost possible significance as an intensive effort to seize upon and express quintessential Canadianism. This movement "back to the soil," back to the wild nature in Northern Ontario or the Rockies, for artistic inspiration, is of great interest, and we may look for important results from it. H.A. Voaden and Lowrie Warrener are leaders in the movement, which aims at developing a distinctively Canadian creative art of the theatre.

Voaden and Warrener had already begun collaborating on a play during their 1929 trans-continental journey. Writing his fiancée Violet Kilpatrick on June 25 of that year, Voaden reported that "Lowrie suggests eight screens—in colour and design gradation from spring through to winter and bitterness—with each screen making the progression in intensity" and that Voaden was "trying to build up a 'colour monologue' to fit this. It would only be a half-hour—but would contain material making it adaptable to movies, talkies, or combination theatre and movie or movie talkie." [1] Though Voaden and Warrener made little progress on this work in 1929, it did suggest the artistic process for their writing of *Symphony* the following summer, perhaps one of the most original playwriting collaborations in Canadian drama. Voaden was aware that he and Warrener were breaking new ground for Canadian theatre, writing Violet Kilpatrick on August 14, 1930 following the completion of *Symphony* that there had been "never anything like it before … a play dance music drama that should be as subtle and beautiful and moving as anything that has come out of Canada."

Symphony is Voaden's most clearly expressionist drama despite its mystical conclusion reminiscent of the symbolist and mystical elements in *The White Kingdom.*

The play, more akin to a scenario for an expressionist silent movie, is completely without dialogue and is unique in 20th century Canadian drama for its imaginative conception and scope. The scenario requires a symphony orchestra, a trained corps de ballet, and an "ample and well equipped stage, with exceptional lighting facilities." Clearly beyond the capacities of the then contemporary Canadian amateur stage and probably even the American professional theatre, *Symphony* is a drama of the imagination that clearly reveals a number of influences on Voaden's theatre aesthetic. From a structural point of view, these are European expressionist writing, acting and production, film and modern dance techniques and the Wagnerian concept of music drama. The title of the play suggests the musical structure of the piece with various *leitmotifs* associated with different characters, moods or images. These European multi-media structural sources are leavened, however, by an idealistic conception of nature derived from the Group of Seven. Of equal importance in the creation of *Symphony* was Lowrie Warrener's own philosophy and visual aesthetic. John Flood indicates in a recent survey of Warrener's career that "by way of compliment, both Harris and Arthur Lismer said of Lowrie—before he went to Europe—that he was the *first* Canadian abstractionist. Lowrie himself refers to his own style as abstract impressionism" (28). [2]

Examining Voaden's collaboration with Warrener on *Symphony* reveals not only the effectiveness of Voaden's attempt to create a national drama through "keen observation, sympathetic study and patient 'awareness' of a new environment." The creation of the play tests Lawren Harris' thesis, expressed in his essay "Creative Art and Canada" (cited by Voaden in *Six Canadian Plays*), that the creative faculty "needs the stimulus of earth resonance and of a particular place, people and time to evoke into activity a faculty that is universal and timeless" (qtd. in Voaden, *Six* xv). As with Harris, the beauty of Canadian nature represented for Voaden not only a particular physical reality but also the ideal beauty of the metaphysical universe. Voaden refers to this dual perception of the Canadian landscape in his introduction to his realistic 1931 "play of the North" *Wilderness* which he "abstracted" in 1932 as *Rocks* for his first "symphonic expressionist" drama. Voaden cited F.B. Housser's comment on Lawren Harris' use of light as a spiritual quality in his northern paintings, "Harris paints the Lake Superior landscape out of a devotion to the life of the soul and makes it feel like a country of the soul," and indicated that to the young Blake, Mary's lover in *Wilderness/Rocks*, the north shore of Lake Superior "*was* a 'country of the soul.'" "The climax of the play is Mary's moment of vision and illumination when she too knows it is her country. In this moment, above all, I used light as actor. Light was at the heart of her mystical experience" ("Introduction" 86). [3]

Symphony: A Drama of Motion and Light For a New Theatre is Voaden's first depiction of Canada as "a country of the soul." Writing Violet Kilpatrick of his collaboration with Warrener on *Symphony* on June 25, 1930, Voaden indicated that "for two years I have been thinking of a new Canadian picture drama. I have come to believe that it can only be when an artist works as co-creator with the dramatist ... I have suggested a deliberate co-authorship in the play—and he has already contributed to it more than I. He is very sensitive—to people as to scene—and feels the action in colour and form and pictorial movement."

Voaden and Warrener's collaboration on *Symphony* was a conscious attempt to interpret artistically the background of the Canadian natural environment and its influence on human character. "We are so anxious to absorb and feel for every mood of the country—to know and speak to its inhabitants—that we dare not actually start to work," Voaden reported to Kilpatrick from British Columbia on July 22, 1930. "And so the ferment proceeds—we discuss—add to, change our ideas—meet new people, watch these interminable lakes and rivers." Noting the differences in climate and both the beauty and occasional inhospitability of Canadian nature as reflected in human character and attitudes, Voaden confided in his diary that he and Warrener would attempt to capture "the 'Totality of things Canadian.'" "We must keep in touch with all of it. It's all part of us—as Canadians. All Canada, all fits in the picture; this is a sub theme to the play."

Voaden's summer 1930 diaries and correspondence with Violet Kilpatrick document the genesis of *Symphony* and the influence of the Canadian landscape on Voaden and Warrener. Already on the second day of their train journey, Voaden wrote Kilpatrick from the north shore of Lake Superior June 19:

> We feel friendly toward the North Shore. We know it a little now humanly as well as "impressionistically." I think of expressionistic symphonic action—someone mad or dreaming—these great forms pulsing and sweeping by. Also of five acts—pastoral—Northern North Shore, Prairie, Rockies (possibly the sea to end it). This country has the height of the Rockies—combined with the feeling of the North—it is the source centre for Canadian "spiritual clarity."

On June 22 Voaden wrote from Crossfield, Alberta, that "we are getting somewhere—getting what we want! Lowrie has just done the first drawing for the expressionistic drama—North Shore. It's fine." While staying at Lake O'Hara, B.C., Voaden reported on June 26 that "the play is developing into a three act thing, 1. Ontario. 2. North and Marine. 3. West (including prairies and mountains). In each I think we'll have both interior and exterior scenes. We'll probably move in the direction of breaking down characters into separate selves—with abstract and pictorial equivalents in character as well as in surrounding scene."

Following a week-long stay with Carroll Aikins in Naramata, B.C., Voaden wrote to Kilpatrick on July 16:

> Lowrie finished a fine sketch of Superior—then we went to work on the first act of the play and got it well outlined—complete. For two hours we worked. It is to be a rhythmic symphony of city life working up to a frenzy of insanity—projecting the central figure on his way across Canada—1. North. 2. West. 3. Mountains. 4. Conclusion—valleys, Natural forms and rhythms and colours are to be the most formidable

protagonists. I am quite pleased with the project as it develops. It should be new, intense, Canadian, powerful.

On their return journey from the west coast, Voaden wrote to Kilpatrick on July 29 from Regina:

> Saturday morning ... we came back with a fine framework for ... the prairie act. The play is essentially taking *one* man and moving him on through these four or five locales or spiritual experiences. In the prairie scene we are using hail and drought with figures and forms and colours and rhythms intensifying to crescendos and climaxes with accompanying words and chanting and music.
>
> Once we felt we had, for the time being, the mood of the prairie, felt the second act (the north) needed more "mood" and "living" in the "atmosphere." Saturday afternoon Lowrie did work out a scenario, but we both felt we wanted to go on. You see, I didn't want to actually start work on the dialogue till the structure and organization was fairly definite in our minds and clearly stated.

After a week's stay in Winnipeg during which Warrener completed painting "Coldwell Harbour" for the Canadian National Exhibition and a large expressionistic bust of Voaden, the two departed for Port Coldwell on August 7 where they rented "the schoolteacher's little shack" to complete *Symphony*.[4] On August 12 Voaden wrote Kilpatrick:

> Today we rewrote the fourth prairie act and planned the last or "mountain act." We shall have finished the last act of the play tomorrow in full outline or resume, and we'll be able to size up the whole thing and see how much longer it is going to take us ... the play may finally work out as a Canadian rhythmic-dance-colour-music-light-pantomime drama, without need for dialogue or poetry or libretto and requiring only more careful restatement and a musical score to be complete. At times I think it is very impressive.

Two days later he added:

> last night and this morning I created the last act of the play ... a powerful thing. A certain spontaneity and capacity for sudden thought and emotional release I am getting from Lowrie. It is a subtle and intangible thing but very real nevertheless ... As it is turning it will be pantomime emotional colour music choral rhythmic light dance drama without dialogue ... as such we are sure to finish it.

On June 26 Voaden had momentarily "doubted Lowrie and our ability to create something great in two months." Yet in his letter to Kilpatrick of August 14, he was able to report that "the big fight is over ... I think the summer will have a rich harvest after all ... possibly the richest yet. We are both anxious to have you read the play." Besides his correspondence with Kilpatrick, Voaden's summer 1930 diaries further clarify the several influences which helped to give *Symphony* its unique dramatic shape and which transformed Voaden and Warrener's perception of a natural Canadian background into an abstract and symbolic "country of the soul." The expressionistic form of *Symphony* was suggested in part by the expressionist silent film. Already on June 18, Voaden recorded in his diary, *"from the screen:* (1) flash-back. (2) kaleidoscopic staccato episodes. (3) symbols. (4) accompanying musical score. (5) violent dynamic assaults on the various nerve centres of the auditor. (6) refusal to be limited by physical handicaps of stage." A July 4 diary entry indicates that *Symphony* would be "four circles of forms surrounding character action—(1) buildings, skyscrapers—traffic. (2) Northern hills and maritime—forests—lakes, (3) Prairies. (4) Mountains" and that the drama would be "part play and part movie. Murnau—a combined structure to give the journey 'conception.'"

Because *Symphony* has already been published in *Canadian Drama* 8.1 (1982), only a brief description of its dramatic structure, moods and images is necessary to indicate Voaden and Warrener's collaboration on the play. *Symphony* portrays an Everyman figure on a pilgrimage that concludes in his death and mystical transformation. The quest nature of the play anticipates the form and content of Voaden's 1931–1932 symbolical *Earth Song*. The depiction of the mother's death in the third movement is further developed in his 1933–1934 *Hill-land*. The theme of man's mortality and transubstantiation into nature is also dramatized in the 1931–1932 *Wilderness/Rocks*, in *Hill-land* and the 1935–1936 *Murder Pattern*. What differentiates *Symphony* from these plays is the more overt political and economic comment of the drama and the expressionist abstraction and grotesqueness (Lowrie Warrener's influence) used to make that political and artistic statement.

Symphony's first movement is the most expressionist section of the drama, a nightmarish depiction of physical and spiritual squalor and deprivation in "a large eastern city." This nightmarish quality is evoked through the distorted, multi-layered physical setting of a basement apartment under a city and huge office buildings connected by series of steps suggesting an infinite impersonal urban landscape. The focus of the scene is on the excessive materialism, approaching idolatry, of city life and the sensual deprivation this materialist pursuit engenders. The only individualized character is the representative Man whose dishevelled hair, haggard face and eyes of a madman express the effect of his environment. The other figures in the scene are an undifferentiated collective mass whose faces "show dissipation, lust, greed and desire." "Swaying drunkenly and moving slowly the masses unite at the steps, climb them and wind through the city like a dark serpent, twisting and disappearing into the night." The masses ritually worship "an ominous disk" which "half rises in the gloom above the buildings." The mysteriously flashing disk is eventually revealed to be the huge steel-gray ticker tape machine of a stock exchange which drives its worshippers to destruction.

> Terror turns to panic, the music swells, and the shapes and figures, moved as if by an unseen force, rush up the steps, face each other, hesitating for a moment as the disk flames into a red ball of fire casting a light that flows down the stairs to meet them, are drawn together at the

foot of the stairs, and in a body follow the light that seems to pull them up and suck them into the disk. These shapes and figures are followed by lines of worshippers, who rush into the disk, impelled by the same magnetic force. All are picked up and whirled dizzily in a circular motion from the top of the disk to oblivion in the void below.

In this hell-like environment, Man can find neither peace, happiness nor love, only sensual lust. "The light grows and reveals more clearly Man, head bent, writhing in agony in front of a woman whose face, convulsed with anger and tortured with jealousy, is that of a demon. Man slowly backs away and melts into the shadows. The woman, gliding like a cat, climbs the steps, moves up through the city, and is lost in the shadow of the disk." Deprived of love and a meaningful life, Man staggers from the symbolized stock exchange determined to escape this urban madness, "accompanied by music, tragic, but prophetic of hope" as the first movement comes to a close.

The extant drafts of the first movement indicate a development from an initially more realistic treatment towards greater abstraction, revealing the influence of Lowrie Warrener's nightmarish dreamlike visions in shaping the play. In an introduction to *Symphony* written in 1983 for a planned anthology of his works, Herman Voaden indicated that while he played "a considerable part in planning and writing the First Movement," Lowrie Warrener "developed the approaches we used in the next three movements, peopling the stage with strange, moving shapes, shadowy forms and patterns of changing music, colour and light." *Symphony's* second movement, "the northern wilderness," represents Man's encounter with the wilderness, the fear it inspires, and the strength Man gains by conquering his fear. The movement is based on a frightening incident in which Warrener had been lost in the Kilarney area while on a painting expedition. The Northern landscape of this brief scene is not yet the stark and serene North of Lawren Harris' semi-abstract paintings like the 1922 "Above Lake Superior" or the abstract 1930 "Mt. Lefroy," but represents a "low swamp area, a tangle of dark depressing undergrowth" in which Man is trapped "like a wounded, frightened animal." As in O'Neill's *Emperor Jones*, Man's fears are externalized. "The tree forms sway into more grotesque and menacing attitudes, and the whole north takes on motion. Then Man's inner imagination transforms the shapes and figures that terrorize him into huge overpowering shapes that close in upon him." Near madness, he "stretches himself to his full height in a gesture of defiance and courage, and slumps heavily to the ground." As Man conquers his fear, "the light upon him grows in warmth, refuelling his vitality and lending him new vigour and energy." He assumes an almost heroic stature, standing on a ridge of rock in momentary triumphant oneness with nature. "In its sturdiness his figure resembles one of the dark wind-blown jack pines that crown the ridge."

The third movement of *Symphony*, "fishing village on a Northern lake," reflects Warrener and Voaden's experiences in Port Coldwell where they became acquainted with the head of the Nicoll family fishing enterprise. "We rented the school teacher's house, roamed the big hills, and came to know the few inhabitants, including a fisherman's wife. She, with her fears and dislike of the country, suggested the old mother in 'Rocks' feeling, fearing and hating the wilderness" (Voaden, "Symphonic" 3). But this fearful fisherman's wife inspired not only Ella Martin in *Wilderness/Rocks* but also the Woman in *Symphony*. In a letter of June 26 to Violet Kilpatrick recalling Voaden and Warrener's encounter with Port Coldwell and its fishermen inhabitants, Voaden indicated that "we felt the vastness of the north; we came out upon the strong clear shore; we watched the coast line from the throbbing panting motor boat; we lived into the dim life of the Hullers—the woman's nervous clutching for her home and happiness—the man's solidarity."

Voaden's diary outlines the expressionistic treatment of the third movement of *Symphony*. It notes the fisherman's wife's "frantic attempt to hold to happiness—form of insanity—rising to screams—dread—almost shouts out that no one can take it from her" in contrast with "the quiet strength of the husband—master more than she of the north." His notes for the scene also indicate, "have the child drown or run over by train" and suggest "a continuous net—enveloping—symbolical—feeding happiness or poverty to them ... in contrast—the austere quiet of the hills brooding above." The third movement of *Symphony* introduces this apprehensive Woman figure whose only solace for her fear of nature and the weariness of a fisherman's life is her love for her husband and child. The Woman's fears are not only externalized through "nerve" dance figures but through descriptive music, light and sound as Voaden and Warrener bring the North itself on stage to evoke the mood of the coming disaster. "The music begins on a low note, prophetic of impending disaster, growing stronger, more foreboding and intense. Winds come up and heavy cloud shadows sweep across the stage. Once more the nerve figures weave in and out around the loft, which sways, totters dizzily, and almost falls." When Man appears carrying the limp and dripping body of their child, "elements and music suddenly break out again and sweep to a climax of fury and despair, while the dancing figures work themselves into a similar rage of movement" until "silence and complete darkness engulfs the scene."

Unlike Arthur's revelatory mystical encounter with a spiritual void at the end of his journey in *The White Kingdom*, *Symphony* dramatizes death concretely on stage. The third movement closes with the death of the Woman. The conclusion of the scene already suggests the theme of Voaden's later symphonic expressionist plays, the transcendence of death through nature, particularly in the austerity and spiritual clarity of the North toward which *Symphony* moves geographically and symbolically. "As the curtain drops the outlines of the great austere hills in the background are barely distinguishable." *Symphony*'s fourth movement, "a Prairie farm," is an extended dance drama with contending representational characters such as light green grain figures, grotesque sales agents, brown sun figures, heat waves, winds and fear forms. Man, now seen as a farmer, sows his grain but is eventually defeated by hail and heat. "Lights go out and come up on a bare stage, with the farmer standing, in a drooping crucified posture, with a yellow light playing about him. On all sides of him the great dry plains stretch away endlessly." Voaden and Warrener found it difficult to dramatize their encounter with the prairie landscape for *Symphony*, "The North and North Shore I have fairly got hold of, I think. The prairies are eluding us, however," Voaden wrote Kilpatrick on June 26. Crossing Saskatchewan Voaden had written

Kilpatrick June 21, "Prairies all day long. An immensity engulfing me. This is vaster than the North Shore—intangible—elusive—a fugitive powerful illimitability." Voaden and Warrener briefly interrupted their trans-Canada journey June 22, stopping at Crossfield, Alberta, to inspect the town and to "take a long walk around a country section of land. We were looking for prairie mood—how to paint it—how to dramatize it." They also went on a car ride towards the mountains and ranch country "searching the Prairies for mood and meaning."

Voaden's diary indicates that he and Warrener were partially successful in experiencing the prairie mood in order to create the fourth movement of *Symphony*. Recording a walk across the open prairie at night near Ogema, Saskatchewan, the end of July, Voaden noted that "outside the prairie waited for us, unhurried—buried in deep grass. Prairie night brooded about the village—vast and inscrutable … The grass was wet to our waists. A thousand subtle fears and essences moved toward us from the dark field … Too lonely a country for anyone but a God to dream of—much less create." But the final dramatic action of the fourth movement was suggested by a rancher who informed Voaden and Warrener of a recent storm in which crops had been extensively damaged by wind, early frost and hail, "a strip 80 miles wide—sweeping through to Regina—rain storms on either side … stones as big as eggs." Voaden's diary also contains an unidentified newspaper clipping dated Winnipeg, July 8, with the headline "Cyclonic Storms Hit Grain Areas, Heavy Damage to Western Crops Reported at Many Points." Voaden's diary entry, "yellow bleached fields—and a crucified Christ arising from them," points to his own and Warrener's metaphysical orientation evident in the conclusion of the fourth and the final movement of *Symphony*.

The concluding fifth movement, "the mountains," culminates in Man's death and transfiguration, a Whitmanesque oneness of body with nature and the universal spirit. The movement is a recapitulation of previous moods, images and character figures and initially recalls the grotesque sensuality and brutal vision of the play's first movement. The tragedy of Man's mortality and the drama's symbolist and mystic conclusion is already suggested in the opening orchestral prologue. "Slow, mournful music, touching a dim faraway note of sadness and loneliness. Austere sombre echoes of another world. At times there is a note of desolate langour and weariness. Then a sudden change is made up to a sharper, more bitter mood. But always there is the feeling of remoteness, of an immense yearning to be satisfied, of sorrow never to be assuaged."

The setting of this final movement consists of "great dark towering shoulders of rock" whose summit, however, "is still shrouded in darkness, mist and gloom." Man is discovered on a narrow ledge; "he seems to be caught up in a turmoil of dizziness and fear. The elements rage about him," until finally "his body is seen to sway for a moment and drop out of sight in the mist below. Sudden appalling silence. Sudden darkness." Despite this second encounter with death, both Man and nature are transfigured, however. The transformation of the mist figures into a life-giving force suggests the cyclical rebirth of nature. They momentarily form a great white cross, a symbol found in several of Lowrie Warrener's mystical paintings, suggesting a

Christian redemption.[5] More characteristic of Voaden's own philosophy is the drama's concluding image of radiant mountain summits and peaks evoking, like Harris' abstract mountains, the austerity and beauty of eternal life in which man is at one with the universe.

> High up on the mountain the mist forms sway together for a moment and take the form of a great cross, white in the vast gloom. As this appears, the music, still sad and tender, becomes exultant, prophetic. The cross disappears; light increases steadily. The music grows stronger, more confident. Finally the sun's rays strike the mist figures, warm, bright and life giving. The mist figures become radiant … leaving the mountain summit, visible at last, radiant with the morning light. The music is tumultuous and triumphant. On either side of the great lifting shoulders of the summit can be seen other peaks in the distance, likewise caught in the matchless radiance of morn.

Voaden's correspondence and diaries reveal not only the genesis of *Symphony* but also clarify his perception of man's encounter with the natural environment which transformed the beauty and austerity of Canadian nature into the ideal beauty and truth of "a country of the soul." Because Voaden's transcendentalism is not always clearly comprehensible in his dramas, an examination of his attitude towards nature while writing *Symphony* also clarifies his later dramatic works. To a degree, Voaden and Warrener's reaction to the Canadian landscape on their transcontinental journey could still be shared by most Canadians today. Encountering the Canadian Rockies near Calgary, they marvelled at "the clear view of the mountains—the feeling of immanent wonder as you approach them—the crazy desire to get over them—never to be contented till you are through them and have seen what is on the other side." At Lake Louise Voaden felt that "these mountains are capable of magic," querying "who can be small in stature ringed with mountains and silence, living in contact daily with inexhaustible beauty in form and colour?" Voaden's reaction to mountain climbing at Lake O'Hara as recorded in his diary and correspondence is also easily comprehensible: "An eternal grey silence brooded over me and around me. The excitement that is so closely akin to fear and exultation was sweeping over me. The stillness caught my breath." "There was a decided exhilaration to this. I felt in close fearsome company with the silent sand and white forms towering all about me. Something in the stillness—the 'above-worldliness'—that caught my breath."

But Voaden's diary also records a conception of nature as both beautiful and malign, probing his reaction to the mountains, "would you have them as companions—day by day? Do they inspire you?—to romance—serenity? Or do they give you deep dark moods?" The diary indicates that he and Warrener were not only inspired by the beauty of the Canadian landscape but were also frequently oppressed by its massiveness and austerity. Near Port Coldwell where they found the spot where Lawren Harris painted "Above Lake Superior," "dead trees stood stark and upright against the dead pattern of soundless grey sky and rolling deepening greying hills. There were moments of dreadful immanence … the colossal dimness of twilight engulfed us." On June 29 Voaden wrote Kilpatrick from Lake O'Hara that "last night Lowrie saw the lake late at night for the first time. Two patches of snow across it by the falls were like two terrible eyes. The hills and mountains seemed to be crushing in on us—a savage and horrible feeling. Neither of us wanted to stay out for long." Voaden confided in his diary, "do not carry too far the emotional intimacy with nature: it will make you mad!"

The perception that nature can be both evil and good is reflected in *Symphony* in the symbolism of the mountains and man's death and transubstantiation in nature. Echoing Lawren Harris and Bertram Brooker, Voaden's diary speaks of "'the still steady flame of aspiration' kindled by the north—by the hills and mountains— passionate belief that they hold an ideal better unattained." This identification of ethereal mountain ranges with the ideal of beauty, massiveness and eternal permanence (attainable for man only in death by becoming part of nature) also underlines the quest form of *Symphony* on both a literal and symbolic level. "The real actors in Canada are the elements—man feels—is responsive to them, he has not dominated them," Voaden continued in his diary. Of all the possibilities open to Warrener and Voaden to dramatize their trans-Canada journey, "the memory persists of the whirl of the city maelstrom in youth—the test of the north in early manhood— the vigor and full-blown power of the prairies—the sharpness, exultation and despair of the mountains."

But this encounter with the Canadian environment would not merely be a geographic one but would be "intimate—personal—spiritual ... the pictorial equivalent of an inner search for meaning—serenity—power—achievement—abstract landscape and figure forms symbolizing this. In each area—find something good—something yet unanswered and unanswerable—always the quest." The nature of the drama as mystic quest is also suggested by many of the over two dozen titles considered for *Symphony* such as "Ultimate Search," "Pilgrimage," "Spirit Progress," "The Vision Beautiful," "The Pulse of the North," "Soul and the North," "Wakening," "Soul to Light" and "Prelude to Canada." Voaden had indicated his mystical perception of mountains to Violet Kilpatrick already in August of 1929, describing a perilous night crossing of the Bitter Root mountain range in Wyoming by car with Warrener and Gordon Alderson, "a fearful and exultant thing to me."

> As we went higher I grew more excited—thrilled. The thing had a grandeur and mysticism that stirred me beyond words. We approached the summit. The moon was there—riding clear and windy. Hardly any trees.
>
> It was an ultimate moment. All the intangible forces of life rushing to sudden recognition. We were at the top! All around us were calm untroubled summits—towering—gigantic—silent forms. A moment of ecstasy. We will go and stand there—and that moment will live again. You can feel it now—can you not? Something imperishable in us— something as undeniable, massive, and glittering as those crowns of darkness.

It is interesting to note that in the development of his playwriting, which fluctuated from 1930 to 1932 between the expressionist *Symphony*, the realistic *Western Wolf* and *Wilderness*, and the highly stylized, symbolical *Rocks* and *Earth Song*, Voaden did not abandon *Symphony*. For the first time, he actively sought a production for one of his plays, submitting *Symphony* on November 5, 1930 to John Murray Gibbon, himself a librettist, Publicity Agent for the Canadian Pacific Railway, and organizer of the CPR's Canadian Folksong and Handicraft Festival in Quebec City and other music festivals along the CPR line. Gibbon, who had supplied Voaden and Warrener with free tickets for their trans-Canada journey, wrote Voaden January 2, 1931 regarding *Symphony*: "I do not see how we could make any use of the latter, as it does not appear to have the slightest relation to the Canadian Pacific Railway, which is essentially an optimistic undertaking and could not be identified with anything so gloomy and morbid, quite apart from the question of cost of production."

Symphony was better received at Yale University where Voaden revised the play in October of 1930. Though he attempted to encourage Voaden to write realistic plays, George Pierce Baker was sufficiently impressed by the drama to provide letters of introduction to the noted stage designer Norman Bel Geddes and Irene Lewishon of the New York Neighborhood Playhouse. Bel Geddes wrote Voaden January 6, 1931 that he found the play "most interesting." "It offers great pictorial opportunities for staging. My chief regret was a lack of grip and power in the action itself. I have taken the liberty of forwarding it to Mrs. Clair Reis and Leopold Stokowski, who are the leading factors of the League of Composers. They do one or two productions annually on a large scale in cooperation with the Philadelphia Symphony Orchestra and if interested are the most likely people to help you." Claire Reis wrote Voaden January 31 indicating that she too found *Symphony* "very interesting." "I believe it would lend itself to very unique stage setting and I am sure that one of our contemporary composers would find it interesting material to work with. I think it would add to this work to have the central theme emphasized more forcefully and to have more opportunity for action in the central characters."

Voaden's reply to Bel Geddes of January 21 acknowledged his criticism of *Symphony* and agreed that "a good deal of more definite pantomime and action can be written into it. The play to me is as yet only a first draft, not carried further because I felt that the exigencies of production, and the character of the music and choreography that is created, will inevitably change the problems of revision" ("Letter to Norman"). Voaden's notes and *Symphony* correspondence indicate that he felt the composer for the drama should preferably be a Canadian since "thoroughly Canadian in its birth ... I could see no reason why it should be clothed with alien music" ("Letter to Percival"). On July 6, 1932 Voaden wrote Kilpatrick: "I saw McMillan today—youthful, quiet, clear-eyed. He read *Symphony* rapidly, exclaiming once or twice in praise. 'Well done', he said when he put it up. He would like to do the music— but it is a year's work and he is *very* busy. He kept the script. In any case the interview was keen and interesting. We had much in common—our youth—our idealism. It was all worthwhile" ("Letter to Violet").

Voaden had not submitted *Symphony* to Healey Willan since "the majority of my musical friends felt that he was too interested in academic composition" ("Letter to Percival" 1–2). Voaden again worked on the play in London in January of 1933, hoping to interest the Camargo Society into producing the dance drama. He considered approaching Vaughan Williams or Gustav Holst to compose the music but decided instead to abandon his work on the play until he could study composition himself and to concentrate on writing *Hill-land* during his nine-month journey around the world. When the Canadian composer Percival Price won a Pulitzer Prize travelling scholarship in 1934 for his romantic "St. Lawrence" symphony in four movements (Islands, Rapids, Flatlands, Mountains), Voaden thought he had found his composer. In his letter to Price, Voaden referred to his month-long stay at the Jooss School of Dancing in Essen, Germany, in March of 1933 and pointed to Jooss' acclaimed "The Green Table" as a model for creative collaboration. The highly theatrical dance piece had been choreographed and danced by Jooss in collaboration with the composer Frederic Cohen. "The result was a ballet representing a perfect fusion between the two arts—a ballet which indeed constituted a new art form" ("Letter to Percival" 2). Voaden suggested a similar collaboration between himself, Price and the dancer-choreographer Boris Volkoff. "I am interested in experimental light and staging, and feel that I can add considerable in the way of visual background—the vital light and meaningful colour of the painter—to the production" ("Letter to Percival" 2).

As in the case of Stokowski, there is no extant correspondence to indicate Percival Price's reaction to *Symphony*. What is nevertheless of interest is Voaden's suggested application of "symphonic expressionist" directional methods he had begun developing in 1932 with *Rocks*, particularly in the use of lighting and the cyclorama, to attack the production difficulties of *Symphony*. In his letter to Price, for example, he indicated that "the settings described in the manuscript at present are too elaborate and costly. They can be greatly simplified. Light and colour would take their place. Similarly, the story would have to be simplified and developed" ("Letter to Percival" 2).

Perhaps stimulated by the possibility of collaborating with Price, Voaden attempted to simplify *Symphony* by designing a single all-purpose setting for all five movements. He had begun using interior monologues in *Northern Song*. *Symphony*, even in its original summer 1930 version, alerted Voaden to the use of light and darkness as a dramatic component of stage action as opposed to being merely a means of creating atmosphere and mood. Voaden's increasing use of light and darkness beginning with *Rocks* and other symphonic expressionist plays is evident in the revised scenario for *Symphony*. For the fourth prairie movement, for example, "the wind gusts will be suggested by light beams sweeping over the grain dancers. The rain—by a slight darkening of the stage" ("Outline" 4).

The interaction between Voaden's dramatic works is also suggested by a completely different conclusion of the revised *Symphony* scenario, echoing the ecstatic finale of *Earth Song* produced by the Sarnia Drama League in December of 1932.

Perhaps remembering J.M. Gibbon's criticism of the "gloomy and morbid" nature of *Symphony*, Voaden revised the play to conclude not in Man's death but in a more easily comprehensible triumphant oneness with nature. The fifth movement in the revised scenario culminates in "The final triumph and transfiguration, Man asleep at first. Then he rises to his knees. Finally he stands, lifting his arms to the sun in the glory, while the music and dancers recapitulate and sublimate his experience in triumph" ("Outline" 5).

Though never produced, Voaden and Warrener's *Symphony* holds an important place in the history of Canadian drama. The play tested Lawren Harris and Voaden's thesis, proclaimed in *Six Canadian Plays*, that a Canadian national drama and a distinct "Canadian 'Art of the Theatre'" could be created from an aesthetic awareness of Canadian nature and a philosophic and artistic idealism. Voaden and Warrener's non-realist aesthetic and neo-platonic idealism transformed their observations of Canadian nature and actual individuals and events during their two month trans-Canada journey into a highly abstract and symbolical work which probes beneath the "banality of surfaces" to examine man's fundamental relationship with society, nature and the cosmos in a "country of the soul."

Symphony also marked an important stage in Voaden's own development as a playwright and director. In his subsequent dramas, he would continue to contrast the materialism and decadence of modern North American society with the spirituality and ideal purity of the Canadian North. With *Rocks* he publicly stated his thesis, already evident in *Symphony*, that "the North possesses unique vitality—an elemental strength which uplifts and sublimates the strong ... while it warps and beats down the weak and those foreign to its spirit" ("Canadian" 18). He continued using the quest form in his dramas, "the pictorial equivalent of an inner search for meaning— serenity—power—achievement." Like Man in the fifth movement of *Symphony*, Adam in *Earth Song* also travels "beyond that far hill to the north" where he is blinded by the absolute truth, "the face of light," he has been seeking. Mountain tops, places of earthly and metaphysical vision, truth and beauty reminding man of both his finiteness and mortality and the eternal permanence of nature, also feature promi- nently in *Hill-land*. Writing extensive notes on his "New Play—Faith" while working on *Hill-land* after viewing the ancient temples of Angkor Watt in Cambodia in July of 1933, Voaden declared that "your plays are epics, prophetic calls—not *dramatic entertainment* ... Create your own signs, symbols, language, ritual—simply, honestly *but fearlessly!*—as all the prophets have done! ... a new faith is born to us—to whom at last the earth and soul-kingdoms are one!" ("New Play"). In January of 1931 Voaden had described *Symphony* to Claire Reis as "a very sincere attempt to combine music, design, the dance, and pantomime in a single synthesis" ("Letter to Claire"). In his subsequent playwriting and productions from 1932 to 1942, Voaden attempted to express "an original relation to the universe" using "symphonic expressionism" as a means of making "the earth and soul-kingdoms" one.[6]

(1983)

Notes

1 Sixty-two boxes of archival materials documenting Herman Voaden's work in the theatre, education and politics from the 1920s to the present are available to researchers at the York University Archives. The summer 1930 correspondence between Voaden and Violet Kilpatrick and the diaries "Cross Canada Summer 1930" and "Cross Canada Summer 1930: June–July" are still in Herman Voaden's possession. [Voaden passed away in 1991, eight years after the first publication of this article—Ed.]

2 In his 1983 introduction to *Symphony*, Herman Voaden paid tribute to Warrener indicating, "I am happy that *Symphony* was published before his death and that he knew he had a prime role in writing an important early Canadian theatre work." Warrener died in Toronto February 8, 1983.

3 The F.B. Housser citation is from his *A Canadian Art Movement: The Story of the Group of Seven*: 187.

4 A photo of Warrener's bust of Voaden can be found in Flood 15.

5 See for example his 1928 linocut "Pilgrim's Progress" and 1929 oil "Cross Worshippers" reproduced in *Northward Journal* 25 (1982).

6 For an analysis of Voaden's symphonic expressionism, see Grace.

Works Cited

Bel Geddes, Norman. Letter to Herman Voaden. 6 January 1931.

Denison, Merrill. "Nationalism and Drama." *Yearbook of the Arts in Canada 1928–1929*. Ed. Bertram Brooker. Toronto: Macmillan, 1929: 49–55.

Farmer, Harcourt. "Play-Writing in Canada." *Canadian Bookman* 1 (April 1919): 55–56.

Flood, John. "Lowrie Warrener." *Northward Journal* 25 (1982). 11–28.

———. "Northern Ontario Art: Part 3—Franklin Carmichael and Herman Voaden." *Boréal* 11–12 (1978): 5–8.

Gibbon, J.M. Letter to Herman Voaden. 2 January 1931.

Goldie, Terence. "Canadian Dramatic Literature in English 1919–1939." PhD Thesis. Kingston: Queen's University, 1977.

———. "A National Drama and a National Dramatist: The First Attempt." *Canadian Drama* 3.1 (1977): 9–19.

Grace, Sherrill. "A Northern Quality: Herman Voaden's Canadian Expressionism." *Canadian Drama* 8.1 (1982): 1–14.

Housser, F.B. *A Canadian Art Movement: The Story of the Group of Seven*. Toronto: Macmillan, 1926.

Jacob, Fred. "Waiting for a Dramatist." *Canadian Magazine* 43 (June 1914): 142–46.

Mason, Lawrence. "Theatre and Concert Hall Brief Comment." *Globe* 19 April 1930: 24.

Reis, Claire R. Letter to Herman Voaden. 21 January 1931.

Voaden, Herman. "Canadian Plays and Experimental Stagecraft." *Globe* 23 April 1932: 18.

———. "Introduction to *Wilderness.*" *Canada's Lost Plays, Vol. 3: The Developing Mosaic*. Ed. Anton Wagner. Toronto: Canadian Theatre Review Publications, 1980.

———. Letter to Claire Reis. 21 January 1931.

———. Letter to Norman Bel Geddes. 21 January 1931.

———. Letter to Percival Price. N.d. (Spring 1934).

———. Letter to Violet Kilpatrick. 6 July 1932.

———. "New Play—Faith." MS July 1933.

———. Outline for Revisions in *Symphony*. 1934.

———. "Symphonic Expressionism: A Canadian Adventure in the Direction of a More Musical and Expressive Theatre." Unpublished TS, 1975.

———, ed. *Six Canadian Plays*. Toronto: Copp Clark, 1930.

Between Empires:
Post-Imperialism and Canadian Theatre

by Alan Filewod

> We thought it deeply significant to hear repeatedly from representatives
> of the two Canadian cultures expressions of hope and confidence that in
> the common cultivation of things of the mind, Canadians—French- and
> English-speaking—can find true Canadianism. (Royal Commission
> 271)

The search for "true Canadianism" has always been an imperative project of Canadian theatre, and the continued failure to "find" an essential national principle suggests one of the defining conditions of post-colonial nationhood. Because Canada is a product of Victorian state-making, any appreciation of the history of the legitimization of the theatre as a public enterprise requires an investigation into the complexities coded into the very formulation of "Canadian theatre," complexities which expose the contradictions of colonialism and nationalism.

As an historical and cultural process in any social context, colonialism is pervasive and complex, and consequently the commonly used term "post-colonialism" rewards vastly different readings and applications. Despite its currency, "post-colonialism" is a problematic formulation, in part because it reductively equates very different historical experiences, and in part because it implies a state of emergence from colonialism, whereas in fact post-colonial societies find themselves defined and often confused by numerous intersecting and very present colonialisms.

For that reason, "post-imperial" is a more appropriate term to refer to the development of nationalism and nationhood in Canada, from its imperial origins to the constitutional crises of the 1990s. "Post-colonial" then refers to the cultural experience of societies (and communities) struggling for definition after having identity displaced through colonialism, or (as is the case of the settler dominions of the British Empire) seeking an essential definition to legitimize the founding of the colonial state. Post-imperialism is, by definition, one particular post-colonial experience, but it is by no means the only post-colonial reading of Canadian culture —especially if the notion of colonialism is applied to ethnic, class, and gender, as well as political, hegemony.

The post-imperial narrative suggests that the theatre in Canada has been both a site of post-colonial definition and the material expression of changing ideologies of nationhood, and has been institutionalized—funded, promoted, and studied—precisely because it has legitimized those ideologies. It is an indication of the cultural instability of post-colonial society that the phrase "Canadian theatre" must be differentiated from "theatre in Canada," because "Canada" is not merely the site of conflicting readings of the nation (as is the case with any country). The very phrase "Canadian theatre" has for over a century carried an implicit value of anti-colonialism—as did "imperial" to the generations of Canadians who proudly considered themselves citizens of what the poet Wilfred Campbell called a "Vaster Britain".[1]

The propositions that pride in Empire could be in fact be a gesture of *anti-colonialism* and that, in Canada at least, Imperialism was in itself a post-colonial and anti-hegemonic ideology, can be supported by reference to a representative example of imperial iconography. From 1887 to 1941, the Canadian National Exhibition in Toronto featured patriotic pyrotechnical pageants, staged by the Hand & Teales Spectacular Company (now Hands Fireworks). The 1900 pageant, *The Siege of Mafeking*, was typical of the genre, with crowd-pleasing panoramas, special effects and pleasing sentiment. The climactic scene showed:

> The coming of the relief force under General Plumer and General Mahon. Enter Canadians, Australians, Rhodesians, Artillery and others … The Boers finding themselves discovered open fire. Canadians suddenly rise up and make a run for the first trench. The Boers fly to the higher rocks. Gallant charge on all trenches by the British. (Hand)[2]

For the audiences that cheered the image of Canadian soldiers serving under British command in a colonial war, complicity in British imperialism was not evidence of colonial subservience but proof of post-colonial autonomy: the Empire was an arena in which Canada was recognized as a mature partner but whose difference was acknowledged. Perhaps more importantly in terms of Canadian cultural development, the Empire served as a means of resistance against the rapidly expanding empire of the United States. The very proposition of "Canadian theatre" was an attempt to redress the material fact that by the end of the 19th century, theatre in English-speaking Canada was largely an American enterprise. The theatre was perhaps one of the first economic sectors of Canadian society to have been penetrated deeply by American capital, and consequently it was one of the first sectors to resist that penetration.

The theatre of the Victorian era in Canada was extremely busy but, as contemporary critics noted vehemently, not very Canadian. Ann Saddlemyer has estimated that "by the late nineteenth century there were about 250 touring companies on 'The Road'" in Ontario alone (Saddlemyer 6). Although many of these troupes were in fact Canadian (such as the seven touring companies of the Marks Brothers and numerous local minstrel troupes), some were British (usually booked through New York), and the majority were American, with their competing Tom shows and melodramas. More importantly, the touring circuits were owned or controlled by American booking agencies. Nationalist critics argued that such control would necessarily impede the development of Canadian drama. One of the most vociferous was B.K. Sandwell, who in a series of articles and addresses to business clubs, argued that American control of the theatre jeopardized Canadian cultural development, while exposure to British drama would encourage it:

> There are good reasons why Canadians should familiarize themselves with the social conditions and problems of Great Britain, and there is no better way of doing it than by the serious British drama. Great Britain is the predominant partner in the Empire to which we all belong—a partnership which few of us want to break and which many of us would like to see drawn even closer than it is today. It is possible that at no distant date we may have quite a lot to say about the running of the Empire; and we cannot understand the Empire without understanding the people of the British Isles and their conditions and problems. The British drama is the drama of our own people, or our brothers and fellow subjects. The American drama is an alien drama…. ("Adjunct" 102)

The problem with "the American occupation of our stage" was that American drama expressed social values alien to "the Canadian mind," which Sandwell defined as philosophically and historically opposed to the American mission of "testing certain far-reaching theories concerning man, property and the State" ("Annexation" 24). In that sense, American domination of the stage was subversive precisely because to the New York producers the theatre was no more than a business proposition.

Sandwell was by no means alone in his belief that closer imperial ties would strengthen Canadian national development. Mistrust of American hegemony may have been in part a mistrust of popular taste but it was also the consequence of history. American Loyalist refugees from the United States had been one of the formative components of English Canadian settlement, and their legacy, seemingly confirmed by the War of 1812, was a deep apprehension of American republicanism as rapacious and expansionist. This was the common thesis of the patriotic poetic dramas of the high Victorian era, the best-known of which are Charles Mair's *Tecumseh* and Sarah Anne Curzon's *Laura Secord: The Heroine of 1812*. In these plays even the choice of form—book publication of verse dramas—restated the gap between the material conditions of the American-dominated popular stage and the literary affirmation of the British classical repertoire. Mair's *Tecumseh*, about the doomed aboriginal ally of the British cause in the War of 1812 and his friendship with General Brock, the "Canadian Washington," was an attempt to situate Canadian experience in the larger domain of imperial romantic tradition. [3] It was also a polemical treatise which proposed an essentialist principle of nationhood in the intersection of imperial resistance to American "mobocracy," and the passing of proprietary right to the land from Tecumseh, configured as the last hope of aboriginal sovereignty, to his English Canadian "heirs."

The ideology of Canadian nationhood evolved gradually, from what late Victorian observers termed "colonial nationalism" to a modern pluralist state patriotism. [4] From its beginnings, the Canadian state sought ways to legitimize itself as a nation even though it lacked what E.J. Hobsbawm calls "protonational" conditions: commonality of race, language or religion (45–79). To that extent, the Canadian

Confederation prefigured the modern pluralist state, but it was legislated into being at a time when a new form of nationalism was redefining the state in Europe. Noting an increasing equation of nationalism with self-determination based on ethnicity and language, and a concurrent "sharp shift to the political right" (102), Hobsbawm argues that

> ...the type of nationalism which emerged towards the end of the nine-teenth century had no fundamental similarity to state-patriotism, even when it attached itself to it. Its basic loyalty was, paradoxically, not to the country but only to its particular version of that country: to an ideological construct. (93)

In these terms, the colonial nationalists of the new Dominion of Canada promoted imperialism as one such construct to legitimize their ethnic and class vision of what a nation-state should be. The commonly expressed rhetoric of the dominions as sibling "sisters" and "daughters" of the crown offered the new Canadian state a legitimizing national sentiment in the anthropomorphic terms of nineteenth-century racialism. Accepting the biological determinism of Victorian "race-science," nation-alists spoke of the country's "evolution" into "maturity": Canada was frequently portrayed as a young woman coming into age, loyal to her mother and wary of her "cousin Jonathan." [5] The terms may have shifted since that time but the fundamental trope that equates national "growth" with a maturation from dependent infancy to autonomous adulthood is still very much part of the rhetoric of Canadian nationhood. [6] To the original generation of Canadian nationalists like Mair, the identification of race and nation supplied the essentialist principle demanded by the ideological forces of the day. Imperial sentiment did not survive the changing political and economic conditions of the early 20th century (except for a lingering but declining fondness for the monarchy, revived periodically by carefully staged royal visits) but the equation of nation with family did, and succeeding generations of Canadian nationalists continued to redefine the "true Canadian" principle according to their ideological contexts.

The changing value of nationalism directly influenced the cultural formation of Canadian theatre. The rhetoric of nationalism became increasingly secular as the British Empire was gradually reconstituted as the Commonwealth, but the formative role of British experience has continued to shape the notion of Canadian theatre. When Sandwell attacked the American commercial stage, he proposed a remedy in the form of civic repertory theatres along the British model. Through the first decades of the century, the argument in favour of public subsidy was invariably linked to the proposition of a national theatre, again following recent British developments. [7] In the Canadian case however, the national theatre idea was not merely a defence against degraded commercialism, it was a defence against degraded American com-mercialism. Consequently, the class assumptions of the British national theatre debate were grafted onto the idea of a distinctly Canadian theatre, which would thereafter carry with it the assumption that the theatre and drama should uplift the populace and (in the words of the Royal Commission on National Development in the Arts,

Letters and Sciences 1949–51) stand as "not only the most striking symbol of a nation's culture but the central structure enshrining much that is finest in a nation's spiritual and artistic greatness" (193). The various proposals for a national theatre (most of which were informed by the National Theatre proposals in Great Britain) that came and went unfulfilled through the first half of the century all adhered to this principle of an elite culture that would resist American hegemony (with its equation of republicanism and mass taste) by providing an exemplary alternative. The corollary that a subsidized theatre need only appeal to an educated minority to fulfill its purpose is to this day the fundamental justification of public funding.

The development of cultural policy in the mid-century can be seen as a process of nationalizing cultural industries to legitimize an ostensibly decolonized vision of the state. In terms of the theatre, the process of decolonization was also one of rationalizing the diversity of theatrical activity in terms of its relationship to national ideology. The key figure in this regard was Vincent Massey, who was the architect of the cultural policy that created the conditions which enabled the theatre to develop as a professional enterprise in the decades following the Second World War. In 1949 the Liberal government of Louis St. Laurent invited Massey to chair the Royal Commission on National Development in the Arts, Letters and Sciences. Commonly referred to as the Massey-Levesque Commission (as an acknowledgement of the important contribution of Georges-Henri Levesque, one of Massey's four commissioners), this body was empowered to survey the state of Canadian culture (including the fine and performing arts, mass media, crafts and scholarship) with a view to making recommendations to the federal government regarding cultural policies. Massey's credentials were widely known: in his youth he had vigorously championed the cause of Canadian playwriting as an actor and director at the University of Toronto's Hart House Theatre (which his family foundation had built), and he was one of the first anthologists of Canadian drama. Later, while High Commissioner to Great Britain during the Second World War, he had served as Chairman of the British National Gallery. To a government anxious to legitimize itself with a national culture, Massey was the ideal choice. A gifted amateur who personified the idea of high culture, he had educated taste, Liberal politics and a substantial fortune. As Claude Bissell has exhaustively demonstrated, Massey's nationalism was formed on the basis of a profound cultural allegiance to Great Britain: his deep loyalty to the monarchy and friendship with King George VI (who inducted him as a Companion of Honour in 1946), his close affiliations with Oxford, his service as High Commissioner to Britain, and his term as Governor General of Canada (the vice-regal representative of the crown) all attest to his abiding faith in British culture. In his memoirs Massey made the point that

> It is significant that movements in Canada such as the Dominion Drama Festival, and the Shakespearean Festival at Stratford, have very close connections with England. Although New York, a great theatrical centre, is so near, it is to London that we have turned for experience, expertise and training in the sphere of drama. (198)

For two years the commission travelled across the country and heard from hundreds of groups and individuals. When it turned its eye towards theatre the commission concluded that "In Canada there is nothing comparable, whether in play-production or in writing for the theatre, to what is going on in other countries with which we should like to claim intellectual kinship and cultural equality" (Royal Commission 193). Relying heavily on the opinions of the playwright and novelist Robertson Davies, who like Massey was born into a wealthy family, had studied at Oxford, and understood the theatre in terms derived from British cultural experience, the commission's survey of the arts omitted mention of theatrical activity that did not fit the explicit project of nation-building. In effect it can be read as an attempt to establish a genealogy of the theatre that reinforced state ideology. Massey was concerned above all with the need to recognize and support national culture, but his insistence that Canadian nationhood proceeded from the historical marriage of two founding cultures reflected the ideology of the Liberal party. Massey applauded attempts to create a national dramatic repertoire, and saw the Dominion Drama Festival, which since 1933 had provided an annual festival for amateur theatres, as a truly national enterprise. But his survey erases as much as it includes, primarily on the basis of class and ethnicity. There is no mention, for instance, of the Theatre of Action or any of the other left-wing worker's theatres of the 1930s. Nor is there any concession that professional theatre could operate in languages other than English or French, although there had been active theatrical traditions in many of the immigrant communities.

For Massey, Canadianism was built on the foundation of British civilization (modified to include francophone Canada) and his ideal of the theatre was a Canadian refinement of a British prototype. The chief recommendation of his commission was of course the Canada Council, founded six years after the submission of the report on the model of the British Arts Council. The founding of the Canada Council is normally seen as a watershed in cultural history, a move which superseded the inadequacies of the colonized past and established the conditions for the autonomous future. It may be more useful to look at it from the opposite perspective, which posits the founding of the Council as the final realization of an imperial vision first pronounced at the turn of the century. The issue is not just one of the acceptance of state patronage as a principle, but of the notions of culture the state saw fit to patronize and the institutional structures it established for that purpose. In its own operations and its policies, the new Canada Council embodied an elitist concept of culture which had not changed in substance since Vincent Massey's student days at Oxford.

Throughout the twentieth century the signifiers of imperial experience were gradually eradicated in Canadian life, but in the arts its substance was given renewed vigor. In English-speaking Canada the professional theatre funded by the Canada Council unabashedly relied on the "experience and expertise" of British directors, designers and actors. By the late 1960s, the vision of the Massey report had been realized insofar as English Canada boasted a dozen or so civic theatres. Their dependence on British experience, so welcomed by Massey, would in the ensuing decade be the site of renewed post-colonial anxiety. Fifty years earlier critics had identified American popular drama as the factor that retarded Canadian playwriting; in the 1970s, in a Canada deeply implicated in the new American empire, American drama was no longer a threat to the notion of an elite theatre (although it was the site of controversy in broadcasting and film distribution). In the theatre, the once-liberating force of British culture was now perceived as the colonizing agency. The polarity of Canadian/American had now been superseded by the new antitheses of Canadian and "international"; and the call for increased "Canadian content" in the theatre was a threat to the class assumptions inscribed in the civic theatre network. The large theatres in the 1950s and '60s had a dismal record of producing new work, and when challenged, responded in terms that suggest the continuing instability of Canadian nationality. Even as the Liberal government was promoting the Centennial year of 1967 as a post-colonial coming-of-age, Eddie Gilbert, the artistic director of the Manitoba Theatre Centre, justified his lack of interest in Canadian playwriting with the comment that,

> I don't see how a play can be Canadian. I mean, what is a Canadian play? Is it a play written by a Canadian, is it a play written in Canada? What happens if a Canadian writes a play in Bermuda? Is that a West Indian play or a Canadian play? The whole issue seems to me to be a total red herring. (Chusid 14)

Two years later, Gilbert's successor at MTC, Kurt Reis, used the same rhetorical strategy to answer a similar criticism:

> Frankly, I don't think there is any way to suddenly cause good Canadian plays to appear. What does the phrase mean? Does it mean the author was born in Canada? Writes in Canada? Writes about Canada? Once visited Canada? (qtd. in Hendry 13)

Such attitudes, which displaced the responsibility for developing new playwrights to small non-funded theatres, played a major role in defining the temper of the great surge of creativity and reorganization in the theatre of the 1960s and '70s. Commonly referred to as the "alternative theatre movement," this reconstitution of the theatre profession was the result of many interconnected historical factors. In the post-colonial context it was a nationalist revolt against the perceived dominance of an imperial model which expressed itself as "international." At the same time it revealed the changing terms of nationalism. The alternative theatre was heavily influenced in its formative stages by the American experimental theatre: in terms of cultural ideology and theatrical techniques, companies such the Living Theatre, the San Francisco Mime Troupe, Bread and Puppet, and the Open Theatre gave the post-war generation of artists the artistic vocabulary to repudiate the model of culture institutionalized in the civic theatres. Politically, this generation was closely aligned with its American and European counterparts (in fact, the new Canadian theatres included many American war resisters), and it expressed itself in similar ways. In the 1969–70 season in Toronto the most popular plays showed the strong affinity between Canadian and American counter-culture politics: Studio Lab Theatre's production of

Dionysus in '69 was the first outside of New York; *Hair* played for a year at the Royal Alexandra Theatre (twenty years later to be the home of *Les Miserables*); Theatre Passe Muraille, which would soon become the vanguard of the new nationalism, began with Foster's *Tom Paine* and Rochelle Owens's *Futz*. Within two years the new force of nationalism had asserted itself with unprecedented creative energy: by mid-decade dozens of new small theatres had produced hundreds of original works. Many of them followed the example of Theatre Passe Muraille, which from 1972 began exploring the application of collective creation to localist history and culture.

This new nationalism may have accorded with federal policy but it also met with strong resistance. The provincial and federal arts councils were caught in a bind: on the one hand they promoted new work but on the other they had an enduring investment in the idea of "showcase" culture, which apportioned the greater share of public funding to "world-class" institutions such as the Stratford Festival (which because of its reputation and size was frequently identified as the *de facto* national theatre) and the National Ballet; such institutions normally turned to Great Britain for artistic expertise, and commonly hired British directors. But the appointment of Robin Phillips as artistic director of Stratford in 1974 was the first in a series of controversies regarding preferential hiring of British directors that marked the decade. Perhaps for the first time in Canadian theatre, a British artist found himself opposed as alien when, in its inaugural issue, *Canadian Theatre Review* editorialized that "no other country in the world has a foreigner running its 'national' theatre" (Rubin 5).

The new theatre movement of the 1970s was the expression of a nationalist generation that came to the theatre after the founding of the Canada Council and which perceived public subsidy as a right. The new theatres that survived the decade were institutionalized out of their underground beginnings by the cultural policies of Pierre Trudeau's Liberal government, which encouraged nationalism and provided easily obtained grants through job-creation programs. Many of the theatre companies that began with these grants turned to the Canada Council for support when the original programs lapsed; invariably those that survived the decade did so by tempering their original radicalism to meet the institutional demands of the arts councils. The signal example is that of the Toronto Free Theatre, founded in 1971 as a radical company to present new works free of charge; by the end of the decade it was one of the largest of the new generation of theatres, with prices to match; by the end of the 1980s it had merged with its former nemesis, the bourgeois CentreStage (the mainstream tenant of the St. Lawrence Centre) to form the Canadian Stage Company, one of the two largest civic theatres in the country. In this way it was the alternative theatres that finally realized the vision of the Massey Commission by establishing a network of civic companies that balanced obligations to the "world" repertoire (still largely British and American) with a proven commitment to Canadian playwrights. But just as the theatres of the 1970s challenged institutional culture as colonized, so were the confidently "Canadian" theatres of the 1980s challenged in turn; now the terms of colonization had more to do with gender and ethnicity than with imperial affinities.

By the end of the 1970s, the nationalism that inspired the new theatre movement no longer seemed adequate, except in Québec. And even the rise of Québécois nationalism and separatism merely confirmed the collapse of the essentialism of the Trudeau years; in terms of the theatre, Québec and (English) Canada were obviously separate. Outside of Québec, nationalism no longer seemed to define cultural difference; in fact it seemed to obscure it. The change can be measured in the shifting values of key words: in 1974 the terms "native" and "indigenous" meant "Canadian" as opposed to British or American; by 1984 they had acquired a much more specific value (pertaining to aboriginal peoples) which challenged the very meaning of "Canadian" as it was understood only a decade earlier.

The adoption of multiculturalism as a national theory and policy was intended as the final stage of repudiating the imperial tradition, in part as a response to changing demographics, and in part to constrain the separatist tendencies of Québécois nationalism. The doctrines of bilingualism and multiculturalism promoted by federal governments since the 1960s attempted to replace the defining signifier of the principle of nationhood. In the fundamental relation of nation and state, multi-culturalism serves the same purpose for today's governments as imperialism did for yesterday's, by defining the conditions of national distinctiveness and imbuing the state with a national mission. The development from imperial to multicultural nationalism is an historical process that Canada shares with its former "sisters" of the Empire because of changing political realities. In a parallel example, Stephen Alomes and Catherine Jones point out in *Australian Nationalism: A Documentary History* that, "The discovery that Australia was a multicultural society was not only a sign of a new openness and tolerance in a changing society after generations of migration and inter-marriage. It was also a recognition by the political parties that the 'ethnic vote' was becoming politically important" (370). Both Canada and Australia were of course multicultural societies since their founding, and the ethnic vote had always been important in regional pockets: what matters here is that in both countries post-imperial governments promoted multiculturalism as an ideology of nationalism to satisfy the post-colonial need for a defining national principle. The fact of official multiculturalism however had little impact on the theatre, which as an institution continued to reflect the actual distribution of wealth and power in Canadian society. In the 1980s the cultural assertions of previously silenced and marginalized commu-nities began to destabilize the official meaning of "multicultural" and showed the nationalism of the 1970s to have been the artifact of a particular segment of Canadian society—or, to repeat Hobsbawm's words, "a particular version of [the] country, an ideological construct." So too were the cultural enterprises that legitimized that nationalism.

The Liberal ideology of the Trudeau years needed an active, nationalist theatre as one of the proofs of its vision of Canada as a true federation which was post-colonial in the technical sense of the term: a culture that had moved beyond colonial signifiers to "true Canadianism." The Progressive Conservative government of Brian Mulroney that followed has as a result of its own ideological program exposed that vision as a post-imperial stage of unresolved colonialism. Mulroney's attempt to complete

Trudeau's failed mission to obtain Québec's agreement on a constitutional accord resulted in ongoing negotiations with the ten provinces as well as aboriginal groups in which it became clear that "Canada" was still an unstable construct that defied consensual definition, and which could quite conceivably break apart. At the very least, if the prospect of an independent Québec recognized that Québec had achieved nationhood but not autonomy, then this forced the question of whether English Canada might be considered a nation as well, although a majority of its population had been steeped in the Liberal principle that defined Canadianism as the historical marriage of two founding cultures. In the renegotiation of federalism there appeared to be the potential for a postnational state, and as cultural minorities found renewed opportunity to express their experience (and win the rhetorical status of nationhood, as was the case of the First Nations), funding programs in the arts gradually opened to accommodate them. Still, cultural policies continued to favour the monumental showcases of "national" as opposed to "community" importance. In 1992, the Stratford Festival was still the most heavily subsidized theatre in the country.

In the mid-1980s, the Mulroney government embarked on a program of economic integration with the United States in which the idea of nation was subordinated to an idea of the state as economic competitor in a world defined as a marketplace. The very notion of countries as "markets" has had profound implications for the theatre. Although the North American Free Trade Agreement deliberately excluded cultural enterprises, at the same time federal cultural policies have emphasized the importance of market economics in the arts.

The two major developments in Canadian theatre in the 1980s show a shifting perception of the arts as a business rather than a public enterprise. The development of entrepreneurial commercial theatre, particularly with Canadian productions of Broadway and West End "megahits" has created a marked disparity between public and private sectors in the theatre. As the theatre business becomes more lucrative, the subsidized theatres—the large civic companies as well as the small "community"-based companies—have been forced to justify themselves in business terms defined by "popular" hits of the order of *The Phantom of the Opera*. In this the Canadian experience parallels similar developments in the United States and Great Britain—with the familiar complication that the commercial theatres invariably rely on imported West End or Broadway repertoires.

The second development is that of the Fringe festivals, which began in Edmonton in 1981 and by 1992 had become annual events in seven Canadian cities. The festival programs typically feature several dozen participating companies selected on a first-to-apply basis; after paying a small initial fee, the companies keep their entire box office. With a minimal amount of public funding, the Fringe festivals market new work and talent in a competitive arena where reputations can be made quickly and success is measured mainly in terms of box office popularity. In effect the Fringe functions as an entry-level trade show for the theatre industry. Significantly the success of the Fringe festivals coincides with the decline of initiative funding for new theatre companies; the Fringe provides entry into the profession in manner analogous to the make-work projects of the 1970s.

These two developments, at both ends of the theatre's financial spectrum, disprove a fundamental assertion of the Massey report, that a professional theatre must be a public enterprise. But they do so by reconstituting the same theatrical conditions that Massey inveighed against. The commercial theatre continues the enterprise of the touring syndicates of a century ago, and the Fringe festivals take place outside of the domain of the professional unions; the artists earn only what they make at the box office and therefore rarely make a living at their art. Massey, like many others, believed that public funding would diminish, if not eradicate, those conditions from the theatre.

In the theatre then, the power of market economics shows the notion of public funding to have been an ideological strategy rather than the realization of a national imperative. Although one might well think that the more tenuous the sense of nation, the more importance will be placed on public funding, the opposite has been the case in Canada, because the survival of a professional theatre *in any form* satisfies those who see the arts as a showcase of national maturity. The existence of a profitable commercial theatre has in fact been used as a justification of reduced subsidy by the conservative governments of the 1980s and '90s. For the Mulroney government, the most overtly pro-American and continentalist in history, the expressions of nationalism (and of cultural difference) that seem to result from public subsidy are seen as an embarrassment. In the 1992 constitutional talks, the federal government agreed in principle to allocate ("devolve") jurisdiction over "culture" to the individual provinces, retaining control only over a few unspecified "national institutions." To the government mind of 1992, the arts were increasingly irrelevant to "true Canadianism." If the cultural assumptions of the Massey *Report* derive from the imperial traditions of Great Britain, the assumptions of public funding in the 1990s reflect a tendency to conform to the ideological priorities of the United States.

Like so many of the other national narratives that are the historical products of late 19th- and early 20th-century state-making, "Canada" has become a decentered text, and in consequence the cultural enterprises that legitimized the state have been exposed as artifacts rather than essential principles. Although some Canadians take an ironic pride in claiming that the recurring inability to define the state as something more than a legislative compromise may itself be the defining characteristic of Canadian nationhood, we need only look at Eastern Europe to recall that seemingly stable national ideologies are very quickly overturned. If the experience of the Canadian theatre shows that cultural enterprises serve to legitimize the state and lose their centrality (and too often their funding) when they are no longer needed, that merely restates an historical principle all too familiar to students of Soviet or East German theatre.

The evolutionary patterns of Canadian theatre and drama in the twentieth century can be read as the expression of a post-colonial impulse that failed to transcend the contradictions of colonialism. Post-imperial nationalism may in the end be little more than nostalgia for a sense of historical belonging, for the essential principle which must always remain elusive. Not only is that principle itself the projection of a certain historical phase in the notion of nationalism, but the *desire* for it is the articulation of a constantly changing understanding of nationhood. In that sense, "true Canadianism" (or to use its more recent signifiers, "Canadian identity" or "national unity") can never be achieved: it is the constant projection into the future of a nostalgia for a perpetually re-invented past.

(1992)

Notes

1   Campbell used the formulation "Vaster Britain" in the title of his 1914 collection, *Sagas of Vaster Britain.*

2   The archives of Hands Fireworks Company, Milton, Ontario include several such scripts, as well as designs, correspondence and programs. Most of the pageants depicted chapters of imperial and Canadian history; some, like *Nero and the Burning of Rome* (1913) turned to classical history, following the popular Victorian construction of Imperial Rome as a template for the British Empire.

3   Mair was not entirely removed from the appeal of the popular stage; his depictions of the American invaders as crude bumpkins may have been the first instance of what would become a popular character type in Canadian drama, although the invading soldier has been more commonly revived as an invasive tourist or businessman.

4   The phrase "colonial nationalism" was proposed in the specific context of emerging national sentiments in the settler colonies of the British Empire by Richard Jebb at the turn of the century. See Eddy and Schreuder.

5   The empire as family was a common motif in poetry and art of the day; its most familiar version may be Kipling's poem "Our Lady of the Snows"(1897), with its refrain:

> A Nation spoke to a Nation,
> A Queen sent word to a Throne;
> "Daughter am I in my mother's house,
> But mistress in my own .... "

The Toronto satirist J.W. Bengough drew numerous cartoons for *Grip* and *Punch In Canada* illustrating this relationship. In a typical example from 1869, a sturdy young Miss Canada embraces a helmeted Britannia while a sneering Uncle Sam figure smokes a cigar nearby. The caption reads:

> Mrs Britannia: "Is it possible, my dear, that you have ever given your cousin Jonathan any encouragement?
> Miss Canada: Encouragement! Certainly not, Mamma. I have told him we can *never* be united." (Bengough 27)

⁶ The prevalence of anthropomorphism as the defining metaphor of nationalism can be seen in numerous references to Canada's "coming of age" at various points in the country's history, and by the federal government's practice of celebrating Canada Day ("Dominion Day" until 1989) as "Canada's Birthday." Such practices reinforce the state's powers to control the terms of nationalism by configuring the relationship of the government and the citizens as familial: the government serves as the parents of the "Canadian family" and, like parents, enforces unity.

⁷ For discussion of the ideological formation of the national theatre, see Filewod; Salter.

Works Cited

Alomes, Stephen, and Catherine Jones. *Australian Nationalism: A Documentary History.* North Ryde: Angus & Robertson, 1991.

Bengough, J.W. *A Caricature History of Canadian Politics.* 1886. Ed. Doug Fetherling. Toronto: Peter Martin, 1974.

Bissell, Claude. *The Young Vincent Massey.* Toronto: U of Toronto P, 1981.

———. *The Imperial Canadian: Vincent Massey in Office.* Toronto: U of Toronto P, 1986.

Campbell, Wilfred. *The Poetical Works of Wilfred Campbell.* Ed. W.K. Sykes. London: Hodder, 1922.

———. *Sagas of a Vaster Britain.* Toronto: Musson, 1914.

Chusid, Harvey. "Nationalistic Labels Stifle Development." *The Stage in Canada / La Scène au Canada* May 1967: 9–18.

Eddy, John, and Deryck Schreuder, ed. *The Rise of Colonial Nationalism.* Sydney: Allen & Unwin, 1988.

Filewod, Alan. "National Theatre / National Obsession." *Canadian Theatre Review* 62 (1990): 5–10.

Hand & Teals Spectacular Co., *The Siege of Mafeking* t.s., 1900. Hand Fireworks Company archive, Milton, Ontario.

Hendry, Tom. "Regional Theatre Works." *The Stage in Canada / La Scène au Canada* November 1969: 10–14.

Hobsbawm, E.J. *Nations and Nationalism since 1780.* Cambridge: Cambridge UP, 1990.

Massey, Vincent. *What's Past Is Prologue: The Memoirs of the Right Honourable Vincent Massey, C.H.* Toronto: Macmillan, 1963.

Royal Commission on National Development in the Arts, Letters and Sciences 1949–1951 *Report.* Ottawa: The King's Printer, 1951.

Rubin, Don, Stephen Mezei, and Ross Stuart. "Aside: An Editorial Viewpoint." *Canadian Theatre Review* 1 (1974): 4–5.

Saddlemyer, Ann, ed. *Early Stages: Theatre in Ontario 1800–1914.* Toronto: U of Toronto P, 1990.

Salter, Denis. "The Idea of a National Theatre." *Canadian Canons: Essays in Literary Value.* Ed. Robert Lecker. Toronto: U of Toronto P, 1991. 71–90.

Sandwell, B.K. "Our Adjunct Theatre." *Addresses Delivered Before the Canadian Club of Montreal: Season* 1913–1914. Montreal: The Canadian Club, 1914. 95–104.

———. "The Annexation Of Our Stage." *Canadian Magazine* November 1911: 22–26.

Reading Material: Transfers, Remounts, and the Production of Meaning in Contemporary Toronto Drama and Theatre

by Ric Knowles

Criticism and analysis of Canadian drama has focused on published scripts, treating them as plays. Most dramatic criticism, that is, deals with Canadian drama as dramatic literature, a stable body of literary texts whose meanings, or potential meanings, are contained in (and often by) the words on the page, to be released by theatrical production or revealed by scholarly interpretation without reference to the social, cultural, historical, or theatrical contexts in and through which those scripts and their meanings are produced. At the same time, Canadian theatre history, and writing about contemporary theatre in Canada, has focused on the records of theatrical production with little reference to the ways in which specific material conditions and cultural contexts shape the production of meaning by theatre workers and audiences alike.

As a corrective to this situation, I will consider plays not as the autonomous works of individual creators—products of the determinable intentions of playwrights, directors, and other theatre artists—but as the results of a more complex mode of production that is rooted, as is all cultural production, in specific social and cultural contexts. At its most basic level, this approach means that the work of a playwright such as Nova Scotia's Christopher Heide, who has worked almost exclusively with small rural Maritime theatre companies, is not in any meaningful way comparable to that of, say, Sky Gilbert, who speaks out of the context of Buddies in Bad Times Theatre and Toronto's gay community, or to that of Maenad Theatre Company, a Calgary-based feminist collective. It also means, for example, that the British-born Michael Cook can more usefully be seen as a "Newfoundland" playwright in the 1970s than can the Newfoundland native David French. Cook's play's produced their meanings through Newfoundland theatre workers and audiences—through, that is, their Newfoundland theatrical and cultural context—while French's works produced their meanings in the context of the burgeoning alternative theatre scene in Toronto. One *can* understand French, in part, by understanding the ways in which his plays express his Newfoundland background, heritage, and experience, as one *can* understand Cook, in part, as a product of his background in the Irish theatre and the British army. Equally, however, one can read their works as taking part in the mutually transformative struggle for meaning within the social and theatrical contexts through which the plays were and are produced; one can look at the scripts, that is, not as stable texts in a body of dramatic literature or as prescriptive of performance, but as pre-texts; and one can look at their performances not as theatrical *interpretations* of pre-existing plays, evidence that certain readings work and are therefore genuinely in the plays, but as *themselves* cultural productions, performance texts that serve specific cultural and theatrical communities at particular moments as sites for the negotiation, transmission, and transformation of cultural values.

I

I want to focus on this circulation of cultural values, in particular on the negotiation between culturally dominant, conservative forces and potentially subversive or transgressive texts, structures, and theatrical languages that can intervene as agents of social change. I want, that is, to look at how versions of society, history, class, race, or gender can be both instantiated and contested in a given performance text, and the degree to which the transgressive or transformative potential of a particular script can be realized or contained by the changing material conditions within and through which it is produced. [1]

In the final sections of my essay, I will look at what Baz Kershaw defines as the "[p]erformance efficacy" (257–58 and elsewhere) of four Canadian scripts that have been taught, written about, and celebrated (through literary awards) as dramatic literature, that were clearly intended by the playwrights to engage in transgressive cultural intervention, but whose ideological work has been mediated in complex and ongoing ways by the cultural and, specifically, theatrical conditions through which they have been produced. But I will first look briefly at some of those theatrical conditions and the ways in which they can shape meaning in contemporary productions.

I want to focus on the theatrical rather than the cultural conditions that shape meaning on Canada's stages because it is important for readers of a literary journal to construct strategies for reading as actors, directors, and audience members, to notice how the material conditions of production shape the meanings of the plays that we write about and teach as dramatic literature. These conditions include: theatre and stage architecture, which silently inscribe specific and ideologically coded ways of seeing; the training of actors, directors, designers, and other theatrical practitioners, the effects of whose naturalized assumptions about character, action, and audience perception are often mystified in productions whose meanings they help to shape or subvert; the processes of new-play development, which privilege particular forms and genres and often inscribe the conservative wisdom of received traditions; rehearsal and production processes, through which meaning is negotiated and produced, but whose shape and duration are dictated by organizational and funding structures unrelated to the project; these structures themselves often determined by the financial and ideological interests of the corporate or political status quo—which determine shaping factors such as production budgets and cast sizes, ticket prices and audience amenities; the discourse of the host theatre, produced through its mandate, programming, playbills, posters, and publicity releases, each of which plays a major role in determining an audience's horizons of expectation and, therefore, its production of meaning; and the location of the venue, which shapes an audience's experience of what Kershaw, following Richard Schechner and Victor Turner, calls the "gathering" and "dispersal" phases of performance (257). [2]

In Canada, most of these material conditions work in one of two ways: either they construct the performance as a product, packaged and delivered with efficiency and clarity to a paying public; or they construct the experience, process, and product as a free exploration of "universal" human nature. On the one hand, for example, most Canadian theatres employ some sort of proscenium arch arrangement: the audience sits in the dark, watching the lighted action through the frame of a real or imagined proscenium. Many theatres, such as Toronto's Factory Theatre and the Berkeley Street Theatre of the Canadian Stage (formerly Toronto Free Theatre), have moved to modifications of a proscenium structure after having started out in the "experimental" 1960s and early '70s with flexible spaces. These moves have often been constructed somewhat condescendingly by critics as signs of promising new maturity for the companies in question and for Canadian drama. The proscenium, however, inscribes a model of pictorial illusion and depth perspective that is to the theatre what Catherine Belsey, following Roland Barthes and Bertolt Brecht, has suggested "classic realism" is to fiction, and that similarly constructs the "readers" of a performance as "passive consumers" rather than active producers of meaning (125). [3] The dominance of the proscenium in Toronto theatres is closely related not only to the dominance of a particular kind of play that has been produced in the city, often referred to as "poetic naturalism" and associated with Tarragon Theatre, but also to the ways in which Toronto audiences and critics have produced meaning.

Not all Toronto theatres employ proscenium arrangements, however, and many, often at second stages devoted to what is called experimental work, use variations on the black box, a room that is constructed, in Peter Brook's famous phrase, as an "empty space," unencumbered by social, cultural, and architectural accidentals. These spaces are promoted as neutral, audience-friendly, and therefore democratic, allowing the playwrights and theatre companies to communicate directly with their audiences, and allowing theatrical productions to be interpreted "freely" by audiences unburdened with inappropriate environmental or scenic decoration or distraction. But ideology abhors a vacuum, and there is no such thing as an empty space. Empty spaces are to theatre what common sense is to critical practice: vacuums to be filled by the unquestioned because of naturalized assumptions of ideology. [4] Plays produced in and by these theatres, whatever their particular social or artistic goals, often serve as safety valves for potential unrest, allowing disruptive energies to be released in a kind of neo-Aristotelian, socially sanctioned catharsis.

A similar division of experience obtains in the work and training of directors in Canada. Directors are hired in Canadian theatres, usually from among the professional-managerial class, by boards of governors, general managers, and artistic directors, and they work in hierarchical corporate structures from positions that might be constructed as middle management. They are trained, moreover, to function in rehearsal processes as autocrats or creative geniuses whose vision shapes a theatrical production in which actors, designers, and technicians—constructed in this model as the theatre's worker bees—are trained to deliver. I pored over the standard textbooks available and used in Canada when preparing to teach my first course in directing in 1990, and I found the bulk of them astonishingly prescriptive. They casually employ metaphors of the director as "a good general" (Morrison 15), a "ship's captain," "missionary," "benevolent dictator" (Catron 25), and "guiding genius" (Catron 29); and they invariably describe the "director's job" (Morrison I) as being to arrive at a single, unifying concept (Catron 8). He (it is always "he") must analyze the script and "find" in it a structure that must include "the inciting incident," "exposition," "foreshadowing," "the point of attack," "the protagonist's goal," the "complications," the "climax," and the cigarette afterwards, or "resolution" (see Catron 39–49). Characters must be analyzed in terms of their "objectives" and categorized according to "type": "the protagonist," "the antagonist," "the confidant(e)," "the foil," "the raisonneur," and "the utilitarian character" (see Catron 55; 61–67). Other aspects of these books are equally logocentric, involving such things as the achievement of unity, clarity, and control through the director's "plan of attack" in making "the play's [sic] intellectual concept clear to the audience" (Catron 8, 9).

These texts may seem like easy targets, but they represent what is taught in North America and Britain, and they are thought to provide the basics for directors of whatever ideological stripe intending to work in any type of theatre. There are other approaches, however, but they are usually acknowledged in brief chapters about "experimental" methods. Most of these are to the textbook what the black box is to the proscenium. They aspire to create a rehearsal process that is open and free from preconceptions; they are celebrated by most scholars and critics; and they usually result in productions that are the recognizably opaque products of modernism. Maurice Good has described Robin Phillips (at the first rehearsal for his 1979 production of *King Lear* at the Stratford Festival) asking members of the assembled company to introduce themselves in turn and say what they thought the play was about. Phillips, speaking last, said "My name is Robin Phillips, and I don't know what the play is about" (Good 3–4). But the prime exemplar of this approach is Peter Brook, whose 1970 production of *A Midsummer Night's Dream* and 1968 book *The Empty Space* have become landmarks. Thanks to writings by Brook and his associates, his approach is familiar. But it becomes clear in reading these works that what presents itself as free and open exploration designed to liberate actors from their inhibitions turns out to be the construction of a rehearsal process as empty space; that is, it is likely to be silently filled with cultural and historical imperatives that rush in like fools to fill the void left by the silence of a historicized interpretation of the script or performance score that is openly and self-consciously engaged. Far from offering unfettered access to universal or transcendent truths, or to a collective unconscious, these productions can easily become the unconscious conduits of ideology. They can function, in spite of themselves or their directors' intentions, as what Marcuse calls "affirmative culture." Is it any wonder that Canadian playwrights such as Judith Thompson, and George F. Walker, whose *Love and Anger* I discuss below, are increasingly choosing to direct their own work? Or that others, such as John Krizanc,

Ann-Marie MacDonald, and Tomson Highway, each of whom I treat below, tend to select and repeatedly work with directors whose sensibilities and methods they trust?

Performance as either consumer product or empty space is also inscribed in the training of actors, and considerable attention has been paid to this construction in recent years as cultural materialists, feminists, and others move "towards a materialist theatre practice" (see McCullough), "performable feminist critiques" (see O'Brien), or "gestic feminist criticism" (see Diamond). The dominant approaches to actor training in Canada are variations on, or mediations between, "the American Method" and "the Stanislavski System"; and, like most theatre training, they tend to represent themselves as apolitical, pure, and transcendent techniques adaptable for use in any type of theatre (see Salter, "Body Politics"). In discussing the Method or System (words that are invariably capitalized in handbooks), I draw on a representative chapter from Sonia Moore's influential handbook *The Stanislavski System*. A glance at the chapter "Work on the Role: Building a Character" reveals a concept of identity that is individualist, naturalized, ideologically based, linear, and prescriptive. The following are representative samples that employ words, metaphors (particularly organic and spiritual), and concepts of character, action, and dramatic structure that recur throughout the book:

> Life will be created on the stage if an actor follows the laws of nature. (65)

> If an action helps to express the character, it is artistically right; if it does not, it is wrong. (66)

> The choice of actions must be guided by the *main idea* of the play and of the role. (66)

> An action on stage, if it has no purpose, merely diverts the audience's attention from the essence of the play. The purpose is what determines the action, and that purpose is to express individual life. (66)

> The continuous line of the character's actions, leading to the solution of the super-objective, builds *perspective* in a role. [5] (67)

> Work on the role means study of the spiritual content of the play and understanding of the "kernel" from which it came to birth. It is this kernel that determines the essence of the play. (70)

> The main idea is the spine and pulse of the play ... ; the actor must know his [sic] mission in the chain of events of the play .... [E]very thought and gesture must be imbued with the light of the main idea of the play. (70–71)

> [The actor] must complete the life of his character in his imagination and see a continuous, logical, unbroken chain of events. (71)

> A valuable dramatic work is always based on struggles between different persons. [6] (76)

>An actor must find the obstacles in the way of his character and try to overcome them. (76)

>Each character has its own main objective of struggle. (76)

In these examples, following "the laws of nature" is conflated with psychological consistency, narrowly defined; with the pursuit of linear objectives through conflict; and with the logocentric pursuit of one *"main idea"* as it unfolds in "a continuous, logical, unbroken chain of events." Is it any wonder that a Canadian playwright such as John Krizanc complains that his play *Tamara*, discussed below, was distorted and its political implications contained by "American emotionalism" (Swan 67) as inscribed in "the American style of method acting," and in Method-trained actors who are "so literal ... [that t]hey won't tolerate ambiguity" (64)? Is it any wonder that productions featuring actors with this training, directed by directors functioning as autocrats on the proscenium stages of corporately structured theatres, tend to function as illustrated lectures?

Other modes of actor training exist for Canadian actors, of course, and many of them are celebrated as innovative, liberating, and experimental in much the same way that "experimental" directors and "empty spaces" are celebrated. These methods—which in Canada notably include clowning techniques deriving from L'École Jacques Lecoq in Paris, in Toronto often by way of the late Richard Pochinko and the Theatre Resource Centre (see Allan; Cashman; Hayden)—present themselves as being less prescriptive and logocentric than Moore or Stanislavski. And, like the black box or some of the more exploratory directing styles, they claim openness and neutrality. These methods attempt in various ways to bypass cerebral, learned actions, reactions, and emotions in order to draw on the actor's natural or neutral voice and body. They therefore provide direct access to purely physical responses to the world, unmuddied by cultural accidentals and therefore closer to a universal humanity and collective unconscious. They claim, that is, to "free the natural voice" and body (see Linklater) in order to allow text, character, or emotion to speak *through* the actor unmediated, ahistorically constructing the actor's body as empty space much in line with the other empty spaces that I have been discussing. But like other so-called freedoms (free trade comes to mind), this one favours the powerful and privileges a hegemonic status quo. Without otherly directed and conscious shaping, these techniques simply allow the cultural context to speak the actor, "naturally" to reinforce hegemony, and often to undermine the transgressive potential of a radical or subversive script.

I have described elsewhere how communist playwright David Fennario resorted to working with untrained actors in his working-class community in Montreal after seeing his plays "improved" within the context of Centaur Theatre and the traditional processes and wisdoms of director Guy Sprung (Knowles, "Voices" 103–04). It is similarly interesting that radical Toronto director Hillar Liitoja refuses to work with professional actors, fearing the ideological inscriptions of Canadian actor training that I have outlined here. Even within the established dramatic canon, such as it is, the lack of production history or successful production for much-taught and studied socially conscious plays, such as George Ryga's *The Ecstasy of Rita Joe* and

Michael Cook's *Jacob's Wake*, might convincingly be attributed to a failure of training and rehearsal processes to accommodate their expressionist styles. Margaret Hollingsworth hints at this failure to break out of accepted practice in an interview about the creation and production at Toronto's Theatre Resource Centre of her powerful and innovative feminist play *Poppycock*, which she describes as expressionist in her introduction to the published script (50–51). She admits in the interview with Rudakoff,

> We got scared and tried to handle the power of what we were seeing in rehearsal by using more conventional means, which, of course, you cannot do .... We were exploring areas in that rehearsal process that teetered on the brink of something very ... new and exciting ... But we simply weren't strong enough to ... carry through. [T]here were deadlines to meet and a show to put on. ("Margaret Hollingsworth Interview" 158)

If it is this difficult to break from established procedures at one of Toronto's most flexible and consistently innovative venues and training centres, then the difficulty of mounting and communicating radical theatre in the city's more established venues may be virtually prohibitive.

In addressing this difficulty, I will focus on transfers or remounts of three potentially transgressive scripts that have emerged from Toronto since 1980 in order to assess the material conditions that changed with different theatrical or cultural contexts. Each production considered below was either transferred from one venue to another or remounted in a new production by the same director, usually the same designer, and most of the original cast. Some roles were recast, and some of the scripts were revised for a remounting in the new venue—revisions that tended to render the scripts more univocal and less interrogative in order to accommodate, presumably, different audience expectations. But my major interest here is less in the playwright's production of the script, or in the director's production of the performance text, than in the audience's production of meaning. Where appropriate, I will briefly consider script revisions and production changes, but my focus will be on the material conditions that shaped the ways in which audiences read the productions.

II

The most spectacular example of a small-scale politically alternative play to emerge from an alternative theatre in Toronto in the 1980s and be picked up for large-scale production was *Tamara*. It was created in 1981 for Onstage 81: The Toronto Theatre Festival by the virtually unknown environmental theatre company, Necessary Angel, its director Richard Rose, and its resident playwright John Krizanc. After two months, *Tamara* was taken on by media mogul and self-proclaimed hipster Moses Znaimer, who refinanced it, extended its run, and moved it to Dundurn Castle in Hamilton before eventually producing lavish and long-running remounts in Los Angeles and New York.

As the president of Toronto's trendy CityTV, and the executive producer of MuchMusic, Znaimer may at first seem to be a surprising backer of an experimental theatre piece such as *Tamara*. The play is set in 1927 in Il Vittoriale degli Italiani, where the Italian nationalist poet Gabriele d'Annunzio was held in virtual house arrest by Mussolini and kept silent by a steady supply of food, sex, and cocaine. The play was designed by Krizanc to be "a critique of Fascism" and an interrogation of the artist's responsibility to society. Krizanc felt that because "one of the problems with theatre is that you're subjected to the particular politics of the authors or directors," not to mention the tyranny of traditional wisdoms about blocking and focus on the proscenium stage, "the best way to write a critique of Fascism was to give people more democratic freedom than they've ever had in the theatre" ("Interview" 34). The play, then, was staged throughout a large house—Strachan House in Toronto, Dundurn Castle in Hamilton, and increasingly elaborate locations in Los Angeles and New York—with characters travelling from room to room, scenes occurring simultaneously, and members of the audience following characters of their choice, coming together to compare notes only at an intermission buffet, served in the dining room of the house as part of the admission price. In a sense, the audience was given control, each member constructing his or her own play; *Tamara* becomes, as Alberto Manguel suggests in his foreword to the published script, the theatre's "first democratic play," "the exact antithesis of fascism, because it condemns the audience to the unbearable freedom of a concerned and active witness" (5, 7). In a script whose "premise ... is choice" (Swan 45)—in that, as Krizanc says, "What you learn depends on the choices you make ... " (Kaplan 137) the playwright not only explores the *theme* of fascism but also metatheatrically explodes what he calls "the Fascism of theatre" itself (Michael 14). "The freedom of self-discovery," he says, "is true democracy" (Kaplan 137).

The first production, despite what Znaimer later called a "pathetic little budget" of $29,000 (Swan 43), became the surprise hit of the 1981 festival, and reviewers praised not only its novelty but also the effectiveness of its structure in helping the audience to "understand the ideas and themes that fuel the movement of the piece" (Blackadar). Most, such as Don Shewey in the *Soho News*, praised the "incessant intellectual stimulation" of the play's exploration of "the moral consequences of remaining neutral in times of political turmoil" (44, 21); and most, according to Richard Plant,[7] recognized the open, interrogative nature of the production text.

Based on the evidence in the reviews, it seems safe to conclude that the Toronto production, at least to some extent, served Krizanc's stated purposes, which were explicitly nondeclarative and, if not subversive, then at least "cautionary" ("Interview" 34) to Canadians living, like the characters in the play, in a satellite relationship to a superpower:

> "I don't think things *can* be explained. I think it should be 'curtain up,' and then you spend the whole time thinking 'what the hell are they talking about?'" Krizanc is interested in the audience as *investigators*, not passive spectators, and his greatest concern is with complacency ....
> "[O]ne of the reasons why I would write a play like *Tamara* is I still don't

understand why people didn't see what was happening. I wonder whether *I'll* see, in *my* lifetime …. People go along doing their thing," he says, "and one day the tanks come in." (Knowles, "The Truth" 29)

Things changed in Los Angeles and New York, however. Reviewers were again overwhelmingly positive, but they made little mention of the serious concerns in the piece and were unaware that the staging was anything more than innovative and gimmicky. Krizanc complained that "the incomprehension of reviewers drove me crazy" ("Interview" 36), lamenting the fact that the play was reviewed "as an event but never as a play" (Swan 63), and commenting that "American critics missed the boat as to what the whole experience was about and its implications for theatre" (Garebian 15). The director, Richard Rose, referred to the "poverty of the mind" of American theatre critics (Garebian 16). But as early as the transfer to Hamilton, shortly after Znaimer became involved as executive producer, evidence suggests that the play's impact had changed and provides clues about some of the reasons for this change. In Toronto, on its "pathetic little budget," the production had been mounted with borrowed furniture and volunteer labour in a decaying mansion on its way to becoming a city-run residence for men:

> The toilets at Strachan House were broken. The actors read in the dark because there was no power. After an eight-hour rehearsal, they would stay to paint walls, lay tile, or cook dinner. This zeal soon spread to friends, even strangers in the park. Everyone wanted to help: a grade-eight class spent an afternoon gathering up garbage, a carpenter volunteered labour in exchange for tickets …. With only $2,000 to create d'Annunzio's villa [designer Dorian Clark] had to borrow beds, tables, a grand piano, my entire library. (Krizanc, "Innocents" 35)

When the show moved to Hamilton, after an injection of funds from Znaimer that doubled the actors' salaries and gave Krizanc a royalty payment, it was housed in Dundurn Castle, ticket prices went up, and, as Martin Knelman noted, the show changed:

> Finally ensconced in a genuine castle, the show gained another dimension. It was no longer necessary to pretend that the surroundings were opulent; they really were. There was room for an extra twenty-five customers a night, and almost immediately the entire run was sold out. (60)

Not surprisingly, as Knelman's remarks suggest, the shift from representing opulence to embodying it was accompanied by an altered construction of the audience: in the early days in Toronto, the audience was seen as a community taking active and to some degree independent part in a critique of fascism, but henceforth it was considered to be, as Knelman said, "customers." And, of course, the trend continued, escalating as the show found ever more opulent venues in Los Angeles and New York. The design budget alone was $100,000 in Los Angeles, where the show was housed in the "massive" (Krizanc, "Innocents" 36) Hollywood American Legion building, decorated with original Tamara de Lempicka art borrowed from celebrities such as Barbra Streisand (Swan 46). As described by Jon Kaplan,

> The Los Angeles location is a 1920s edifice, centred around a high atrium complete with sky-blue ceiling in which hangs a gold cherub, roses in hand. There's also an enormous auditorium area, dubbed the Oratorio, which is complete with d'Annunzio's coffin, a pulpit from which he pontificates, a piano, a statue of winged victory, and an altar. Scenes occur on all three floors and in more than a dozen rooms, as well as in various stairways and hallways. The atrium is surrounded one floor up by a gallery; some of the more special theatrical moments occur when audience members watch the action on the floor below from the vantage point of the balcony. It gives a sense of eavesdropping on a scene, which ideally suits the mood and theme of the work. (136)

In New York, if reviews are any indication, the 66th Street Armory became the indisputable star of the show. A review in the *New York Times*, entitled "The Park Avenue Armory Is Home to a 10-Room Villa for 'Tamara,'" focused on the venue itself and the way that it was modified and used (see Giovannini).

As the opulence of the venues increased, so did ticket prices, escalating from a pricey-but-possible $20 in Toronto (for an audience of 40) to a prohibitive $135 (for an audience of 200) for a weekend performance in New York, and thereby virtually guaranteeing an economic elitism that belied the ostensible intentions of the show's creators. Moreover, what in Toronto had been environmental theatre, deconstructing the totalizing experience standard on the proscenium stage, became what Znaimer called a "living movie," recontextualized and marketed as part of his "InterActive Entertainment Inc." empire, which included the virtual-reality tourist show, *Tour of the Universe*, at the base of Toronto's CN Tower (qtd. in Miller 50). Reviews and feature articles, which showed up in such places as *People* magazine, conditioned by sensationalist marketing,[8] no longer focused on themes, meanings, or intellectual challenges; they turned instead to the stars in attendance, often including descriptions of their wardrobes and accounts of the show's venues and menus. In Los Angeles, the intermission buffet was provided by Ma Maison; the New York production (where a Tamara champagne cocktail was served at the beginning of the show, the "Intermezzo") was catered by Le Cirque, the menu for which appears in the play's published text (176). *Newsday* sent its restaurant critic to review the buffet (Alaton). Krizanc was horrified; as he remarked to Ann Jansen, "it was never our intention that [Tamara] should be about running around the house and drinking champagne" ("Interview" 34).

There were script changes, too, made to accommodate the new locations, audiences, and producer's expectations. Some of these changes were practical—when a script depends on the arrival of a character from one scene into the midst of another, the length of a hallway can determine the length of a speech—but many were substantial and significant, and most reduced the script's complexity, eliminated its interrogative qualities, and made it a more marketable product. Even in the show's

Hamilton run, for which Krizanc had done rewrites at Znaimer's request, Martin Knelman noted a "sharper focus," which made it possible more readily to "get a fix on the characters" (60). The rewrites continued throughout rehearsals for the Los Angeles opening, and again for the New York production, all of them serving to clarify things for audience members who at "fifty dollars a ticket ... have a right to know what's going on," according to Znaimer (Krizanc, "Innocents" 38). Krizanc describes Znaimer as "a great editor ... [who] can cut to the heart of a story and make you tell it in half the time ... [and who] knows what people want because he asks them." [9] And "Znaimer wanted one climax," rather than the two simultaneous endings of the Toronto script ("Innocents" 38). With the ending tightened up, a character eliminated along with a potentially confusing doubling, other characterizations made more clear and consistent, and other housekeeping changes to accommodate the new opulence and larger budget, Krizanc felt that the script was "better," but he ironically worried "that the Americans are missing the point that *Tamara* is an examination of the artist's role" (Swan 63). It seems clear, however, that these changes were partly responsible for the problem, rendering the script more contained and marketable while depriving it of its disturbing contradictions and complexities, and much of its politics. [10]

More significant are the ways in which the script changes conspired with the changes in casting, venue, and marketing to construct the audiences differently for the different productions and thereby to change the ways in which the productions meant. The combination of declarative script, opulent venues, sensationalist publicity, and star-studded casting tended to position the audiences less as investigators, critics, or even voyeurs, and more as invited guests—the social equals of d'Annunzio and his guests—who read the production as a party. This tendency was reinforced by the serving of pre-show champagne and the strewing of welcoming rose petals, neither of which was a part of the Toronto production. [11] In New York, it was explicitly reinforced by the management, which "encourage[d] the paying guests to wear evening dress" to performances (Lapham, qtd. in Harvie 16). Moreover, publicity stressing the casting of such stars as Anjelica Huston and Karen Black, the frequent presence in the audience of artists, celebrities, and stars, and the reservation of houses for private parties by Hugh Hefner, Norman Jewison, and others reinforced the sense of the production as an exclusive, if not decadent, event, the plaything of the rich and famous. Such publicity reduced its chances of accomplishing any kind of effective political intervention.

While *Tamara* in Toronto was designed in form and content to be about choice, in Los Angeles and New York it seems to have presented only the *illusion* of choice, functioning hegemonically in much the same way as other parts of Znaimer's entertainment empire. Even the script and the original production function in this way. The rules of the production are set out clearly in the opening scene (particularly so in the Los Angeles and New York versions), and any real audience participation is precluded because the cast does not acknowledge its existence. The audience has no influence on the outcome of the plots, and the script is carefully constructed in order to provide the "essential" information for each member no matter what plot or character he or she chooses to follow. As Richard Plant argues, "The spectator creates his/her art within what is at root a manipulated set of circumstances, a state of artistic 'fascism' where the choices are dependent upon the conventions set up by the production" (13). Like "zapping through the channels" on television, then, to which the Polish novelist Jerzy Kosinski has compared the audience's experience in *Tamara*, much to Znaimer's delight (qtd. in Alaton); or like playing video games (Czarnecki); or like experiencing Znaimer's simulation spaceport, *Tour of the Universe* (Miller), the experience of *Tamara* is a carefully orchestrated creation and manipulation of the audience's illusion of freedom and control, marketed as a consumer product. The play functions, in fact, like Znaimer's CityTV, which presents a heterogeneous, multicultural image that in fact effaces difference by imposing a Queen-Street-West Toronto brand of slim-and-hip sameness. Like *Tamara*, CityTV purports to democratize its medium by turning the city into its studio, placing cameras on street corners and "broadcasting the people," while carefully constructing an image that is similar to that projected by the American *Tamaras*: "inclusive, exotic, sexy, and ultimately closed" (McKinnie 5). [12] Indeed, Znaimer is conscious of the connection, as he indicated to Susan Swan: "I make a living movie at City every day." Swan then notes,

> Moses sees all his projects as one body of work. For him; there is a link between the drama-oriented news at City, in which reporters ... live the part they play on air, to a production such as *Tamara*, which gives the audience a chance to participate by exercising the choice of character to follow, to the Tour of the Universe, in which the audience buys a ticket to have an experience. (66)

The conclusion seems to be clear: *Tamara*'s potential for political critique or subversion, at least in Los Angeles and New York, was effectively co-opted, contained, and reversed by the lethal embrace of Moses Znaimer's media empire. That John Krizanc felt this was the case is perhaps evidenced by the fact that he has not returned to the form of *Tamara* in subsequent plays, even though Znaimer suggested that he write two more "*Tamara*-like plays" for InterActive Entertainment Inc. (Miller 51)— and perhaps a murder mystery (Knelman 60). Krizanc's response to his experience with Znaimer may also, perhaps, be read into his portrayal, in his most recent play *The Half of It*, of the relationship between the environmentalist Peter Malchuk and the capitalist Freddy Boise, who hires Peter to manage a profitable environmental stock fund and in the process compromises and contains his efforts on behalf of the environment. As I suggested in a draft of my afterword to the published script of *The Half of It*, moreover, Boise and Znaimer share many tricks of speech. (The suggestion was cut by the publishers.)

Despite the apparently all-consuming appetite of a dominant consumer capitalism for anything new and innovative, however, there is always a level in the public and unstable forum that is theatre at which the genuinely innovative, particularly in form, resists containment and has the potential to negotiate genuine cultural intervention. *Tamara* in Toronto functioned in carnivalesque fashion, and at least one Toronto reviewer discussed it in the context not of video games and virtual reality but of the city's multicultural, citywide "Caravan" festival (Blackadar). That the productions in Los Angeles and New York functioned differently is not surprising, but it is unlikely that they failed completely to open fissures in Znaimer and company's containment, if only because the play's form generally fractures any audience's monolithic gaze and thus the social, textual, and sexual politics and pleasures that are traditionally constructed by that gaze (see Mulvey). A scene in the bedroom of Tamara or Luisa, for example, means differently if women alone constitute the audience on a given night. Even the inevitable breaking up of the groups in which audience members arrive can have this effect.

There were, I suggest, other negotiations played out in these productions. For one thing, there were the contextual accidentals that often occur around good productions of theatre, changing the ways in which they mean and creating frissons and fissures that refuse to sit still for comfortable containment and closure. Krizanc describes the most remarkable and political accidental surrounding *Tamara* in Ronald Reagan's America, one that occurred because of the fortuitous location of the Los Angeles production:

> Early in act two, the Fascist captain, Finzi, interrogates the suspicious-looking new chauffeur, Mario:
>
> > FINZI. "Are you now, or have you ever been, a member of the Communist Party?"
> > MARIO. "No."
> > FINZI. "I ask again: are you a Communist?"
> > MARIO. "No."
> > FINZI. "Have you ever known a Communist?"
> > MARIO. "No."
> > FINZI. "Three times you answer no."
>
> When that scene was first rehearsed, the temperature in the room seemed to drop twenty degrees. Everyone got goose bumps. The actor playing Mario broke character and asked, "Can *you* feel it?"
>
> We could. Thirty years ago, the building had housed the hearings concerning the Hollywood Ten. Those words have become synonymous with McCarthyism and I had put them in the play to draw the parallel between McCarthyism and fascism. Every house has its ghosts. ("Innocents" 37–38)

Such resonances in the theatre have happened in ways that have resisted censorship, or more frequently benign containment, for centuries, if not always so dramatically.

Contextual accidentals aside, not all accounts of the American productions accepted that *Tamara* failed entirely as cultural intervention. Canadian critic Keith Garebian, reviewing the New York production and taking into account the script and production changes, the excessive opulence of the venue, and the horizon of expectations created by the "crassness" of the "hypertrophic" marketing devices (15), nevertheless argues that "*Tamara* contradicts or sabotages the Fascist aesthetic by provoking an audience's reflective, critical and pluralistic responses." He concludes that "there are enough anomalies of experience and attitude to erase Fascism's insistence on submission and containment" (16). Richard Plant also comments on the play's resistance to closure, in spite of its revised ending, arguing that "Ironically, the choices available to the audience all end in the same state of chaos and incompleteness." The form itself, he suggests, is contradictory in being both "illusionary" and metatheatrical, and he argues that the show "deconstructs the move toward apparent freedom" and urges the audiences "to be critical or detached about what they are experiencing" (33).

I suggest that Plant, Garebian, and one other contextual accidental point to a way in which the American *Tamara*s worked differently than the Toronto production, but nonetheless worked. [13] Plant's suggestion that both audience and characters share a sense of "chaos and devastation" (10) at the end of the play derives, I think, from a sense that the audience's choices parallel those of the characters. Garebian quotes Jerzy Kosinski's comment that "This is the most ethical theatre I could imagine, because I was always torn. Should I sympathize with Luisa dying here, or should I follow my voyeuristic instincts and see this guy [Mario] get shot?" (16). Finally, Jennifer Harvie cites Clive Barnes's trenchant observation that "while you are enjoying your excellent buffet meal during the evening's half-hour 'intermezzo,' or your crème brulée served after the performance with coffee and strawberries, you can have the dramatic/political frisson of realizing that only two floors up in this very same Armory are being housed some of New York's homeless" (12).

These comments ultimately suggest, I think, that the impotent self-indulgence of the play's artists in response to the larger political situation of fascist Italy may have been echoed by the indulgence of an elite, champagne-sipping, artsy Hollywood or New York audience in Ronald Reagan's and George Bush's America. Possibly the artists, stars, would-be stars, and stargazers that constituted so large a percentage of *Tamara*'s American audience may have looked, at the end of the evening, at the pathetic figure of their fellow artist Gabriele d' Annunzio on his hands and knees, snorting cocaine from the feet of a corpse, and seen themselves.

III

At the end of the 1980s, three potentially subversive scripts were mounted in Toronto, then transferred to, or remounted at, larger theatres in 1990–91. In each case, a complex negotiation similar to that of *Tamara* was played out along the continuum between subversion and containment. Ann-Marie MacDonald's feminist revisioning of Shakespeare, *Goodnight Desdemona (Good Morning Juliet)*, was first mounted at Nightwood Theatre in March 1988 and later picked up for a production and tour by the Canadian Stage Company; Tomson Highway's provocative Native-Canadian play *Dry Lips Oughta Move to Kapuskasing* was first produced by Native Earth Performing Arts at Theatre Passe Muraille in April 1989, and it was remounted at the Royal

Alexandra Theatre and the National Arts Centre as a co-production with David Mirvish, the producer of *Les Miserables* and *Miss Saigon*; and George F. Walker's anti-capitalist comedy *Love and Anger* opened at the Factory Theatre in October 1989 before being picked up and transferred to the Bluma Appel Theatre of the Canadian Stage by Toronto's other major producer of megamusicals, Garth Drabinsky. Each show displays the "love and anger" of Walker's title: each uses comedy to mount an attack, from a different angle, on dominant patriarchal, white, capitalist forces in Canadian society and institutions; and each contains—and, in its second incarnation, was in danger of having its efficacy contained by—an attempt to create a unifying sense of community in order to empower a group that is marginalized by these forces.

Goodnight Desdemona is a feminist revisioning of Shakespeare, a sophisticated deconstruction of the authority of authorship and an enactment of resisting reading. The central character, Constance Ledbelly, is a lecturer and PhD candidate at Queen's University. MacDonald introduces the play with a stinging portrayal of academic life for women before plunging her unlikely heroine into the central action, a metadramatic revisioning of *Othello* and *Romeo and Juliet*, the subjects of Constance's dissertation. She has broken the code of a mysterious "Gustav manuscript" that, she thinks, contains the unknown sources of Shakespeare's unlikely tragedies, sources that Shakespeare "colonized," in Ann Wilson's phrase, transforming the original and subversive comedies into patriarchal tragedies and, in the process, "constituting women as passive subjects, both as characters in the plays and as readers" ("Critical" 4). The body of the play deals with Constance's encounters with Shakespeare's characters as she searches, in the worlds of the plays themselves, for the original foolscap manuscript, the author, and the fool that she posits was cut from the originals as they were transformed from comedies to tragedies. After encountering a powerful Desdemona and a passionately randy and bisexual Juliet, Constance discovers that she herself *wears* the fool's cap and *is* the author. She assumes "authority," that is, for her own production of meaning in the plays, for it is not, as she learns, the "man you seek" *in* (literally) the script, but the man-u-script yourself, "A lass" (MacDonald 73).

Love and Anger is a very different kind of script, but it shares with *Goodnight Desdemona* its indictment of a patriarchal establishment, taking the form of "old-fashioned, revolutionary rage—against the money-grubbers, against parasitical lawyers, [and] against sleazy politicians" (Crew, "Love and Anger") in what is clearly Toronto, "a city that has gone the way of all Boomtowns" (Donnelly). Walker's central characters are "the marginals and the disturbed" (Crew, "Love and Anger"): a born-again lawyer, Petie Maxwell, who lost half his brain but found his integrity when he suffered a stroke; his long-suffering secretary, Eleanor; a rightly paranoid and practicing schizophrenic, Sarah, who thinks that she's Black; and Gail, who really is Black and comes to Petie for legal help because her husband has been framed for a crime that was committed on behalf of "Babe" Connor. Connor, the central, melodramatic bad guy, is the publisher of a sensationalist "fascist rag" (21) and the friend of Petie's former partner, a self-confessed "greedy prick" named Sean Harris (67), who is running for Parliament.

Dry Lips Oughta Move to Kapuskasing sets out to indict "the destructiveness of patriarchal Christianity" (Drainie), particularly the systemic misogyny that results in the abuse of Native women. Centering around the response of the men on The Wasaychigan Hill Indian Reserve to the formation of a women's hockey team, the script combines realistic portrayals of life on the reserve, sequences of comic exaggeration, a drunken delivery in a tavern of a child with foetal alcohol syndrome, a brutal rape-by-crucifix, and several symbolic/spiritual sequences involving a female Nanabush, or trickster character, who intervenes in the action incarnated variously as all of the play's female characters.

Each script also combines with its criticism of the dominant order an attempt to construct an alternative sense of community and empowerment among its marginalized characters and its audience. In doing so, each in its way becomes attractive to "mainstream" or commercial producers, thereby potentially broadening its audience appeal but watering down its efficacy as cultural intervention. Each risks sentimentality by inviting what Alan Filewod calls, in an article on Native theatre, the "colonizing gaze," in "the colonizing formality" of a large mainstream theatre, letting the audience off the hook and leaving its power *as* colonizers unchallenged ("Averting" 25). In their first productions, these plays were variously judged by reviewers to be "loosely structured ... and sometimes hurt by a lack of clarity" (Crew, "Dry Lips"); lacking "stylistic unity" because their "many strands ... are not satisfactorily drawn together" (Conlogue, "Emotionally Riveting"); in need of "some objective editing" (Donnelly); far "too long" (Crew, "Goodnight"); or "far from being a completed script" (Conlogue, "New roles"). At the same time, however, reviewers found each production powerful, moving, and effective in making its political point. Reviews of these first productions also noted their criticism of white, patriarchal, and/or capitalist forces at work in Canadian society, and noted with approval or dismay transgressive elements such as *Love and Anger*'s "Marx and Malice" (Pennington),[14] *Goodnight Desdemona*'s bisexual sensuousness, or the searing attack on Christianity presented by *Dry Lips*.

The three plays also seem to have succeeded in their first productions in forging a sense of community among their variously marginalized characters, and between them and the audiences. But something changed after the moves to more opulent surroundings. Apparently containment occurred in the new settings: what had been empowerment devices in the first productions became ways of constructing a kind of unity and universality that effaced difference. In any case, the focus of reviewers after the transfers was on the uproarious comedy and aesthetic quality of the productions. While the anticapitalist diatribes of Petie Maxwell in *Love and Anger* had been greeted with cheers at the Factory Theatre—where the play had been "catching the crest of a wave" of anger at Toronto's politicians and developers (see Conlogue, "Love and Anger: Catching the Crest")—the same production at the Bluma Appel Theatre and under the sponsorship of Drabinsky was read as being more polished and contained, and was greeted more with sympathetic laughter than with cheers. Reviewing it in *The Globe and Mail*, Ray Conlogue noted that the play's villains get trounced "stylishly," and he focused on the cathartic release provided by Petie's death, which he found to be "more moving than ever" ("Love and Anger, One More Time"). The coming together at Petie's death of the play's three marginalized women, which at the Factory had been an empowering image of solidarity, became at the Bluma a sentimental gesture, invoking a conventional closure on the work of a playwright whom Michael Feingold described in the *Village Voice* review of the play's New York production as "A subverter of genres by trade" (qtd. in Vincent).

Reviewer response to *Goodnight Desdemona* was similarly soft compared to reviews of the first production, and focus shifted from feminist issues to the "delicious fun" (Crew, "Desdemona") of presenting a "comic Shakespearean romance" (Illustration). Noting that the script had been "trimmed and tightened" (Crew, "Desdemona"), reviewers now downplayed or overlooked the transgressive sexuality of the show, which they had earlier (softly) called "Sapphic" (Conlogue, "New Roles"; Crew, "Goodnight"), in order to focus on its "stylish pace" and on the comic audacity (Conlogue, "Of Heroines") with which the "agreeably silly comedy ... pokes fun at the Bard" (Crew, "Desdemona"). What had been a radical feminist revisioning of Shakespeare and a direct attack on compulsory heterosexuality—subject to extended and admiring academic analysis of its "genderbending and genrebending" in *Canadian Theatre Review* (see Fortier)—dwindled to saucy and irreverent parody of "the Bard," who survived with his patriarchal cultural authority intact. What had been a forging, in the first production, of a peculiarly feminine and empowering sense of identity based on a feminist reading of Jung [15] seems to have been read, in this production, as a generalized humanist fable that failed to confront the colonizing gaze of its new audience. Apparently what the playwright intended as an expansive feminist "humanism," challenging an audience that was constructed as heterogeneous (Fortier 50–51), became smothered by the embrace of a more traditional, patriarchal, and monolithic consumer humanism that denies difference.

Perhaps the most radical change in response, however, was to *Dry Lips*. As was the case with the other plays, *Dry Lips* was considered more polished in its remount (at the Royal Alex), more aesthetically pleasing, with comfortable closure provided by a combination of *Goodnight Desdemona*'s use of awakening-from-dream and *Love and Anger*-style sentimentality in the final image of the perfect Indian family: strong but conforming woman, sensitive man, and healthy baby. Reviews, interviews, and news features concentrated on the theatrical "magic" with which the production "beautifully, comically, and with enormous theatricality" created a "style" (Cushman). Many zeroed in on Highway's training as a classical pianist and his knowledge of classical forms, in the way that they had concentrated on the Shakespearean antecedents of *Goodnight Desdemona*—and to similar effect. Despite Highway's claim in some forums that he had not merely applied white forms to Native subjects (Morgan 131), he is quoted in many interviews and articles as saying that he had done just that: "I put together my knowledge of Indian reality in this country with classical structure, artistic language. It amounted to applying sonata forms to the spiritual and mental situation of a street drunk, say, at the corner of Queen and Bathurst" (Wigston 8). At the Royal Alex, at least, this apparently meant accommodating what Robert Cushman calls "a general audience," constructed in his review as "us," and clearly set apart from an "ethnic" them:

> Sometimes he [Highway] suggests a grown-up Sean O'Casey. Urban-sharp this Highway may be, but he belongs in the line of ethnic comedy that periodically rejuvenates the Anglo-American theatre. When this line breaks through, as Indian writing now has, it does us a double service; it introduces us to new scenes and puts us in touch with old ones.

Clearly, for Cushman, the value of *Dry Lips* at the Royal Alex lay in what it could contribute to a firmly entrenched "Anglo-American" tradition. Any political efficacy that it may have had as cultural intervention was swallowed by the march of that tradition's avant-garde, consuming "primitive" works in order to renew itself in the way that modernism once consumed African art. Other critics were similarly welcoming. Denis Johnston noted that "we need to learn from" "this Native resurgence" (263), and Bronwyn Drainie went so far as to state that the play's real "quality" rests in its ability to be "comprehensible or interesting to white audiences," "to move native experiences successfully across cultural borders."

But the Royal Alex production of *Dry Lips* evoked another and, to the playwright, surprising response. What at Theatre Passe Muraille had been enthusiastically greeted as a powerful play about misogyny was attacked in its new incarnation as being misogynistic *itself*. This response was related to a general tendency, supported by Highway's comments, to see aesthetic value and universal symbolism precisely where the first production had been noted for its shockingly brutal portrayals of the plight of women on the reservation. Highway was quoted by more than one writer as claiming, for example, that the play's rape scene is about the rape of Native culture and of "all women" ("Interview" 17): "In the rape scene ..., a woman is raped with a crucifix. On a metaphorical level, the scene symbolizes the matriarchal religion raped by the patriarchy" (qtd. in Steed). A Native woman might be forgiven for saying, as Ann-Marie MacDonald has about what she calls "the new misogynist art," "Good going, boys, but get your fucking metaphors off of my body" ("Ann-Marie MacDonald Interview" 143); and the production was, in fact, attacked in this way. [16] Stephen Godfrey, reviewing it at the National Arts Centre before it moved to the Royal Alex, noted that "A horrible abuse of a woman focuses not on the woman abused, but on the suffering of the abuser" ("Trip from Comedy"); and Marian Botsford Fraser, similarly pointing out that "our attention is drawn not to the women who are suffering but to the men who are watching," argued that "the weight of loathing for women that this play carries is almost unbearable."

It is interesting that Fraser, whose column sparked a lengthy debate in *The Globe and Mail*, introduced her comments by noting the "focus" and energy of a production that she describes as "brassy and exuberant and slick." The following week, in the same paper, Jay Scott picked up on this and provided an explanation for the change in response to *Dry Lips* that may have a broader application. He began by observing that there had been no suggestion of misogyny with the Passe Muraille production, where "a funky awkwardness and emotional messiness ... pushed the audience's face into an alien world that turned out not to be alien at all." At the Royal Alex, he argued, a "Broadway-(s)ized stylization" and "slick show-biz assurance and emotional precision," together with a "loss of intimacy" in the new space, "transformed visceral images into picturesque tableaux":

> A rape with a crucifix, for example, has had its horror softened:
>
> The choreography of the rape, contemplated through a proscenium arch many yards away rather than witnessed in the same room a few feet away, takes on the distanced artifice of modern dance.

"[T]he megaphone," he concludes, "has mangled the message."

Scott's analysis is perceptive, and it begins to account for the changes in reception and meaning between the first production and the transfer or remount of each play. Each underwent minor changes either to script or production—there were cast changes to include more marketable actors in *Love and Anger*, the script of *Goodnight Desdemona* was shortened, and the design was more polished for *Dry Lips*—but, for the most part, the significant changes were contextual: they constructed the plays as self-contained and unthreatening products of the theatre industry for the con-sumption of audiences that were newly constructed as consumers or voyeurs. [17]

In each case, there was a shift in relationship between stage and audience from social equality and shared space to sharply divided space in which the audience patronized the theatrical performance and, in Alan Filewod's terms, "translate[d] it into a self-congratulatory discourse: See how sophisticated I am; I appreciate this work" ("Averting" 23); or even: See how generous and tolerant I am; I support this work. Factory Theatre, for example, where *Love and Anger* was first produced, is located on the edge of working-class Bathurst Street and, together with the decor and architecture of the building, created a sense of shared space, values, and comfort level with the warehouse neighbourhood and decor of Petie Maxwell's basement office, as represented by the shabbiness of the set. The audience travelled through the play's world to get to the performance, and the line was not clear where the run-down set stopped and the equally run-down auditorium began. When the capitalist "greedy pricks" showed up in their tuxedos, there was no ambiguity as to who were the out-siders. In the upscale brick-and-brass ambience of the St. Lawrence Centre, however, next to the flagship O'Keefe Centre and far from the grubby realities of anybody's daily life, the audience physically and metaphorically looked down on the same set from plush and pricey seats to which it had been lured by Garth Drabinsky's "bold, aggressive marketing" (Kucherawy). As with *Dry Lips* at the elegant Royal Alex and under the sponsorship of the Mirvishes, the audience of *Love and Anger* was constructed by the setting as voyeurs.

The change in space was not as radical for *Goodnight Desdemona*, though it was similar in kind and effect, but MacDonald's play did share with *Love and Anger* and *Dry Lips* the effects of a new discursive context as constructed by the advertising, pro-grams, ticket prices, mandates, and seasons of the producers or producing companies.

While the *Love and Anger* transfer recontextualized the play as a production of Garth Drabinsky's Live Entertainment Corporation, and *Dry Lips* became part of a subscription season, on the same billing as the Old Vic's *Carmen Jones*, the Schubert Theatre's *Buddy: The Buddy Holly Story*, and *Les Misérables*, *Goodnight Desdemona* became part of the newly-formed Canadian Stage, with its stated aspiration of being Canada's national theatre. This company, "dedicated to mirroring our city, deepening our perception of Canadian reality and reflecting our unique identity," was constructed by its founding co-Artistic Director, Guy Sprung, as "another natural and very necessary milestone in the evolution of English theatre in Canada" (qtd. in Crew, "New Theatre"). *Goodnight Desdemona* was thereby recontextualized within this and other evolutionary, federalist, and nationalist rhetoric.[18] It was also part of the company's subscription "freedom package," and it sported a program featuring elaborate thanks to Air Canada, Imperial Oil, and other major corporate sponsors, including several (such as Alcan) with questionable human rights or ecological records. The program also listed, in decreasing order of dollar-value importance, the company's "premiere performers," "benefactors," "patrons," "donors," "contributors," and "supporters."

While the not-for-profit Canadian Stage program for *Goodnight Desdemona* positioned the play's audiences as real or potential patrons of the arts, benefactors whose support was tax deductible as "charitable donations," the commercial-theatre *Dry Lips* program astonishingly framed Highway's portrayal of poverty, alcoholism, and misogyny on the reserve within the context of glossy, full-colour ads for Cadillac and Mercedes Benz and eroticized photographs of scantily clad (white) women selling Smirnoff vodka. The program also included among the high-market advertisements articles on *Les Miz* and on the glorious history of the Royal Alex, together with a feature article by the dean of New York drama reviewers, Clive Barnes, legitimizing as a serious art form the Broadway-style musical "From the Beef Trust to Miss Saigon," the latter, of course, coming soon to a Mirvish theatre near you.

These and other contextual circumstances suggest, then, that any potential the productions had for cultural intervention was effectively contained and institutionally neutralized when they transferred to their new venues. But was containment complete and efficacy denied? Or did the shows mean *differently* for their differently constructed audiences? All cultural production is to some degree culturally productive. The primary efficacy of the original productions of these plays may have been their empowering construction of community among the socially marginalized groups that they represented, and this construction may have been what invited the colonizing and neutralizing patronage of their commercial or mainstream producers and audiences. At the same time, however, evidence suggests that in their new contexts other elements of these productions gained new resonance and opened fissures in the institutional veneer, fissures that could serve as potential sites of negotiation and change. These shows constructed the audience as voyeurs, but they also frequently pushed audiences beyond that construction to the point of conscious and uncomfortable confrontation with their own attitudes; that is, audience members potentially became *conscious* voyeurs, aware of the gap between the venue and the performance, conscious of the colonizing nature of their gaze. On the night that I saw *Goodnight Desdemona* at Canadian Stage, for example, there were titters of discomfort rippling through the house during the relatively restrained and extremely brief love scene between Constance and Juliet. Reviews reported a much stronger reaction to *Dry Lips*: regular subscribers were said to have walked out, left at intermission with requests for refunds, or otherwise "voic[ed their] disapproval" (Godfrey, "Trip from Comedy"). Bronwyn Drainie reports a reaction that I believe was typical, that suggests a degree of self-conscious anxiety in its disapproval:

> The Toronto audience on Tuesday night seemed stunned and pretty unhappy. They tittered nervously at the nudity ... and the foul language, and gasped in disbelief at the brutal examples of misogyny .... A lot of seats were empty for the second act, and a well-dressed older woman in the washroom commented, "I don't know how they can allow them on the stage."

And, of course, *Dry Lips* registered the significant achievement of placing a controversy over misogyny on the front page of the Entertainment Section of *The Globe and Mail* for three weeks.

I suggest that the efficacy of these productions derived in part from an element in their scripts that resisted easy containment and neutralization, or any simple unitary and colonizing interpretation. Each play included at least one wild-card character in a role that was central to any audience's reading of the play but that tended to fracture the unified subjectivity of characters and audiences. In *Love and Anger,* this role was shared by Petie and Sarah, stroke victim and schizophrenic respectively, whose skewed views of themselves and the world resisted the traditional unitary approaches of method acting, along with any final act of self- or Aristotelian recognition, including the affirming closure toward which the play's final image gestures. [19] Sarah, of course, even refuses to acknowledge the closure of Petie's death, and her unpredictability resists any confident projection of a hopeful future. But most significantly, perhaps, the play suggests that Petie's irrational anger and Sarah's schizophrenia are more *appropriate* as responses to the world that the play portrays than would be any normalcy to which a more conventional reversal and recognition might return them.

Their function in *Love and Anger,* I suggest, is comparable to the one more explicitly played by Constance as fool in *Goodnight Desdemona* and Nanabush as trickster in *Dry Lips:* both serve authorial functions that nevertheless resist authoritative readings. They maintain, that is, the "ambiguous and equivocal character" that Claude Levi-Strauss assigns to the trickster, and they serve the trickster's culturally "mediating function" as he describes it (248). In *Goodnight Desdemona*, the audacity of the play and its Shakespearean parodies function as disruptive play, what Stephen Greenblatt describes in referring to Christopher Marlowe as play "beyond estrangement from ideology, a fathomless and eerily playful self-estrangement":

> The will to play flaunts society's cherished orthodoxies, embraces what
> the culture finds loathsome or frightening, transforms the serious
> into the joke and then unsettles the category of the joke by taking it
> seriously, courts self-destruction in the interest of the anarchic discharge
> of its energy. This is play on the brink of an abyss, *absolute* play.
> *(Renaissance Self-Fashioning 220)*

In addition, *Goodnight Desdemona* assigns the role of author and fool to the act of
interpretation itself; and the containment made possible by the structure of Jungian
dream-vision, and partly effected at Canadian Stage, is made problematic to the
degree that the audience recognizes that its interpretative role is inscribed within the
play as a resisting one.

Dry Lips similarly writes its resisting trickster into a dream-vision play-within-
the-play—though the revelatory role of "dream power" in Native culture (Highway, "A
Note") is largely lost when played before a white audience for whom the vision
becomes "just a dream." Like *Goodnight Desdemona*, however, it assigns its trickster a
larger and less comprehensible (or containable) role, that of the slippery Nanabush,
the central figure in Native mythology, who metatheatrically performs the parts of
all of the women in *Dry Lips*. This foregrounded doubling of roles, the exotic and
heightened disruption both of method acting and of the psychologism of clowning
that it invites, and the use of a separate platform level upstage for the Nanabush
character: all invite a kind of interpretative fracturing that is lent authority by
Nanabush's stature as a "comic, clownish sort of character ... [who] straddles the
consciousness of man and that of God, the Great Spirit" (Highway, "A Note").

In these plays, then, the images of solidarity that served their first audiences as
focal points for empowerment and resistance invited the patronizing or colonizing
embrace of larger audiences in different material contexts. But they also employed
elusive and disruptive comic play, together with trickster characters that were central
to their meanings even for mainstream audiences as sites of negotiation, mediation,
and even transformation. None of these plays meant for mainstream audiences what
it did for its home community, but each was culturally productive insofar as it served
as a public site at which meaning and value, if not directly contested, were at least
rendered contestable. Poisons, if they are to work, can neither be rejected as incom-
patible by the organisms to which they are given nor be assimilated by them as
entirely compatible. The efficacy of any cultural production as intervention, like the
efficacy of the fool or trickster, depends on its adopting a mediating role that is
pre-textual rather than pre-scribed and is, of necessity, unstable.

(1993–94)

Notes

I would like to thank my undergraduate and graduate students in Canadian drama and theatre at the University of Guelph over the past two years, whose insights and analyses have directly influenced mine. In particular, I would like to thank my researcher Martin de Jonge and to acknowledge the assistance and resources of the University of Guelph's Theatre Archives.

[1] Although my largest theoretical debts are to Louis Althusser, Bertholt Brecht, and Antonio Gramsci, my approach derives more immediately from the politicized theory of the contemporary theatre, particularly the work of Susan Bennett, Herbert Blau and Baz Kershaw; and from recent cultural-materialist and new-historicist criticism of the drama of early modern England, notably the work of Jean Howard, Louis Montrose, Alan Sinfield and other contributors and to Jonathon Dollimore and Sinfield's *Political Shakespeare*, Graham Holderness, Christopher J. McCullough, and, of course, Stephen Greenblatt.

[2] Not all of these material conditions have received much scholarly attention in Canada or elsewhere: see, however, Salter ("Body Politics"); Allan; Flaherty; and Wilson ("Starters"). See also Wallace on government organizations and funding structures.

[3] See Salter ("Seeing Things") for a detailed analysis of the ideological work of the proscenium stage.

[4] I use *ideology* here and throughout this essay in the Althusserian sense as Jean Howard defines it:

> Ideology in my understanding is the obviousness of culture, what goes without saying, what is lived as true. It is therefore precisely not a set of beliefs known to be "false" but cynically sold to others to hold them in an inferior position, nor does it originate from a conspiratorial power group (or author) bent on dominating or deceiving others. This does not mean, however, that ideology does not function to produce unequal social relations ... stratified by race, gender and class. It simply means that ideology does not lie in anyone's conscious control, nor can it be opposed to "truth," simply to other ideological modalities of knowing. (226)

[5] The concept of "perspective" in a role, of course, has significant and mutually rein-forcing analogies to pictorial perspective, directors' notions of focus, proscenium stagecraft, and so on.

[6] The slip from "characters" to "persons" in this passage is significant and revealing, as is, of course, the equation of value with conflict in the forging of "character" (in both senses of the word) and dramatic action.

[7] Plant notes that "Many [reviewers] acknowledged the … sense of chaos and fragmentation; some treated that as a flaw" (11).

[8] Keith Garebian discusses the effect of the New York marketing on audience's horizons of expectations with Krizanc and Rose. Ads focused on " … Cocaine, World Politics, Sex, Love, Sadism, Questionable Morals, Decadence, Voyeurism, … and so on" (15), while marketing gimmicks included a "Tamara collection" line of products that included a Tamara perfume, Tamara watches, and Lucite paperweights containing tickets from the show's first anniversary in Los Angeles, as well as postcards, T-shirts, and books (Godfrey, "The Little Play"). The "Theatre Directory" listing for the show in the *New York Times* (2 January 1988) is representative of the publicity for the show and is worth transcribing in full:

TODAY & TOM'W MAT
(Cocktails 1:30 *Perf 2)*
TONIGHT & TOM'W
(Cocktails 7:30 *Perf 8)*

"'TAMARA' IS A SHOT OF ADRENALINE … IT'S UNLIKE ANY OTHER SHOW CURRENTLY IN NEW YORK.

"A TOTAL THEATRICAL EXPERIENCE ON EVERY LEVEL WHICH NO DESCRIPTION CAN DO JUSTICE. AUDIENCES WILL WANT TO SEE IT OVER AND OVER"

—*Gloria Cole, UPI*

The Story You Follow
From Room to Room
TAMARA
'The Living Movie'

A spectacular evening—story, food, drink—in One place for One price

Champagne by Perrier Jouet, Cocktails by Seagram, sumptuous buffet banquet presented by Le Cirque, designed by Chef Daniel Houlud, catered by Remember Basil.

Mon–Wed & Fri–Sun 8; Mats Sat & Sun 2
TICKETMASTER
212-307-7171/516-888-9000/914-965-2700
Groups 398-8383
THE PARK AVE ARMORY
643 Park Ave. at 66th St.

[9] An interesting parallel between Znaimer as editor and as Canadian nationalist surfaces in Susan Swan's account of his "Taking Hype to Hollywood." She discusses his free-market nationalism and quotes his criticism of the Secretary of State, who, "Despite all the huffing and puffing, … has never taken very seriously the *business of creating a focus* and *building a mythology*" (47, emphasis added). The comparison

perhaps reinforces any suggestion that John Krizanc in Hollywood played d'Annunzio to Znaimer's Mussolini.

[10] I am indebted in this paragraph to a seminar and paper presented by graduate student Liz Snyder at the University of Guelph in 1992, in which she undertook a comparative analysis of the script for the Dundurn Castle production and the published version of that used in New York. She concluded that "Any traces of ambiguity have been erased from *Tamara* as Znaimer has effectively contained any politics which Krizanc and Rose put into the original text" (22–23).

[11] I am indebted to Snyder (19) for this observation.

[12] Michael McKinnie, a senior drama student at the University of Guelph to whom I am indebted throughout this section of my paper, usefully undertakes a comparative semiotic analysis of the operations of CityTV and *Tamara*, noting that "both City and later *Tamara*s communicate through objects and images that read as fetishized representations of unattainable desire" (12). I am also indebted here to Snyder's discussion of CityTV news programming (9–11) and her example of the station's "Speaker's Corner" show,

> which broadcasts selected statements from people who speak into the "videobooth" located on the street by the station .... "Speaker's Corner" starts with Moses Znaimer's signed statement that:
>
>> One of the original objectives of CityTV was to broaden the range of voices in Toronto television. This means not only different style and content in programs but also expanding the number of real people who get on the air .... Open 24 hours a day. Every day of the year. Forever. (10–11)

Snyder goes on to comment that "anyone can pay their loonie, sit in the isolation of the booth and speak their mind, but not everyone will be seen on TV." In Znaimer's quoted words, only "The most compelling," however defined, "will be run," and, as Snyder points out about the commodification of democracy, "there is a prize for the 'best' spot on the show which consists of a package of 'Muchwear' and Much products. The prize itself is a promotional tool" (11).

[13] I am using "worked" here not in the usual (and vague) theatrical sense but in the politicized sense of "performance efficacy" defined by Kershaw (257–58).

[14] Perhaps it is not surprising that Pennington considered the play to be a "mean-spirited diatribe": his review appeared in the *Toronto Sun*, which, though not named, was clearly the model for the "fascist rag" that the play attacks.

[15] MacDonald refers to the play as a "Jungian fairy tale" ("Ann-Marie MacDonald Interview" 141).

[16] See Baker, a Saulteux poet, playwright, and teacher, who responded in almost precisely this way in an article in *Canadian Theatre Review*'s special issue on Native theatre, but her comments were made about the Winnipeg production.

[17] As far as I know, the phrase "theatre industry" dates, interestingly, to Gramsci's use of it, in 1917, in an article in *Avanti*, parts of which could have been written about Toronto in the 1980s and '90s, including his remark that "actors are being forced to turn to the cinema to make a living" (57).

[18] See Salter, "The Idea of a National Theatre"; and Filewod, "National Theatre/National Obsession," for analyses of the history and implications of these aspirations and this rhetoric. See also note 9.

[19] See Knowles, "The Dramaturgy of the Perverse," for a discussion of Walker's use of fragmented subjectivity in the character of Sarah.

Works Cited

Alaton, Salem. "Mixed Reviews for Tamara." *The Globe and Mail* [Toronto] 4 December 1987: C3.

Allan, Katherine. "Columbus and the Neutral Mask." *Canadian Theatre Review* 71 (1992): 20–25.

Althusser, Louis. *Lenin and Philosophy and Other Essays.* Trans. Ben Brewster. New York: Monthly Review, 1971.

Baker, Marie Annharte. "Angry Enough to Spit but with *Dry Lips* it Hurts More than You Know." *Canadian Theatre Review* 68 (1991): 88–89.

Barnes, Clive. "From the Beef Trust to Miss Saigon." *Dry Lips Oughta Move to Kapuskasing.* Program, Royal Alexandra Theatre, Toronto, n.d. 40–59.

Belsey, Catherine. *Critical Practice.* London: Routledge, 1980.

Bennett, Susan. *Theatre Audiences: A Theory of Production and Reception.* London: Routledge, 1990.

Blackadar, Bruce. "Tamara a Brilliantly Staged Play." Rev. of *Tamara*, by John Krizanc. Strachan House, Toronto. *Toronto Star* 1 June 1981: E3.

Blau, Herbert. *To All Appearances: Ideology and Performance.* New York: Routledge, 1992.

Brask, Per, and William Morgan, eds. *Aboriginal Voices: Amerindian, Inuit, and Sami Theater.* Baltimore: Johns Hopkins UP, 1992.

Brecht, Bertolt. *Brecht on Theatre: The Development of an Aesthetic.* Ed. and trans. John Willett. 2nd ed. 1974. New York: Hill; London: Methuen, 1987.

Brook, Peter. *The Empty Space.* 1972. Harmondsworth, Eng.: Penguin, 1976.

Cashman, Cheryl. "Toronto's Zanies." *Canadian Theatre Review* 67 (1991): 22–31.

Catron, Louis E. *The Director's Vision: Play Direction from Analysis to Production.* Mountain View, CA: Mayfield, 1989.

Conlogue, Ray. "An Emotionally Riveting Dry Lips". Rev. of *Dry Lips Oughta Move to Kapuskasing,* by Tomson Highway. Theatre Passe Muraille, Toronto. *The Globe and Mail* [Toronto] 24 April 1989: C1.

———. "Love and Anger: Catching the Crest of a Wave." Rev. of *Love and Anger,* by George F. Walker. Factory Theatre, Toronto. *The Globe and Mail* [Toronto] 13 February 1990: C 10.

———. "Love and Anger. One More Time." Rev. of *Love and Anger,* by George F. Walker. St. Lawrence Centre for the Arts: Bluma Appel Theatre, Toronto. *The Globe and Mail* [Toronto] 4 May 1990: C3.

———. "New Roles for Classic Heroines." Rev. of *Goodnight Desdemona (Good Morning Juliet),* by Ann-Marie MacDonald. Annex Theatre, Toronto. *The Globe and Mail* [Toronto] 4 April 1988: C9.

———. "Of Heroines and a Comic Quest." Rev. of *Goodnight Desdemona (Good Morning Juliet),* by Ann-Marie MacDonald. The Stage Downstairs, Toronto. *The Globe and Mail* [Toronto] 31 March 1990: C9.

Crew, Robert. "Desdemona Delicious Fun." Rev. of *Goodnight Desdemona (Good Morning Juliet),* by Ann-Marie MacDonald. The Stage Downstairs, Toronto. *Toronto Star* 29 March 1990: C3.

———. "Goodnight Desdemona Puts a Twist on the Bard." Rev. of *Goodnight Desdemona (Good Morning Juliet),* by Ann-Marie MacDonald. Annex Theatre, Toronto. *Toronto Star* 4 April 1988: C5.

———. "Hope Flickers in Disturbing Probe of Native Spirit." Rev. of *Dry Lips Oughta Move to Kapuskasing,* by Tomson Highway. Theatre Passe Muraille, Toronto. *Toronto Star* 23 April 1989: CI.

———. "Love and Anger Simply Stunning." Rev. of *Love and Anger,* by George F. Walker. Factory Theatre, Toronto. *Toronto Star* 12 October 1989: CI.

———. "New Theatre Company to Boost Canadian Works." *Toronto Star* 26 March 1988: J2.

Cushman, Robert. "From Ideal to Painfully Real" Rev. of *Dry Lips Oughta Move to Kapuskasing,* by Tomson Highway. Royal Alexandra Theatre, Toronto. *The Globe and Mail* [Toronto] 15 April 1991: C3.

Czarnecki, Mark. "Tamara Wins in Hollywood." *Maclean's* 30 July 1984: 6.

Diamond, Elin. "Brechtian Theory/Feminist Theory: Toward a Gestic Feminist Criticism." *TDR [The Drama Review]* 32.1 (1988): 82–94.

Dollimore, Jonathan, and Alan Sinfield, eds. *Political Shakespeare: New Essays in Cultural Materialism*. Ithaca: Cornell UP, 1985.

Donnelly, Pat. "T.O. Takes It on the Chin from Canada's Foremost Playwright." Rev. of *Love and Anger*, by George F. Walker. Factory Theatre, Toronto. *Gazette* [Montreal] [6 October 1989: F6.

Drainie, Bronwyn. "Highway Play a Challenging Stop on the Road to Understanding." Rev. of *Dry Lips Oughta Move to Kapuskasing*, by Tomson Highway. Royal Alexandra Theatre, Toronto. *The Globe and Mail* [Toronto] 20 April 1991: C1.

Filewod, Alan. "Averting the Colonizing Gaze: Notes on Watching Native Theater." Brask and Morgan 17–28.

———. "National Theatre/National Obsession." *Canadian Theatre Review* 62 (1990): 5–10.

Flaherty, Kathleen. "Table Stakes: Gambling with New Play Development." *Canadian Theatre Review* 71 (1992): 26–31.

Fortier, Mark. "Shakespeare with a Difference: Genderbending and Genre-bending in *Goodnight Desdemona*." *Canadian Theatre Review* 59 (1989): 47–51.

Fraser, Marian Botsford. "Contempt for Women Overshadows Powerful Play." Rev. of *Dry Lips Oughta Move to Kapuskasing*, by Tomson Highway. Royal Alexandra Theatre, Toronto. *The Globe and Mail* [Toronto] 17 April 1991: C1.

Garebian, Keith. "Success or Excess?" Rev. of *Tamara*, by John Krizanc. Park Avenue Armory, New York. *Performing Arts in Canada* 26.1 (1990): 13–16.

Giovannini, Joseph. "The Park Avenue Armory Is Home to a 10-Room Villa for 'Tamara.' " Rev. of *Tamara*, by John Krizanc. Park Avenue Armory, New York. *New York Times* 12 November 1987: C1, C10.

Godfrey, Stephen. "The Little Play that Grew." *The Globe and Mail* [Toronto] 26 December 1985: A 10.

———. "Trip from Comedy to Drama Is a Worthwhile, if Bumpy, Ride." Rev. of *Dry Lips Oughta Move to Kapuskasing*, by Tomson Highway. National Arts Centre, Ottawa. *The Globe and Mail* [Toronto] 9 March 1991: C5.

Good, Maurice. *Every Inch a Lear: A Rehearsal Journal of "King Lear" with Peter Ustinov and the Stratford Festival Company Directed by Robin Phillips*. Victoria: Sono Nis, 1982.

Gramsci, Antonio. *Selections from Cultural Writings*. Ed. David Forgacs and Geoffrey Nowell-Smith. Trans. William Boelhower. Cambridge: Harvard UP, 1985.

Greenblatt, Stephen. *Renaissance Self-Fashioning: From More to Shakespeare*. Chicago: U of Chicago P, 1980.

————. *Shakespearean Negotiations: The Circulation of Social Energy in Renaissance England.* Berkeley: U of California P, 1988,

————. "Towards a Poetics of Culture." Veeser 1–14.

Harvie, Jennifer. "Taking Responsibility for *Tamara.*" Unpublished honours essay, McGill U, Montreal, 1990.

Hayden, Gene. "Lecoq Tales." *Theatrum* 26 (1991–92): 17–20.

Highway, Tomson. *Dry Lips Oughta Move to Kapuskasing.* Saskatoon: Fifth House. 1989.

————. "An Interview with Tomson Highway." With Barbara Nahwegahbow. *Beedaudjimowin* (1991): 7, 17.

————. "A Note on Nanabush." *Dry Lips Oughta Move to Kapuskasing.* Program, Royal Alexander Theatre, Toronto., n.d. 11.

————. "The Trickster and Native Theater: An Interview with Tomson Highway." With William Morgan. Brask and Morgan 130–38.

Holderness, Graham, ed. *The Shakespeare Myth.* Manchester: Manchester UP, 1988.

Hollingsworth, Margaret. *Endangered Species.* Toronto: Act One. 1988.

"Margaret Hollingsworth Interview." With Judith Rudakoff. Rudakoff and Much 144–64.

Howard, Jean E. "Scripts and/versus Playhouses: Ideological Production and the Renaissance Public Stage." Wayne 221–36.

Howard, Jean E. and Marion F. O'Connor, eds. *Shakespeare Reproduced: The Text in History and Ideology.* New York: Methuen, 1987.

Illustration. *Toronto Star* 29 March 1990: C1.

Johnston, Denis W. "Lines and Circles: The 'Rez' Plays of Tomson Highway." *Canadian Literature* 124–25 (1990): 254–65.

Kaplan, Jon. "Los Angeles: Tamara Takes Off." Rev. of *Tamara,* by John Krizanc. Hollywood American Legion, Los Angeles. *Canadian Theatre Review* 44 (1985): 135–38.

Kershaw, Baz. *The Politics of Performance: Radical Theatre as Cultural Intervention.* London: Routledge, 1992.

Knelman, Martin. "Upstairs, Downstairs." *Saturday Night* January 1982: 59–60.

Knowles, Richard Paul. "The Dramaturgy of the Perverse." *Theatre Research International* 17.3 (1992): 226–35.

————. "'The Truth Must Out': The Political Plays of John Krizanc." *Canadian Drama/L'art dramatique canadien* 13.1 (1987): 27–33.

————. "Voices (off): Deconstructing the Modern English-Canadian Dramatic Canon." Lecker 91–111.

————, ed. *Canadian Theatre Review* 71 (1992).

Krizanc, John. *The Half of It.* Toronto: Anansi, 1990.

————. "Innocents Abroad." *Saturday Night* November 1984: 34–38.

————. "Interview: John Krizanc." With Ann Jansen. *Books in Canada* March 1988: 34–36.

————. *Tamara.* Toronto: Stoddart, 1989.

Kucherawy, Dennis. "Garth Drabinsky: Getting Behind Love and Anger." *Metropolis* 26 April 1990: 5.

Lecker, Robert, ed. *Canadian Canons: Essays in Literary Value.* Toronto: U of Toronto P 1991.

Levi-Strauss, Claude. "The Structural Study of Myth." *European Literary Theory and Practice: From Existential Phenomenology to Structuralism.* Ed.Vernon W. Gras. New York: Dell-Delta, 1973. 289–316.

Linklater, Kristin. *Freeing the Natural Voice.* New York: Drama Book, 1976.

MacDonald, Ann-Marie. "Ann-Marie MacDonald Interview." With Rita Much. Rudakoff and Much 127–43.

————. *Goodnight Desdemona (Good Morning Juliet).* Toronto: Coach House, 1990.

Manguel, Alberto. Foreword. *Tamara.* By John Krizanc. Toronto: Stoddart, 1989. 13–17.

Marcuse, Herbert. "The Affirmative Character of Culture." *Negations: Essays in Critical Theory* By Marcuse. Trans. J. Shapiro. Boston: Beacon, 1968. 88–133.

McCullough, Christopher J. "The Cambridge Connection: Towards a Materialist Theatre Practice." Holderness 112–21.

McKinnie, Michael. "The Hip and the Led: *Tamara* and CityTV." Unpublished essay, U of Guelph, 1992.

Michael, Patricia. "Will the Real Tamara Please Stand Up?" *Performing Arts in Canada* 24.1 (1990): 14–15.

Miller, Robert. "All Aboard the Stairway to the Stars." *Maclean's* 2 September 1985: 50–51.

Montrose, Louis A. "Professing the Renaissance: The Poetics and Politics of Culture." Veeser 15–36.

Moore, Sonia. *The Stanislavski System: The Professional Training of an Actor.* New rev. ed. Harmondsworth.; Penguin, 1976.

Morrison, Hugh. *Directing in the Theatre.* 2nd ed. 1984. London: Black; New York: Theatre Arts Books, 1989.

Much, Rita, ed. *Women on the Canadian Stage: The Legacy of Hrotsvit.* Winnipeg: Blizzard, 1992.

Mulvey, Laura. "Visual Pleasure and Narrative Cinema." *Visual and Other Pleasures.* By Mulvey. Bloomington: Indiana UP, 1989. 14–26.

O'Brien, Ellen J. "Mapping the Role: A Means to Performable Feminist Critiques." Paper presented at the Feminist Theatrical Practice seminar at the Shakespeare Association of America Conf. Philadelphia, 12 April 1990.

Pennington, Bob. "Love and Anger's Marx and Malice." Rev. of *Love and Anger,* by George F. Walker. Factory Theatre, Toronto. *Toronto Sun* 13 October 1989: 88.

Plant, Richard. "The Deconstruction of Pleasure: John Krizanc's *Tamara,* Richard Rose and the Necessary Angel Theatre Company." Unpublished essay. Trans. and pub. as "Die dekonstruktion des vergnugens: John Krizanc's *Tamara,* Richard Rose, und die Necessary Angel Theatre Company." *Das Englisch-Kanadische drama.* Ed. Albert-Reiner Glaap. Düsseldorf: Schwann, 1992. 257–68.

Rudakoff, Judith, and Rita Much, eds. *Fair Play: 12 Women Speak: Conversations with Canadian Playwrights.* Toronto: Simon 1990.

Salter, Denis. "Body Politics: English-Canadian Acting at NTS." *Canadian Theatre Review 71* (1992): 4–14.

———. "The Idea of a National Theatre." Lecker 71–90.

———. "Seeing Things: Shakespeare, Imperial History, and the Ideological Formations of the Proscenium Stage." Paper presented at Beyond the Shakespeare Revolution seminar at the Shakespeare Association of America Conf. Kansas City, 18 April 1992.

Scott, Jay. "Dry Lips' Loss of Intimacy Transforms Visceral Images into Picturesque Tableaux." Rev. of Dry *Lips Oughta Move to Kapuskasing,* by Tomson Highway. Royal Alexandra Theatre, Toronto. *The Globe and Mail* [Toronto] 22 April 1991: C1.

Shewey, Don. "Adventurousness Rewarded." *Soho News* 3 June 1981: 21, 44.

Sinfield, Alan. "Royal Shakespeare: Theatre and the Making of Ideology." Dollimore and Sinfield 158–81.

Snyder, Liz. "As Much as You Can Afford: Moses Znaimer and *Tamara.*" Unpublished essay, U of Guelph, 1992.

Steed, Judy. "Tomson Highway My Way." *Toronto Star* 24 March 1991: n.p.

Swan, Susan. "Taking Hype to Hollywood." *Toronto Life* September 1984: 43–67.

Veeser, H. Aram, ed. *The New Historicism.* New York: Routledge, 1989.

Vincent, Isabel. "Love and Anger Reaction." *The Globe and Mail* [Toronto] 18 December 1990: C3.

Walker, George F. *Love and Anger.* Toronto: Coach House, 1990.

Wallace, Robert. *Producing Marginality: Theatre and Criticism in Canada.* Saskatoon: Fifth House, 1990.

Wayne, Valerie, ed. *The Matter of Difference: Materialist Feminist Criticism of Shakespeare.* Ithaca: Cornell UP, 1991.

Wigston, Nancy. "Nanabush in the City." *Books in Canada* March 1989: 7–9.

Williams, David, compiler. *Peter Brook: A Theatrical Casebook.* London: Methuen, 1988.

Wilson, Ann. "Critical Revisions: Ann-Marie MacDonald's *Goodnight Desdemona (Good Morning Juliet).*" Much 1–12.

———. "Starters: A Theatre Program and Its Audience." *Canadian Theatre Review* 71 (1992): 49–54.

Healing the Border Wound:
Fronteras Americanas and the
Future of Canadian Multiculturalism

by Mayte Gómez

"Here we are. All together. At long last." With these words, Guillermo Verdecchia, author and performer of *Fronteras Americanas*, welcomed his audience to the Tarragon Theatre's Extra Space in Toronto on a cold winter evening of 1993. The same words served to welcome audience members to a larger space, a metaphorical one perhaps, one whose name has been misused and abused, and in which people are still alienated from one another. Welcome to the Americas, the continent of borders, of *fronteras*.

Fronteras Americanas, perhaps one of the most successful one-person shows in Toronto in recent years, is a humorous but poignant look at the Latino stereotypes which have been created in North America and which serve to deepen the alienation between North and South, an alienation which in economic and political terms translates into exploitation. But the play is also about the personal story of one of those Latinos, Verdecchia himself, born in Argentina and living in Canada from an early age, on the border between two cultures without fully belonging to either one of them. Thus, the borders explored in the play are those within the continent and within the individual.

Fronteras, originally performed by Verdecchia himself, was extraordinarily well-received by Toronto audiences and critics alike and was an impressive box-office success. Since then it has been produced in other parts of the country, and it has won Verdecchia a 1993 Governor General's Drama Award and a 1994 Chalmers Award for Best Canadian Play. The explanation of this outstanding success might seem to be quite simple at first. The play is well-written and Verdecchia is an inspiring performer. The text is funny, witty and profound, all in the right doses. The original production was sponsored by a well-established theatre in Toronto with a long tradition of workshopping new Canadian scripts and supporting new playwrights, and it was put together by a winning team of professionals. Finally, being easy to produce and tour, the text has caught the imagination of other artists and audiences across Canada.

However, there are more profound reasons for *Fronteras'* success, reasons which cannot be found in its literary and production values alone. At some level, I believe, it has brought to life some profound contradictions latent in Canada as a country and in Canadians as individuals. These contradictions have to do with the way Canadian society is shaped by the federal policy of Multiculturalism.

Elsewhere[1] I have argued that all aspects of Canadian life, but most obviously the arts, have been affected by what I have called "the ideology of Multiculturalism," an apparently liberal discourse of "integration" of and respect for all cultures underneath which lies a reality of acculturation into a mainstream. My main argument in this discussion has been that this ideology was established and is continuously recreated by both the official and the popular use of the terms "cultures" and "ethnic groups" to describe the different inhabitants of Canada. In my work I have attempted to analyze how Canadian cultural policy as well as the work of minority[2] artists in Toronto is affected by the subtle workings of this ideology of acculturation. Whether they reproduce it or attempt to consciously subvert it, they are bound to be framed by it, and often they comply with it and challenge it at the very same time. As a play dealing with relations among cultures, both inside and outside Canada, *Fronteras Americanas* is also framed by the ideology of Multiculturalism, and it also serves to reproduce it and subvert it in different ways.

In *Fronteras*, the negotiation between ideological compliance and challenge is found in the content of the play as well as in some of its means of production, such as venue and language. In each of these means of production this negotiation is firmly grounded in an ongoing shift among the two kinds of borders present in the script, borders within the continent and within the individual. But *Fronteras* also manages to go a step further, as the issues which result from the exploration of these borders are transferred to Canada itself. I would like to suggest that the image of Canada presented toward the end of *Fronteras* is the play's most powerful ideological subversion.

In 1967, the Royal Commission on Bilingualism and Biculturalism established by Prime Minister Lester Pearson published Book 1 of a Report which defined Canada as a "bilingual" and "bicultural" country, the home of two cultures—British and French (already known as "Charter cultures" since they are recognized by the British North America Act of 1867)—each with its respective language. Groups which were neither British nor French were dealt with in other books of the Report, which classified them all together under the rubric of "ethnic groups."

The Report defined culture as "a way of being, thinking, and feeling ... a driving force animating a significant group of individuals united by a common tongue and sharing the same customs, habits and experiences" (1:xxxi). This definition seems to be in line with others put forward by modern social scientists who see culture as "a way of life that a group of people develops in order to adapt to a set of external and pre-existing conditions" (Li 8). What matters in these definitions is that culture is a notion which denotes *material practice,* since it seems to make reference to a social system of customs, norms, and institutions, a system which can change and can be chosen.

The Report's definition of "ethnic group" also seemed to be in line with those offered by modern social science, which has defined it as a group "bound together by common ties of race, nationality, or culture, living together in an alien civilization but remaining culturally distinct" (Ware 607).

As much as modern social science has been successful in revealing the notion of race as a social construct, it has failed to approach the notion of "ethnic group" in the same fashion. The essence of the definition of an ethnic group lies in the fact that it lives in an "alien civilization," that is, it is a minority within a majority, its social and political position being constructed in relation to others. In Canada, the British and the French are called "cultures" because they have a social impact, being the creators and safeguards of the material practice of this country. Other groups are simply "ethnic groups," because their material practice has a limited influence outside their own communities. In Canadian society at large, they have a merely symbolic function. Their presence is recognized but they are not necessarily allowed to influence the over-all cultural practice.

Although in the 1970s Pierre Trudeau's policy of Multiculturalism introduced an apparently new vision of Canada—not with *two* but *many* cultures—the ideology remained the same, for the new policy included no discussion of how these groups would have an impact on the practice of Canadian society. It simply encouraged all Canadians to honour their ancestors and their own ways of life, as long as they affected their communities alone. "Cultural pluralism" simply meant to regulate "equality of opportunity for all *within the existing system*" (Hawkins 11; emphasis added). Instead of allowing for pluralism, the policy of Multiculturalism continued to frame Canada's peoples as "cultures" and "ethnic groups," perpetuating the division between their spheres of influence, and thus re-instituting acculturation.

If ideology can be defined as ideas which help to "legitimate a dominant political power" (Eagleton 1) and if this political power may legitimate itself, among other ways, "by *naturalizing* and *universalizing* such beliefs so as to render them self-evident and apparently inevitable" (5), the ideology of Multiculturalism in Canada has re-instituted the power of the British and French cultures (already self-granted in 1867), keeping other groups unable to influence the material practice of the country as a whole. Furthermore, it has served to promulgate this status quo as the natural way things are in this country. This is the ideology which shapes modern Canadian society and all practices within it. It is also the context in which I wish to look at *Fronteras Americanas.*[3]

As I suggested in the introduction to this essay, *Fronteras* deals with two kinds of borders, which for the sake of clarity I would like to call the "continental border" and the "individual border." The continental border divides the Americas into North and South and is grounded in colonial relations which translate into stereotyped representations of the "other," representations which, in turn, legitimate hegemonic relations of power. This border, Verdecchia argues, using Carlos Fuentes' words, is a "personal frontier" which "can be nourished by ... knowledge ... [or] can be starved by suspicion, ghost stories, arrogance, scorn and violence" (30). Verdecchia discusses well-known stereotypes (the "Latino lover," the "Latino dancer" or the Colombian "drug lord") and performs some others (the Mexican "bandito"[4] and Wideload, a Chicano immigrant in Canada) as a strategy to make those who have created the stereotypes laugh at them. This strategy works quite effectively, for at many times during the course of the performance it is not clear whether the audience is laughing at the stereotype or at themselves laughing at it.

The individual border acknowledges the presence of two cultures alive within an individual, as he struggles to find his [5] "identity," his "Home." Verdecchia, born in Argentina, is going back home "after an absence of fifteen years." He repeats the words to himself: "Going Home ... I am going Home—all will be resolved, dissolved, revealed, I will claim my place in the universe when I Go Home" (36). But once he is "Home," he is as confused as he was when he left Canada, and he feels he needs to go ... home: "[B]ut I'm already there aren't I?" (50).

On the border between the two cultures, Verdecchia feels "different," "wrong," "out of place," "not nowhere," "not-neither" (51). Pressured by an Argentinian friend, he goes to visit "El Brujo," a medicine man (presumably Argentinian as well) who also finds himself "on the border" (El Brujo himself thinks this border is in Mexico, but Verdecchia knows they are just near Bloor and Madison, in Toronto). "El Brujo" asks Verdecchia to "remember" the pieces of his life and finally tells him he has "a very bad border wound" (70). He also tells him that the wound, the border "is ... home" (48). [6] With "El Brujo," Verdecchia finally discovers his "problem": "I'm not in Canada; I'm not in Argentina! I'm on the Border/I am Home ... *Je suis Argentin-Canadien!* I am a post-Porteño [7] neo-Latino Canadian! I am the Pan-American Highway!" (74).

The exploration of the continental border serves to debunk myths about the supremacy of English-speaking cultures in the Americas. In the context of Canadian society, however, ruled by the ideology of Multiculturalism, the use of stereotypes as a performative strategy necessarily re-inscribes the binary opposition "we and them" established by the hegemony of this ideology. The use of stereotypes might allow "Canadians" (those who occupy this subject position) to realize that their under-standing of the "other" is deeply grounded in ignorance and prejudice, but it also allows them to see the "others" still as "foreigners" who come to Canada as "immigrants." In this sense, the final point of the play for "Canadians" might still be that "they" must change their prejudicial view and "accept" "others" as they are, in which case the final action is still one of containment.

The exploration of the individual border, however, begins to challenge this binary opposition by acknowledging the existence of two *practised* and *living* cultures (as opposed to one of them being a "symbolic" ethnic background) in a person. The individual who experiences two cultures defies acculturation, as he searches for a place where two cultures interact with one another equally, creating an identity which is "not-neither" (51). When he is finally able to look at his "border wound" not as a "problem" but as the potential to find "Home," he has found a third space where he is truly himself. The personal border is the site where this interaction takes place.

In the non-linear expositional mode which he uses to shift time and space, Verdecchia also shifts from border to border in his performance. The means of pro-duction used by the play both reproduce and subvert the ideology of Multiculturalism as a result of this negotiation of emphasis among borders. To illustrate this idea, I will focus on two of those means of production: venue (Tarragon Theatre) and language (English versus Spanish), paying special attention to the use of stereotypes as a performative strategy.

One of the first alternate theatres to appear in Toronto during the height of Canadian nationalism in social and cultural life, the Tarragon Theatre was founded by Bill Glassco in 1971 with the goal of achieving "production excellence for contemporary Canadian plays, in order to build an appreciative audience" (Johnston 150). Although the Tarragon has consistently pursued its policy of presenting Canadian work, it could be argued that its understanding of the word "Canadian" has been rather narrow until quite recently. This is perhaps explained by the history of the theatre, founded during the years in which to be "alternate" meant to be "national," that is, Canadian, and in which a lack of awareness about cultural diversity in the arts (despite the fact that the policy of Multiculturalism was released also in 1971) resulted in "Canadian" theatre in Toronto being largely English Canadian. [8] In the following decades, the "alternate" theatres—Tarragon, Passe Muraille, Factory Lab and Toronto Free, [9] for instance—came to be part of the establishment of Canadian theatre, if not because of their economic structure certainly because of their institutionalization of English Canadian culture.

While this institutionalization was taking place, the work of minority artists in Canada (which has often been referred to as "immigrant" art), was considered "amateur." This classification, which is still being fought by cultural activists across the country, meant, among other things, that this work did not need to be judged by professional standards of quality, because it was only relevant to a reduced community, to an "ethnic group," not to society at large (see Harney and Government of Metropolitan Toronto). [10]

The fact that the Tarragon became the home for *Fronteras*—not only the work of an Argentinian Canadian but also a theatre piece dealing with intercultural relations—can be read in two different ways. On the one hand, it could be argued that the play was co-opted and contained by a symbol of the English Canadian cultural establishment, *de facto* giving in to the power of acculturation coming from the official culture. Perhaps many Latin American artists and members of the audience wondered why the show was not done in a place which would be recognized as "Latino" or at least Spanish-speaking. Alternatively, it could be argued that to have produced it in a Spanish-speaking venue would have re-established the "ghettoization" of non-Anglo-Saxon artists, for such a place does not exist as part of the professional theatre in Toronto and it would have made the production to be seen as "amateur."

I would suggest this question is far from being an either/or proposition, for each venue would have made *Fronteras* reproduce and subvert the ideology of Multiculturalism in different ways.

Produced at the Tarragon, *Fronteras* was mostly about the continental border, where an Anglophone audience received the play as a criticism of the way North

Americans have constructed stereotypes of Latinos. [11] Presumably, the audience followed Verdecchia's strategy to make them laugh at the stereotype first and then have them consider (however reluctantly) what it was they were laughing at. At moments this strategy worked extremely well, as when Verdecchia/Wideload admitted he had been calling Anglo-Saxons "you," "painting [them] with the same brush" and finally asked his audience in quite a cunning tone: "Is it starting to bug you yet?" (75). The most common response to this question has been an uneasy silence.

This focus on stereotypes reproduces the ideology of Multiculturalism by re-establishing the dichotomy "we-them," as I have already suggested, but it also subverts that ideology by making the audience aware of it, since it is a strategy to bring the audience's attention to the construction of stereotypes. In order to bring their awareness to the creation of "Latino" stereotypes, Verdecchia makes his audience experience the position of victim themselves, making them a target of how Latinos would see a stereotyped Anglo-Saxon. One of such stereotypes is the "Saxon" dancer, who, Verdecchia/Wideload argues, makes "a big effort to move his hips independently of his legs" and flaps his arms "like a flamenco dancer" (40).

This strategy, however, contains a double bind; in the first place, because it still depends on the creation of a stereotype; more importantly, however, because, although it might reveal the absurdity of the stereotyped Latino dancer, it might also re-inscribe it. After all, to suggest that a "Saxon" is a bad dancer, even acknowledging that this is a stereotype, only re-inscribes the notion that Latinos are born dancers themselves.

The strategy to disclose the creation of stereotypes, however, is strengthened to some extent when Verdecchia/Wideload points out the way "Saxons" re-inscribe their cultural supremacy by referring to every other cultural group as a "community." To do this, he only needs a single line, uttered casually in the middle of an intervention about the song "La Bamba": "Like sometimes, I'll be out with my friends from de [sic] *Saxonian community* and we'll be out at a bar… " (39–40; emphasis added).

What further strengthens Verdecchia's strategy, I would argue, is the way in which his stereotypes function as self-reflexive tools, for, ultimately, Verdecchia himself seems to be quite conscious of the double bind in which he is caught, not only by dealing with stereotypes but also by presenting them humorously. Toward the end of his piece, he unveils his strategy and the heart of its contradictions:

> It doesn't really matter what I say does it? Cause it's all kind of funny, cause I'm just a clown. Well, dat [sic] has been my mistake. For some stupid reason, I want you to like me—so I've played the clown. Well, no more. Because de [sic] times are tough and when the going gets tough, clowns get dead (51, original punctuation). [12]

The production of *Fronteras* at the Tarragon further subverted the ideology of Multiculturalism by refusing to have the play "ghettoized." This, I think, has to do with Verdecchia himself. As a theatre artist in Toronto, he has rarely been identified with the "Latin American theatre community," and, therefore, has never been seen as "amateur." He has worked with other well-known Toronto theatre artists like Daniel Brooks or Jim Warren, and has performed at the Tarragon several times before. His reputation in the Canadian professional theatre community grew even stronger when his play *The Noam Chomsky Lectures,* co-written with Brooks, had an extremely successful run at Theatre Passe Muraille's Backspace. Their production won a Chalmers Canadian Play Award in 1991 and the published script was a finalist for the Governor General's Award for Drama in 1992.

By being produced at the Tarragon, *Fronteras* made a statement about not being only for Latinos, about being "professional" theatre and not "amateur," about not being "ethnic" theatre for a reduced "community," of no interest to Canadian society at large. Yet the fact that Verdecchia's career cannot be "ghettoized" as that of an "ethnic" does not necessarily mean he has been "co-opted" or "embraced" by the English Canadian artistic "norm," as is proven, I believe, by the stylistic and conceptual distinctiveness of works like *Fronteras* or *The Noam Chomsky Lectures.*

There is always a double bind, however, for it is also important to consider Verdecchia's position as an "ethnic." He is a Latin American of European (Spanish) descent, is white, speaks "unaccented" English and has been in Canada for most of his life. In sum, many might see him as a "non-ethnic" Canadian. It is unlikely that a newly-arrived Latin American Canadian of mestizo or mulatto blood and speaking with an accent would have been "accepted" in the same way.

If *Fronteras* had been produced in a Spanish-language venue in Toronto the use of stereotypes as a performative strategy would not have re-established the binary opposition "we-them" in the same way as at the Tarragon, but it would have still re-established the "truth" of the stereotypes themselves. Indeed, Verdecchia did seem to give in to what appeared to be an implicit acknowledgement of the "essential truth" in the stereotypes he performed. For instance, he (as Wideload) first said that "Latinos are no sexier dan [sic] Saxons," but then he added in playful conspiracy: "well maybe just a little" (42); the difference being, of course, that "we like it. A lot. And we practice. A lot" (ibid). Latinos laughing at this stereotype in a theatre venue considered "their own" would re-inscribe a sort of "essential" truth about themselves. For, a Latino would perhaps think, it is the "others" (the "Saxons") who see "us" the wrong way and make fun of "us," but that is because "we" are better than "them"; the truth is that "we" are better lovers, because "we" like it. Thus the dichotomy "we-them" would hardly disappear. It would simply be redrawn, with the Latinos occupying the subject position (that of sexier lovers), while at the same time adding more weight to the Latino stereotype created by Anglo-Saxons in the first place.

In fact, even at the Tarragon, Verdecchia/Wideload reinscribed this "essential truth" when he talked about the "fact" that "whenever a Latin and Saxon have sex it's usually a mind-expanding experience *porque Nosotro sabemos hacer cosas que ni se imaginaron en la* Kama Sutra *porque nosotro tenemos un ritmo, un calor un sabor un tumbao de timbale [sic] de conga de candomble de kilombo. Una onda un dos tres, un dos*" (41; original punctuation),[13] acknowledging that the Latinos' "rhythm" and "heat" are essential attributes which make them better lovers.

In the performance of *Fronteras Americanas*, language also served to negotiate the play's compliance with and challenge of the ideology of Multiculturalism. Produced in a Spanish-language venue, the play would have emphasized the individual border more than the continental one, for presumably the audience would have identified with Verdecchia's experience as a first-generation Canadian. Although the exploration of this border would have subverted the ideology of Multiculturalism in its acknowledgement of two living cultures, such a message would have been contained by virtue of the venue, for it would have framed that issue as one of concern only to a particular "ethnic group."

It would have also re-inscribed the notion of Latinos as an "ethnic group" (a totalizing category, at best), separated from Canadian society at large exploring an issue which is of concern only to them, and one which could not have access to the "professional" theatre venues or be of relevance to Canadian society at large.

Fronteras was conceived, written and delivered in English with a few interventions in Spanish. The use of the English language was a necessary strategy for a performance which aspired to criticize the way "Saxons" have constructed Latinos. At the Tarragon theatre, Verdecchia/Wideload seemed to be mistakenly referring to all Anglophones as "Saxons," apparently unaware that for many people in the audience English was a second or third language, and that perhaps most of them were "immigrants" like himself and might have no Anglo-Saxon blood at all. This might have temporarily contradicted the effect of his earlier speeches in Spanish, which acknowledged the presence of Spanish-speakers in the audience and seemed to be a conscious refusal on Verdecchia's part to construct his audience in a monolithic subject position.

I would suggest that this "mistake" was another performative strategy. In this strategy, the word "Saxon" meant more than just an ethnic origin, [14] it meant a cultural system which has not only created stereotypes about Latinos but has also effaced difference and instituted acculturation.

When Verdecchia admitted that the thought "stupid drunken Mexican" (72) crossed his mind when a man bothered him in the park, he was acknowledging he had "adopted" the view of the cultural system in which he lives; he was admitting he had been "co-opted" by a "norm" which discriminates against that Mexican man. When the entire audience was addressed as "Saxons," many people from other cultures could also relate to that word and could think of how they believe those stereotypes as well, or of how they themselves create others. In other words, although the use of the word "Saxon" might have suggested that the performance was effacing difference in the audience, it was really pointing at the reality of acculturation into the Anglo-Saxon cultural system which the many "ethnic groups" in Canada have experienced to different degrees. [15]

The use of Spanish in the title, I think, suggests as well a possible subversion of the widely-spread identification of the word "America" with English-speaking or Anglo-Saxon culture. During the first few minutes of the show, Verdecchia said:

"*Somos todos americanos,*" first in Spanish, and after that in English: "We are all Americans" (20). The audience who repeats a title like *Fronteras Americanas* in Spanish will come to understand that the word "America" also exists in the Spanish language (in fact, it is a Latin word) challenging the notion of America as an Anglophone culture, [16] and, as a result, challenging the power which North America has granted itself to control the South politically and culturally.

As it approaches its end, *Fronteras* makes a sudden shift. The play no longer seems to be about Latino stereotypes or about the Argentinian Canadian who struggles to find his home on the border. Suddenly, the play is about the entire country, about all those Canadians who live on borders. The Argentinian Canadian is no longer in the "backyard." He, says Verdecchia, is now "flesh and blood": "I am across the street. It's me ... your neighbour" (76). In a very emotional speech, Verdecchia urges his audience to "[c]onsider the English ... the Russian, Polish and Hungarian Jews ... those from the Caribbean ... the Irish ... the Chinese ... the Latin Americans ... Consider those here first. Consider those I have not considered. Consider your parents. Consider the country. Consider the continent. Consider the border" (52–53). [17]

I would suggest that in this final shift *Fronteras* is effectively moving the personal border, proposing that it affects all of Canada. Consider the country, made out of individuals within whom cultural practices are alive and struggling to fuse, to find new identities. If that struggle could be extended to Canada, it would mean that all cultural practices would perhaps be able to participate in the creation of a new country—not one with two official "cultures" and many symbolic "ethnic groups," but one with ever-changing cultural formations in a continuous search for a new personality.

This is not simply multiculturalism, a notion which seems to imply static, unchanging cultures, living side by side without touching one another. Instead, it might be called *interculturalism,* as it is grounded on the interaction among living, practised cultures. [18]

Although *Fronteras* focuses on the continental border—the exploration of stereotypes—and the individual border—the exploration of a personal struggle—I believe its greatest subversion of the ideology of Multiculturalism is to suggest that these two borders must affect the way in which we think of Canada.

In considering these borders, in considering a new vision of this country, we begin to break away from some borders, while acknowledging the possibilities others have to offer. Once we do that, we might all be able to say with Verdecchia: "Here we are. All together. At long last."

(1995)

Notes

This essay is a revised version of a chapter from the MA thesis "Shifting Borders: A Project of Interculturalism in Canadian Theatre," which in turn was a revised version of a paper read at the Conference of the Association for Canadian Theatre Research in Ottawa in 1993. I am indebted to Prof. Ric Knowles, chair of the Drama Department of the University of Guelph and my thesis supervisor, for his invaluable support in the writing of both the paper and the thesis. I am equally indebted to Guillermo Verdecchia, author and performer of *Fronteras Americanas*, who in February 1993 gave me permission to read and quote from the production script used for the Tarragon performance in Toronto. *Fronteras Americanas* has since been published by Coach House Press and this essay has been modified to show page numbers from the published version unless otherwise noted.

[1] See my Master's Thesis, "Shifting Borders," and the essay "Coming Together in Lift Off '93."

[2] I use the word "minority" here for lack of a better one. What I mean is artists, like myself, whose ethnic background is neither British nor French. Other terms which attempt to describe these artists as one group—"multicultural," "allophone," or even "non-British, non-French"—are extremely problematic. "Minority" is also problematic, but seems to me the least so.

[3] The analysis of *Fronteras Americanas* I offer in this essay is, primarily, of a *performance*. Although I have read several versions of the script, both unpublished and published, my ideas are based on observations made about the effectiveness of certain performative strategies the three different times I saw the show, which were during different runs. I first saw *Fronteras* during its run at the Tarragon's Extra Space in Toronto, where the audience was culturally diverse; the following June, I saw it as part of Le Festival de Théâtre des Amériques in Montréal, where the audience was mostly French-speaking, although with some English and Spanish speakers as well. Finally, I saw it a third time during its second run at the Tarragon the following October, this time in the Mainspace, where the audience was again quite diverse.

[4] This is probably Verdecchia's conscious appropriation of a stereotyped use of Mexican culture in North American television. "Bandito"—which is really "bandido" (bandit, outlaw)—is misspelled and mispronounced in order to rhyme with "frito" (fried), for a television commercial for corn chips.

[5] In the context of *Fronteras*, I choose to refer to the individual as "he" for the sake of simplicity, since the writer/performer is male.

[6] The page number indicated here is that of the production script, in which the word "home" actually appears. In the published version, this passage reads: "The Border is your ..." (p. 73).

[7] "Porteño" is Argentinian slang for a man born in Buenos Aires.

[8] The best known exception to this has been the Tarragon's historical support of Québécois playwrights, especially Michel Tremblay. Even so, the term still means Canadian as belonging to the two Charter cultures. This, of course, is not symptomatic of the Tarragon alone, but of all theatres—commercial and alternative—in Toronto. In recent times the Tarragon seems to have expanded its understanding of "Canadian" culture to include the work of artists of other cultural backgrounds, although this is done mostly in the Extra Space and through a rental agreement. I can think particularly of the 1993 production by the CanAsian Theatre Company of *Dance and the Railroad* about the life of two Chinese railroad workers in Canada, and the celebration of Lift Off! '94, a festival of plays written by playwrights of diverse cultures, produced by Cahoots Theatre Projects, a local intercultural company. The recognition of work by artists of other cultures is also taking place in institutions like Theatre Passe Muraille and the Theatre Centre.

[9] Toronto Free joined CentreStage in 1988 to become the Canadian Stage Company.

[10] Recently the work of many committed cultural activists and artists across the country has served to introduce a new definition of "professional" in the arts councils.

[11] In recent years, the word "Latinos" has been used in progressive circles as a term of empowerment to describe the people of Latin America. In this way, it has taken the place of other terms such as "Spanish" Americans, "Latin" Americans or "Hispanic" Americans, terms which emphasize the imperial connection to Spain (and Portugal, in the word Hispanic). Recognizing the need for such an attempt and agreeing wholeheartedly with its political goal, I would like to point out some problems with the use of this term. In Spanish, the word "Latino" means anything related to the Latin language and the countries where Latin languages are spoken, and therefore has historically been used to refer to countries like Spain, Portugal, France and Italy. It is only because the southern part of the Americas was conquered by the Latin peoples of Spain and Portugal that Latin America ("Latino" America, in Spanish) was given that name. In the English language, "Latino" might be a different word from "Latin," but the connection to the meaning in Spanish is, I believe, too strong to be ignored. In this way, the imperial connection is not erased, I would argue, but further re-inscribed. Second, "Latino" is often used as an all-embracing term which serves to identify any inhabitant of South America and is often used as if it were a race. Within the "Latino race," however, there are four different races: indigenous, white, mestizo and mulatto. Certainly an indigenous Guatemalan individual has little to do with a Chilean whose parents are from Spain. I believe that a true term of self-empowerment needs to abandon all connection to the Latin cultures, but also needs to account for the variety of races and cultures in the continent and for the colonial relations which exist among them.

[12] The page number given here is that of the production script. In the published version, this speech is slightly different (pages 75–76).

[13] The bits in Spanish read: "because we know how to do things that nobody could even envision in the *Kama Sutra*, because we have a rhythm, a heat, a taste of … "

The rest is untranslatable, as it refers to different musical rhythms of the American continent.

[14] And Anglo-Saxon is an ethnic group, of course, despite the fact that in Canada they might absurdly be constructed as "non-ethnic," since they are the majority.

[15] Because *Fronteras* was created in Toronto, it deals with Anglo-Saxons as the ruling power. Although certainly Québécois culture has instituted a similar kind of acculturation, Anglo-Saxons remain as the focus here.

[16] This notion is particularly inscribed by the English language, and not necessarily by others, especially Spanish. In Spanish, the word "americano" is often used to refer to anybody from any country in the Americas, but *especially* Latin America; and the word "América" is often used to refer to the entire continent (as in "the Americas") but *especially just* Latin America. The rest of the continent is referred to as "Norteamérica." Unlike English, Spanish does have an adjective to name those who live in the United States. They are not "americanos," they are "estadounidenses."

[17] The page numbers indicated here are those of the production script. In the published version, this speech was slightly different (page 77).

[18] In my master's thesis I explore the possibility of such a cultural system in more depth. In the last chapter I begin to explore how this might be possible in Canada. I also emphasize the difference between the way I use the word "interculturalism" and the way it is used and put into practice in intercultural performance

Works Cited

Eagleton, Terry. *Ideology: An Introduction.* London: Verso, 1991.

Gómez, María Teresa (Mayte). "Shifting Borders: A Project of Interculturalism in Canadian Theatre." MA Thesis. Guelph: University of Guelph, 1993.

Gómez, Mayte. "'Coming Together' in Lift Off! '93: Intercultural Theatre in Toronto and Canadian Multiculturalism." *Essays in Theatre/Études Théâtrales* 13.1 (1994): 45–59.

Government of Metropolitan Toronto. *Policy Statement of the Multicultural and Race Relations Division.* Toronto, 1978. n.p.

Harney, Robert F. "Immigrant Theatre." *Polyphony* 5.2 (1983): 1–4.

Hawkins, Freda. "Canadian Multiculturalism: the Policy Explained." *Canadian Mosaic: Essays on Multiculturalism.* Ed. A.J. Fry and C. Forceville. Canada Cahiers no. 3. Amsterdam: Free UP, 1988. 9–24.

Johnston, Denis. *Up the Mainstream: The Rise of Toronto's Alternative Theatres.* Toronto: U of Toronto P, 1991.

Li, Peter S. "Race and Ethnicity." *Race and Ethnic Relations in Canada.* Ed. Peter Li. Toronto: Oxford UP, 1990. 3–17.

Multiculturalism and Citizenship Canada. *The Canadian Multiculturalism Act: A Guide for Canadians.* Ottawa, n.d.

Royal Commission on Bilingualism and Biculturalism. *General Introduction: The Official Languages.* Vol. I of *Report of the Royal Commission on Bilingualism and Biculturalism.* Ottawa: Queen's Printer, 1967.

———. *The Cultural Contribution of the Other Ethnic Groups.* Vol. 4 of *Report of the Royal Commission on Bilingualism and Biculturalism.* Ottawa: Queen's Printer, 1967.

Verdecchia, Guillermo. *Fronteras Americanas/American Borders.* Toronto: Coach House, 1993.

———. "Fronteras Americanas (American Borders)." Production Script, Tarragon Theatre, 1992–93 season.

Ware, C. "Ethnic communities." *Encyclopaedia of the Social Sciences.* Vol. V. New York: Macmillan, 1931. 607–13.

Theorizing a Queer Theatre:
Buddies in Bad Times

by Robert Wallace

> ... a performative is that discursive practice that enacts or produces that
> which it names.
> —Judith Butler (13).

Sky Gilbert, founder and artistic director of Toronto's Buddies in Bad Times Theatre, begins a letter to the Theatre Advisory Committee of the Ontario Arts Council in March 1994 by explaining that the name of his company has become "more and more apt as the years go by." He writes: "what with AIDS, and with the plagues of various right-wing fundamentalists bearing down upon us, the mandate for Buddies in Bad Times Theatre has become curiously apt also. Our commitment to innovative/ gay and lesbian theatre is now more necessary than ever" ("Artistic Director's Letter 1994" 1).

For people not involved with the creation of innovative or gay and lesbian theatre in Toronto, Gilbert's reflection on his company's name and mandate might seem disingenuous. Quite probably, many of these would consider Buddies' current situation burgeoning, not beleaguered. In 1992, only thirteen years after its inception, Buddies was selected to organize and manage the activities of The Alexander Street Theatre Project, a large and ambitious operation that includes a 2.2 million dollar renovation of the facility that, for two decades, housed the venerated Toronto Workshop Productions. As Tim Jones, Buddies' general manager, explains in a submission to the Canada Council written in February 1994, the eight arts funding bodies and service organizations responsible for selecting an operator for the 12 Alexander Street facility "had the opportunity not only to view [Buddies'] renovation plans, but also to scrutinize Buddies' operational objectives of making the building accessible to alternative theatre and dance companies at heavily subsidized rental rates." Because of their decision to award the coveted operation to Buddies, Jones understandably reasons that "the will for Buddies to carry out the objectives ... [has] already received resounding approval in the community" (2).

How, then, is Buddies a theatre "in bad times," as Sky Gilbert would have it? To answer this question, one must remember that Buddies operates within a complicated matrix of social and material conditions, many of which are beyond its control. As the company enters a new phase of its development, it both reveals and reshapes this matrix. That a building undergoing renovation—the 12 Alexander Street facility exists at the centre of Buddies (re)configuration in the mid-1990s—is serendipitous inasmuch as "Buddies," as an "innovative / gay and lesbian theatre," already is an imaginative construction that has been in process since the company started to produce work in 1979. Buddies' theatrical "subjectivity," like its mandate, was not fixed with its inception; both have changed over the years, and they continue to change, partly as a result of activities and statements made by Gilbert and others connected with the company and partly by the reactions of those who observe and respond to these. To examine how Buddies has situated itself through promotional materials such as grant applications and advertising campaigns during the last few years, as well as through its programming, and to consider how this activity has been regarded by funding bodies, the press and the theatre-going audience, is to study not only the place that the company occupies in Toronto theatre but, additionally, the ways in which this place marks the "times." This is my primary purpose in this paper. My introduction of the term "subjectivity" is meant to signal another, parallel, aim. Using ideas about identity formation offered by contemporary theorists—especially those writing under the rubric of "queer theory" [1]—I plan to interrogate the idea of gay and lesbian subjectivity itself. This is crucial, I think, if the term "gay and lesbian theatre" is to be used meaningfully. Currently, the words "gay" and "lesbian" are undergoing a process of cultural renovation or, at least, resignification, central to debates about the construction and constitution of the subject. It is not coincidental that this process intersects with the literal and figurative reconstruction of Buddies' theatrical subjectivity. If, as Gilbert argues, Buddies' name and mandate have become more apt, this is one of the reasons.

To suggest that a company or a building can demonstrate subjectivity might seem strange given that the word "subject," at least in the discourse of critical theory, usually refers to a human individual. [2] In *Discerning the Subject*, Paul Smith offers a common definition of the term by explaining its use in psychoanalysis: here "subject" signifies "the complex of psychical formations which are constituted as the human being is positioned in relation to language" (xxxiii). More pertinent to my use of the term in this essay is Brenda K. Marshall's elaboration of Smith's idea in which she explains that a subject, by being positioned in relation to language, is inescapably "subject to" ideology; indeed, it is the work of ideology to suppress the role that language plays in the construction of the subject. Working with ideas originally put forward by Louis Althusser and Jacques Lacan, Marshall is led to state that "we are each assigned a subject position according to gender, race, ethnicity, family, region, as well as according to a variety of other discourses (as a woman, as white, as Irish, as daughter, as a Midwesterner, as a consumer, etc.)" (82).

Significantly, Marshall does not mention sexual orientation in her list, a subject position particularly important to people whose same-sex sexual activities situate them outside the dominant cultural order—what Michael Warner calls the "hetero-normative understanding of society" (xi). Since the mid-nineteenth century, the primary category assigned to these people was "homosexual" [3]—a clinical term that was rejected during the late 1960s in favour of "gay" and, subsequently, "gay and lesbian." The growing acceptance of these terms throughout the western world has led to their metonymic signification of group identity; terms that once applied only to sexual behaviour now are used regularly to signify "a people" or even "a nation." As Teresa de Lauretis explains in "Queer Theory: Lesbian and Gay Sexualities":

> ... male and female homosexualities—in their current sexual-political articulations of gay and lesbian sexualities, in North America—may be reconceptualized as social and cultural forms in their own right, albeit emergent ones and thus still fuzzily defined, undercoded, or discursively dependent on more established forms. (iii)

In his Introduction to *Fear of a Queer Planet*, Michael Warner argues that "In the United States, the default model for all minority movements is racial or ethnic" (xvii). I would expand his idea to suggest that this model has been used by the majority of gay activists in the Western world since the late 1960s—if only to explain why it currently weathers attack across the same terrain. For many people, certainly most heterosexual people, "sexual behaviour is clearly not the determining factor in finalizing a self-nomination" (Meyer 4), let alone in formulating a social identity. As a result, an increasingly large number of gay and lesbian people, along with others, are choosing to "renominate" themselves in other terms; the most important of these to this paper is "queer." In his introduction to *The Politics and Poetics of Camp*, Moe Meyer offers two reasons for the substitution of this word for "gay" and "lesbian":

> "Queer" does not indicate the biological sex or gender of the subject. More importantly, the term indicates an ontological challenge to dominant labelling philosophies, especially the medicalization of the subject implied by the word "homosexual," as well as a challenge to discrete gender categories embedded in the divided phrase "gay and lesbian". (1–2)[4]

Meyer goes on to present his definition of "queer," one "based on an alternative model of the constitution of subjectivity and of social identity" in which "queer" signifies "an oppositional critique of gay and lesbian middle-class assimilationism ... " (2).

While I do not wish to debate the merits of this renomination in this paper it is important to problematize the category "gay and lesbian" at its outset just as it is essential that I clarify the idea of subjectivity. For during the last few decades, the words "gay" or "lesbian" have been used not only to label social groups but also to modify things—films, books and plays being the examples most appropriate in this instance. Although these things are products of human creativity, they do not, of course, have a sexuality; *ergo*, buildings in which they exist—cinemas, libraries, theatres—cannot legitimately be modified by words that signify sexual behaviour. Can we then talk of "gay and lesbian" textuality of any sort? And, if so, how? What constitutes a gay film, a lesbian novel, or, more to my point, a gay and lesbian theatre?

Elsewhere, I have argued that all texts are "neutral" until a reader invests them with meaning, noting that "In this line of reasoning (which constitutes a theory of reading), the idea of a 'gay text' is problematic" ("Making Out Positions" 20). While I still maintain that a text is inherently without meaning and, consequently, that the author's sexuality, like his or her gender, does little to affect the interpretations that readers make of his or her text, [5] I now want to give more attention to the *place* of the text in the reader's "negotiation" of its meaning. In saying this, I mean to be quite literal: working with the trope of location that weaves throughout this essay, I want to consider more carefully where a text is placed—in what cinema, what bookstore and what theatre—for these sites also are texts open to interpretation.

Texts, while they may lack meaning until they are read, never exist in a vacuum but, on the contrary, operate within contexts, both literal and figurative, that seriously affect how they are read. Nor do texts simply "emerge" in contexts on their own; rather, they are positioned by their creators and those who market them, as well as by the reviewers and readers who make meaning of them in written and spoken comments. A reader approaching a text that is labelled, marketed or discussed as lesbian and/or gay will have a set of expectations that affects the way s/he reads it. In an essay titled "Reading Past the Heterosexual Imperative," Kate Davy addresses the implications of this for theatrical performance, her premise being that "the theatre as a social technology that includes its spectators is still firmly embedded in the sociosymbolic systems and discourses of the dominant culture" (166). A play that is performed in a theatre that is positioned as "lesbian" and/or "gay," is placed in a context that can't help but affect the ways it is read. Consider the fact that a spectator, just to watch a play in this context, must enter a space specifically marked as alternative to the heterosexual norm. [6]

That the context of a production space affects the meaning that a spectator makes of a performance is succinctly illustrated by a review of a Buddies' production that was published in *The Globe and Mail* in 1991. Writing about *Steel Kiss*, a play by Robin Fulford that dramatizes the social and psychological forces that lead four teenage boys to murder a gay man in a Toronto park, critic Liam Lacey comments that in its original production at another venue, *Steel Kiss* "seemed primarily a play for straight audiences about the background to a terrible incident. At Buddies, which is a gay-oriented theatre, the play takes on a much stronger point of view: it is enraged and histrionic" (C5). A year later in *eye*, a weekly arts and entertainment newspaper, Sky Gilbert acknowledges the same idea but gives it a different spin. Gilbert states: "A lot of gay and lesbian people are frightened to set foot in a gay and lesbian theatre. Because they're not out of the closet, there are a lot of people who don't think they're defined by the term 'gay,' they think it's ghettoizing. The straight community thinks to some extent that [Buddies] represent[s] the gay and lesbian community—well, we don't. We represent a radical fringe of the gay and lesbian community … " (Hunt 29).

Gilbert's recognition that different audience members approach his theatre (if they approach it at all) with differing expectations is based on the premise that Buddies, as both a company and a facility, has a subjectivity in which sexuality is central. His comments also imply that the "meaning" of this subjectivity is not fixed but, rather, is multiple, dependent upon the subject positions of the spectators who decide what the company "represents" and, as a result, do or do not attend one of its productions. Perhaps more important, Gilbert's comments indicate his understanding that Buddies' subjectivity is linked to its positioning—hence his concern to situate the theatre in a context of his own making, to supply it with imaginative coordinates that reject those of "the straight community."

Most certainly, Buddies does not exist in a vacuum; it occupies literal and figurative positions within Toronto culture of increasingly high profile. In the report by Tim Jones quoted earlier, Buddies' general manager suggests that the company's new space at 12 Alexander Street "holds great potential in developing a much larger audience base" than its previous location at 142 George Street. He reasons that "situated at the very heart of the lesbian and gay community, in a high traffic area, and in close proximity to subways, the location alone has given us the confidence to project growth in attendance of 5,000 people next year" (8). Gilbert, in his comments to *eye*, situates Buddies in a less literal location; indeed, by positioning Buddies on "the radical fringe of the gay and lesbian community," he not only moves the company far from the centre of Toronto's lesbian and gay neighbourhood where Jones puts it, but places it on a different map altogether.

Whereas Jones situates Buddies within geographic and economic contexts, Gilbert places it within political and aesthetic ones. This is evident not only in the example quoted above but also in Gilbert's letter to the Ontario Arts Council cited at the beginning of this essay. In his letter, Gilbert suggests aesthetic consequences of the material conditions that he considers synonymous with "bad times." Ignoring the social circumstances to which he alludes in his opening paragraph, Gilbert proceeds to isolate two trends in Canadian theatre and their results: "1. the decreasing amount of funds available for new Canadian Theatre … and 2. the tendency for companies on operating funding to avoid taking risks." That "new, Canadian, experimental work is relegated, at best, to the 'second' 'smaller' 'back' 'extra' or 'other' space," at least in Toronto, is the consequence to which Buddies is opposed and to which, Gilbert argues, its new facility provides an alternative. Gilbert describes the new theatre as "a 100 to 300 seat flexible black box of a space with surrounding catwalks and pit, a space which can be transformed (including its lobby, and rehearsal areas) to suit almost any environment, any approach, any theme which an imaginative director may choose." He affirms that the theatre is "totally dedicated to new Canadian work which is experimental and innovative," explaining that

> Artists at Buddies who are questioning the bounds of theatre and dance, or theatre and performance art, artists who are dealing with forbidden controversial topics, artists who wish to stage work in the audience or quite near the ceiling, will not be relegated to the "second" space. At Buddies they will have affordable space in the prime of the season with the kind of technical support which is rarely provided for this kind of dangerous work. ("Artistic Director's Letter 1994" 1–2)

Gilbert's remarks, when viewed beside Jones', indicate Buddies careful management of the strategy of "positionality" [7] which, as Jill Dolan notes in an essay published in *Theatre Journal,* is common with political activists. Dolan explains that positionality "locates one's personal and political investments and perspectives across an argument, a gesture toward placing oneself within a critique of objectivity, but at the same time stopping the spin of post-structuralist or postmodernist instabilities long enough to advance a politically effective action" (417). How does a subject utilize positionality to "advance politically effective action?" The question not only relates to subjectivity but to larger issues of power. Who governs the development of subjectivity—whether of a person or a theatre company? Who controls how the subject is named, treated and (dis)empowered?

Such questions are important to all theatre companies that regularly are "treated" to reviews and audience response. And they are especially important to not-for-profit companies whose "treatment" also includes peer evaluations for financial subsidies from the public purse. [8] The questions are not just important to companies that produce gay and lesbian work. However they are crucial—if only because the words "gay" and "lesbian" still signify sexuality even as they become metonymies of social identity. As signifiers of sexual behaviour, "gay" and "'lesbian" remain highly volatile. In Canada, as in all heterosexist cultures (are there any cultures that are not?), most gay men and lesbians cannot afford to "come out"—that is, publicly affirm their desire for same-sex sexual relations—for fear of discrimination, harassment and often violent abuse. This alone would allow Sky Gilbert to characterize the "times" as "bad" for his theatre. Indeed, given the ingrained homophobia of Canadian society, it is fair to ask what happens to a theatre company that declares its commitment to gay and lesbian work. What happens, in other words, to a theatre that "comes out?"

The answer, at least in Buddies' case, is that it operates much like the human subject who uses "coming out" as a tactic for social change: it makes sexuality a political issue. This has been Buddies' strategy since the mid-1980s when, not coincidentally, Gilbert himself came out as a gay man in public statements. While Gilbert possibly had political intentions for Buddies when he founded the company with three other graduates of York University's theatre programme, these had nothing to do with lesbian or gay subjectivity but, rather, were firmly focused on theatrical experimentation. [9] That this remained the case for some years Gilbert substantiates in an article published late in 1983 in which he states that Buddies "was formed in 1979 to explore the relationship of the printed word to theatrical image in the belief that with the poet-playwright lies the future of Canadian theatre" (Keeney-Smith 35). Certainly this was the operative principle behind Buddies' first event, a six-play festival called *New Faces of '79*, the prototype of *Rhubarb!* which the company renamed the festival the following year. [10] In an article in which he outlines the history and aesthetic of *Rhubarb!* to 1986, Gilbert notes that "'to rhubarb' is to complain, and we were complaining about Canadian theatre" from the start ("Inside the Rhubarb! Festival" 40). Explaining how he selects work for *Rhubarb!*, Gilbert links complaint to experimentation: "The criteria are these: that the piece be a half-hour or less in length and that the creators (writers, directors, whatever) are experimenting theatrically. The experiment can be for the artist, for the audience, or for both" ("Inside the Rhubarb! Festival" 42). [11]

In the mid-1980s Buddies began to rework its mandate to emphasize gay and lesbian material. Before this time, Gilbert's co-founders departed the company and

Buddies joined ranks with five alternative theatres to form the Theatre Centre, an artist-run organization set up to produce work by its members and other small companies lacking space and facilities. Although Gilbert wrote and directed plays concerning gay artists during the early 1980s,[12] only with *The Dressing Gown* in 1984 did he overtly position himself as a gay playwright interested in promoting gay and lesbian work. The sold-out run of *Drag Queens on Trial* the following year raised both his and Buddies' profile. Not coincidentally, 1985 also saw Buddies inaugurate its 4-Play Festival in which the company commissioned four new plays, two by lesbians and two by gay men.

With 4-Play, Buddies officially came out as a theatre company openly engaged in the production of work by and about lesbians and gay men. While Gilbert was to write and direct a number of successful productions during the next few years—most notably, *The Postman Rings Once* (1987), the company's first mainstage production, mounted at Toronto Workshop Productions—he allowed the focus of his company to shift to other artists whose talents emerged through the company's various festivals. By 1988, when Buddies celebrated the 10th anniversary of *Rhubarb!*, work by Audrey Butler, David Demchuk, Hillar Liitoja, Ken McDougall, Marcie Rogers, Robin Fulford, Ed Roy and others had expanded the company's reputation to include not only "innovative" but "gay and lesbian" as well. But while the audience for Buddies' programming had grown concomitantly, funding had not. In an article in *what* magazine published in 1988, Gilbert connected the company's financial problems with its reorientation towards gay programming citing, in particular, difficulties in funding 4-Play. Rather than abandon the festival, however, Gilbert announced that, in 1989, Buddies would bring back 4-Play "with a vengeance" ("What's coming" 5). 4-Play, he explained, would form the centrepiece of QueerCulture, a city-wide event integrating social, political and cultural activities sponsored by gay and lesbian organizations ranging from the Canadian Gay Archives to the Inside Out Collective which annually hosts Toronto's festival of lesbian and gay film and video.

The proactive, political stance that Gilbert assumed in 1988 has been performed by Buddies ever since. My use of the verb "perform" here is meant to connect Buddies' sexual subjectivity from this time to the present with theories of identity formation advanced in queer theory—specifically, those that view subjectivity as performance. In his introduction to *The Politics and Poetics of Camp*, Moe Meyer explains that

> Whether one subscribes to an essentialist or constructionist theory of gay and lesbian identity, it comes down to the fact that, at some time, the actor must do something in order to produce the social visibility by which the identity is manifested. Postures, gestures, costume and dress, and speech acts become the elements that constitute both the identity and identity performance. When we shift the study of gay and lesbian identity into a performance paradigm, then every enactment of that identity depends, ultimately, upon extrasexual performative gestures. Even the act of "coming out," that is, the public proclamation of one's

self-nomination as gay or lesbian, is constituted by an institutionalized speech act. (4)

To develop this argument, Meyer cites the work of Judith Butler for whom categories of sex and gender are neither innate nor stable but, rather, "performatives" continually in process. Theories of identity formation that utilize such ideas invariably stress not only that sexual subjectivity is constituted in and by its performance but that its performance, by necessity, is repeated. Certainly this is true for the gay or lesbian subject who wishes to be distinguished from the heterosexual norm. As Butler explains in her introduction to *Bodies that Matter:* On *the Discursive Limits of "Sex"*, extrasexual gestures such as posture, dress and speech acts both cite and signify differences from heteronormative behaviour—they both repeat and refer to other and previous performatives.

Elsewhere, writing about gender identity, Butler makes a point that is useful to my argument here:

> if gender ... is an imitation that regularly produces the ideal it attempts
> to approximate, then gender is a performance that *produces* the illusion
> of an inner sex or essence or psychic gender core; it *produces* on the skin,
> through the gesture, the move, the gait (that array of corporeal theatrics
> understood as gender presentation), the illusion of an inner depth ... it
> is always a surface sign, a signification on and with the public body ...
> ("Imitation and Gender Insubordination" 28)

In her introduction to *Bodies that Matter*, Butler addresses the term "queer" directly, suggesting that "the contentious practices of 'queerness' might be understood ... as a specific reworking of abjection into political agency." She continues with a statement particularly appropriate to Buddies' evolution since the late 1980s: "The public assertion of 'queerness' enacts performativity as citationality for the purposes of resignifying the abjection of homosexuality into defiance and legitimacy" (21).

Moe Meyer also makes a statement that applies to Buddies' positioning in the 1990s, as well as to the activities of Sky Gilbert whose performances, both onstage and off, are central to its efficacy. Meyer writes: " ... queer identity emerges as self-consciousness of one's gay and lesbian performativity sets in" (4). This application is warranted given that Gilbert has performed numerous versions of "queerness" since announcing QueerCulture in 1988. In the *what* article quoted above, for example, Gilbert offered his first published rehearsal of the term:

> Growing up in a heterosexually dominated culture, the gay man or
> lesbian woman finds a need to express (what by necessity become) the
> deepest darkest secrets of their sexual and emotional lives. The result is
> queer culture. Just as Canada is multi-cultural, it is multi-sexual, and
> the encouragement of queer culture (as opposed to its oppression)
> encourages a lively exchange of ideas and images about our sometimes
> very different experiences of life. ("What's coming" 5)

Gilbert's interest in the multi-sexuality of culture and the differences that prefigure artistic expression has shaped Buddies' subjectivity during the 1990s. The company repeatedly performs its subjectivity in its marketing materials, as well as its programming. In 1992, for example, Buddies stated QueerCulture's mandate in a succinct note that also applies to queer subjectivity: "QueerCulture is a three week-long celebration of alternative visions of lesbian and gay life which are sexual, brazen, radical and unconventional" (Buddies, 1992 *Calendar*, inside front cover). By this time, the company was performing positionality with confidence—and for good reason: QueerCulture had grown to encompass thirty-two events at ten different venues across the city including film, theatre, visual arts, music, literary readings and dance. It also had generated controversy which, in a move that Buddies was to repeat in 1993, the company turned to its advantage.

In a speech to the Milton, Ontario, Chamber of Commerce in December 1989, Otto Jelinek, then the National Revenue Minister for Canada's Conservative government, commented on federal arts funding by saying that "it is incumbent on the Canada Council, as it is on all agencies, to be accountable to the public." Threatening that "whether the arm's-length funding policy is considered sacrosanct or not, we're going to tamper with it," he went on to single out the grant of $61,000 that Buddies had received from the Canada Council that year. Specifically, he cited Buddies' production of *Drag Queens on Trial* and then remarked, "That's homosexuals, I take it" (Dafoe C8). Buddies, rather than simply protest the comments (which, along with many other arts organizations, it did), adopted Jelinek's offhand remark as the title of its second QueerCulture Festival in 1990, brandishing the comment on thousands of posters which, shaped as triangles, were printed on neon-pink paper. [13] The company's ironic use of a homophobic phrase provides a clear paradigm of the performative strategies that it would develop during the 90s. In this instance, like many to follow, queer subjectivity and its homophobic context are made visible through an extrasexual sign that both signifies and cites performance. For Moe Meyer, this performative strategy—one "used to enact a queer identity, with enactment defined as the production of social visibility" (5)—is the foundation of Camp.

In 1992, the evolution of Buddies' queer subjectivity took another turn when Gilbert implied that the mandate of QueerCulture had become the mandate of Buddies' programming in general. In a letter copied to various funding organizations he wrote:

> The work that goes on at Buddies is not only new work but work which exists outside of mainstream culture and goes anywhere from poking fun at "fine art" and popular culture to seriously frightening the audience and making them sincerely angry. For a long time I have been searching for a sense of QUEER [sic] Theatre which encompassed gay and lesbian issues as well as radical art. I think we are creating this art, and these artists, at Buddies. ("Artistic Director's Letter 1992" 7)

The following year, Buddies acknowledged its evolution from a "lesbian/gay" nomination to one more specifically "queer" in a variety of promotional materials.

One of the most important is Gilbert's Artistic Director's Message published in the 1993 QueerCulture Guide where he establishes that the company's queer aesthetic now is unequivocal. Because he most completely supplies his definition of the word "queer" in this message, I quote it at length:

> Let's talk about the word Queer. Because it doesn't always mean gay or lesbian. It means sexual, radical, from another culture, non-linear, redefining form as well as content. It means power and ownership of power, images of human bondage and submission (because power is sexual and so is queer, and all good theatre is about power and the manipulations of it but that's another essay.) So. What has been happening at Buddies in Bad Times Theatre in the last two years has been the definition of an aesthetic, as people learn that one doesn't have to be gay or lesbian to get involved, when people learn that queer theatre has as its common denominator a unique relationship with the audience—you come into the theatre assured of who you are and what you believe, but you leave the theatre all shook up. We are not into explaining comfortable, politically correct moral lessons here. We are, in contrast, at Buddies, providing a space and more importantly environment where radical, sexual work can be developed ... If I was a sweeter nicer guy, I'd call Buddies in Bad Times Theatre a "gay and lesbian theatre for all people." But I'm not that nice. I'm an orgiastic poet and a drag queen, and I feel compelled to call something queer what it is. ("Artistic Director's Message" inside cover)

Earlier in this essay I suggested that the process of Buddies' reconfiguration during the 1990s parallels challenges to gay and lesbian subjectivities represented by the increased use of the word "queer." To a large part, this increase has been stimulated by Queer Nation, the movement of activists that came into political consciousness during the 1980s through the struggle against bureaucratic indifference to the fight against AIDS. While Buddies has not aligned itself with Queer Nation in any direct manner, the company's definition of the term "queer" is similar to that used by Queer Nation in the early 1990s. In their introduction to an edition of *Out/Look* that covers the "birth of a queer nation" in 1991, Allan Berubé and Jeffrey Escoffier suggest that Queer Nation calls itself "queer," not "lesbian, gay and bisexual," because the latter are "awkward, narrow, and perhaps compromised words." Their reasoning for Queer Nation's use of "queer" applies equally to Buddies' use of the term: "*Queer* is meant to be confrontational—opposed to gay assimilationists and straight oppressors while inclusive of people who have been marginalized by anyone in power" (Berubé and Escoffier 12). In acknowledging that Queer Nation's task is made extremely difficult because it is fraught with contradictions, Berubé and Escoffier could be describing Buddies where paradoxes also make the company vulnerable to misunderstanding:

> They are trying to combine contradictory impulses: to bring together people who have been made to feel perverse, queer, odd, outcast,

different, and deviant, and to affirm sameness by defining a common identity on the fringes. They are inclusive, but within boundaries that threaten to marginalize those whose difference doesn't conform to the new nation. These contradictions are locked in the name Queer Nation:

QUEER = DIFFERENCE

NATION = SAMENESS

(Berubé and Escoffier 12)

In the same article in which Sky Gilbert acknowledges that Buddies represents "a radical fringe of the gay and lesbian community" (Hunt 29), he also describes an event called *Jane Goes Shopping* that was part of QueerCulture's 1992 programme. Dressed as Jane, a flamboyant drag queen who makes no attempt to disguise her gender-blur, Gilbert and an entourage of "other drag queens and leather dykes" (Hunt 29) visited the Eaton Centre, a shopping mall in downtown Toronto, where Jane shopped for a new spring frock. Gilbert explains in the *eye* article that "if people shopping in those stores are offended, they'll have to deal with it. It's an in-your-face political act … " (Hunt 29). As part of QueerCulture the previous year, Jane led a similar group on a tour of various outdoor haunts in Toronto's gay neighbourhood where s/he had performed sex. These excursions are similar in their tactics and effects to those of Queer Nation that "play on the politics of cultural subversion: theatrical demonstrations, infiltrations of shopping malls and straight bars, kiss-ins and be-ins" (Berubé and Escoffier 14). They also illustrate Camp which Meyer argues *(pace* Susan Sontag [14]) "has become an activist strategy for organizations such as ACT UP and Queer Nation, as well as a focus in utopian movements like the Radical Faeries" (1). As Camp, Jane's performances—whether scheduled or not—provide an "oppositional critique embodied in the signifying practices that processually constitute queer identities" (Meyer 1).

The idea that the meaning of all texts and, indeed, of all contexts, depends upon the subject position of the reader is especially problematic for the Camp performance that Buddies presents. In Buddies' short history, this became most apparent during its 1993 QueerCulture festival when the company's funding was jeopardized because of public reactions to press depictions of its programming: these reactions, I presume, are what Sky Gilbert refers to, in the letter that begins this essay, as "the plagues of various right-wing fundamentalists" ("Artistic Director's Letter 1994" 1). To a large degree, the reactions were incited by Christina Blizzard, a columnist with the *Toronto Sun* who, on April 1, 1993, announced that Buddies had received a grant from the City of Toronto for $58,908 in a column headed "Live sex group gets city bucks" (14). Blizzard was concerned that Buddies would use its funding to "present sado-masochism seminars as well as a 'female ejaculation Pajama Party'" ("Live Sex" 14) during its 1993 QueerCulture festival.

Despite the facts that these seminars were only three of 36 events programmed for the ten venues included in the four-week festival, and that none of the seminars was funded by Buddies itself, Blizzard used excerpts from descriptions of the seminars published in the 1993 QueerCulture Guide to represent Buddies' activities in general.

In a series of columns that sustained her attack on the company, Blizzard generated enough public anxiety about Buddies' programming and funding that the budget committee of Metro Council—the body of elected politicians representing the six boroughs of Metropolitan Toronto—decided to debate its response to Buddies' annual application for a grant when it met in early July. A news story published in the *Sun* in late April, reports Alan Tonks, Chairman [sic] of Metro Council, as saying, "I can tell you the concerns raised by the reports that you and others have been making on this QueerCulture festival have given serious rise to a heightened concern for the manner in which public money is being expended" (Blizzard, "Hard look" 16).[15]

What interests me about this fracas, at least in the context of this essay, is that Blizzard did not need to misquote Buddies' descriptions of these events to incite her readers' outrage and lobbying tactics. She could rely on descriptions of the seminars to excite her readers' homophobia. Quoting the QueerCulture Guide in her column, Blizzard notes that the S/M seminars will present a "hands-on, pants down approach to SM techniques and safety." She also explains that the female ejaculation party invites participants to "bring sex toys, your pillows, your girlfriends and your sisters to a hands-on, girls-only party and learn to ejaculate" ("Live sex" 14). While such performances may not have been understood as Camp by many of her readers, they certainly were perceived as "queer."[16]

On July 7, 1993, Metro Council granted Buddies its request for $26,500 after a heated debate that led to a 15-13 vote by its members.[17] Ostensibly, this debate concerned arts funding but, invariably, it focused on the sexuality of the artists applying for subsidy—or, more accurately, on the performance of sexuality enacted by descriptions of the seminars. As a result, the debate provides invaluable material for theorizing the social circumstance of queer relations in Canadian culture today. For Tim Jones, there was no need to theorize; as he said, "This was homosexuality on trial ... " ("Restore Funding" A16). Much to the chagrin of Metro politicians, Jones' claim was supported by an editorial in the *Toronto Star*, beginning with the comment that "Metro's gay and lesbian community is right to be wondering why its cultural groups were the only ones left out of the grants bonanza at Metro Hall last week,"[18] the editorial concluded: "Unfortunately, homophobia, not economic concerns, seems to have been the driving force behind the committee's decision" ("Restore Funding" A16).

To begin his 1994 General Manager's Report to the Canada Council, Tim Jones, like Sky Gilbert, refers to the "times" in which Buddies operates. After noting the "generally bleak economic climate," he comments that Buddies successfully undertook the responsibility of managing the 12 Alexander Street Project "while withstanding an ongoing assault on its freedom of expression and funding by homophobes and anti-arts funding advocates." To substantiate his belief that Buddies has emerged "profoundly strengthened as an organization," Jones cites the positive support of public organizations like the *Toronto Star*, and an impressive statistic: " ... an overall growth in box office revenues of more than 30% this season" (1).

Ironically, this growth partially results from the funding fracas or, more precisely, from the ways in which Buddies responded to attacks with an aggressive performance of protest. Buddies' press releases, posters, public demonstrations and a variety of activities at its theatre galvanized a unified outcry from Toronto's arts constituencies and mobilized the anger of Toronto's gay and lesbian communities into political action. As a result, Buddies not only won its grant from Metro Council but exposed the homophobia that made its funding an issue.[19]

These, then, are the "times" that affect how Buddies operates in the mid-1990s. For many who identify with Toronto's gay and lesbian communities, the times are neither new nor unexpected; as a result they cannot celebrate Buddies' move into 12 Alexander Street without some concern. As Sue Golding, the president of Buddies' board of directors, eloquently puts it in her letter to the Ontario Arts Council in February 1994,

> Over the past three years, the artists, producers, administrators and technical staff—even the audiences—at Buddies have undergone a remarkable metamorphosis. We have transformed from being a nomadic theatre company attempting to put on the best avant-garde/ experimental, gay and lesbian theatre in this city, to one which has set its sites [sic] on creating one of the most accessible, provocative and vibrant art centres in the province. Despite incredibly difficult times, including relentless attacks by right-wing media, the move has not been without its sweet victories: for we have brought together people from all walks of life—people who might not have ever rubbed shoulders with each other in different settings—and we have done this during one of the most devastating crises to hit our community. We have tried to offer, and I think for the most part succeeded, to those who have been wreaked [sic] by the untold death and destruction of HIV/AIDS, a tiny bit of respite, a "little night magic," as we've said in our season brochures; and we've tried to do this not simply by ripping apart old myths around sex and race or gender or class, but by playing with and against new forms of art itself, pitching that play at the highest professional standards available. (1)

Setting sites, citing sets, playing difference, pitching play: these are the performatives of a queer theatre.

(1995)

Notes

[1] One of the first theorists to introduce the idea of "queer theory" in a published text was the American academic Teresa de Lauretis who, in a special issue of the scholarly journal, *differences*, introduced a collection of essays "generated in the context of a working conference on theorizing lesbian and gay sexualities that was held at the University of California, Santa Cruz in February 1990" (iii) under the title "Queer Theory: Lesbian and Gay Sexualities." In her introduction de Lauretis explains her decision to use the term:

> The term "queer," juxtaposed to the "lesbian and gay" of the subtitle, is intended to mark a certain critical distance from the latter, by now established and often convenient, formula. For the phrase "lesbian and gay" or "gay and lesbian" has become the standard way of referring to what only a few years ago used to be simply "gay" (e.g., the gay community, the gay liberation movement) or, just a few years earlier still, "homosexual" (iv).

Since this early instance of sanctioned usage, many other theorists have advanced the term "queer theory" in a wide range of published texts. For recent, notable examples pertinent to this essay, see the anthologies edited by Michael Warner, R. Jeffrey Ringer, and Martha Gever, John Greyson and Pratibha Parmar listed in Works Cited.

[2] Antony Easthope and Kate McGowan discuss the relationship between the terms "subjectivity" and "individual" in their introduction to "Section Three (Subjectivity)" of *A Critical and Cultural Theory Reader*. Here they explain that

> the concept of subjectivity decentres the individual by problematizing the simplistic relationship between language and the individual which common sense presumes. It replaces human nature with concepts of history, society and culture as determining factors in the *construction* of individual identity, and destabilizes the coherence of that identity by making it an *effect* rather than simply an origin of linguistic practice. (67)

[3] In *Sexuality*, Jeffrey Weeks explains that

> homosexual activities are of course widespread in all cultures and there is a sustained history of homosexuality in the West. But the idea that there is such a thing as the homosexual person is a relatively new one. All the evidence suggests that before the eighteenth century homosexuality, interpreted in its broadest sense as involving erotic activities between people of the same gender, certainly existed, "homosexuals" did not. (33)

⁴ Perhaps because she is a lesbian, Teresa de Lauretis gives more weight or, at least, explanation to Meyer's second point. Writing about the term "lesbian and gay" in "Queer Theory: Lesbian and Gay Sexualities," she states that

> our "differences," such as they may be, are less represented by the discursive coupling of those two terms in the politically correct phrase "lesbian and gay," than they are elided by most of the contexts in which the phrase is used; that is to say, differences are implied in it but then simply taken for granted or even covered over by the word "and". (v–vi)

⁵ In proffering this theory of reading, I align myself with Catherine Belsey who calls for "a new critical practice which insists on finding the plurality, however 'parsimonious,' of the text and refuses the pseudo-dominance constructed as the 'obvious' position of its intelligibility ..." In *Critical Practice*, Belsey goes on to state that "As readers and critics we can choose actively to seek out the process of production of the text: the organization of the discourses which constitute it and the strategies by which it smoothes over the incoherencies and contradictions of the ideology inscribed in it" (129).

⁶ The focus of Davy's paper is *Dress Suits to Hire*, a play by Holly Hughes, an American lesbian playwright who attracted considerable attention as one of "the NEA four"—four American artists whose funding from the National Endowment for the Arts was rescinded in 1990. Davy explains that "from its inception, *Dress Suits* was made to be performed at P.S. 122, an East Village [New York] venue for new, or non-mainstream, theatre, dance, music, and performance art." As such, it represented a departure for Hughes and her collaborators who usually created work for the WOW Cafe, a theatre space in Manhattan's East Village whose address, Davy states, "is clearly lesbian" (153). Davy further explains that in the WOW context, " ... artists create a theatre *for* lesbians, a theatre that responds to lesbian subjectivity" (154). She then proceeds to examine *Dress Suits* in performance at P.S. 122 and, eventually, in a university theatre in Ann Arbor, Michigan, her goal being to answer the question "What does it mean, then, when lesbian theatre is performed in venues outside of lesbian performance spaces?" (166).

⁷ This idea is further substantiated by a long programme note written by Sue Golding, the president of Buddies' board of directors since 1986, published in 1992 in which she overtly situates Buddies on a map of "radical geography." Because of the metaphoric intricacy of her statement, as well as its clear use of "positionality," I quote it in full:

> In the face of a cruel and relentless recession—replete with our bureau-crats proclaiming at every turn, its imminent end—a peculiar laughter refuses to be destroyed. It is a laughter filtered through the bright lights of the city and nurtured on the very anonymity of being "urban." It is not by accident that this urbanity, utterly fractured and diverse at its very core, is the strange dome to queer-ness itself. And we begin to map its routings: no longer constituted by community politics, community

aesthetics, community ethics; we have here, instead, little cities: the little cities of drag; the little cities of S&M; the little cities of vanilla sex; the little cities of celibacy. We weave ourselves against and through and alongside these cities, with pleasure (and pain) being our only guides. Sometimes public, sometimes private, sometimes underground, sometimes fictional and sometimes all or none of these at exactly the same moment, we toast to life (and death) in all its profane and impure ways.

Along the strange routings of this radical geography sits a little inn, a little roadside hut where queers of every ilk can take a rest, a drink, a joke, a fuck—and do more than simply survive. At Buddies, these kinds of urban refreshments are available to all those attracted to and propelled by the crazy throbs of the city ... ("President's Message" back cover).

[8] For a fuller discussion of the relationship between marketing, reviewing and funding of small theatre companies, see my essay "Producing Marginality: Criticism and the Construction of Canadian Theatre." For a useful critique of the systems of "peer evaluation" used by Canadian funding bodies, see Ann Wilson, "A Jury of Her Peers."

[9] The name of the company is taken from a lyric by French songwriter and singer Jacques Prevert.

[10] This first version of *Rhubarb!* was co-produced by Buddies and Nightwood Theatre, a feminist theatre with which the company became associated as part of the Theatre Centre in 1979. By the mid-1980s, Buddies had become *Rhubarb!*'s sole producer. Exactly when, and why, Buddies assumed exclusive "ownership" of *Rhubarb!* is unclear, as are many other details about the relationship between the founding members of the Theatre Centre during its early years.

[11] *Rhubarb!*'s combination of experimentation and complaint has made the festival an annual hit with artists and audiences alike—and it has more than fulfilled Buddies' mandate to produce innovative work. In an article titled "Towards a New Dramaturgy" published in *Canadian Theatre Review*, Paul Leonard comments that "Buddies' insistence that *Rhubarb!* pieces be given genuine, if somewhat undernourished productions has enabled the event to establish itself as a festival, with the characteristics of other theatre festivals—variety, concentration, and unusual fare—rather than as a developmental series for theatre insiders only" (45). For his part Gilbert argues that "by allowing artists to test their work before an audience, Buddies has engendered a unique approach to Canadian dramaturgy" (Buddies, "Supplementary Information" 2)—a statement that warrants consideration given that, by 1992 *Rhubarb!* had produced 205 different shows under its banner.

[12] For example, *Cavafy* (1981), *Pasolini/Pelosi* (1983) and *Life Without Muscles or Growing Up Artistic* (1983), a play about the life and work of David Hockney.

[13] A pink triangle was used by the Nazi party to signify homosexual prisoners held in concentration camps during World War II. Since the late 1960s it has been used internationally as a symbol of lesbian and gay liberation movements.

[14] Meyer suggests that Susan Sontag's influential essay, "Notes on Camp," first published in 1964, complicated interpretations of the term camp "by detaching the signifying codes from their queer signified" (5). The result is that camp (Meyer distinguishes his use of the word by capitalizing it) usually is defined as "apolitical, aestheticized, and frivolous" (1), a signification he intends this book to challenge. For another "authorized account of camp" (Sedgwick 250), see Andrew Ross; also useful is Jack Babuscio's "Camp and the Gay Sensibility."

[15] By late June, the grant application of the Inside Out Collective also had come under scrutiny by Metro Council. At issue in its case were descriptions that the Collective published in its Programme Guide for the 1993 festival of gay and lesbian film and video held during QueerCulture. The Collective had distributed the Guide to a large number of locations throughout Metropolitan Toronto including public libraries in mid-May. Ironically, Metro Council had made distribution of the Guide a requirement of its 1992 grant to the company.

[16] At the denotative level of signification, "queer" remains pejorative in general usage. *The Concise Oxford Dictionary* defines the word as "strange, odd, eccentric; of questionable character, shady, suspect; out of sorts, giddy, faint" (Oxford 846). The *Oxford* restricts its definition of "queer" as a noun to its "slang" usage as "homosexual," noting that it is "Esp. male." The two definitions, I suggest, are intermingled in contemporary alternative or oppositional discourse where both the sexual signification of nominal use combines with the "strangely suspect" qualities signified by the adjectival form.

[17] In the same meeting, Metro Council voted to reject the grant application of the Inside Out Collective in a 14-14 tie.

[18] Of the 203 arts organizations that submitted grant applications to Metropolitan Toronto Council for public funding in 1993, only two were subjected to special scrutiny—Buddies in Bad Times Theatre and the Inside Out Collective.

[19] A further irony ensued: in 1994, Buddies relinquished control of QueerCulture, explaining that the festival "has not only ballooned in size, it has taken on a mandate to include cultural activities which are not necessarily art. In effect, the mandate of the festival has eclipsed that of Buddies" (Jones 8). Although Buddies continues to contribute 4-Play and other performance events to the festival, QueerCulture now is managed by an independent company with its own programming committee and board to which Buddies contributes.

Works Cited

Babuscio, Jack. "Camp and the Gay Sensibility." *Gays and Film.* Ed. Richard Dyer. New York: Zoetrope, 1984. 40–57.

Belsey, Catherine. *Critical Practice.* London: Routledge, 1980.

Berubé, Allan and Jeffrey Escoffier. "Queer/Nation." *Out/Look* 11 (Winter 1992): 12–14.

Blizzard, Christina. "Hard look at grants to troupe." *The Toronto Sun* (22 April 1993): 16.

———."Live sex group gets city bucks." *The Toronto Sun* (1 April 1993): 14.

Buddies in Bad Times Theatre. 1992 *Calendar.* Toronto: Archives of Buddies in Bad Times Theatre.

———."Supplementary Information." Application to the Laidlaw Foundation, 1 April 1992. Toronto: Archives of Buddies in Bad Times Theatre. 3 pages.

———. *QueerCulture Program* 1991 (6–28 April 1991). Toronto: Archives of Buddies in Bad Times Theatre. 3 pages.

Butler, Judith. *Bodies That Matter: On the Discursive Limits of Sex.* New York: Routledge, 1993.

———."Imitation and Gender Insubordination." *inside/out: Lesbian Theories, Gay Theories.* Ed. Diana Fuss. New York: Routledge, 1991. 13–31.

Concise Oxford English Dictionary, 7th ed. s.v. "queer."

Dafoe, Chris. "Jelinek Under Fire for Remarks on Grants." *The Globe and Mail* (2 December 1989): C8.

Davy, Kate. "Reading Past the Heterosexual Imperative: Dress Suits to Hire." *The Drama Review* 33.1 (1989): 153–70.

de Lauretis, Teresa. "Queer Theory: Lesbian and Gay Sexualities. An Introduction." *differences* 3.2 (1991): iii–xviii.

Dolan, Jill. "Geographies of Learning: Theatre Studies, Performance, and the 'Performative'." *Theatre Journal* 45.4 (1993): 417–41.

Easthope, Anthony and Kate McGowan. "Introduction: Section Three." *A Critical and Cultural Theory Reader.* Ed. Anthony Easthope and Kate McGowan. Toronto: U of Toronto P, 1993. 67–70.

Gever, Martha, John Greyson and Pratibha Parmar, eds. *Queer Looks: Perspectives on Lesbian and Gay Film and Video.* Toronto: Between the Lines, 1993.

Gilbert, Sky. "Artistic Director's Letter 1994." Letter to the Theatre Advisory Committee of the Ontario Arts Council, 01 March 1994. Toronto: Archives of Buddies in Bad Times Theatre. 13 pages.

———. "Artistic Director's Letter 1992." Letter to the Theatre Advisory Committee of the Laidlaw Foundation, 1 April 1992. Toronto: Archives of Buddies in Bad Times Theatre. 7 pages.

———."Artistic Director's Message." *Programme Guide: QueerCulture* 1993 (10 April–09 May 1993). Toronto: Archives of Buddies in Bad Times Theatre. Inside front cover.

———."Inside the Rhubarb! Festival." *Canadian Theatre Review* 49 (1986): 40–43.

———."Rhubarb in your face." Programme for *Rhubarb!* (20 January–16 February 1992). Toronto: Archives of Buddies in Bad Times Theatre. Inside front cover.

———. "What's coming: Spring, 1989." *what* 17 (February 1989): 5.

Golding, Sue. Letter to Jan McIntyre, Ontario Arts Council, 01 February 1994. Toronto: Archives of Buddies in Bad Times Theatre. 3 pages.

———. "President's Message." Programme for *Rhubarb!* (29 January–16 February 1992). Toronto: Archives of Buddies in Bad Times Theatre. Outside back cover.

Goodwin, Joseph P. *More Man Than You'll Ever Be: Gay Folklore and Acculturation* in *Middle America.* Bloomington: Indiana UP, 1989.

Hunt, Nigel. "He's here, he's queer and he's sometimes Jane." *eye* 9 (April 1992): 29.

Jones, Tim. "General Manager's Report." Letter to the Theatre Advisory Committee of the Canada Council, 01 February 1994. Toronto: Archives of Buddies in Bad Times Theatre. 11 pages.

Keeny-Smith, Patricia. "Living With Risk: Toronto's New Alternate Theatre." *Canadian Theatre Review* 38 (1983): 33–43.

Lacey, Liam. "Steel Kiss confronts audience with reality of homophobia." *The Globe and Mail* (22 November 1991): C5.

Leonard, Paul. "Towards a New Dramaturgy." *Canadian Theatre Review* 49 (1986): 44–50.

Marshall, Brenda K. *Teaching the Postmodern: Fiction and Theory.* New York: Routledge, 199.

Meyer, Moe. "Introduction: Reclaiming the Discourse of Camp." *The Politics and Poetics of Camp.* Ed. Moe Meyer. New York: Routledge, 1994. 1–22.

"Restore Funding." *Toronto Star* 6 July 1993: A16. [Editorial]

Ringer, R. Jeffrey, ed. *Queer Words, Queer Images: Communication and the Construction of Homosexuality.* New York: New York UP, 1994.

Ross, Andrew. "Uses of Camp." *Intellectuals and Popular Culture*. New York: Routledge, 1989.

Sedgwick, Eve Kosofsky and Michael Moon. "Divinity: A Dossier, A Performance Piece, A Little-Understood Emotion." *Tendencies*. Durham: Duke UP, 1993. 215–51.

Smith, Paul. *Discerning the Subject*. Minneapolis: U of Minnesota P, 1988.

Sontag, Susan. "Notes on Camp." *A Susan Sontag Reader*. New York: Vintage, 1983. 105–19.

Wallace, Robert. "Making Out Positions: An Introduction." *Making, Out: Plays by Gay Men*. Toronto: Coach House P, 1992. 11–40.

———. "Producing Marginality: Criticism and the Construction of Canadian Theatre." *Producing Marginality: Theatre and Criticism in Canada*. Saskatoon: Fifth House, 1990. 107–76.

Warner, Michael "Introduction." *Fear of a Queer Planet: Queer Politics and Social Theory*. Ed. Michael Warner. Minneapolis: U of Minnesota P, 1993. vii–xxxi.

Weeks, Jeffrey. *Sexuality*. New York: Ellis Horwood, 1986.

Wilson, Ann. "A Jury of Her Peers." *Canadian Theatre Review* 51 (1987): 4–8.

Degrees of North: An Introduction
[to *Staging the North: Twelve Canadian Plays*]

by Sherrill Grace

When Herman Voaden published *Six Canadian Plays* in 1930 and "dedicated [it] to the north" (xviii), he wanted to encourage the writing of Canadian plays about Canadian subjects and places. He wanted to foster a *Canadian* theatre, and he believed that such a theatre would spring from a desire to dramatize "the north." Voaden did not ask what "the north" meant or where it was because he identified it with the country north of Lake Superior, the country painted by the Group of Seven; it was up and out there; it was, ultimately, for Voaden, synonymous with Canada. Voaden's Canadian theatre would be naturally (he thought) a northern theatre, whether as realist exploration of human relations and social issues, historical romance and adventure recreating actual events, or an experimental "art" theatre with symbolic or expressionist qualities and strong links with music and the other arts *(Six Canadian Plays* xx–xxiv).

Much has changed since 1930. We now have Canadian theatre with all the types of plays that Voaden envisioned, and many others besides. We have several anthologies of Canadian drama, many presses that publish Canadian plays, and we can see our playwrights' work performed on all the main stages of the country and reviewed in the newspapers. Canadian drama is taught in our schools and universities, studied by scholars, and analyzed in an ever-growing secondary literature. So the publication of a new collection of Canadian plays should not be a surprise.

What may come as a surprise is that, sixty-nine years after Voaden's *Six Canadian Plays*, a new volume appears that is "dedicated to the north." But much has changed on this score as well. It is no longer possible to assume that there is *a North* that can be the subject of a Canadian theatre or that can be *staged*. In fact, a number of fundamental questions and assumptions about North and about staging inform and surround this collection, and these must be posed and exposed before I can talk about the plays themselves. To claim that one can put the North on stage is immediately to ask: Whose North? What stage? And these questions open out to reveal others: Which playwrights? Staging for whom? The "true North," like the "we" who guard it in the Canadian national anthem, is a complex, changing, and problematic term.

There are, in fact, almost as many Norths in this volume as in the country, and Armand Tagoona's cover drawing [on *Staging the North*] of drum-dancing reminds us of their power. These Norths come to life for us—readers, listeners, audience—in the voices and movements of the story-tellers. Indeed, it is this visual concentration of the basic elements of staging the North that makes Tagoona's image such an apt metaphor for the volume. What Tagoona shows us is less a staging of the North than the North as a stage on which we can dance, sing, and communicate with each other across time, space, and cultural difference. Tagoona's story-telling-drum dancer is a figure of the playwrights and the characters who take to the stage in this volume and before whom we sit spellbound.

Before saying anything further about this volume, however, I must return to those questions and assumptions because considering the questions and teasing out the assumptions, which underlie any attempt to write plays *about* or *set in* the North, prepares the stage for the plays themselves, highlights what they have in common, underscores the many ways in which they differ, and reminds us of where we have come from since 1930.

* * *

Over the past century and a half, Canadians have consistently thought of themselves as a northern nation. As early as 1869, R.G. Haliburton, lawyer, man of letters, and founding member of the Canada First Movement, lectured publicly on what he saw as *our naturally* northern identity and superiority; his lecture, *The Men of the North and their Place in History*, was reviewed and excerpted in the major papers of the day and published in pamphlet form. Haliburton's ideas of North and Canadian identity were not original, but they were influential, and they can be traced from the 1860s to the present (see Grace, "Re-inventing Franklin"). Haliburton's North of white racial purity, romantic idealism, spiritual inspiration, and masculinist adventure is fundamentally the North of Lawren Harris and the Group of Seven, of Herman Voaden, Grey Owl, and Stephen Leacock, and of more recent thinkers and artists such as W.L. Morton, Glenn Gould, R. Murray Schafer, Margaret Atwood, Aritha van Herk, and Judith Thompson.[1] Above all, this North is a southern construction that has little to do with what James Lotz calls "Northern Realities" or Louis-Edmond Hamelin defines, in precise geographical indices, as Canadian nordicity.

There have always been other Norths, of course. Quebec has a long cultural and literary tradition of North as *le pays d'en haut* (see Warwick); W.L. Morton, taking his cue from Harold Innis's study of the fur trade, was the first Canadian historian to put a wider concept of North (which included the northwest and the territories north of sixty), and, thus, of Canada, on our historiographic map; and the Norths of the Klondike Gold Rush, of oil and mineral exploration along the Mackenzie to the Beaufort Sea, and of "Eskimo" art from Baffin Island have steadily expanded the parameters and the images of where and what *North* is and means. Repeatedly, in what I call the discursive formation of North, the dominant culture produces images of North that are creations of a southern imaginary and that serve and legitimize southern needs and interests. What are those billboard ads for beer and mutual funds selling us with their majestic Inukshuks and pristine lakes surrounded by mysterious, untouched pines? And who is *us*? The answers were quite clear in the 1995–96 retrospective exhibition of the Group of Seven, which opened in Ottawa at the

National Gallery and travelled to Montreal, Toronto, and Vancouver: according to the sub-title, it was *Art for a Nation, L'Emergence d'un art national* (see Hill). The *us* was southern Canadians, especially those in the national capital and the three major cities strung along the country's southern border, who buy beer and mutual funds or visit galleries. The *what* was national history, pride, identity, and unity as represented by a selection of powerful icons of that identity, the great majority of which depict Canada as North and North as northern Ontario.

The problem, if problem it be, is not that southern Canadians have imagined North in particular ways, usually without having ventured any further north than Algonquin Park or the West Edmonton Mall. As the 1998 ice storm reminded sophisticated, southern, urban Canadians, we are northerners by virtue of our geographical location and meterological reality. There is nothing wrong with these representations: the ads are very clever because they touch us subliminally; the Group of Seven exhibition was expertly mounted and the art shown was excellent. Moreover, these icons of cultural identity, using powerful images of a deeply felt nordicity, contribute directly to the construction of what it means to be Canadian. They function as patriotic reminders to Canadians who have been here for generations and they train newer Canadians to recognize where they are (see Brand). What is sometimes forgotten is that they are *representations* of North and that they do crucial ideological work. As representations, they have great power over our imaginations; we repeat them unconsciously and come to believe in them. As representations, however, they change over time, while maintaining a central core of meaning, and that meaning will work, will be put to work, as long as it resonates in some notion of a shared, public mind. [2]

For many southern Canadians, North has come to signify a place of adventure, and of physical and moral challenge. Wally Maclean, the narrator/philosopher in Glenn Gould's *The Idea of North*, put it very well when he said that the North was "the moral equivalent of war" (liner notes). It is also viewed as a place of spiritual beauty, silence, even transcendence, and of terror—a place of isolation, madness, and death. To the southern mind, the North is a paradox: it is at once empty—with nothing but lakes, rivers, forests, muskeg, taiga, tundra, and ice—and full—full of exotic peoples, caribou, mineral riches, unsolved mysteries, and ghosts. Many southern Canadians fear and dread it, running to the beaches of more southern climes at every opportunity, and yet they cannot live without it because, whether as *terra incognita* or as a hinterland playground for summer holidays, it is there ... and here.

But North has never been solely the preserve of southern Canada. The Inuit, Dene, Inu, northern Cree, and many other First Nations have occupied the provincial Norths, the territories, and the high Arctic for millennia. Slowly, southern Canadians have come to understand that their imaginary North is not *north* but *home* to these peoples as well as to those Canadians, of many ethnic backgrounds, who have gone north, settled there, and stayed. How that understanding has grown is a story too long for this essay. It reaches back to the 17th century and to a colonial history of exploration and trade, and it is an understanding that is still growing. Northern constructions of North are both older and newer than southern ones, older insofar as they spring from the oral traditions and cultures of indigenous northern peoples and newer insofar as they are now being articulated in ways that make them more accessible south of sixty. Northerners represent their Norths in stories about a way of life, in myths about an ancestral homeland, or in images familiar in the South from sculpture, prints, and other arts. Increasingly, they are representing themselves in magazines like *Up Here*, in radio and television programs made by and for northerners, and in political developments, the most important of which is Nunavut. Northern historians have called for and begun to write a northern history from a northern perspective (see Coates and Morrison). And while this realization may come as a shock, northerners construct representations of the South and of the *us* targeted by those beer ads and national exhibitions (see Freeman, Ipellie, and Highway).

Within the broad distinction between southern and northern representations of North, there are many further distinctions, refinements, and complexities, some of which emerge from the plays themselves. The key point is that North is not a monolithic concept or fixed set of images; Canadians living south or north of sixty, from whatever ethnic and cultural background, imagine a variety of Norths in widely differing geographical areas. Wherever North is located and however it is represented, it is a cultural construction. Being North, going North, imagining North, like staging North, are human activities, and to some degree they contribute to a collective understanding of who Canadians are. The more inclusive and diverse the Norths we construct, the richer will be our image of Canada as "*our* home and native land."

* * *

In his 1977 essay, "Is There a Canadian Drama?" Brian Parker argues that a key reason for the slow development of Canadian theatre is our lack of an appropriate myth. According to Parker, Canada's frontier myth of the North is "antidramatic" (155), and while he accepts the centrality of the North for Canadian identity and recognizes the capacity of poets, novelists, and painters to represent the North, he cannot conceive of a dramatic art that can put such a resistant, non-human landscape on stage. He dismisses early attempts by Voaden, Merrill Denison, and Gwen Ringwood to stage the North or to represent, on stage, the experiences of living in and with such a landscape. But Parker misses the point: North can be and has been staged. The challenge is not the myth, which is highly dramatic, but the audience for which a play is written and the stage upon which it is played.

As Voaden knew, plays about the North can take many forms to enact many different kinds of stories; the subjects are not limited by a northern landscape but embedded in it. What matters is how the drama is presented and where it is situated, whether within the social interaction of individuals, within a historical context, or within a single human mind. To be sure, trying to transplant a detailed forest set or a live dog-sled team to the stage can have disastrous or comic results, but good theatre has never been hobbled by such reductive literalism. More importantly, different stagings create different Norths, and different concepts of acting and production styles necessarily produce different stagings. What may have slowed the development of Canadian theatre is not something inherently antidramatic in the landscape or the myth of North, or in the stories that arise from that mythology, but the inhibiting influence of such demographic and economic factors as theatre spaces, audience size and demand, and the costs of production. Despite these obstacles, however, Canadian drama has flourished over the past sixty years, and a tradition of plays about the North is a component of that growth.

The strongest tradition of northern plays is still one grounded in southern Canada, and its genealogy, to which I will return, begins with Voaden and continues into the 1990s with Thompson's *Sled*. There are alternatives to this version of Canadian theatre history, of course, and they come from theatre companies based in the North. To date, very few of the plays written and produced in the North have been published *down south*, and few of these plays have been produced south of sixty. Over the past fifteen years, Playwrights Union of Canada has published working scripts of some of these plays. In 1992 two publications appeared that introduced southern readers to northern plays by northern playwrights: *Canadian Theatre Review*'s special issue on the Arctic called *Beast of the Land* (see Cowan and Rewa) and *Writing North: An Anthology of Contemporary Yukon Writers* (see Friis-Baastad and Robertson). In addition to valuable commentary on northern theatre and many splendid production photographs, *CTR* includes scripts by Inuit writers and *Hornby* by Yellowknife playwright Bruce Valpy; *Writing North* includes scripts by Philip Adams, Patti Flather and Leonard Linklater, and Leslie Hamson.

The emergence of a northern tradition is very recent. Nevertheless, there are lessons to learn about Canadian theatre, generally, and about northern theatre, in particular, from comparing the experiences of theatre groups like Nakai in Whitehorse and the Northern Arts and Cultural Centre (NACC) in Yellowknife. If success is to be measured in productivity and longevity, then Nakai is the northern theatre success story. It began in 1978 as a bottom-up adventure with community and Native roots outside and independent of Whitehorse. From the beginning, it developed a vital tradition of workshopping scripts, training local talent, and sponsoring writing competitions and story-telling festivals. It does not rely on imported plays for its main season or privilege plays by southern Canadian, American, or British playwrights. Moreover, the subjects of Nakai's plays are of local, regional relevance and interest. By big city standards, this philosophy should be the kiss of death, leading audiences and reviewers to sneer: regionalism, parochialism! But on this point NACC's history provides an interesting contrast.

The Yellowknife experiment has faltered and failed. NACC started in 1984 with a great deal of money, a new theatre, and enthusiastic volunteers. However, it soon lost sight of its original stress on local talent and its close ties with the Dene community. It failed to workshop and train. And it put money, time, and effort into mounting imported plays by playwrights with an international reputation (see Francis Thompson 48–49). NACC tried to create theatre in the North from the top down, and the absence of a play from Yellowknife in this collection suggests that northern

Canadian theatre, like Canadian theatre generally, must be home-grown. Among other northern theatre groups, Tunooniq Theatre from Pond Inlet now survives through David Qamaniq, who continues to create community-based scripts about social issues of immediate concern to the Inuit. The Native Theatre Group in Yellowknife and the Igloolik Dance and Drama Group have been less active in recent years, although both are represented in *Beast of the Land.*

* * *

The context for staging the North is complex and multi-faceted. Moreover, it cannot be confined to the theatre. Popular representations of the North, and of Canada-as-North, can be traced well back into the 19th century, but even in this century the genealogy is extensive. Early films used the North as their subject and setting; three examples that come to mind are Nell Shipman's *Back to God's Country* (1919), Robert Flaherty's *Nanook of the North* (1922), and W.S. Van Dyke's *Rose Marie* (1936). As Pierre Berton has told us, this was but the tip of a celluloid iceberg because Hollywood mass-produced hundreds of films about the North or the RCMP.[3]

Radio drama was not far behind film. From the mid-thirties to the late forties, Canadian children were entertained by shows such as *Renfrew of the Mounted,* the all-Canadian *Men in Scarlet,* and the popular *Sergeant Preston of the Yukon;* to the sound of howling blizzards and cries of "Mush," the valiant Sergeant, with his noble dog and horse, pursued his man over the frozen air waves. By the fifties, Preston had moved to television, where he still performs in Saturday afternoon reruns. In 1959, weary of the American bowdlerization of the national symbol, the CBC introduced a highly popular series called "RCMP" starring Gilles Pelletier, and "North of Sixty" has had a very successful run through the 1990s (see Warley). From the early forties, Canadian children have enjoyed northern comic book heroes such as Nelvana of the Northern Lights and North Guard.

None of this material could have influenced the boyhood of Voaden or Denison, of course, but what about later artists and writers? Did the young Glenn Gould thrill to Sergeant Preston? Was it radio drama and films, as much as the Group of Seven and maps of Canada's North, that inspired his lifelong passion for the North? And what about R. Murray Schafer, with his *Music in the Cold* and *North/White,* in which he brings a snowmobile on stage years before Judith Thompson's *Sled?* By the time Gould and Schafer were adults, younger generations of southern Canadians had many sources of inspiration about the North in fiction, non-fiction, poetry, National Film Board documentaries, and in real-life dramas about mad trappers, bush pilots, drowned artists (Tom Thomson being the mythic figure) and exhumed corpses on Beechey Island (see Grace, "'Franklin Lives'"). Canadian feature-length films continue to represent Canada-as-North, either by selling their stories in the Arctic ("Never Cry Wolf," 1983, "Shadow of the Wolf," 1992, and "Map of the Human Heart," 1993), or by exploiting northern imagery ("Thirty-two Short Films about Glenn Gould," 1993). Judging by our popular culture, novels, and documentaries (see Grace, *Representing North*), Canadians are obsessed with the North, and nothing testifies to that obsession more clearly than our annual search for Sir John Franklin and his missing ships, *Terror* and *Erebus*—a subject explored by two of the plays in this volume.

The historical context for a southern tradition of plays about the Canadian North begins with Voaden in the late 20s and early 30s. His initial efforts, such as *Northern Song* (1930) and *Wilderness* (1931), were followed by more complex pieces with a stronger plot line (*Hill-Land*, 1934, and *Murder Pattern*, 1936), but all his plays call for the staging of an idealized northern landscape that attracts but overwhelms human beings (see *A Vision of Canada*). In putting *his* North on stage, Voaden took inspiration from paintings by the Group of Seven, especially those by Lawren Harris and Tom Thomson, and he created sets with stylized rocks, hills, and trees flooded with silver-grey or blue light. But Voaden was not working in a theatrical vacuum. While the positive influences on his plays included the Group and his own love of wilderness, the negative spur to his art came from Denison, who had published a volume of plays called *The Unheroic North* in 1923. Denison's characters are crude country yokels or defeated northern Ontario farmers. In *Brothers in Arms*, for example, any remnant of romantic charm associated with a "hunting camp in the backwoods" (*Unheroic North*, 9), where the action takes place, is stripped away to expose it as a "God-forsaken hole" (*Unheroic North*, 10). And yet, when Denison turned his attention to Canadian history, he was drawn by the excitement of northern adventure and the heroics of exploration; his radio dramas on Henry Hudson and Alexander Mackenzie were historical romances such as Voaden called for in *Six Canadian Plays*.

Gwen Pharis Ringwood also wrote plays with northern settings: her classic *Still Stands the House* (1939) is a psychological drama that is inseparable from the northern blizzard that dominates and destroys her isolated, prairie family, and *The Road Runs North* (1967), with music by Art Rosoman, is a celebration of Billy Barker and the 1860s Cariboo Gold Rush in British Columbia. By going as far northwest as the Cariboo or Hudson Bay, Ringwood and Denison moved the parameters for a southern representation of North well beyond Voaden's boundaries. The only subject matter left to explore—or so it must have seemed at the time—was the exotic world of the Inuit, whose culture was introduced to southern audiences and consumers through James Houston's discovery and development of "Eskimo" sculpture and print-making in the 50s.

During the late 50s and early 60s, the Inuit and their arctic world were put on stage in some striking ways that, by contemporary standards, seem painfully inept. The most problematic attempt was David Gardner's 1961–62 production of *King Lear* with the Canadian Players. In his desire to promote a national theatre, Gardner sought a primitive Canadian setting for the play and decided to mount an arctic *Lear*, complete with harpoons, mukluks, snow-goggles, arctic sets, and a Fool re-cast as "part seal, part penguin [sic], and part wise, old owl" (Garebian 152). *The Great Hunger* (1958), by Leonard Peterson, is a white southern Canadian's attempt to dramatize an Inuit family caught between a traditional lifestyle and Christian teachings, which make little sense in their world. The result is a conventional tragedy interspersed with bits of Inuit myth, legend, and story. Robertson Davies took an entirely different approach to representing the Inuit and the Arctic in *Question Time* (1975), a complex, satiric allegory of Canadian spiritual and political life starring an Inuk Shaman who convinces a Canadian Prime Minister that life is worth living and Canada worth serving, as long as we remember the importance of the North.

A northern tradition of plays about the North may be much younger, but it is no less varied than the southern one. Oddly enough, this tradition, at least as it has emerged in theatre companies like Nakai, has usually heeded Brian Parker's warning about trying to put a northern landscape on stage. A brief comparison of two plays not included in this collection will suggest one reason why northerners often resist this temptation. In *Sled*, Judith Thompson goes to great lengths to specify a number of visual and aural details which, she hopes, will represent North to her southern audience; these include birch trees, the Northern Lights, the semblance of snow, wolf howls and snowy owl hoots, and, of course, the omnipresent "sled" (a snowmobile), suggested, in the production I saw, by simulated headlights and raked "trails." By contrast, Leslie Hamson calls for the simplest of stylized sets, using a scrim and lighting to evoke a feeling of the Yukon bush in *Land(e)scapes* and *Last Rites*. In *Land(e)scapes*, the main set is a cabin, and the sound effects are created by members of the cast using natural objects of wood or stone. Thompson's more elaborate set derives, I suspect, from her need to create an image of an exotic northern locale that her southern, urban audience will recognize as *northern*; Hamson, however, can assume that her northern audience will have no trouble imagining what is all too real in the outdoor world around them.[4]

First Nations and Inuit plays, and here Tunooniq is a fine example, also treat the North as a given. Their primary purpose is education, not entertainment, and the dramaturgy resembles aspects of Brechtian epic theatre. Mimetic representation, as such, is not a concern in a theatre that draws heavily on oral traditions, story-telling, and the physical enactment—or performance—of the story in mime, dance, and song. So deeply is the northern landscape a part of the story being told and of the experiences of the characters/story-tellers, that it demands little representation on stage. As in Tagoona's drawing, the North is the stage. *Trickster Visits the Old Folks Home* and the two Tunooniq plays must be read in this light, whereas *Sixty Below*, which combines native myth and story-telling techniques with western dramaturgy, offers a rich and fascinating hybrid theatre experience. In a sense, the southern and northern traditions I have outlined meet and complement each other in *Sixty Below*.

***

So far I have focused on what North can mean, where it can be located, and how a context and tradition for northern drama can be described. But this particular volume exists as a result of many decisions made in the process of understanding how the North might be staged. It results, as well, from the editor's and publisher's shared conviction that the end of the century, with the inauguration of Nunavut, marks a significant moment in the history of the nation, a moment for reflection on the past and an ideal point for contemplating the future. The North is very much on the political, social, and cultural agenda in Canada. A major, state-supported exhibition like *Art for a Nation* is part of that agenda. Books about the North—fiction, auto-biography, memoir, and history—are as popular as ever, and the centenary of the Yukon Gold Rush has contributed to this renewed interest. Theatre, as this volume demonstrates, also makes an important contribution to this literary, artistic, cultural, political, and constitutional activity.

Inevitably, many worthy plays do not appear in this collection. In addition to earlier plays already mentioned and to plays about the Canadian North by non-Canadians, such as Wilkie Collins' and Charles Dickens' *The Frozen Deep* (1857), there are others we have not included: new scripts by Miche Genest ("The Fasting Girl"); Cristina Pekarik ("Cloudberry"); historical plays, such as Bruce Valpy's *Hornby*; Betty Lambert's play for children about the Cariboo Gold Rush called *The Song of the Serpent*; Edmonton New Heart Company of Artists' script "In the Teeth of the Shore," about the Franklin expedition; and Gerald St. Maur's scripts about Henry Hudson ("Abacuck," and "The Solstice Mutiny"); and musical pieces like *The Shooting of Dan McGrew*, a parodic re-writing of Service's famous poem, with text by John Bertram and music by Jim Betts; or more topical plays like *Running on Frozen Air* about the Yukon Quest dog-sled race, with text by Gordon McCall and music by Cathy Elliott. One of the few Quebecois plays about the far North is Jacques Languirand's *Klondyke*, a lengthy, mock-epic piece with music by Gabriel Charpentier, and there is an older francophone tradition of *pays d'en haut* plays about *coureurs de bois* and historical events, which, like the early anglophone plays, now seem anachronistic (see Dufresne, Ferron, Roux, Savard, and Thériault).

Among works by contemporary Quebecois playwrights, however, there are some powerful plays that might have been included if a quality translation existed. For example, Marie Laberge's *Ils étaient venus pour...*, set in the ghost-town of Val-Jalbert in the Saguenay area, is deeply rooted in regional history and language. Françoise Loranger's téléthéâtre piece, *Un cri qui vient de loin*, while visually stunning, is neither meant for the stage nor translated, and Franco-Ontarian Jean Marc Dalpé's award-winning *Le Chien* (translated by the playwright) is set in northern Ontario and has much in common with [Mansel Robinson's] *Colonial Tongues*. By and large, however, contemporary Quebecois playwrights either do not write about a North or, when they do, that region is abstracted and reduced to the backdrop for a family drama of psychological violence, incest, and artistic rivalry as in the work of Jeanne-Mance Delisle. For example, the father in Delisle's *Un reel ben beau, ben triste* vents his rage and frustration in a monologue about escaping North, like the voyageurs, while, in Laberge's hands, the North of exploitation and internal colonization, represented by "*une ville fântome*" (128), becomes an image of Quebec. Despite their differences, the common ground shared by the *pays d'en haut* and contemporary plays is the construction of a symbolic North as a place for violent, masculine adventure and escape or of bitterness, betrayal, and defeat. This tradition constitutes a subject worthy of another study and another collection.[5]

The plays included in *Staging the North* have been chosen with definite criteria in mind. Each play, we believe, reads well on the page and has had at least one well-received production. Each play has something interesting to say about the theatre—about how to use the theatre and why, about production, dramaturgy, and dramatic subjects. Each play, of course, *stages* a North, and in doing so tells its audience or readers something new about what it is to be northerners—and Canadians.

These plays are about social problems, historical events, and personal conflicts. They offer vehicles for single actors, for two characters, or for a group, and the theatrical styles range from savage social satire in *Esker Mike & His Wife, Agiluk* to poetic lyricism in *Terror and Erebus*. The expressionistic mode of *Free's Point* is ideal for its subject—a man driven mad by his inner demons and the northern bush—and the symbolic, mythic qualities of *Inuk and the Sun* make an Everyman of its hero. There are realist plays here as well, even if they do resist the temptation to recreate a northern landscape on stage—plays about the loss of national identity that are rooted in political and family disintegration (*Colonial Tongues*), or psychological realism that confronts the reader/audience with bitter truths about southern ignorance and indifference (*The Occupation of Heather Rose*), or about hypocrisy in extremity and the necessity of love (*Ditch*). Realism is stripped to its minimalist bones in *Who Look In Stove*, a historical play about the Hornby disaster so understated that it seems to exist, finally, in gesture and silence. Along with *Colonial Tongues*, *Sixty Below* is the most complex and ambitious of the plays collected here. This complexity arises not only from the inter-relations of its characters, but also from the hybridity of its sources, style, and presentation; it is a play that tries to live in two worlds and does a remarkably successful job of it. *Changes, In Search of a Friend*, and *Trickster Visits the Old Folks Home* present southern and northern Canadians with another perspective on North and on theatre; to stage the North in these plays is to tell stories about daily life in the north by enacting them. These are overtly didactic plays in ways that none of the others, not even *Esker Mike* or *Colonial Tongues*, attempts to be.

And yet, despite these differences, a common view of North emerges from these plays with great clarity. North, they tell us, is a topos rich in imagery, story, history, living myth, legends, and ghosts. In fact, of all the possible subjects that I might single out as common to these plays, the one that insists on taking precedence is ghosts: the ghosts of madmen, explorers, past selves, vanished towns, dead fathers and brothers, and unappeased spirits stalk these plays, haunt the living, and dance in the Northern Lights. North is perceived and dramatized as a place of purity and freedom, even when—as is so often the case—purity and freedom collapse into violence, greed, and madness. And it is represented, time and again, as both stunningly beautiful and staggeringly dangerous. It is a landscape of challenge to western concepts of masculinity, and, more broadly, to notions of civilization, truth, and to life itself.

As staged in these plays, North is a landscape of extremity that resists the human need to capture it in words. A significant aspect of such extremity is the challenge it poses to the theatre itself, to language, and to representation. Each of these plays asks fundamental human questions about how we can say what we mean, or make sense of existence *in words* when faced with that extremity, and about how we can represent and embody the distillation of that experience on stage. All the plays gathered here draw upon cultural and social sources to help them in this task, whether from literary intertexts, other plays, myth, music, or political and historical allusions; but in the final analysis, when the lights come up, it is the body, through gesture and voice, that must register and convey the experience, that must remain silent or speak. It is the embodied voice that counts—the words which the dying men in *Ditch* struggle to say aloud, which Edgar in *Who Look In Stove* just barely manages to sound and write, and that Heather throws directly at us in *The Occupation of Heather Rose*. Several of the plays in *Staging the North* use a minimalist style to convey the extremity of the North; *Terror and Erebus, Changes, Ditch,* and *Who Look In Stove* are the clearest examples of the simplicity and stripped-down quality that I associate with minimalism in the arts. Paradoxically, but fittingly, the less *of* the North they put on the stage, the more they represent—through embodying in performance—that phenomenon, place, or idea an audience can recognize as North.

Cindy Cowan, a southerner who has lived in the North, suggests that the land determines how northerners see themselves (3). If this is so, then staging the North will involve an attempt, at least, to represent who we think we are. But *who* is represented in these plays, or, to put the question differently, what is Canadian about them? Perhaps an answer lies in the spare, taut, simplicity of the action, themes, and language, in the emphatic absence of traditional heroes, in the obsession with death and ghosts, in the fascination with history, genealogy, identity, and document, or the rich sub-stratum of myth that comes to the surface in *Inuk and the Sun, In Search of a Friend,* and *Sixty Below*. Or perhaps the answer lies in the stern social ethic that informs all of these plays and that couples the meaning of being human with a respect for the land and the people who are a part of it. It is the loss of this ethic that Hardin portrays in *Esker Mike*, that contributes to the failure of Franklin and Hornby, and that sabotages Mick in *Free's Point*.

To my mind, however, it is Butch Barnett, in *Colonial Tongues*, who articulates this ethic most forcefully by reminding us about the cost of forgetting where we are. "We gave it away," he cries:

> This place. The north. We had everything we needed. We could have built a home. But we volunteered to build our own coffins instead ....
> We turned this place into a colony of a colony. (385)

If there is an answer to my question, of course, it will lie in the plays themselves and in the eye of the reader or theatregoer. Canada is certainly a northern nation, but it also contains many norths. Insofar as the North determines how we define ourselves, then in these plays it is a stage upon which Canadians perform a complex, multiple identity.

(1999)

Notes

[1] Atwood, van Herk, and Thompson, as well as Rudy Wiebe and Robert Kroetsch, critique aspects of this myth; however, by reacting to the dominant discourse of North, which they have inherited, they reproduce, while modifying, its semiotics (see Grace, "Gendering Northern Narrative").

[2] The concept and trope of North has been used deliberately to shape a shared, public mind. In the last century, and through much of this, that shaping has been racist, sexist, and exclusionary, but this collection demonstrates that the North can be shared, without excluding individuals or groups on the basis of race, ethnicity, class, or gender.

[3] According to Berton, between 1907 and 1956 Hollywood made 575 films set in Canada. Many were preposterous tales about the Mounties, and all represented Canada as an unspoiled wilderness of trees, ice, and snow (Berton 51–56).

[4] In the 1994 Tamanhous production of *Land(e)scapes*, Vancouver audiences appeared to have difficulty imagining the northern bush home that Hamson and her characters took for granted. *Last Rites* has not yet been produced south of sixty, but the set for the 1992 Nakai production was a huge abstract mask beneath a semi-circle of branches. In the 1997 Touchstone production of *Sled*, the set was (in my view) a failure because it was too literal.

[5] Quebec plays in which northernness is generalized as winter or as the countryside include: Garneau's *Les Neiges*, Tremblay's *La Maison Suspendu*, where city and country become opposites and the country is associated with a mythic North, and Marie-Claire Blais' *Sommeil d'hiver* (1984), in which a desolate arctic landscape emerges behind transparent scrims to provide the visual metaphor of the play. In the introduction to his translation of Blais' chamber plays, Nigel Spencer notes that the "Nordic sensibility" of these plays is "strong in Quebec writing—though rarely discussed by critics" (10).

Works Cited

Atwood, Margaret. *Strange Things: The Malevolent North in Canadian Literature.* Oxford: Clarendon, 1995.

Bertram, John. *The Shooting of Dan McGrew.* Music by Jim Betts. Toronto: Playwrights Union, n.d.

Berton, Pierre. *Hollywood's Canada: The Americanization of our National Image.* Toronto: McClelland and Stewart, 1975.

Blais, Marie-Claire. *Wintersleep.* Trans. Nigel Spencer. Vancouver: Ronsdale, 1998.

Brand, Dionne. "Driving North, Driving Home." *Canadian Forum.* October 1998: 30–32.

Brannan, Robert Louis, ed. *Under the Management of Mr Charles Dickens: His Production of 'The Frozen Deep'.* Ithaca, N.Y.: Cornell UP, 1966.

Coates, K.S. and W.R. Morrison. "Writing the North: A Survey of Contemporary Canadian Writing on Northern Regions." Grace, *Representing North* 5–25.

Cowan, Cindy. "Beast of the Land." Cowan and Rewa 3.

———. and Natalie Rewa, eds. *Beast of the Land. Canadian Theatre Review* 73 (Winter 1992).

Dalpé, Jean Marc. *Le Chien.* Ottawa: Éditions Prise de Parole, 1987.

Delisle, Jeanne-Mance. *Un reel ben beau, ben triste.* Ottawa: Les éditions de la pleine lune, 1980.

Davies, Robertson. *Question Time.* Toronto: Macmillan, 1975.

Denison, Merrill. *Henry Hudson and Other Plays.* Toronto: Ryerson, 1931.

———. *The Unheroic North: Four Canadian Plays.* Toronto: McClelland and Stewart, 1923.

Dufresne, Guy. *Les Traitents.* Ottawa: Leméac, 1969.

Ferron, Jacques. *Les Grands Soleils.* Montreal: Éditions d'Orphée, 1958.

Freeman, Minnie Aodla. *Life Among the Qallunaat.* Edmonton: Hurtig, 1978.

Friis-Baastad, Erling and Patricia Robertson. *Writing North: An Anthology of Yukon Writers.* Whitehorse: Beluga, 1992.

Garebian, Keith. *William Hut: A Theatre Portrait.* Oakville: Mosaic, 1988.

Garneau, Michel. *Les Neiges.* Montreal: VLB Editeur, 1984.

Gould, Glenn. "The Idea of North." 1967. "Glenn Gould's Solitude Trilogy: Three Sound Documentaries." CBC 2003-3, 1992.

Grace, Sherrill. "'Franklin Lives': More Atwood Ghosts." *Various Atwoods: Essays on the Later Poems, Short Fiction, and Novels.* Ed Lorraine York. Toronto: Anansi, 1995. 146–66.

———. "Gendering Northern Narrative." *Echoing Silence: Essays on Northern Narrative.* Ed. John Moss. Ottawa: U of Ottawa P, 1997. 163–81.

———. "Going North on Judith Thompson's *Sled.*" *Essays in Theatre/Études théâtrales* 16.2 (1998): 153–64.

————. "Re-inventing Franklin." *Canadian Review of Comparative Literature* 22. 3–4 (1995): 707–25.

————, ed. *Representing North. Essays on Canadian Writing* 59 (Fall 1996).

Haliburton, R.G. *The Men of the North and their Place in History* Montreal: John Lovell, 1869.

Hamelin, Louis-Edmond. *Canadian Nordicity: It's Your North Too.* Trans.William Barr. Montreal: Harvest, 1978.

Hamson, Leslie. *Land(e)scapes.* Unpublished script. 1997.

————. "Last Rites." *Canadian Theatre Review* 75 (1993): 55–71.

Highway, Thomson. *Kiss of the Fur Queen.* Toronto: Doubleday, 1998.

Hill, Charles C. *The Group of Seven: Art for a Nation.* Ottawa and Toronto: National Gallery of Canada and McClelland & Stewart, 1995.

Innis, Harold. *The Fur Trade in Canada: An Introduction to Canadian Economic History.* 1956. Rev. ed. Toronto: U of Toronto P, 1970.

Ipellie, Alootook. "Ice Box." Cartoon. *Inuit Monthly,* January 1974–February 1975.

Inuit Today, February 1975–Spring 1982.

Kroetsch, Robert. *The Man from the Creeks.* Toronto: Random House, 1998.

Laberge, Marie. *Ils étaient venus pour ….* Montréal Boréal, 1997.

Lambert, Betty. *The Song of the Serpent. Boneman: An Anthology of Canadian Plays.* Ed. Gordon Ralph. St John's, NFLD: Jesperson, 1995. 178–225.

Languirand, Jacques. *Klondyke.* Musique de Gabriel Charpentier. Montréal: Cercle du livre de France, 1971.

Loranger, Françoise. *Encore cinq minutes et Un cri qui vient de loin.* Ottawa: Le Cercle du Livre de France, 1967.

Lotz, James. *Northern Realities: The Future of Northern Development in Canada.* Toronto: New P, 1970.

McCall, Gordon. *Running On Frozen Air.* Music by Cathy Elliott. Toronto: Playwrights Union, n.d.

Morton, W.L. *The Canadian Identity.* 1961. 2nd ed. Madison, WI: U of Wisconsin P, 1972.

Parker, Brian. "Is There a Canadian Drama?" *The Canadian Imagination: Dimensions of a Literary Culture.* Ed David Staines. Cambridge, Mass: Harvard UP, 1977. 152–87.

Peterson, Leonard. *The Great Hunger.* Agincourt, Ont: Book Society of Canada, 1967.

Ringwood, Gwen Pharis. *Still Stands the House*. New York: Samuel French, 1939.

———. *The Road Runs North*. Music by Art Rosoman. Unpublished script and music, 1967. Ringwood Papers. University of Calgary.

Roux, Jean-Louis. *Bois-Brulées: Reportage epique sur Louis Riel*. Montreal Editions du Jour, 1968.

Savard, Félix-Antoine. *La Dalle-des-Morts*. Montreal: Fides, 1965.

Schafer, R. Murray. *Music in the Cold*. Toronto: Coach House, 1977.

———. *North/White*. Score. Toronto: Universal, 1982 .

Tagoona, Armand. *Shadows*. Toronto: Oberon, 1975.

Theriault, Yves. *Le Marcheur*. 1950. Ottawa: Leméac, 1968.

Thompson, Francis. "From Prestige Project to Simply Shell: The Short History of the Northern Arts and Cultural Centre." Cowan and Rewa 45–50.

Thompson, Judith. *Sled*. Toronto: Playwrights Canada, 1997.

Tremblay, Michel. *La Maison Suspendue*. Trans. John Van Burek. Vancouver: Talonbooks, 1991.

Valpy, Bruce. *Hornby*. Ed. John Rafferty. Cowan and Rewa 60–76.

van Herk, Aritha. *Places Far From Ellesmere*. Red Deer, Alberta: Red Deer College P, 1990.

Voaden, Herman. *A Vision of Canada: Herman Voaden's Dramatic Works, 1928–1945*. Ed. Anton Wagner. Toronto: Simon & Pierre, 1993.

———, ed. *Six Canadian Plays*. Toronto: Copp Clark, 1930.

Warley, Linda. "The Mountie and the Nurse: Cross-Cultural Relations *North of 60*." *Painting the Maple: Essays on Race, Gender, and the Construction of Canada*. Ed. V. Strong-Boag, S. Grace, A. Eisenberg, and J. Anderson. Vancouver: U of British Columbia P, 1998. 309–33.

Warwick, Jack. *The Long Journey: Themes of French Canada* Toronto: U of Toronto P, 1968.

Wiebe, Rudy. *Playing Dead: A Contemplation Concerning the Arctic*. Edmonton: NeWest, 1989.

Urban National, Suburban Transnational: Civic Theatres and the Urban Development of Toronto's Downtowns

by Michael McKinnie

Now, after nearly two decades of continental economics and the recurring threat of federal dissolution, it is sometimes hard to imagine just how celebratory Canadian nationalism was in the late 1960s. Canada commemorated its hundredth birthday in 1967, and the optimism embodied in projects like Expo 67 in Montreal seemed to signal that the country had achieved national maturity and international stature. The centennial celebrations implied—indeed shouted—that the Canadian federation was confident, modern, and secure, and that the able steward for the national project was a benevolent state. Like many Western countries in the late 1960s, Canada's economic expansion was accompanied by legal liberalization, greater immigration, and an increasingly generous welfare state. Unlike many Western countries in the late 1960s, however, the counter-cultural corollary to this modernization project did not seek to challenge significantly the supremacy of the national state. If anything, the centennial best illustrates how the ascendancy of Canadian cultural nationalism was secured by a kind of soft authoritarianism. As one popular commentary observes, "The great Canadian Centennial love-in was definitely a top-down affair: an officially legislated, publicly-sponsored, impeccably choreographed national debutante ball. Compulsory attendance notwithstanding, we loved it anyway: it was probably the most fun the country ever had doing something it was told to do" (Diamond and Pevere 50).

If that kind of national celebration seems unimaginable in Canada today (leaving aside the question of its desirability), everyday life in Canada remains equally unimaginable without the physical legacy of that time. Centennial projects married a familiar practice of pork-barrel beneficence with an oedipal rationale for cultural institution-building: the nation would throw off its colonial inheritance (represented as a kind of infantile disorder) by constructing "something for everyone, everywhere in Canada." Scores of public schools, ice arenas, and swimming pools built across the country would contribute to personal development, while "[c]oncert halls, museums, art galleries, libraries and cultural centres" would, at the local level, redress a perceived lack of collective cultural development (Fortier and Schafer 19). Expo 67 may have been the grandest national symbol of the centennial, but the many smaller civic building projects funded in the name of the centenary remain the most enduring and useful local benefit of national patronage.

The St. Lawrence Centre for the Arts (SLC) was one of the centennial's major cultural projects, and was built as Toronto's first civic theatre facility on the eastern edge of the city's Central Business District (CBD). The $5.2 million complex housed two theatres (an 830 seat auditorium and a 480 seat auditorium) and was the first theatre facility built in Toronto specifically for a resident company, one assembled by the not-for-profit, city-governed agency called the Toronto Arts Foundation. Construction began in 1967 after demolition of a row of nineteenth-century buildings on Front Street East, and the SLC finally opened in 1970 under the directorship of Mavor Moore, a long-time advocate for theatre in Canada and a prominent supporter of the SLC project. Four of the five plays staged that first season were Canadian, a nationalist programming practice for which many theatre practitioners had agitated, but which was only beginning to gain legitimacy among Toronto companies at the time. [1]

While the construction of the SLC marked the beginning of profound changes in theatrical production in Toronto, 1967 also heralded the first major victory for Toronto's nascent urban reform movement. The Friends of Old City Hall helped prevent the sale and demolition of the former city hall, thereby inaugurating a powerful political constituency whose focus was the preservation and streetscape-sensitive development of downtown Toronto. Since 1967 a significant number of the most fractious political struggles in Toronto have been over what former mayor John Sewell calls "the shape of the city" (*Shape*). [2] Well-organized political coalitions and their allies on city council have consistently ensured that city form in general, and downtown in particular, are central preoccupations of Toronto's local political imaginary.

The intersection of these events—one theatrical and one urban—is more than just chronological. If 1967 is the year when urban development assumed a prominent position in Toronto's political consciousness, the centennial also marks the last moment that the nation state built cultural institutions in a systematic fashion, and here I mean "built" both administratively and physically, in the sense of creating what geographers call a "built environment." Though the SLC is a metonym of national cultural development, it is also an act of civic development, and its construction illustrates how a civic discourse may help cement a link between theatre-building and urban development after the nationalist impulse that first brought them together has faded. Furthermore, if the meaning of the civic in Toronto after 1967 signified a struggle over development of the city's built environment, then it is worth asking if the SLC, as a civic theatre, played a role in that struggle. Does the "civic" in "civic theatre" signify a theatrical intervention in Toronto's urban development?

Similarly, it is worth asking if the other, more recently developed, civic theatre in Toronto played a role in the urban development of its neighborhood, and, if so, how it interprets the relationship between theatre and the city. The North York Performing Arts Centre (NYPAC) was completed in 1993 in downtown North York, a suburb north of the old city core built after the Second World War. (Like the City of Toronto, North York was an autonomous municipality within the Metropolitan Toronto federation until Metro's constituent cities were amalgamated into a single city in

1998. [3]) NYPAC was built by North York at a cost of approximately $30 million, and was renamed the Ford Centre for the Performing Arts when Ford Motor Company purchased the right to name it soon after opening. The Ford Centre is a much larger facility than the SLC, and is comprised of a main theatre auditorium that seats 1800 spectators, a concert hall, an art gallery, and a small black box theatre. North York built the Ford Centre as the artistic component of its downtown development scheme, which attempted to create a city centre along a four kilometre stretch of Yonge Street by building public facilities, shopping centres, condominiums, and commercial office blocks.

Though owned by the City of North York, the Ford Centre was operated by the LivEntertainment Corporation (Livent) until its bankruptcy in 1998, and was the first home to productions of *Sunset Boulevard, Ragtime,* and *Showboat* that later transferred to Broadway. Confusingly, the facility was renamed again in 2000 as the Toronto Centre for the Arts (TCA). Unified Toronto, which assumed ownership of the complex after amalgamation, chose not to retain the Ford Centre name once Livent was no longer the resident producing company. [4] The TCA is now marketed as a rental facility, though without a resident commercial producer it is dark most nights and incurs significant losses. The TCA may be a civic arts facility, but meeting its high operating costs was always predicated on its occupation by a major for-profit theatre producer, and without such a producer the complex struggles to find sound economic and artistic footing. My analysis focuses on the period when the complex functioned as the Ford Centre for the Performing Arts, since it is in this guise that the facility best articulates its ideal relationship between the civic and the theatrical.

"Civic theatre" means different things at different historical moments, and by considering the SLC and the Ford Centre as urban developments it is possible to reveal the competing connotations of the designation in Toronto since 1967. As the title of this investigation implies, I see the SLC as a form of national urban development and the Ford Centre as a form of transnational suburban development. By this I mean that the SLC is a last gasp of cultural and urban planning by the Fordist nation state. [5] But the SLC is also a bridge, at the civic level, to the transnational understanding of the relationship between theatre and cities that the Ford Centre represents. These civic theatres, then, have helped mediate macro-economic transformation at the local level through the socially affirmative values they bear, and the built form they embody. Each centre is an index of how civic theatre-building can be used strategically as part of urban core development to soften the upheavals that this development may bring or represent, and to reinscribe the civic ideal of downtown that is so dear to many Torontonians.

Ideologies of Civic Theatre

Civic theatres can provoke the response that theatre and local politics are not, or should not be, compatible. Denis Johnston, in his analysis of theatre in Toronto during the 1960s and 1970s, argues that the SLC "was conceived by civic planners, unlike most Canadian theatres, and has been cursed with civic politics ever since" (9). The implication that the SLC was the brainchild of city planners is not altogether historically accurate, as Johnston himself admits when he calls the St. Lawrence Centre the "Holy Grail of local professional theatre" during the 1960s. Johnston also claims that "civic politics" have "cursed" the SLC "ever since" its construction (12). Theatre practitioners were as much in favour of the St. Lawrence Centre as city planners were, and the involvement of city planners in a civic theatre project does not necessarily mean that their urban concerns were in conflict with the theatrical desires of the time. Johnston assumes that civic politics are opposed to, and, he implies, taint, theatre projects, but this is untrue both in a broad historical sense and in the specific case of the SLC.

Civic theatres, and cultural institutions generally, have historically contributed to the civic as a social and urban ideal. These contributions can be grouped in three ways. First, art's "strong affirmative tendencies toward reconciliation with the established reality," as Herbert Marcuse puts it, reinforce civic ideals of citizenship within an idealized public sphere (10).[6] Second, cultural institution-building often affirms the economic dominance of capitalist urban development within the city. Third, theatre-building in Toronto affirms the centrality of downtown in creating a sense of civic well being. Collectively these affiliations create a sense of urban affluence, where civic theatre-building offers an ideal of civic accord that compensates for the anxieties of economic change.

Citizenship

Stacy Wolf points out that the affiliation of the civic with theatre has not usually been dissonant in Western societies. In her perceptive analysis of the civic arts centre in Madison, Wisconsin, Wolf argues that cultural institution-building plays an important ideological role in creating affirmative civic ideals of citizenship, whether or not people actually attend the theatre:

> Rather than constituting a daily social practice for most people, "the arts" remain in the realm of values. Still, they carry an ethical force, not unlike religion or moral goodness. "The arts," a general, undifferentiated, seemingly unpoliticized notion, are assumed to be significant and positive. Art, in theory, creates good citizens. (11)

Wolf invokes art critic Rosalyn Deutsche, who suggests that cultural production frequently buttresses the civilizing impulse of modern urban development: "The presence of 'the aesthetic'—whether embodied in artworks, architectural style, urban design, or museums—helps give redevelopment democratic legitimacy, since, like 'the public,' 'art' often connotes universality openness, inclusion" (qtd. in Wolf 11). Western theatre history often places the City Dionysia—a type of civic performance—at the core of its narratives, and Marvin Carlson argues that Western theatre practice and cities have frequently comprised a mutually legitimating symbolic economy (particularly in the Middle Ages and the early Renaissance), or have intersected as oppositional spaces through which civil society might be formed (particularly in the nineteenth and twentieth centuries) (14–37).

Urban theorists have also been concerned with how art and urbanization might be linked in creating good citizens, something that is not surprising considering these theorists emerge from an intellectual tradition which frequently considers urbanization a civilizing force in itself. H.D.F. Kitto, whose work has been read within both theatre and urban studies, argues that the Greek *polis* exemplifies a civilized social formation because it attempted to be "an active, formative thing, training the minds and characters of the citizens" through their participation in an urban public sphere. The city, Kitto claims, has been more important as an ideal of "common cultural life" than as a "political unit," and "the drama" played a crucial role in establishing the notion that "the *polis* [was] open to all" (35). Henri Pirenne suggests that cities and cultural products together helped create an ideal of social mobility in late medieval Europe, one that would later inform the egalitarian principles of liberal democracy. He argues that cultural production was the corollary to European urbanization; the development of cultural products helped create an urban laity where "the burgher was initiated … long before the noble" (240). Aesthetic and civic discourses have often been mutually affirmative, and so it is necessary to be skeptical of claims, implicit or explicit, that civic politics taint theatre projects. On the contrary, "the arts" have often helped form the social ideals that civic politics promote.

Place Patriotism

While the affiliation of arts projects and cities has helped create affirmative ideals of citizenship, this affiliation may also help create a chauvinistic sense of the civic that is economically affirmative. Urban sociologists John Logan and Harvey Molotch advance the concept of "place patriotism" to explain this process. They argue that place patriotism occurs when property value inflation is linked with cultural institution-building to create sentiments of local well-being. Logan and Molotch make a compelling case for the building of cultural institutions in the city as part of an urban "growth coalition" of capitalists and their allies in city governments. In their formulation, cultural institutions marshal localist sentiments in favor of projects that can then be used as levers for private capital investment in the areas surrounding them:

> The growth machine avidly supports whatever cultural institutions can play a role in building locality. Always ready to oppose social and political developments contrary to their interests, renters and their associates encourage activities that will connect feelings of community to the goal of local growth …. We do not mean to suggest that the only source of civic pride is the desire to collect rents; certainly the cultural pride of tribal groups predates growth machines. Nevertheless, the growth machine coalition mobilizes these cultural motivations,

legitimizes them, and channels them into activities that are consistent with growth goals. (62)

Logan and Molotch note that arts centres were used as "development leverage" during the 1980s in downtown Miami, Tampa, and Dallas, and cite a Dallas newspaper comment that "[t]he feeling persists that the arts have been appropriated here primarily to sell massive real estate development" (77). One could make the same statement about the Ford Centre in Toronto, the 42nd Street development in New York City, and the State Street development in Chicago. [7] Logan and Molotch argue that the encouragement of place patriotism links arts projects with sentiments of civic well-being, while simultaneously enriching private developers and smoothing the upheavals of economic change (60). If Logan and Molotch allow us to see how arts projects are leveraged into an urban cash economy, they also point to (but do not expand on) the way those projects might contribute to a sense of local well-being. The SLC and the Ford Centre are part of a sentimental urban economy, and this role also requires elaboration.

Downtown

In Toronto, place patriotism and civic theatres meet downtown. Toronto's civic theatres help define and entrench capitalist land use areas that are called downtowns and their presence becomes evidence for an ontological "downtown-ness" that pleases the local urban subject. This practice is not confined to theatre spaces—it is relevant to the function of cultural institutions in downtown redevelopment in general—but civic theatres are particularly useful from an urban planning and security perspective, since, unlike art galleries or museums, they tend to attract affluent citizens to an area at night.

Downtown may be an area where legitimate economic transactions take place (and illegitimate economic transactions are nervously accommodated), but it is also an affirmative spatial and ontological ideal to which many Torontonians are fiercely dedicated. While the cores of many American cities suffered from economic and residential decline after the Second World War, this does not hold true of Toronto. Toronto continues to maintain a vibrant city centre, containing many healthy neighbourhoods comprised of diverse classes and races. As a result, downtown is an ideal to which many Torontonians have become deeply attached. For proof of this attachment, one need only look to the contemporary history of urban activism in Toronto, much of which has been focused on the downtown core. The most recent example is the vocal and well-organized opposition by many residents of the former City of Toronto to the provincial government's amalgamation of the metropolitan federation into a unified municipal government. Although the majority of municipal services were provided to city residents by the metropolitan government, city planning remained in the hands of the local government, and many downtown activists feared that the suburban cities would collectively impose less restrictive planning requirements after amalgamation, effectively eliminating the ideal and form of downtown to which many

Torontonians subscribed. The fight was undoubtedly over who would control "the shape of the city" (for historical perspectives on Toronto's downtown development and urban reform struggles, see Caulfield; Fraser; Sewell, *Shape* and *Up*; Stein).

An allegiance to downtown should not, however, be viewed strictly as the preserve of residents of the former City of Toronto. Downtown North York was built by the City of North York to achieve the sense of civic well-being that seemed to be missing as a result of its low density, post-Second World War suburban planning. North York is Toronto's second city in terms of population, but, in terms of urban planning, was practically indistinguishable from Scarborough and Etobicoke, the other large suburban communities that make up Toronto. North York thought that building a downtown would differentiate it from Toronto's other suburbs by establishing a sense of a distinct civic identity within the former metropolitan federation. North York for many years promoted itself as "the city with a heart," and the construction of a downtown gave an advertising slogan physical and sentimental form; North York could point to its downtown as evidence of its civic identity and self-confidence. Throughout Toronto, then, downtowns are sites where the investment of capital produces both money value and sentimental value that exceed the boundaries of downtown. The benefits of downtown investment accrue beyond its borders and beyond purely cash measure.

There were both theatrical and urban motives for building the SLC and the Ford Centre. For the SLC the major impetus came from a then small and financially precarious profession of local theatre practitioners, and it is germane that the SLC was proposed and built during a liminal period in Toronto's professional theatre economy. For the Ford Centre the major impetus was as much urban as it was cultural; it was conceived as part of North York's checklist of commercial and artistic developments that hoped to inscribe an uninspiring stretch of Yonge Street with the economic and symbolic resonances of a downtown. In the cases of both civic theatres, however, theatrical and urban motives proved amenable to each other.

The St. Lawrence Centre for the Arts

The SLC was adopted as the City of Toronto's official centennial project, and was conceived on a much larger scale than what was finally built. The complex was originally planned as a community centre that would not only incorporate larger auditoria than were actually constructed, but also meeting spaces for community groups, space for "town hall" gatherings, and extensive facilities for technical theatre production. Other theatre complexes built with centennial money and styled in the poured concrete vernacular of Brutalist architecture include the Manitoba Theatre Centre in Winnipeg (1969) and the National Arts Centre in Ottawa (1970).[8] The SLC was bound up in centralized national macro-economic planning, since centennial projects were perhaps the most organized and concentrated extension of the welfare state through physical form that Canada has seen.

It is important to emphasize that the welfare state should not be seen as anti-thetical to capitalism, but, rather, as the means through which public and private capital investment is coordinated at the local level. Michael Piore and Charles Sabel chart the relationship between increasing levels of welfare state provision and rapid economic growth among industrialized countries during the 1960s and 1970s, and their data show that Canada was no different in this regard (11–13). As an element of welfare state provision, the SLC was part of the national state's desire to fuel economic growth through a country-wide building program. But the SLC also illustrates how the sentimental overtures of centennial projects locally resonated: centennial projects linked national patriotism to local place patriotism. A civic theatre bequeathed by the nation accomplishes two things in the national development of localist sentiment. First, the SLC implies that cultural institution-building plays an important role in celebrating the nation. Second, fulfilling that role is predicated on these institutions being granted in the name of the local community, binding national celebration to civic boosterism.

Plans for the SLC, however, were greeted with enormous political and public skepticism. Johnston notes:

> As debates raged and cost estimates rose … the scope of the enterprise was steadily whittled down to overcome vehement political opposition at City Hall. In fact, the Centre had become a political football: it was a major issue in two successive mayoralty campaigns, was subjected to innumerable revisions, and was cancelled entirely at least twice. By 1967, with no agreement in sight, the St. Lawrence Centre had become (to many Torontonians) a symbol of the city's short-sighted stinginess in cultural matters, especially when compared to Montreal's glorious Expo. (12)

Debate over the SLC frequently split along lines that had become well-defined through public responses to the Massey Commission Report in 1951: a high-minded call for state patronage and cultural progress, contrasted with a denunciation of perceived social elites. [9] In fact, it was Toronto's artistic elite, led by Toronto Arts Foundation director Mavor Moore, that persuaded the City to push through the SLC project later in 1967; by that point many members of city council were embarrassed at the possibility of Toronto's civic undertaking being left out of the centennial building boom, and Moore had managed to recruit some private funding for the project. The final result, though, was significantly watered down, and, at a cost of $5.2 million was "far less than other centennial projects of comparable stature" (Johnson 502). The meeting space for community groups was eliminated entirely, along with the technical facilities. The only remnants of the original plan were two multipurpose auditoria, both of which, when opened in 1970, turned out to be concrete boxes whose poor sightlines and dismal acoustics barely acknowledged that performance was their intended use.

Toronto's theatre professionals, however, had won a victory by persuading a reluctant city that cultural institution-building was worthy of national and civic sponsorship. By being built downtown, the SLC provided visible evidence that the professional theatre industry in Toronto was at "the heart of the city," and made the arts a significant concern of the municipal state in Toronto for the first time (the SLC's civic alliance with that state also unwittingly symbolized a cultural coziness against which new small companies would later define themselves). This embodiment of theatrical and municipal confidence was particularly important considering the precarious economic condition of much of the professional and semi-professional—and by "professional" and "semi-professional" I mean waged or part-waged—theatre in Toronto in the mid to late 1960s. Toronto's professional and semi-professional theatre industry through most of the 1960s could be divided into three broad groups: the commercial sector, dominated by Broadway and West End touring shows at the Royal Alexandra Theatre and the O'Keefe Centre; the "serious drama" stock companies, the most prominent of which were the Crest Theatre, Red Barn Theatre, and the Canadian Players; and, finally, a tiny and economically (if not artistically) marginal small theatre sector that mostly consisted of one company, the leftist Toronto Workshop Productions. Because of its emphasis on touring shows, the commercial sector employed very few local theatre practitioners, and the size of the small theatre sector at this time was simply too modest to provide much work.

This left the stock companies to claim the mantle of "Toronto theatre," if for no other reason than they provided local practitioners with the most employment and best embodied an Arnoldian ideal of theatre practice that dominated Toronto's aspirant high culture at the time: the presentation and celebration of the theatrical touchstones of Western cultural development. But the case of the Crest Theatre illustrates how this sector was faltering in the mid-1960s. The Crest was the leading stock company in Toronto during the 1950s and for much of the 1960s, mandated to "provide repertory theatre in Toronto comparable with the best of British repertory companies" (Whittaker 119). The Crest's mandate, then, was both high cultural in its aims and derivative in its repertoire, and though it produced more plays than any other local company in the 1950s and 1960s, its work was increasingly seen as dramaturgically stale and unimaginatively staged. Nathan Cohen, the influential *Toronto Star* newspaper theatre critic, waged a lengthy campaign against what he believed to be the Crest's smug mediocrity; Cohen saw the work of George Luscombe at Toronto Workshop Productions, with its roots in agit-prop and Joan Littlewood's Theatre Workshop, as charting a much more promising path for theatre in Toronto. Even the Canada Council, the national foundation that had been established by Louis St. Laurent's Liberal government in 1957 to fund the type of high culture that the Crest represented, called the Crest's work "indifferent" and withdrew its subsidy in 1964 (Whittaker 120). The company lurched along for two more seasons, merged with the Canadian Players in 1966, and finally collapsed, debt-ridden, before the amalgamated company produced a single show. Apart from a few shows presented by Theatre Toronto, a company formed out of the ashes of Canadian Crest Players, the stock sector in Toronto was exhausted by 1966. The stock companies' artists, however, were still strong local advocates for professional theatre, and the two directors of the Toronto Arts Foundation, Mavor Moore and Leon Major, were Crest veterans. The

SLC provided an opportunity to carry on the mantle of high culture in Toronto, but under the new rubric of a civic theatre company.

However grudging the final result was politically and physically, the SLC provided two badly needed performance spaces downtown and a home for a new theatre company that would take up the gauntlet of "mainstream" drama from the stock companies. The theatrical motives behind the SLC also engendered a shift in the relationship between high culture, the national state, and the municipal state in Toronto: the SLC allied one important stream of Toronto's professional theatre industry much closer with the municipal state than it had been previously. This closeness can be measured in two ways. First, the changes to the built form of the SLC through the planning process indicate that, in the creation of Toronto's civic centre, theatre space was privileged over space for community groups. The most likely explanation for this is that the theatre spaces were not anticipated by the municipal government as being politically dissonant, whereas the community-use space could easily be just that. Toronto's urban reform movement was gaining ground by organizing activist neighbourhood groups to oppose the actions of the municipal government at the time the SLC was being planned, and it is not surprising that, given the political anger directed at city politicians, they would be reluctant to extend civic sponsorship to building space that could be used to organize against them. The theatre spaces, on the other hand, posed no such threat, and this is best illustrated by the fact that the smaller auditorium was named the "Town Hall." Its name demonstrated that theatre space was conceived as civically affirmative space.

Second, the SLC signalled a shift in the way that different state apparati in Canada structured their patronage of high culture. If the Canada Council grew impatient with the artistic work of the Crest, the Council still had an institutional desire to fill Toronto's "regional theatre" quota (the Canada Council provides guaranteed funding to larger companies that it considers to have an appeal beyond their immediate locality). Toronto lacked a regional theatre until the Toronto Arts Foundation formed its company, and the creation of a civic company backed financially by the city lent the project an institutional legitimacy that its artistic predecessors lacked. Moreover, Mavor Moore resigned after his nationalist programming proved financially disastrous in the first season, and his replacement, Leon Major, sharply reduced the "Canadian content" onstage. The abandonment of a nationalist programming philosophy symbolically weakened the artistic connection between the civic theatre and the nation state. Inching toward the civic did not necessarily mean that theatre was wholly embraced by the municipal state—the city government, responsible for the Foundation's deficits, divested itself of the production company and retained control over the SLC as a physical plant—but even in its ambivalence toward the civic theatre project, the implications of the theatrical and urban form of the civic theatre company increasingly registered within in a municipal context. [10]

Insofar as that municipal context meant a changing downtown, the built form of the SLC straddled the national and the local, but was more important in stressing the importance of the civic at a time when downtown Toronto was starting to shed its

Fordist features. The part of downtown immediately adjacent to the SLC illustrates this transformation best. The SLC is located at the southeastern corner of Front Street and Scott Street on the eastern border of Toronto's financial district, an area stretching from Front Street north to Queen Street, and from Simcoe Street east to Scott Street. The SLC was built at the same time as a major development boom in the district, when, according to geographer Gunter Gad, a growing property development industry financed intensive skyscraper-building in the city core on a scale previously unknown. [11] Extrapolating Metropolitan Toronto employment data, Gad argues that it is only in the 1960s that the downtown business core actually became a financial district:

> In 1951 the present financial district was still the general office district of the metropolitan area. Soon afterwards, however, various offices began to relocate, including several life insurance company head offices, the offices of architects, consulting engineers, advertising agencies, publishers, the head and sales offices of manufacturing companies, and others. Only at this stage did the label "financial district" become justi-fied. Office employment figures for 1970 and 1989 show a continuing trend toward specialization. Jobs in the finance, insurance, and real estate group of industries and in business services have more than doubled in the financial district and have significantly increased their shares of employment. (205)

Gad claims, "This small part of Toronto is undoubtedly the focal point of the Canadian financial system," and notes that, of the 100 largest financial institutions listed by the *Financial Post* in 1989, thirty-nine had their head or executive offices in the financial district (and eleven more had their head offices somewhere in Toronto). These financial institutions include "the majority of Canada's chartered banks, foreign banks, and trust companies" (205). The dominance of financial services and real estate development contrasts with the subordinance of manufacturing companies: of the thirty-nine head offices in the financial district in 1989, only three were in manufacturing-based industries, and two have since left (206).

The urban counterpoint to the finance district's development is the stretch of small, upmarket retail shops along Front Street that begins at Scott Street and ends, two blocks east, at the St. Lawrence Market. This part of Front Street, which developed in the 1970s, can be seen as the local compensation for the increasingly transnational development next door. The SLC, in terms of its built form and the audiences it attracts, helped smooth the neighbourhood's transition from one where mercantile wholesalers supplied regional businesses to one where retailing was geared to upscale shoppers and sidewalk *flâneurs*. The SLC is wedged into a lot at the corner of Front Street and Scott Street. Architecture critic Patricia McHugh comments that the complex is in the style of "[a]rchitectural Brutalism, with musty-coloured, right-out-of-the-mold concrete slabs weightily pronouncing a message of 1960s avant-garde vigour" (33). Its form is contextually contradictory: neighbouring buildings are rehabilitated Renaissance Revival commercial buildings constructed in the 1870s. The

SLC's neighbours emphasize mercantile exchange through large display windows, strong vertical lines, and fine decorative embellishment. They are the confident physical articulation of late nineteenth century petty-bourgeois capitalism in Toronto. The concrete exterior of the SLC, however, fits within the architectural vernacular of the post-Second World War Canadian welfare state. But unlike other examples of Brutalism in Toronto—such as the isolated and forbidding John Robarts Library at the University of Toronto—the SLC is not indifferent to its surroundings. The site demolished to allow the SLC was small, and so the Centre squeezes up against its neighbours and opens directly on to Front Street. The SLC only offers a minimal amount of parking in a small, privately-operated lot behind the building, and the public entrance to the Centre is from the sidewalk on Front Street. Though constructed of massive materials, the SLC eschews the usual modernist disdain for the streetscape and maintains both a contrapuntal and complementary relationship to its surroundings.

The SLC and Front Street articulate the change from Fordist to flexible accumulation capitalism through built form. If much of the downtown core was devoted to offices during the 1950s and 1960s, Front Street provided the wholesale goods that the nearby offices distributed or required. Front Street started to decline as a wholesaling street when the offices next door started to disappear, and so the public sector moved in to generate use value through a new kind of petty-bourgeois consumption (the SLC has always housed theatre companies that attract affluent audiences—ticket prices for its current tenant, Canadian Stage Company, are mostly in the $50 range at the time of writing). Five addresses were demolished to make way for construction. These housed a grocery wholesaler, a tea and coffee merchant, a textile supplier, an asbestos installer, and a business furniture manufacturer. None of these business categories is represented in the Central Business District anymore, suggesting that the SLC was constructed as many of these types of companies vacated the financial core.

The SLC was, and remains, a city-owned theatre complex housing a not-for-profit theatre company, but it smoothed the transition from a Fordist to post-Fordist urban economy by training for a new type of commodity consumption. The Centre helped establish the pattern of affluent, individual consumption that transformed Front Street into a strip of artisanal, boutique, and recreational destination shopping, thereby ensuring the presence of *flâneurs* in the central business district as it evolved into a truly national, and then international financial district. The *flâneur* represents a highly desirable type of affluent social activity in the maintenance of vibrant city districts, since the *flâneur* both consumes and spectates, something akin to what a theatregoer does.

The SLC also responded to the neighbourhood's changing use through modifications to its own built form. The City of Toronto closed the SLC in 1981 for major renovations and reopened it two years later after a $5.8 million refurbishment. The Centre had suffered from the familiar problems of multipurpose auditoria built in the 1960s: a spartan, concrete lobby and auditorium, a marked architectural division between audience and stage in the main theatre, and poor acoustics and sightlines. But the renovations reveal the SLC's increasing anticipation of an urban economy which links local and transnational consumption. The façade of the building was opened up somewhat to Front Street, with display windows punched through the concrete that could feature promotional materials for the resident theatre company, and which better incorporated the SLC into the commercial landscape of the street (a renovation in 1999 would dispense with opaque exterior walls altogether in favour of a solid glass façade, further dismantling barriers between the Centre and its neighbourhood). [12] The renovated lobby, with its cream-coloured walls, wood trim, brass rails, and potted plants, now resembles the interior of an early-1980s Sheraton Hotel. The SLC's lobby suggests that renovations were undertaken for an urban subject who is comfortable with both the locality of Front Street and the transience of the transnational hotel chain. Furthermore, the shops on Front Street are beginning to mix the local with the transnational: Starbucks and Blockbuster Video have recently opened outlets amidst Front Street's boutiques and outdoor equipment suppliers. The SLC and Front Street are now part of a financial and service-sector economy that attempts to link local and transnational political and cultural economies seamlessly.

This link, however, is not as easy as Front Street's affluent streetscape implies, and the SLC's marquee can sometimes draw these tensions sharply into relief: when the Canadian Stage Company produced Stephen Sondheim's *Passion* in 1997 on the main stage, the Jane Mallet Theatre (which the Town Hall was renamed in 1985) hosted a public forum on the effects of neo-liberal economics entitled "Workers' Rights: How Low Can Standards Go?" The affluent civic theatre, which produces an increasingly transnational repertoire, coexists with a political forum trying to deal with the economic effects of transnationalism, in whose name neo-liberal governments in Canada have dismantled protections that were at the heart of the post-War Canadian welfare state. The civic theatre building implies that it is a space in which tensions between these two events can be accommodated. But the civic reconciliation it attempts effaces the theatre company's own participation in a transnational theatre economy through which Sondheim circulates, and takes place against the urban backdrop of a solid wall of banking towers, whose occupants have been some of the most powerful advocates for transnationalism. The civic theatre offers a sentimental accord that the transnational economy does not, but its accommodation is at worst naive, and at best a daunting challenge.

The Ford Centre for the Performing Arts

The Ford Centre, in contrast, has no anxieties about transnationalism. It articulates a very different conception of economic investment, urban form, and theatre practice: if the St. Lawrence Centre nervously attempts to bridge the Fordist and post-Fordist city, the Ford Centre culturally embraces an urban capitalism based on international flexible accumulation. The Ford Centre was funded solely by the City of North York primarily for the profit of a transnational theatrical production company— LivEntertainment Corporation—and was the cultural component of a massive downtown creation (and not redevelopment, or renewal) scheme for North York. As with the SLC, imperatives of urban and cultural development intersected in the construction of the Ford Centre, but the Ford Centre is a transnational complex in both motivation and result.

Of the suburbs within the former Metropolitan Toronto, North York emerged as the second city in the metropolitan federation, both in terms of population (563,000) and economic activity (see Filion; Matthew). In 1981 the city began to plan the creation of a downtown on Yonge Street between Sheppard and Finch Avenues in an attempt to transform the geographic centre of the city into its economic and symbolic heart. Urban analyst Peter Gorrie describes the neighbourhood before its development as downtown North York:

> The area remained little more than a local shopping street despite an influx of hundreds of thousands of people .... The newcomers did not consider it an attraction, or the centre of their community. Most worked elsewhere and travelled to downtown Toronto or the growing number of regional malls for shopping and entertainment. (70)

A massive development project knitted together new office construction, a subway station, city hall, the central public library, the board of education offices, an aquatics centre, skating rink, shopping mall, art gallery, and performing arts centre around a central square on Yonge Street.

This frenzy of building, begun in 1984 and completed in 1993, has been called a "high-speed attempt to re-establish the basic physique of the city" (Gorrie 70). This is an intriguing comment because the city cannot "re-establish" an urban form that it never assumed in the first place, so downtown North York's attempt to install an older urban pattern should be seen as civically recuperative. Furthermore, by stating that there is a "basic physique of the city," Gorrie denotes the way in which North York invoked a supposedly agreed-upon urban ideal, for which the old City of Toronto served as model. By centralizing a checklist of civic, commercial, and cultural projects, North York hoped to reinscribe spontaneously an urban area with the economic and sentimental resonances of downtown that the older city core privileges.

The Ford Centre illustrates a change in the relationship between the state and capital between the late 1960s and the late 1980s. By the time the Ford Centre was built, local growth had largely ceased to be a concern of national economic development. Growth had become, instead, an issue largely of municipal development. There are several reasons for this. The burgeoning wealth of the cities that comprised Metropolitan Toronto made sole funding of large-scale economic development increasingly possible during the 1980s. Moreover, if the Canadian welfare state once sought to provide social benefits on a universal basis, the election of a Conservative federal government in 1984 signalled the end of universalism as a state ideal and severed the link between local growth and national economic planning. The 1989 Free Trade Agreement between Canada and the United States, and the 1992 North American Free Trade Agreement that included Mexico, made such planning nearly impossible. Finally, Saskia Sassen charts how global migrations of capital, commodities, and people are increasingly predicated on urban, not national, destinations. In the hope of capturing capital investment (and individual capitalists), Canadian cities now have little choice but to provide elaborate infrastructure out of local funds, infrastructure that once would have been provided mostly by provincial or federal governments.

North York did not simply finance the Ford Centre through the municipal tax base, as Canadian cities normally funded infrastructure projects during the Fordist period. [13] Instead, North York financed the Ford Centre by speculating on Toronto's inflated property market. When the Conservative Ontario government of Bill Davis decided to build SkyDome, a sports stadium, in the old downtown on Front Street West, Mel Lastman, then Conservative mayor of North York (and current mayor of the amalgamated Toronto), extracted a parcel of land next to North York city hall as his political price for not building SkyDome in North York. The City of North York subsequently "flipped" the building density rights on the land by selling them back to the Province at rising market rates, hoping to generate the capital needed to build the Ford Centre. North York actively inflated Toronto's speculative urban economy, something local governments would have been very reluctant to do in the past. But in a political climate that was becoming very sensitive about expenditure from the property tax base, funding what ultimately became a $48 million arts project through the commercial property market usefully mystified the sponsorship of cultural institution-building. It appeared as though the complex were built with "free money" (something Mel Lastman claimed), even though North York's speculative intervention in Toronto's property market only contributed to the inflationary boom of the mid-1980s, a boom which would eventually lead to a devastating collapse in the local property market in the early 1990s. The Ford Centre's form of sponsorship also made the terms on which the local population could claim symbolic ownership of the civic theatre more problematic. Though North York legally owned the Ford Centre, the people of North York played no direct role in its financial sponsorship, and its elaborate design specifications were largely dictated by Livent. The Ford Centre tied the sponsorship of civic institutions directly to commercial property speculation by private developers and by the City of North York itself, and it served as a medium through which North York paid an indirect subsidy to a transnational, for-profit theatre production company. This suggests that civic theatre-building is preferable, and perhaps only permissible, when the municipal state either enters the market economy directly as a speculator (with all the risks inherent in that intervention) or heavily subsidizes the costs of a for-profit company.

Like the SLC, the Ford Centre is owned by the city. Unlike the SLC, the Ford Centre was financed entirely by the city, which then contracted operation of the Centre to Livent, a transnational theatre production company that subsequently operated Ford Centres in Vancouver, New York, and, Chicago. The North York Ford Centre contains two theatres, a recital hall, and the Art Gallery of North York. The large theatre space within the complex was named after a major pharmaceutical manufacturer and the recital hall was named after the dead patriarch of one of world's largest grocery store empires.

Livent and North York developed the Ford Centre together (using city money), but, as a for-profit enterprise, Livent sat outside the institutional network of national, provincial, and municipal arts agencies that the SLC's tenants always have. This institutional network, in which many Toronto not-for-profit theatres reside, includes: the federal Ministry of National Heritage; the provincial Ministry of Culture, Tourism, and Recreation; and, most importantly, funding bodies like the Canada Council, the Ontario Arts Council, and the Toronto Arts Council.[14] Different state apparati are more interested in the Ford Centre as a lure for American tourists: a television advertisement about Toronto's "arts scene" aired in Chicago in 1997 featured the Ford Centre prominently; notably, none of Toronto's not-for-profit theatre companies was represented, in spite of the fact that they account for a large part of the city's theatre scene. Whereas the SLC is largely adjunct to urban capital formation—it buttresses investment in an urban area but generates no surplus value itself—the Ford Centre is designed to create surplus value within itself, and reveals the city's role in supporting transnational capital flows. The civic theatre may be a sign of urban affluence, but it is designed to be governed by a private corporation that generates surplus value through theatrical commodities that circulate internationally.

The Ford Centre's building is a multi-level structure that occupies the southern edge of North York's downtown core, set far back from Yonge Street and surrounded by a large parking lot. If one looks at the Ford Centre from Yonge Street, the building serves as a giant billboard, with much of its exterior surface intended to be devoted to large-scale advertising of the show that is in performance. There is a small electronic marquee over the front entrance that flashes messages about the show in performance, but it is illegible from the street. The marquee is a nostalgic architectural reference, albeit a high-tech one, but it has no urban function because it does not acknowledge the streetscape. Viewing the Ford Centre from Yonge Street, the dominant image is one of corporate logos surrounded by automobiles: when *Ragtime* played at the Ford Centre there was an eerie continuity between the *Ragtime* billboards (with their unintentionally acontextual image of the Statue of Liberty's torch furled in the stars and stripes), the Ford logo over the entrance, and the cars surrounding the complex. From the street, the only fragmentary object is the theatre building itself. Its skin punctuated by corporate logos, the Ford Centre's self-advertisement fractures a holistic view of the theatre building. It denies the civic theatre's role in contributing to the traditional conception of downtown that North York wants to invoke: that is, as an urban space of relational but relatively autonomous urban forms. Here urban forms exist only insofar as they refer to the transnational theatre commodity.

In spite of North York's attempt to mimic an older ideal of downtown, it still privileges trips into its core by car. As Filion demonstrates, ample parking and easy road access mean that North York is particularly welcoming to trips by car, and an avenue directly to the Ford Centre's entrance encourages cars to drive to the door to deposit passengers (1647). The Ford Centre not only fails to bring people onto the sidewalk, it makes them less likely to become *flâneurs* by providing even more parking space in downtown North York, and by sitting back so deeply from the sidewalk.

The Ford Centre can be approached without a car, but the most agreeable way to gain access on foot, whether from the sidewalk or via public transit, means travelling through private commercial space. Insofar as it permits access by *flâneurs*, this access privatizes their consumption and spectating to a much greater degree than accessing the SLC does. Being a *flâneur* on Front Street involves negotiating both private and public spaces. The Front Street *flâneur* may gaze at and enter private shops, but does so from the public street. The presence of public street space is part of what makes being a *flâneur* pleasurable: one looks at displays, one is on display, and consumption is encouraged but not mandated. The public street has a social value above and beyond its role in assisting consumption. The best pedestrian access to the Ford Centre, in contrast, allows no recourse to public space. In order to get from North York Centre subway station to the Ford Centre, one must travel through the North York City Centre. Though its name implies public space, the North York City Centre is a privately owned and operated shopping mall. This mall provides the easiest access to most municipal buildings in North York, including the city hall and the main public library, whose entrances open into the mall as though they were any other retail store.

The North York City Centre encourages citizens to engage civic space and private commercial space as though they were transposable, and this transposability extends transnationally. [15] Whether shopping or going to the theatre, one moves through a retail centre that is dominated by "the same chain stores and franchises found in any suburban mall" (Gorrie 73). Even when reaching the Ford Centre, one enters a lobby dominated by an atrium that evokes the one lighting the City Centre and two other well-known Toronto sites that anticipate transnational exchange: the atrium of the Eaton Centre shopping mall and the atrium of Terminal Three at Pearson International Airport. [16] Downtown North York suggests that commercial and cultural consumption are the same thing, and when the products consumed are transnational commodities that could be found in Chicago, New York, or Vancouver, the civic becomes placeless. Downtown North York and the Ford Centre betray a paradoxical post-Fordist desire: to create a unique ontological space in an historical moment of increasing time-space compression using transnational urban and cultural tools. [17] Downtown North York and the Ford Centre finally, and ironically, achieve the goal that Herbert Whittaker identified for Canadian theatre in the 1960s. "We want to have a culture unmistakably our own," Whittaker commented. "We want to be different, the same as everybody else" (qtd. in Harvie and Knowles 225).

Conclusion

If the civic theatre in Toronto initially sustained the link between cultural institution-building and urban development first made by the nation, it now anxiously attempts to insert theatres into a transnational urban political economy. The SLC and the Ford Centre suggest two different ways in which this interjection is possible. The SLC positions itself as a culturally affirmative broker, easing the urban transition from a national to a transnational economy and nervously reassuring Torontonians that a civic reconciliation between theatre and capital is still possible under trans-nationalism. The Ford Centre, in contrast, recognizes that post-Fordism has made the relationship between urban and cultural development reliant on a flow of money that circulates throughout the world. Attracting this capital may provide a useful rationale for building new civic theatres at a time when there is little political appetite for state enterprise, but it also potentially creates new relationships of dependence: as the building's present vacancy demonstrates, when the civic theatre's transnational operator disappears, the theatre's cultural and urban appeal fail as well. Post-Fordism has placed cities and cultural institutions in the shadow of transnational capital, and civic theatres vividly illustrate different ways of negotiating this capital's towering presence or its sudden absence.

(2001)

Notes

1 Factory Theatre Lab was founded in May 1970 with a mandate to produce only Canadian plays.

2 These struggles include the successful fight to stop the Crosstown and Spadina expressways, which was finally achieved in 1971; the renovation, rather than demolition, of Trefann Court, a working class neighbourhood in the east end of downtown; the development of infill housing in Baldwin Village near the intersec-tion of Dundas Street and Spadina Avenue; the imposition of strict frontage requirements on new commercial office towers in the financial district; and the building of the St. Lawrence neighbourhood, a popular mixed-use and mixed-scale neighbourhood built on reclaimed railway lands in the southeast end of downtown.

3 The cities that comprised Metropolitan Toronto and which were amalgamated into a unified Toronto were: the former City of Toronto, North York, Scarborough, Etobicoke, York, and East York.

4 In a sign of how much control Livent held over the facility, Ford purchased the right to name the facility from Livent and not from the municipal owners; however, this meant that when Livent went bankrupt Toronto was under no contractual obligation to retain the Ford Centre name.

5 By framing this inquiry in the language of "Fordism" and "post-Fordism" I draw on a conceptual framework established by certain Marxist theorists of economic, urban, labour, and artistic transformation: the Regulation School of French econo-mists, the urban geography of David Harvey, the labour sociology of Harry Braverman, and the cultural criticism of Fredric Jameson (see Boyer; Braverman; Harvey; Jameson). Fordism, as its name implies, arrived when the assembly line became the dominant method of organizing a production process for the purposes

of mass producing standardized commodities. Fordism denotes a system of economic production organized on the basis of routinized, manufacturing labour, where international trade is largely between Western nation states. This period stretched, in most Western political economies, from the 1920s to the late 1960s. Post-Fordism, or, to use David Harvey's more precise term, "flexible accumulation," occurs when international capital floats freely across national borders, structuring production, labour, and trade according to the needs of transnational financial speculation. This shift is generally marked historically by the oil shocks and abandonment of the Bretton Woods system of international financial governance in the early 1970s, after which the exchange rates for most tradable currencies floated freely. There is an extensive literature on, and a fierce debate about the merits of, this model as a representation of historical transformations in Western political economies (for even the barest outline of this debate, see Amin; Boyer; Drache and Gertler; Gibson-Graham; Harvey; Lash and Urry; Lipietz). A comprehensive discussion of this literature would require a book in itself, so I can only say that I agree with the paradigm as a broad model of historical transition, with a few clarifications. First, transition is a fragmentary, incomplete, and awkward process. That it is possible to identify the material effects of economic trends does not mean that one system of production simply supplants the other. Automobile production, on which Fordism is modelled, remains a significant part of most Western economies, but the method of work organization that automobile manufacturing usually employs is in steady decline throughout the Western world, and manufacturing in general employs a smaller proportion of these economies' workforces. Second, "post-Fordism" is sometimes related to, but not reducible to, "postmodernism." I am not concerned with whether or not theatre practice has become postmodern as a result of changes in Toronto's urban political economy (perhaps some has and some has not, and the utility of this finding is unclear). Insofar as it has any logic in the context of Canadian theatre studies, postmodernism has usually denoted a complete submission to an aesthetic discourse, and this is exactly the type of submission I want to resist, or, at least, complicate. To ask how theatre practice negotiates a transition to post-Fordism in Toronto's political economy does not mean that Toronto's theatre production then becomes aesthetically postmodern; if anything, much of Toronto's theatre work has been as likely to insist on its liberal humanism and cultural holism as its fragmentation.

6   I do not want to elide the "rebellious" sense of art that Marcuse argues coexists with an affirmative sense, but this sense is more appropriately used in the context of other Toronto theatre companies like Toronto Workshop Productions.

7   It is also notable that the New York and Chicago developments included Ford Centres (as did an additional development in Vancouver).

8   "Brutalism" is the accepted term for the architectural style, most popular in the 1960s and 1970s, where poured concrete exterior walls are left largely in the form that they possess when unmolded. The style emphasizes mass and angularity, and can sometimes appear forbidding and impenetrable from street level.

⁹ For a perceptive analysis of the historical emergence of this discourse in a Canadian context, see Litt. The Massey Commission is the popular name used for the Royal Commission on National Development in the Arts, Letters and Sciences, which was chaired by Vincent Massey. The Royal Commission's Report, issued in 1951, prompted the creation in 1957 of the Canada Council, an arm's-length body established to extend national state sponsorship of the arts and scholarship. Though for many the Commission's recommendations represented a welcome call for increased investment in cultural production, its cultural model had a distinctly paternalist air that others resented.

¹⁰ The City of Toronto created a stand-alone, not-for-profit theatre company called Toronto Arts Productions, to which it then provided an annual subsidy. Toronto Arts Productions was renamed CentreStage in 1983, and CentreStage merged with Toronto Free Theatre to form Canadian Stage Company in 1988. Canadian Stage Company now occupies the SLC's main theatre space and Toronto Free Theatre's former premises on Berkeley Street.

¹¹ Gad suggests that the best architectural marker of Toronto's changing downtown core is the Toronto Dominion Centre, the Mies van de Rohe-designed skyscraper whose first tower opened in 1967.

¹² It is interesting to note that the Hummingbird Centre, the 3223 seat auditorium opened in 1960 as the O'Keefe Centre (O'Keefe Brewery originally built and owned the space) is just west of the Front Street commercial strip at Front and Yonge Streets, but has never seemed to take part in the changes in Front Street. Perhaps this is because its architectural design, a massive block in the International Expressionist style, ensures a high modernist aloofness that is fundamentally irreconcilable with the surrounding area. The building itself, though, has undergone some interesting changes over the years, which suggest that it too has negotiated the transformation from Fordism to post-Fordism. Early in the Centre's life O'Keefe turned the building over to Metropolitan Toronto. O'Keefe Brewery no longer exists as an independent company, having been taken over by Molson in the mid-1980s (this is not insignificant economically, since breweries are big business in Canada, and Molson's purchase of O'Keefe ensured that over ninety percent of the national beer market was in the hands of Molson and Labatt—a move to duopoly capitalism, at least). The name "O'Keefe" became increasingly anachronistic. The metropolitan government renamed the building the Hummingbird Centre in 1994, after a payment of $5 million from the software development company. Perhaps the economic giants of an age can be traced through their inscription on cultural institutions.

¹³ Unlike American cities, Canadian cities are usually prevented by their provinces from issuing bonds to finance infrastructure projects.

¹⁴ Although private sponsorship of the arts is increasingly common in Canada, the amount of this support that is directed through a network of private foundations remains quite small.

[15] North York City Centre also ensures that citizens realize that they are on private property. When I first researched downtown North York, I took a series of photographs inside the City Centre. I was stopped by a security guard, who informed me that the City Centre was private, not public, property, and that if I wished to take pictures I had to request permission from the Centre's owners, a property development and management company.

[16] It is no accident that the architect of the Ford Centre is Eberhard Zeidler, who also designed the Eaton Centre.

[17] On time-space compression as a feature of capitalism, see Harvey.

Works Cited

Amin, Ash, ed. *Post-Fordism: A Reader*. Oxford: Blackwell, 1994.

Boyer, Robert. *The Regulation School: A Critical Introduction*. New York: Columbia UP, 1990.

Carlson, Marvin. *Places of Performance: The Semiotics of Theatre Architecture*. Ithaca: Cornell UP, 1989.

Caulfield, Jon. *City Form and Everyday Life: Toronto's Gentrification and Critical Social Practice*. Toronto: U of Toronto P, 1996.

Braverman, Harry. *Labor and Monopoly Capital: The Degradation of Work in the Twentieth Century*. New York: Monthly Review P, 1974.

Diamond, Greig and Geoff Pevere. *Mondo Canuck: A Canadian Pop Cultural Odyssey*. Toronto: Prentice-Hall, 1996.

Drache, Daniel and Meric S. Gertler, eds. *The New Era of Global Competition: State Policy and Market Power*. Montreal: McGill-Queen's UP, 1991.

Filion, P. "Metropolitan Planning Objectives and Implementation Constraints: Planning in a Post-Fordist and Postmodern Age." *Environment and Planning A* 28 (1996): 1637–60.

Fortier, André and D. Paul Schafer. *Review of Federal Policies for the Arts in Canada (1944–1988)*. Ottawa: Canadian Conference of the Arts, 1989.

Fraser, Graham. *Fighting Back: Urban Renewal in Trefann Court*. Toronto: Hakkert, 1972.

Gad, Gunter. "Toronto's Financial District." *The Canadian Geographer* 35, no. 2 (1991): 203–07.

Gibson-Graham, J.K. *The End of Capitalism (As We Knew It): A Feminist Critique of Political Economy.* Oxford: Blackwell, 1996.

Gorrie, Peter. "North York's Instant Downtown." *Canadian Geographic* 1991, 66–73.

Harvey, David. *The Condition of Postmodernity.* Oxford: Blackwell, 1989.

Harvie, Jennifer, and Richard Paul Knowles. "Herbert Whittaker, Reporting from the Front: *The* Montreal *Gazette,* 1937–49, and *The Globe and Mail,* 1949–1975." *Establishing Our Boundaries: English-Canadian Theatre Criticism.* Ed. Anton Wagner. Toronto: U of Toronto P, 1999.

Jameson, Fredric. *Postmodernism, Or the Cultural Logic of Late Capitalism.* Durham: Duke UP, 1991.

Johnson, Stephen. "St. Lawrence Centre for the Performing Arts." *The Oxford Companion to Canadian Theatre.* Ed. Eugene Benson and L.W. Conolly. Toronto: Oxford UP, 1989. 502.

Johnston, Dennis W. *Up the Mainstream: The Rise of Toronto's Alternative Theatres.* Toronto: U of Toronto P, 1991.

Kitto, H.D.F. "The Polis." *The City Reader.* Ed. Richard T. Legates and Frederic Stout. London: Routledge, 1996. 34–36.

Lash, Scott and John Urry. *Economies of Signs and Space.* London: Sage, 1994.

Lipietz, Alain. *Mirages and Miracles: The Crises of Global Fordism.* London: Verso, 1987.

Litt, Paul. *The Muses, the Masses, and the Massey Commission.* Toronto: U of Toronto P, 1992.

Logan, John, and Harvey Molotch. *Urban Fortunes: The Political Economy of Place.* Berkeley: U of California P, 1987.

Marcuse, Herbert. *The Aesthetic Dimension: Toward a Critique of Marxist Aesthetics.* Boston: Beacon P, 1978.

Matthew, Malcolm R. "The Suburbanization of Toronto Offices." *The Canadian Geographer* 37.4 (1993): 293–306.

McHugh, Patricia. *Toronto Architecture: A City Guide.* 2nd ed. Toronto: McClelland and Stewart, 1989.

Piore, Michael J., and Charles F. Sabel. *The Second Industrial Divide: Possibilities for Prosperity.* New York: Basic Books, 1984.

Pirenne, Henri. *Medieval Cities: Their Origins and the Revival of Trade.* Princeton: Princeton UP, 1925.

Sassen, Saskia. *Cities in a World Economy.* 2nd ed. Thousand Oaks, CA: Pine Forge P, 2000.

Sewell, John. *The Shape of the City: Toronto Struggles with Modern Planning.* Toronto: U of Toronto P, 1993.

———. *Up Against City Hall.* Toronto: J. Lewis and Samuel, 1972.

Stein, David Lewis. *Toronto For Sale: The Destruction of a City.* Toronto: New P, 1971.

Whittaker, Herbert. "The Crest Theatre." *The Oxford Companion to Canadian Theatre.* Toronto: Oxford UP, 1989. 119.

Wolf, Stacy. "Civilizing and Selling Spectators: Audiences at the Madison Civic Center." 39.2 (1997): 7–23.

"No, the Centre Should be Invisible": Radical Revisioning of Chekhov in Floyd Favel Starr's *House of Sonya*

by Rob Appleford

In his survey entry on "American Indian theater," C.W.E. Bigsby offers an insightful comment on the advantages of live performance over cinematic representation for Native peoples:

> Not merely does the public stage appear to operate as the political platform which, iconographically, it resembles, but it offers a model of group strength, of imaginative purpose and of a confident identity ... The vertiginous excitements of theatre ... the sense of genuine risk, is liable to be closer to the experience of a threatened group than is the aesthetic closure of the film .... (365)

While I readily take issue with his rejection of film as a potent medium for Aboriginal representation, I just as readily agree with Bigsby that the stage offers a unique opportunity for Aboriginal peoples to model both political affirmation and "genuine risk" for immediate public consumption. What I find intriguing when examining Aboriginal theatre is the complex relationship between the traditional and the contemporary in this modelling of Aboriginal identity on stage. At one end of the spectrum, "traditional" Aboriginal performance, involving ritual, orality, local histories, and cultural/spiritual information, has been understood by scholars and critics as either replicating or renewing traditions of performance specific to indigenous regions and cultures. [1] At the other end, "contemporary" Aboriginal performance, utilizing Western theatrical techniques and exploring more overtly political themes, has been viewed in relation to global examples of performance-as-resistance by other "threatened groups" (see Wasserman). Both local/traditional and international/contemporary definitions of performance can serve to illuminate how Aboriginal theatre resists the dominant by pointing to local or international contexts for interpretative frames. Yet, these two frames—the local/traditional and the international/contemporary—are difficult to disentangle, and bifurcate clearly hybrid modes of Aboriginal performance. For myself, as a non-Aboriginal spectator, it remains a difficult task to frame such hybrid theatre so that both the local and international contexts are taken into account. This difficulty is made plain when one examines the 1997 play *House of Sonya*, an adaptation of Anton Chekhov's *Uncle Vanya* by Saskatchewan Cree playwright Floyd Favel Starr. His play forcefully demonstrates the need to view Aboriginal theatre not as being somehow divorced from Western tradition, but rather as being engaged in exploring what Favel Starr calls "the sources of the rivers of our cultures"("Artificial Tree" 83).

Aboriginal theatre in this country is frequently informed by traditional, and therefore localized, knowledges and aesthetics. And yet, to suggest that this theatre is not just as frequently shaped by cultural and material forces that can be loosely termed Canadian and/or Western caricatures its uniqueness and denies its connection to other traditions. Aboriginal performance, rather than experimenting with new ways of representing culture, risks being judged against largely normative and internalized ideas of what Aboriginal stories should be like, in terms of both form and content. When faced with the work of Aboriginal playwrights, many non-Aboriginal critics (including myself) seek to understand how this work fits into an evolving but nevertheless recognizable Canadian or Western theatrical tradition. One strategy that is frequently employed is to discuss how Western theatre is cited by Aboriginal playwrights. If these playwrights are understood to cite Western theatrical traditions, either covertly or overtly, it then becomes possible to analyze Aboriginal theatre in relation to the traditions cited and their aesthetic or political histories. The most obvious example of covert Western citation is the work of Cree playwright Tomson Highway. Many critics have recognized the clear debt Highway owes to Western theatre, most notably to Greek theatre and to the more direct antecedents, Michel Tremblay's *Les Belles Soeurs* and John Murrell's *Waiting for the Parade* (Knowles, *Theatre of Form* 62). Highway also cites the influence of Western musical forms, especially the sonata, on his writing. By identifying these antecedents, covertly signalled in Highway's work, critics can place him, at least provisionally, within a recognizable Canadian or Western theatrical tradition.

When seen as part of a tradition, in this case either a national or an international one, such playwrights can be discussed as either fulfilling or challenging the reputed aims of this tradition. Thus, the formal pedigree of Highway's work becomes vital when critics attempt to gauge the political effects of his theatre. Postcolonial theorists and Aboriginal activists have long stressed the importance of the local/traditional for indigenous peoples as an effective counter to the forces of globalization and assimilation (see Alfred). By challenging the local/traditional, its unique connection to environment and history, indigenous discourse is seen to resist incorporation into universalist humanist discourse. When examined in this light, Highway, with his more than passing nod to the Greeks, Tremblay, Murrell, and others, often invites the label of political conservative. Agreeing with Alan Filewod's analysis of Highway's "problematic" reception by non-Aboriginal audiences (see Filewod 21), Ric Knowles suggests that "perhaps it is the capacity of the [theatrical] form for the comfortable containment of potentially disruptive social concerns" that accounts for the success of Highway's play *The Rez Sisters* ("Look" 62).

Unlike Highway, many Aboriginal playwrights employ citation of Canadian/ Western form/content in order to critique non-Aboriginal notions of theatrical mimesis. These playwrights employ overt or direct citation of non-Aboriginal theatrical form/content frequently to capitalize upon the aesthetic dissonance between the citation and the narrative that contains it. For example, Delaware playwright Daniel David Moses places great emphasis upon overt theatrical citation as parodic subversion, in such plays as *The Indian Medicine Shows* and *Almighty Voice and His Wife*. Similarly, such overt and self-conscious citation invites political reading. In this case, more often than not, self-conscious citation is conflated with radical politics. By using non-Aboriginal theatrical form against itself, exposing how narratives are determined as much by dominant desire as local/traditional need, such work is frequently read as being part of an oppositional theatrical tradition (see Appleford; Knowles, "Look").

While this neat distinction between conservative and radical citations of international/contemporary theatre would appear to answer one question about how to frame Aboriginal theatre (and has served me well in the past), it does little to address the challenges of more hybrid forms. One such hybrid is *House of Sonya*. It demonstrates how Aboriginal performance can explore Western theatrical tradition in a fundamentally radical way. The term "radical" here is used not in the sense of revolutionary, which would imply a political departure from Chekhov's play, but rather in the sense of "radical" as "root", a delving into the deep structure of the play in order to reveal a universal core of meaning.

In an interesting way, Anton Chekhov has been employed as a marker of theatrical coming-of-age in Canada. When, in 1956, Toronto's Crest Theatre mounted a production of *The Three Sisters*, Herbert Whittaker wrote not one but three glowing notices for *The Globe and Mail*, such was his giddiness. Each of his notices was infused with the patriotic certainty that this Toronto production of a Russian play—directed by an American who had trained under a French director at a British theatre school—was proof positive that Canadian theatre was indeed world-class. Twenty-two years later, the urge to master Chekhov persists but is filtered through a requisite cultural nationalism. The Stratford Festival's 1978 production of *Uncle Vanya*, co-directed by Robin Phillips and Urjo Kareda, was a smash hit with audiences and critics alike, as much for the "rare, fresh springiness" of John Murrell's translation of the play as for the acting or direction (Wyman). According to J. Douglas Clayton, Murrell's translation

> represented an important step forward in the Canadian theatre's assimilation of Chekhov. It took away the Russian writer's "'foreign accent'" and focussed on the theatrical values of his play. Since the previous translations used in the Canadian theatre were (presumably) of British or American origin, the translation also represented another step in the long and arduous process of creating a Canadian national theatre, free of its British and American colonial past. (161–62)

The old joke that the three most successful Canadian playwrights pre-1960s were Shakespeare, Ibsen, and Chekhov indicates Chekhov's importance in this country's struggle to see itself as possessing a "mature" theatrical scene. The question of why Chekhov has been seen to play such a role is a difficult one and one which is beyond the scope of my discussion here. That Whittaker could see the Crest Theatre's production of *The Three Sisters* as an indication of international status and theatrical craft and Clayton could see the Stratford Festival's production of *Uncle Vanya* as a vindication of national/local translation suggests that the mastery of Chekhov, either as international or national symbol of prestige, represented an almost Oedipal triumph in Canadian theatre.

And like any Oedipal figure, he's had to watch his back when the children are around. "Chekhov has been ennobled by age," lamented critic Spencer Golub in 1983. "He is as soothing and reassuring as the useless valerian drops dispensed by the doctors in all his plays [...] an article of faith, like all stereotypes [...] the Santa Claus of dramatic literature" (qtd. in Senelick 12). Given this ossification, recent international productions of Chekhov have been less reverential in their treatment of his work, rejecting the poetic-realism or symbolist-morality-play legacy of Stanislavsky in favour of more deconstructive approaches, based on new ways of reading his plays. The fashion now is to see Chekhov's method as "the patient building up of patterns, discontinuous fragments of expression adhering to each other like molecules in a magnetic field, rather than through any ordinary logic of 'development'" (Gilman 17). Genrietta Ianovskaia's 1993 Moscow production put *Ivanov* on rollerskates (see Borden). The Wooster Group's 1990 production *BRACE UP!* employed the conceit of a travelling Japanese theatre troupe performing what may or may not be *The Three Sisters* in a burned-out hotel in New York City (see Arratia). Such revisionist productions capitalize on the more recent readings of Chekov's drama, which emphasize the performative particle over the dramatic wave.

In important ways, the motivations behind Floyd Favel Starr's adaptation of *Uncle Vanya* are convergent with this historical tradition. Favel Starr, briefly artistic director of Toronto's pre-eminent Native Earth Performing Arts, left Toronto (and what he saw as a stagnant Aboriginal theatre scene there) and returned to his roots in Saskatchewan. Actress Doris Linklater soon followed him out west for similar reasons. Favel Starr and Linklater, joined by actor Mark Dieter and performance artist Robin Brass, formed Red Tattoo Ensemble, a troupe dedicated to producing experimental theatre with international themes. *House of Sonya* was their first production, staged at a well-known "hippie bar" called The Other Side (also known as "The Club") in Regina in 1997.

Thus, Chekhov is once again a marker of theatrical arrival—in this case, for Aboriginal artists who wish to escape what they perceive to be a ghettoizing of expression and to redefine the boundaries of what Aboriginal theatre is thought to encompass. Speaking of the future of Aboriginal theatre in Canada, Doris Linklater warns, "The well is dry. ... There is only so much we can do with the material before we repeat ourselves. It's time to expand the vision" (qtd. in Elton 64). Significantly, Linklater is best known for her premiere performance as Nanabush in Highway's *Dry Lips Oughta Move to Kapuskasing*, a play that seems to epitomize the very approach she is now reacting against.

Returning to the distinction between covert and overt citation of non-Aboriginal form/content, *House of Sonya* appears, on the surface at least, to be very much overt in its use of citation. But the vital difference here is that the typical pattern of Western theatre cited within Aboriginal narrative is reversed. Here we have a Western classic riddled with "Indianisms." Heather Elton, who reviewed the Regina production, describes the odd bricolage of the set designed by Métis artist Edward Poitras (who also acted in the production):

> [The set] looks like both an elegant mansion and a low budget rez home. There is Russian samovar for drinking tea and a blow torch for hot-knifing hash. ... Value Village costumes give the play a retro chic aesthetic. ... [Vanya] and Sonya sit on tacky vinyl kitchen chairs and play chess [while] [s]age brush encroaches the stage ... (64)

The choice of venue for the play reinforced the hybridity of the performance. Formerly known as the Saskatchewan Cultural Exchange Society, The Club, as it was called, was the organizational hub for many of the province's cultural festivals. The owners of The Club at that time were avid supporters of Aboriginal artists, and the hall was decorated with an imposing, steel buffalo skull sculpture made by local Aboriginal artist Blair Gerard. In this way, The Club was a perfect venue for Favel Starr's adaptation; it epitomized both cross-cultural activity and aesthetic experimentation by Aboriginal artists.

Continuing this cross-cultural fusion, the text of *House of Sonya* mingles Russian and Aboriginal Canadian, often with bewildering results. In many instances, the text itself is altered to point up local/cultural issues specific to Aboriginal communities. Yelena and Serebryakov, who in Chekhov's original are a peasant bride and her dissipated literature professor husband, are here a half-breed former prostitute and a white academic who has made his career writing on Aboriginal culture. Typhus, the scourge of the Russian peasantry that Dr. Astrov battles against, is replaced by references to diabetes and heart disease, present-day scourges of the Aboriginal population. But there is also much new dialogue that punctures the delicate melancholia with heavy parody. In his wooing of Yelena, Vanya (played by Mark Dieter) enthuses, "you remind me of one of those Indian postcards, a beautiful Native woman with long dark hair and a body like Pamela Anderson!" (*Sonya* 10). Vanya strolls through the snowy garden with his niece Sonya, now both smoking a joint. Vanya exclaims, "I feel so ... Canadian. Farley Mowat! This is like in one of his books!" (34). This self-conscious citation of pop and canonical culture would appear to be in aid less of contemporizing the play than of capitalizing upon the aesthetic dissonance between the citation and the narrative that contains it. Despite his fondness for the non sequiturs of human frailty, one wonders what Chekhov would have thought of Vanya's new question to Sonya: "Man, I'm so stoned, even my ears are stoned. Does that ever happen to you?" (33). If these types of alterations were the extent of Favel Starr's adaptation, *House of Sonya* could be seen as an example of overt citation, self-conscious, anti-mimetic, parodic, and politically radical. But Favel Starr has gone beyond this overt type of citation. He has changed *Uncle Vanya* in a fashion more radical than one might have expected.

The "Canadianized" 1978 translation of *The Three Sisters* at the Stratford Festival sought through language to reclaim Chekhov as a "landed immigrant" on the Canadian stage. Favel Starr's adaptation of *Uncle Vanya* is motivated by a desire to assimilate not simply through translation, but through transplantation. He writes about this impulse:

> I have been thinking for some time now on the need to bury all drama that we do in Canada into the sources of this country. We should not only perform plays that are exiles or colonials to this land, but actually transplant these classical dramas to the soil of this country. We are all from this country and we should accept this. ("House" 1)

This plea is a familiar one, of course. But Favel Starr's rhetoric of transplantation in this case is supported by his culturally specific approach to adaptation. In his early work with Red Tattoo and later with Takwakin Theatre, Favel Starr sought to develop dramaturgical methodologies that could be applied to dramatic texts, regardless of their cultural origin. His approach is indicated by the example he gives of learning to play the hand drum in the Plains Cree Round Dance style:

> The rhythm of the dancing and singing was explained to me in the image/action of "a duck bobbing in the lake water." This image, I understand now, is the basic DNA of the dance step, the voice, the drumming. This image is the technical and spiritual core of the dance and step, the voice, the drumming. ... The spirit of the dance and singing is actually contained in the spaces between the waves of the water and the movement of the duck, between the drum beats and steps, between the dancers. ("Artificial Tree" 83)

Taking his cue from this traditional relationship between image and action, Favel Starr believes that [t]hrough precision and firm precise guidelines, the [theatrical] performer can then approach the mysterious aspects of his/herself in relationship to an image, a classical or contemporary text, or a memory (83). In order to develop this relationship between performer and image, on the one hand, and what he calls "dramatic techniques that are informed by this land" ("House" 1), on the other, he decided to experiment with the performative possibilities of what is known as the "Plains Indian Winter Count" system.

The Winter Count was used by Plains Indians for centuries to record time using pictographs or glyphs painted onto stretched animal hide. Each glyph represents an event agreed upon by the community's elders as being the most significant for that year: great natural disasters, battles, sickness, and so on. Much like the beads of a wampum belt, each glyph is mnemonic rather than mimetic. Each glyph triggers in the mind of the tribal historian several stories related to that year's image. The historian, as a public rememberer, must then pass these stories along to the next generation (Red Horse Owner 5–10). Not simply a calendar in pictographs, the Winter Count is, in Favel Starr's words, both "the fruit of, and fodder for, memory" ("House" I).

In rehearsal, Favel Starr asked his cast to consider the play *Uncle Vanya* as if it were a year that had just ended. Just as Plains Indian elders would confer in the winter season and agree upon the key image to encapsulate that past year, the cast broke down the units of the text into specific images. These images included "Vanya in the garden" and "Yelena in the thunderstorm at night" ("House" 2). The cast members then isolated specific images in the text that resonated on a personal level with them. Just as the Winter Count system sets in motion a highly personalized series of interconnected stories in the mind of the historian, the cast members used the key images found in the play as catalysts for their own personal remembrances, many of which generated new improvised material or staging techniques. This is unlike the technique of "affective" or "emotional memory" used by Stanislavsky, where visual images in the mind of the actor create a corresponding mood, which influences his/her spirit and arouses in him/her a corresponding inner feeling. Favel Starr's approach renders the *text itself* eminently pliable and subject to the transformative power of the actor's memory. For example, Vanya's brief remembrance of Yelena as a naïve but comely young girl in the original text—"To think that ten years ago I used to meet her at my sister's when she was only seventeen and I was thirty-seven" (Chekhov 35)—was transformed into a more involved story about a wild drug party where Vanya first saw Yelena:

> I met her ten years ago at my sister's. It was at a party and it was packed with all these people, anybody who was anybody. There was booze all over, people blasting in the kitchen, slamming in the stairways. I was young, just got out of jail, had money in my pocket. She had jumped up onto the speakers and she was dancing, she had on a short little dress and she was ripped out of her mind, on acid or something. (*Sonya* 16)

This remembered image, in turn, stimulates a highly charged visual image enacted on stage, that of Yelena, in a stylized tableau, shooting up as the action unfolds around her. In this way, *House of Sonya* is neither an aping nor a parody of Chekhov's original work. It is an attempt at revisioning *Uncle Vanya* as a multivalent chronicle of time past.

This revisioning often results in changes that one wouldn't immediately expect. The samovar, so recognizably Russian, remains in Favel Starr's adaptation and, in fact, plays an even greater role in the *mise en scene* than in the original text: the samovar comes to represent tradition in its most tangible form. In what reviewer Heather Elton calls the play's most powerful image, Sonya, played by Doris Linklater, wheels the samovar slowly across the stage while speaking in Anishnaabe/Ojibway (Elton 67). Thus, the samovar becomes an icon of traditional culture associated with traditional language. One does not explicate the other. They are shown to be inseparable as an image.

Another important revision is the elimination of Astrov's famous speech lamenting the disappearance of his beloved trees on the estate. Given dominant stereotypes of Aboriginal environmentalism, one might have expected that such a speech would figure prominently in Favel Starr's version. But consider the significance in Chekhov's original of Astrov's supposed "righteousness." The character is miserable less over the loss of foliage, as such, than over the fact that nothing better has resulted from its destruction. In typical Chekhovian fashion, Astrav's apparent praise of trees is, in fact, a way for him to illustrate yet again his misanthropic thesis that "everything's gone downhill because people have found the struggle for existence too much for them, because they're backward and ignorant, because they haven't the faintest idea what they're doing" (48). Favel Starr replaces this abstract rant with one more directed to real loss of control over Aboriginal land. In *House of Sonya*, Astrav shows Yelena a chart of Peepeekeesis Reserve in northern Saskatchewan, pointing out how the reserve's land base has been appropriated by neighbouring farmers:

> And now it's all gone. ... Gone, because according to rivaling neighbors, we were sitting on their property, farmland. ... This page shows just that. There is absolutely no indication that there was ever a yard or a house there. No house, yard, fence line, or bush line. It's all gone, plowed away, wiped out. (26)

As with that of the original Astrov, the revised Astrov's affection for the past is coloured by a nostalgia necessarily unreal and necessarily predicated on irretrievable loss:

> I would sit on the porch steps facing westward into the sunset and dream. I was surrounded by beauty, gifts. We had very little money but what a life. All those colors and smells, the buzz of bees and that stuff that floats on the air from pussy willows and other plants that have just bloomed. It was like I was living in a movie, circa 1968. And now it's all gone. (26)

And like Chekhov's precious trees, the revised Astrov's "land claim" is less about the land itself than about the human value attributed to it, which has forever passed away. He laments that "all those memories of laughter and summer evenings are now buried beneath the soil by some other family's plow" (27).

In this way, I think, Favel Starr's adaptation of *Uncle Vanya* finds the heart of Chekhov's often frustrating approach to symbolic meaning. In his analysis of Chekhov's symbolism, Peter Holland argues that the playwright is less concerned with constructing a "system of images" than with "question[ing] the process by which certain natural objects are given such artificial symbolic values (227). Favel Starr's adaptation renews this questioning in relation to Aboriginal traditional values and the political or emotional weight these values are understood to possess. This indicates, perhaps, why he is so adamant that the future of Aboriginal theatre lies in the cross-pollination between local/traditional and international/contemporary performance techniques. He relates a dream he had that articulates this relationship:

> I and a group of people were working in a studio; our director told us that our work had no centre, and so we must find a centre. The director went away so we could have time to complete our task. The actors then placed an artificial tree in the middle of the stage as we understood that

> in many Native ceremonies, there is often a central votive image, like a fire or a tree, The director came back to see the results of our work. Horrified, he said, "No, the centre should be invisible." ("Artificial Tree" 84)

Favel Starr interprets this dream to mean that "when we put aspects of our rituals on stage, we are putting up artificial trees. The tree has no roots, and no animating spirit" (84). Just as Chekhov's dramaturgy is seen to demand "a continual testing of each aspect of the play against the actions of the characters" (Holland 227), Favel Starr's adaptation forces the spectator to test his/her premises of what constitutes an Aboriginal story. Like Chekhov's trees, which act as invisible centres for signification in his plays, this adaptation of *Uncle Vanya* has a traditional centre that is unseen yet organizes the nostalgic desires of the characters on stage.

It is this exploration of nostalgia that leads to the most sweeping change in *House of Sonya*. As the title indicates, Sonya has become the main character of the work. The entire play is, in fact, taking place in the memory of Sonya, now an adult, who has returned from her new life in the city to the now-abandoned estate for the funeral of Vanya, found stabbed in a Vancouver alleyway. All the action is filtered through Sonya's bittersweet nostalgia for what she has lost. But isn't Chekhov about the future, the inescapable lure and tantalizing promise of Moscow, the future, where all hope is placed, or even about the ultimate future state of death, where, as Sonya says to comfort Vanya at the end of the play, "we shall find peace" (Chekhov 67)? By revealing the fates of the characters—Vanya stabbed, Yelena dead from AIDS, Sonya living in sad comfort in the city—Favel Starr robs the play of its delicate temporal equipoise. But he also taps into the radical, the root of the play. It is, of course, not the future that will give Chekhov's characters their peace, but rather the turning of the future's deferred hope into real action, real work, in the present. The future for Chekhov is in reality a way for people to grapple with what Richard Gilman calls "the grief of the actual" (123). Importantly, it is not the "grief of the actual" that Favel Starr's adaptation grapples with. It is the ever-presence of the past in the present, in memory, that causes the characters such pain. Favel Starr believes that "pain seems to be the sentiment of memory. Anyone who has left their home or their culture to live in a foreign environment can recognize this" ("House" 1). If *House of Sonya* is a tragedy, it is the "tragedy of people of my generation trying to make a living in the larger society yet longing for our home, homes which stir such strong feelings of nostalgia" (3). Walter Benjamin wrote that "in order for the past to be touched by the present, there must be no continuity between them" (qtd. in Taussig 176). Favel Starr makes the point that for Aboriginal people, and for all people, that the past lives in the present in a way the future cannot because there can *only be continuity between them.*

Chekhov's grief is of the actual, and Favel Starr's grief is of the bittersweet ever-presence of the past. Both articulate the complex notion of human beings seeking moments of pure living but finding instead these moments pre-occupied. When his cast had difficulty finding the right emotional tone in the final ghost dance sequence of the play, Favel Starr told them a story about Hijikata, a Japanese Butoh master:

"When Hijikata dances he feels his sister who lives inside him and he dances for her. Think about the people in your past. Then the work will be lifted up and have another dimension. Theatre is about remembering" (qtd. in Elton 67). *House of Sonya* is successful in that it engages with both Western theatrical tradition and Aboriginal concepts of remembrance. In the words of Jo-Ann Thom, an Aboriginal scholar who attended the only performance of the play in Regina, "having read a little bit of Chekhov as a student, I felt that the play was more true to him as being uniquely Indian." Ultimately, the distinction between international and local, contemporary and traditional, becomes radically unimportant.

(2002)

Note

[1] For an example of this, see Petrone, who, in her historical narrativizing of Aboriginal literatures, creates an evolutionary model of discourse, where the cultural values of the oral traditions precipitate into literary forms.

Works Cited

Alfred, Taiaiake. *Peace, Power, Righteousness: An Indigenous Manifesto.* Don Mills, ON: Oxford UP, 1999.

Appleford, Robert. "Making Relations Visible in Native Canadian Performance." *Siting the Other: Re-Visions of Marginality in Australian and English-Canadian Drama.* Ed. Marc Maufort and Franca Bellarsi. Brussels: Peter Lang, 2001. 233–46.

Arratia, Euridice. "Island Hopping: Rehearsing the Wooster Group's *Brace Up!*" *TDR* 36-4 (1992): 121–42.

Bigsby, C.W.E. "American Indian Theater." *A Critical Introduction to Twentieth Century American Drama.* Vol. 3. Cambridge: Cambridge UP, 1985. 365–74.

Borden, Richard C. "The Comic Chekhov on the Russian Stage, 1993–94." Clayton 93–102.

Chekhov, Anton. *Uncle Vanya. The Oxford Chekhov.* Vol. 3. Trans. and Ed. Ronald Hingley. London: Oxford UP, 1964. 15–67.

Clayton, J. Douglas, ed. *Chekhov Then and Now: The Reception of Chekhov in World Culture.* New York: Peter Lang, 1997.

———. "Touching Solitudes: Chekhov in Canada 1926–1980." Clayton 151–72.

Elton, Heather. "Lynx from the Past: Chekhov Goes Native." Rev. of *The House of Sonya,* by Floyd Favel Starr. Red Tattoo Ensemble. The Other Side, Regina, SK. *Border Crossings* 17.1 (1998): 63–67.

Favel Starr, Floyd. "The Artificial Tree: Native Performance Culture Research 1991–1996." *Canadian Theatre Review* 90 (1997): 83–85.

———."House of Sonya." *alt.theatre: Cultural Diversity and the Stage* 1.1 (1998): 1–3.

———. *House of Sonya.* Unpublished playscript, 1997.

Filewod, Alan. "Averting the Colonizing Gaze: Notes on Watching Native Theater." *Aboriginal Voices: Amerindian, Inuit, and Sami Theater.* Ed. Per Brask and William Morgan. Baltimore, MD: Johns Hopkins UP, 1992. 17–28.

Gilman, Richard. *Chekhov's Plays: An Opening into Eternity.* New Haven, CT: Yale UP, 1995.

Holland, Peter. "Chekhov and the Resistant Symbol." *Drama and Symbolism.* Themes in Drama 4. Ed. James Redmond. Cambridge: Cambridge UP, 1982. 227–42.

Knowles, Ric. "'Look. Look again': Daniel David Moses' Decolonizing Optics." Maufort and Bellarsi, *Crucible* 187–98.

———. *The Theatre of Form and the Production of Meaning: Contemporary Canadian Dramaturgies.* Toronto: ECW, 1999.

Maufort, Marc, and Franca Bellarsi, eds. *Crucible of Cultures: Anglophone Drama at the Dawn of a New Millennium.* Brussels: Peter Lang, 2002.

Petrone, Penny. *Native Literature in Canada: From the Oral Tradition to the Present.* Toronto: Oxford UP, 1990.

Red Horse Owner, Moses. *Red Horse Owner's Winter Count: The Oglala Sioux, 1786–1968.* Ed. Joseph S. Karol. Martin, SO: Booster, 1969.

Senelick, Laurence. "Chekhov and the Bubble Reputation." Clayton 5–18.

Taussig, Michael. *Mimesis and Alterity: A Particular History of the Senses.* New York, Routledge, 1993.

Thom, Jo-Ann. E-mail to the author. 12 February 2001.

Wasserman, Jerry. "Where Is Here Now? Living the Border in the New Canadian Drama." Maufort and Bellarsi, *Crucible,* 63–74.

Whittaker, Herbert. "Crest's *Three Sisters* Enriches Busy Season." *The Globe and Mail* 27 October 1956: 12.

———. "Crest Theatre Scores in Classic by Chekhov." Rev. of *The Three Sisters*, by Anton Chekhov. Crest Theatre, Toronto. *The Globe and Mail* 24 October 1956: 23.

———. "Showbusiness." *The Globe and Mail* 31 October 1956: 24.

Wyman, Max. "Theatre to Make the Heart Glad." Rev. of *Uncle Vanya*, by Anton Chekhov. Avon Theatre, Stratford, ON. *Vancouver Sun* 9 June 1978: C3.

Theatre as a National Export:
On Being and Passing in the United States

by Erin Hurley

> [O]ne of the most venerable principles in the world of negotiation and diplomacy is at issue in [Canada–United States cultural relations] ... Getting along ... requires understanding of each by the other and what that other perceives to be his [sic] needs.
>
> —Allan Smith, *Canadian Culture,*
> *the Canadian State, and the New Continentalism* 21

> We want [Americans] to think about Canada, which they don't often do, and we want them to think about it in the context of excellence. If they leave the theatre thinking, "Wow, that was a really good play, as good as it gets here," then they think more positively in general about Canada. They stop thinking about us as: The same, but not as good.
>
> —Cultural attachée Louise Blais,
> quoted in Simon Houpt, "Enter Canada Stage Left" R3

These two epigraphs suggest that Canada has suffered in its relations with the United States from US misreadings of Canada. While this concern about US failures of perception vis-à-vis Canada has a long history (see Berton), it has taken on a new urgency since the ascendancy of the global economy, dating from the late 1980s. As economies and cultures are integrated in an overarching global system, the risks of misreading Canada by (and as) the United States increase. Many worry that as globalization advances and Canada's satellite-economy relationship to the US is codified in agreements like the North American Free Trade Agreement (NAFTA), Canada's cultural reality will come to reflect the US's (mis)understanding of Canada as a derivative copy of itself—"the same, but not as good" (Blais qtd. in Houpt R3). For instance, in his article about the deleterious effects on Canadian theatre of the Canada/US Free Trade Agreement (FTA), William Peel cautions that "the selective bi-directional filter that we call the 49th parallel may soon become the line of demarcation between a flourishing society to the south and a culturally moribund land to the north" (19).

Peel, Smith, and Blais's concerns have significant merit in light of the impact of globalization on the very idea of national culture. The category nation is no longer as foundational to cultural production and identity structures as it was even twenty years ago (see Buell; Bélanger). In short, globalization revalues the role of the nation state, dissociates culture from nation, and restructures national identities. Characterized by neo-liberal economic, political, and social policies which facilitate the flow of capital between networked, metropolitan and/or regional archipelagos of economic activity, globalization's most pervasive effect has been to diminish the boundary-function and signifying power of national borders. Recent work on the diasporic cultures of the Black Atlantic and Asian Pacific provide important examples of how global networks produce and sustain trans-national cultural communities (see Gilroy; Joseph; Joseph and Fink; Wilson). As globalization decouples nation and culture and limits the import of the nation to identity, nation-states lose their hold on the tools through which they represent themselves to the world.

Smith and Blais proffer transparent self-representation, understanding, and right perception as solutions to the increasingly fraught cultural relations between Canada and the United States which are catalyzed by globalization. However, these solutions continue to rely on a series of assumptions undermined by globalization's very processes: that clearly identifiable nation-states exist, that they have expressive national cultures, and that a stable system of signification would allow for truthful representations and accurate readings of those representations. I take as axiomatic Robert Schwartzwald's assertion that this "new globalist paradigm" of international relations and identitarian formations "compels new thinking about Canada" that does not rely on these three assumptions (12). I would add that the globalist paradigm also compels new representational modes for nation-states and new reading strategies for Canadian theatre studies, particularly in their relationships to the US.

In this discussion, I begin to explore what it might mean to think of Canadian culture, and Canadian theatre in particular, outside of the national(ist) paradigm promoted by policy-makers and commentators. How might theatre scholars theorize Canadian theatre and performance without relying on the idea of the autonomous nation as the foundational category of analysis? How might they do so in the charged arena of the world stage, an arena that relies on national distinctions? I take as my case study the example of Canadian theatre exported to and practiced in the United States. I ask, if the national category is no longer determinative, what counts as Canadian theatre in that context? What is the nature of the relationship between nation and culture in the globalist paradigm? And, when freed from a nationalist project of the kind envisioned by Smith and Blais, what other kinds of work might Canadian theatre be available to do?

To explore the possibilities of this interpretive shift, I first analyze the predominant features of Canada's current cultural export policy, conceived as an antidote to the changes wrought by globalization on national formations. After pointing out the limitations of federal government initiatives and the realist mimetic structure on which they are based, I focus on alternative mimetic strategies employed by Canadian artists and cultural workers in the United States. I argue that the strategies by which Canadians cross the border into US culture insist, not on the accurate representation of Canada or Canadianness, but rather on the performativity of those categories. Their place on the US cultural stage depends less on the traditional structure of mimesis predicated on the reproduction of the same than on the turned mimetic structure of the *pass*—successfully occupying the identity of another. The pass opens the field of Canadian theatre studies to new objects and new modes of interpretation because it alters not only what can be recognized as Canadian but also the conditions of perception for Canadian theatrical work.

The Canada Brand

The showcase of contemporary Canadian plays is a common strategy by which Canadian theatrical work enters the United States, particularly in the northeastern corridor (roughly, Washington, DC to Boston, MA). Small groups of Canadian plays or performances are presented together, generally in repertory, as part of a mini-season or festival billed as "Canadian." [1] This national branding strategy is employed to increase the likelihood that Canadian work will stand out in a crowded and diverse US cultural scene. Not coincidentally, it also serves what political theorist Charles Taylor has identified as the pre-eminent need of the modern nation-state: the need for *recognition.* "The need for recognition," Taylor explains, is

> for an acceptance by the world community that one counts for some-
> thing, has something to say to the world, and is among those addressed
> by others the need to exist as a people on the world stage ... If this
> is denied or set at nought by those who surround us, it is extremely
> difficult to maintain a horizon of meaning by which to identify
> ourselves. ("Why do Nations" 52, 53)

Canadian-branded theatre is deployed in a nationalist project to help secure Canada's recognition as an actor on the world stage and, in so doing, to assure that Canada can continue to produce its own national identity.

In this strategy, Montreal's Centre des auteurs dramatiques (CEAD), in concert with the Quebec government, has taken the lead, sponsoring Quebec theatre festivals in the US, Europe and beyond since the mid-1980s (Pavlovic 43; Culture et Communications, "Délégation générale du Québec"). The Canadian federal govern-ment, through its funding institutions, embassies, consulates, and Department of Foreign Affairs and International Trade (DFAIT), with the cooperation of theatres, playwrights' centres, and companies across Canada, has recently begun to follow Quebec's lead. [2] For instance, in the fall of 2000, the Canadian Cultural Service sponsored readings of four contemporary Canadian playwrights' work at New York's Blue Heron Arts Center Theatre (Carlson). That same season, various Washington, DC theatres produced four plays and some readings funded, in part, by grants from "The Canada Project," a program developed by the Canadian Consulate in Washington (Houpt R3). Mini-seasons of Canadian work have been presented by venues as diverse as New York City's Brooklyn Academy of Music (BAM) in 1990 and Ubu Repertory Theater (Ubu Rep) in 1984, as well as Washington, DC's Studio Theatre in 2000, and in Philadelphia in 1998. [3]

Despite the proliferation of the national branding strategy, there is little evidence to suggest that it is successful at garnering the recognition Canada courts. On the contrary, much Canadian theatre seems to receive more attention when presented under other brand rubrics. For example, although BAM's "New Currents from Montreal" season fared respectably at the box office, its receipts do not match those from subsequent "Next Wave" seasons (Brooklyn Academy of Music). On the other hand, under BAM's own branding device—the "Next Wave" festival—BAM has remuneratively presented many of Robert Lepage's works since *Polygraph* in 1990 (Hurley 11–13). A recent special issue of *L'Annuaire théâtral* indicates that many Quebecois theatre productions are also more warmly received when integrated into contexts and performance categories other than the national; for instance, performances by the Théâtre Sans Fil and the Théâtre de l'Oeil are quite popular on the marionette and children's festival circuits in the United States and beyond (see Landes 35–39; see also Beauchamp). Moreover, those Canadian theatre artists whose work has been most frequently exported to and warmly received by the United States tend not to trumpet their national affiliations but instead create their own global performance or corporate brand. For example, Robert Lepage's troupe, Ex Machina, and the Cirque du Soleil have seized upon the new conditions of possibility occasioned by globalization to great US acclaim. Their shows are populated, not by recognizable national subjects, but by international casts of characters, and they incorporate global cultural forms in their internationally financed touring productions (see Harvie and Hurley).

Nor does branding Canadian theatre expedite Canadian theatre artists' border crossings. Despite Canadian cultural policymakers' desire to increase Canada's recognition south of the 49th parallel through Canadian-branded theatre, in practice, theatre functions more as a figure of foreign policy than an object of it. The "world stage" metaphor (Taylor 53) has not enabled Canadian theatre practitioners to surmount significant obstacles to touring in international trade law and funding. First, theatre artists do not qualify for the temporary work visas called NAFTA or "TN" visas readily available to other professional classes of workers ("TN Visas").[4] According to William Peel, visa approval for a Canadian performer wishing to tour the US typically takes at least two months (16).[5] Second, theatre and the live performing arts are not designated as cultural industries by the Department of Foreign Affairs and International Trade (DFAIT), nor by the most recent iterations of NAFTA or WTO agreements, thereby eliminating certain classes of subvention and tariff-facilitated protection available to other cultural industries (see Cultural Industries Sectoral Advisory Group on International Trade). Statistics from DFAIT reinforce this conclusion: from 1995/96 to 1998/99, the number of Canadian plays produced in the US and funded by DFAIT dropped by almost 60% (Stephens).

Even more far-reaching in its implications than these technical obstacles is the outmoded national-realist paradigm on which the theatrical export model is based. As implied above, this national branding strategy for entering the US upholds an increasingly compromised relationship among nation, national identity, and culture as coextensive. Prefacing Canadian theatre work in the US, this representational strategy recapitulates a Romantic model of "expression/blockage" which presumes a self behind it (Eagleton 28); the nation occupies the position of subject and its expressive culture is evaluated according to the accuracy of its depiction of that subject. In other words, culture and nation are engaged in a naively mimetic relationship: culture acts as the signifier that represents the signified nation, which is presumed stable in its composition and meaning.

This naively mimetic relationship is intended to be pedagogic. In their representative function, Canadian plays teach audiences about what Canada *is*, so that it might be better understood and appreciated. Canadian-branded theatre in the US functions similarly to the way Sherry Simon says Quebecois literature translated into English functions in English Canada. Arguing that the translation into English of Quebecois works is often seen as an ethnographic enterprise, she outlines the pedagogy of understanding it is intended to engender. "*Les préfaces des traductions adopteront souvent deux thèmes reliés: l'oeuvre que vous allez lire est une représentation authentique de la société canadienne-française; en lisant cette traduction vous comprendrez (et aimerez?) mieux cette société*" (53). The national branding strategy in exporting Canadian theatre likewise underscores the authenticity of the cultural product, ties that authenticity to its expression of a particular societal formation—the nation—and exhorts its audience to read the product in a realist framework: the plays that you are about to see are an authentic representation of Canadian society; when the curtain falls, you will "think more positively in general about Canada" (Blais qtd. in Houpt R3). One brief example helps illustrate this point about the ethnographic gaze invited by the national branding model. In her essay on Pollock and Walker in India, Geeta Budhiraja writes that "the productions ... offered a glimpse into the Canadian way of life and ... were appreciated" (26). Budhiraja directly connects the ethnographic gaze with the pedagogy of appreciation that leads to understanding.

These pedagogic imperatives are consistent with the history of Canadian cultural policy (Smith 8–10) and with the history of theatre as a Canadian national enterprise. As Denis Salter has shown, early 20th-century advocates persuaded the government of the need for federal involvement in supporting Canadian theatre by their Arnoldian depiction of theatre as morally uplifting and educational (71–75; see also Knowles). With the advent of globalization, Canadian theatre's mimetic and educative mission does not undergo any substantial rethinking; it merely expands to include the people of other nations. In the 1999 foreign policy document on Canada's role in the changing context of globalization, *Canada in the World*, the federal government made culture the "third pillar" of foreign policy, along with the "promotion of prosperity and employment" and "protection of our security, within a stable global framework" ("Summary"). According to *Canada in the World*, "a country that does not project a clearly defined image of what it is and what it represents, is doomed to anonymity on the international scene. Only Canadian culture can express the uniqueness of our country, which is bilingual, multicultural, and deeply influenced by its Aboriginal roots, the North, the oceans, and its own vastness" ("Projecting Canadian Values and Culture"). Bulwarks against anonymity on the world stage, cultural products "[project] Canadian values and culture" ("Summary"), and are collectively positioned as a response to globalization's threat to Canada's visibility and proper recognition. According to the federal government, culture's role in the new globalist paradigm remains what it was in the nationalist paradigm: that is, figurative; culture, as signifier, reflects and disseminates "Canada," as a unique, discernable signified.

The catch in Canada-US cultural relations—both historically and in the globalist paradigm—is that Canada has not often been recognizably distinct to or from its neighbour. The nation is more cipher than signified, [6] hence the failure of the branding policy and, more fundamentally, the problem with perpetuating the figurative relationship between nation and culture in the "third pillar" policy. "Canada" is not often a recognizable signified to many US theatre institutions. For example, US regional theatres program few Canadian plays because they are neither sufficiently American nor sufficiently not American; Canadian plays are semantically indistinct, making them difficult to categorize and, hence, difficult to program in predefined season slots. [7] Moreover, Canada's neither/nor position does not mark it as a *distinct* signified from the United States. Françoise Kourilsky, founder and artistic director of New York's Ubu Repertory Theater, noted that even Quebecois plays are not perceived as being distinct enough from US texts to draw a significant crowd to their readings (Kourilsky). In *Star-Spangled Canadians, The Globe and Mail* columnist Jeffrey Simpson reports on focus groups of politically active Americans who were unable to produce any "'top of the mind' associations to Canada" (67).

This failure to achieve fullness of signification makes misreadings of Canada by and as its more powerful neighbour that much more likely. However, it also opens up the possibility of exploring other models of the nation/culture relationship, based not in mimesis and ontology, but rather in practice and epistemology. The failure of the ethnographic gaze in these misrecognitions could be construed as generative of alternate paradigms for *Canadian* representation practices and critical reading formations, instead of as misunderstanding and betrayal.

The need for an exploration of alternative models is particularly acute in the case of Canada-US relations. In 1981, Margaret Atwood captured the difficulty of the mimetic model of national representation in her famous characterization of the Canada/US border as a "one-way mirror" (385). In this mirror, Canadians see only Americans; Americans see only themselves. Jettisoning the traditional mimetic/mirror paradigm might enable Canadians and Americans to see Canadian culture and theatre differently. Moreover, the ontological model of the nation based on clearly definable boundaries and distinct national personalities is profoundly compromised by the history of mutual—if not often equal—influence between Canada and the United States. As former Canadian Radio-Television and Telecommunication Commission Chair John Meisel has said, "Inside every Canadian, whether he or she knows it or not, there is, in fact, an American. The magnitude and effect of this American presence in us varies considerably from person to person, but it is ubiquitous and inescapable" (qtd. in Taras 192). Where does Canadian culture end and US culture begin?

In the next section of this paper I will attempt to sketch the features of one alternative model that is more finely attuned to the structuring principle of the Canada-US relationship (i.e. blur) and that acknowledges the impact of globalization's effects (i.e. trans-national, extra-territorial cultural products). Acknowledging globalization's recombinatory effects on the nation's form, culture, and identity, this strategy strives to embody its reconstituted representational strategies and reading formations. The pass supplants Atwood's one-way mirror with a refracting mirror. Using examples from American popular culture, I argue that the misrecognition inherent in the pass expands the definition of Canadian theatre beyond the concept of a theatre that reflects Canada and provides an alternate reading strategy beyond the mimetic for Canadian theatre studies.

Invasion of the Body Snatchers: This American Life

Elise: I guess it's the whole, uh, invasion-of-the-body-snatchers-syndrome. You know, "They look like us, but they're not us." It's weirdly like people hearing that someone they didn't know was gay, is gay. And it turns them back on themselves—that they could have brushed so close and not known. ("Who's Canadian?")

This epigraph is drawn from a popular radio program called "This American Life," broadcast on the United States' National Public Radio network. Every week, its host Ira Glass weaves thematically-related stories into a one-hour show documenting "everyday life in this country [the United States]" ("Never heard us?"). By May of 1997, Canadians had apparently infiltrated everyday American life to such a degree that their presence merited its own episode. "Who's Canadian?" is a five-part meditation composed of interviews, testimonials, and essays on the place and impact of famous Canadians (by birth and/or citizenship) on American life. It presumes that their place is in the United States' quotidian and that their impact is immeasurable.

My interest in this epigraph—and the episode from which it is drawn—lies in the centrality of Canadians to American life, and the possibility that this centrality is achieved, in part, by their successful passing strategies. Surreptitiously occupying the intimate terrain of the American national body, Canadian body snatchers inflect America's everyday. They read its national news (Peter Jennings), popularize its "new country" music (k.d. lang; Shania Twain), influence its neo-conservative values (Danielle Crittenden; David Frum), theorize its liberal policies (John Kenneth Galbraith), and define its generations (Jack Kerouac; Douglas Coupland). Instead of simply buttressing the signified of *Canada*, they also act as signifiers of the *United States*, sometimes embodying the zeitgeist of an era: Mary Pickford was America's Sweetheart in the 1930s; Lorne Greene pursued manifest destiny on TV's "Bonanza" in the space-exploration oriented 1960s; Michael J. Fox depicted an enthusiastic Reaganite in the conservative 1980s; Pamela Anderson embodied the image of the American blonde bombshell in the 1990s. These foreigners, and others like them, have become emblematic American locals, influencing how the US imagines and images itself on national and international stages. Though the US may still be seeing itself in the one-way mirror provided by famous Canadians, its self-seeing is refracted through misrecognized performances of Americanness.

The passer forces the examination of default assumptions concerning national *being*. In so doing, it takes up the representational challenge posed by globalization to "[portray] … local/global historical encounters, co-productions, dominations, and resistances" with all of their ambivalences, power-inequities, contradictions and possibilities (Clifford, "Travelling Cultures" 110). Passing's structure and its outcomes point toward new representational and reading strategies for North American identities founded in the anxieties and pleasures of misrecognition.

Who's Canadian?

To *pass* is to assume the identity of another without benefit of ontological connection. As Elaine Ginsberg puts it,

> the genealogy of the term *passing* in American history associates it with the discourse of racial difference and especially with the assumption of a fraudulent "white" identity by an individual culturally and legally defined as "Negro" or black by virtue of a percentage of African ancestry. … By extension, "passing" has been applied discursively to disguises of other elements of an individual's presumed "natural" or "essential" identity, including class, ethnicity, and sexuality, as well as gender. (2–3)

The threat of national passing—Canadians passing for Americans—is not simply assimilable to the taboo of racial passing as articulated by Ginsberg—American blacks passing for American whites. Although these two types of passing are not mutually exclusive—for example, a black Canadian might pass for a white American and vice versa—the US's history of slavery and of injunctions against miscegenation forcefully distinguish inter-racial passing from intra-racial national passing. That said, the cultural anxiety Elise registers about Canadians passing for Americans gets its charge and derives its humour, in part, from the historical connotations of passing in North America, some of which Elise references: blacks passing for whites, homosexuals passing for heterosexuals, women passing for men.[8]

A secondary source of the national pass's humour, and of the anxiety it registers, comes from the presumed emptiness of the signified, Canada. The prologue of "Who's Canadian?" charts Elise's growing concern over the illegible national markers of famous Canadians living in the United States. When prompted by Glass to catalogue the markers of Canadianness—those characteristics that would reveal their subject as Canadian—Elise is at a loss:

> It's just a sense of, um, that they're a little off somehow, in some way that you don't understand and you can't pin it down and that makes it all the more unsettling. You can't put it anywhere and just have it rest there; it's just sort of continually surprising and disturbing. ("Who's Canadian?")

As she learns about more and more Canadians whom she assumed were Americans, her (mock?) outrage at their trickery escalates. The example of William Shatner is the straw that breaks Elise's proverbial back. When told by her Canadian dinner companion, Paul, that Shatner (a.k.a. Captain Kirk) is Canadian, she blurts out, "That's just wrong!"

> ELISE: The problem [with William Shatner being Canadian] is that I grew up watching "Star Trek" and he is my American ideal. I mean, he represented for me everything that's good about America.
> PAUL: She freaked out …. Elise was saying, "If William Shatner is Canadian, I might as well be Canadian." ("Who's Canadian?")

Exchanges like these articulate the central challenges of the pass to standard practices of performing and reading national identity. First, in the pass, visual or legible markers of national identity do not exist. Elise figures that, like Canada-branded theatre, the Canadian passer should emit some signal as to her/his true national identity, something Elise could pin down as Canadianness. Second, in the pass, that signal is not recognizable according to the tenets of realist aesthetics in which national identity markers scan mimetically, as expressions of a self/subject and as evidence of its identity. Just as globalization decouples the nation and culture, exposing the nation-form as a construction, the pass likewise decouples ontology from visible sign-expressions. The national pass demonstrates the fallibility (and potentially, the emptiness) of the national sign—both Canadian and American. In the successful pass "the difference between the subject [in this case, Canadian] and the image assumed [American] becomes unrecognizable" (Ahmed 92). In Elise's words, "They look like us, but they're not us" ("Who's Canadian?").

The pass strategy capitalizes on the emptiness of the Canadian signifier and Canadians' correlative unrecognizability. In passing, the problem of Canadian identity for national branding—that it is not often clearly distinguishable from that of its southern neighbour—becomes an asset for Canadian cultural producers. So too does the issue of Canada's asymmetrical relationship with the US. Lacking national distinction, Canadian citizens and their cultural products can more readily pass for American. Because of the US's hegemonic position in North America, American identity occupies what Peggy Phelan calls the "unmarked" position (4). American identity becomes the normative North American identity, as is evident in the arrogation of continental designations—North, Central and South America—for a particular national geography called America, and its national identity, *American*. As such, American identity is "left unremarked, in discursive paradigms and visual fields. [It] is the norm and therefore unremarkable" (Phelan 5). The combination of Canada's indistinct national identity markers and America's normative identity position creates the conditions of possibility for Canadian passing. Unless one appears to be manifestly outside the US norm, one is taken for American.

The example of Shatner/Kirk illuminates the features of the unmarked American norm. Shatner's performance as Captain James T. Kirk gave every indication of Americanness. He played a smart and empathetic leader taking manifest destiny into space, leading the aptly named Starship Enterprise to "boldly go where no man has gone before." [9] To a hegemonic reader, nothing in his short-haired, blue-eyed, physically expressive and insistently heterosexual performance belied Shatner's non-normative national identity. The requirements of a successful national pass seem to have changed little in forty years. The overwhelming majority of famous Canadians in the United States today reflect a similar American ideal and possess the following features: they pass singly, by which I mean, they do not pass as part of a group; they are (or appear to be) Caucasian; they are Anglophone; and they require a mediated image, often working in television, film, or the recording industry. [10] Inasmuch as they share in the unmarked categories of *individuality, whiteness* and *Anglophone-ness,* their assimilable characteristics facilitate false recognitions, skewed but mimetic readings of their national identity as *American.*

Passing recommends itself as a generative model for thinking about Canadian culture to theatre scholars for the deconstructive work that passing undertakes. Bearded by the default assumption of American identity, Canadian body snatchers turn Americans back on themselves, in effect re-marking the unmarked identity category of *American.* Elise's reported exclamation—"If William Shatner is Canadian, I might as well be Canadian!"—is a prime example of this function. Her default assumption of Shatner's Americanness is exposed as merely that, a default assumption, instead of an ontological, or an epistemological certainty. When Elise looks in passing's refracting mirror of Shatner/Kirk, she is forced to see both American identity (mimetic sameness) and the creation of American identity through performance (performative difference). As Phelan says, "the one who passes then does not 'erase' the mark of difference, rather the passer highlights the invisibility of the mark of the Same" (96).

Thus, the pass offers not only an alternate strategy for *being* in the United States but, more importantly, a means for entering and altering the realm of the visible, of what is given to view in the United States. As the failed federal "third pillarization" of culture evinces (see Belanger), being *seen* in a crowded US cultural marketplace has proven difficult, making Canada's *recognition* on the US stage in the national-realist mode virtually impossible. The challenge, then, for exported Canadian theatre is less one of accurate representation correctly recognized by American consumers (the goal of national-realist paradigms) than one of provocatively altering the conditions of the visible. The work of the pass offers a potent example of how this might be done by deconstructing the relationships between appearance and ontology, appearance and epistemology, and by throwing mimetic reading formations into question. In other words, passing has the potential to "produce modes of representing [and I would add, reading] that effectively alter the standard frame of reference and visibility, the conditions of the visible, what *can* be seen and represented" in the United States (de Lauretis 224).

What, then, can be seen and represented through the strategy of the national pass which takes misrecognition as its purpose? I propose that what the national pass makes available to view is Canada's potentially deconstructive and performative role on the world stage. The emptiness of the signified, *Canada*, in the US forces a rethinking of nation/culture relations, changing them from signified/signifier to construction/deconstruction. In this reconceptualization, culture acquires a more active role, a performative role, displacing the figurative role it has been asked to play in federal policy. In addition, the national pass makes available new objects of analysis and avenues of inquiry for Canadian theatre studies. Those objects might be defined more capaciously as, for instance, the North American theatre of national identities. This is a theatre in which national identities (singular and hyphenated, mimetic and deconstructive) are performed on countless theatrical, social, political, and economic stages by a wide array of actors. Attuned to the means by which identity transformations are effected and skilled in reading written, visual, verbal, and kinaesthetic texts simultaneously, theatre scholars are well situated to analyze this kind of object.

In the North American theatre of national identity, the pass is the site where national-realist and, what I would call, "global-performative" reading strategies are brought to bear on a single object. In "'It Takes One to Know One': Passing and Communities of Common Interest," Amy Robinson theorizes the pass as a triangular theatre of identity comprised of "the passer, the dupe, and a representative of the in-group" (723). In the spectatorial triangle elaborated above, William Shatner is the passer, Elise occupies the position of the dupe, the unknowing, believing witness to a passer's deceptive performance, and I am a representative of the in-group, someone of the group from which Shatner is passing.

Each of the two witnesses of the pass employs a different reading strategy. The dupe presumes mimesis and therefore "reads the passer's appearance (in this case [Americanness]) as evidence of her [national] identity" (Robinson 726). Shatner is misrecognized as American. On the other hand, the in-group representative presumes performance and therefore "reads the apparatus of the pass" (Robinson 726). As an alternate epistemology or way of seeing, presuming performance "grants the in-group clairvoyant access to the illusionistic apparatus that for the dupe remains [obscured]" (Robinson 727). Shatner's *performance* of Americanness is recognized (and, possibly, misrecognized).

It is important to stress that the interpretive work of the in-group clairvoyant is not like that of a detective in a thriller; s/he does not see the passer's true identity (in this case, as Canadian), correctly recognizing and revealing ontology through its hidden markers. This search for "true identity" is the premise that makes a dupe out of the realist reader. The distinction between the dupe's and in-group clairvoyant's reading strategies might be profitably recast as the difference between J.L. Austin's "constative" (3) and "performative" (4) utterances. The dupe accepts Shatner's identity statement of "I am American" (delivered verbally, visually, kinaesthetically, contextually, etc.) as a constative utterance: a description of some action or reality, "inner or outer, prior or posterior, occurring elsewhere other than the utterance itself" (Gould 20). In other words, his implied statement, "I am American," is taken by the dupe as referential to his *being* American and read mimetically. On the other hand, the in-group clairvoyant accepts Shatner's identity statement as a performative or illocutionary utterance: an utterance that in itself constitutes an action, as in the oft-cited example: "I now pronounce you husband and wife." Shatner's utterance, "I am American," is seen by the in-group clairvoyant as performative, as the means by which Shatner passes as American. In both reading formations, national identity becomes a matter of a way of seeing, a skill in reading, available to a community of people who share a certain cultural literacy; as Robinson puts it, "the question of the passer's 'real' identity [is] a function of the lens through which it is viewed" (723–24).

Altered States

In her 1993 keynote address to the Association for Theatre in Higher Education, performance artist Anna Deavere Smith declared: "Now, I think, is the time to create ways of moving between the fortresses, and in so doing to encourage a new generation of artists [and I would add critics] who live [and] work ... in *boats*" (86). She encouraged a shift away from traditional mimesis to performativity in contemporary university acting training, noting that "we have spent too much time training our students to mirror ourselves, to show the world what's *inside* the artist" (81). Emphasizing movement between ethnic, racial and national fortresses, Smith challenged those present to train their acting students to show difference instead of sameness, to show "the world *around* the artist" (81). I submit that Canadian theatre, as recast by passing's *refracting* mirror, meets this challenge; it shows the world *around* itself, through itself.

A similar shift of emphasis in Canadian cultural policy might be equally useful and generative. The national branding strategy limits both what counts as Canadian theatre and that theatre's purview. It sacrifices theatre's actantial function for its representative function, thereby severely curtailing the scope of what Canadian theatre might be and do in an increasingly networked world. In the globalist paradigm, Canadian theatre in the United States re-marks unmarked identity categories, making them available to view, and it highlights Canada's potentially deconstructive and performative role on the world stage.

As witness to the passer's performative action, the in-group clairvoyant provides a way to think about the role of the Canadian theatre scholar alongside the nationalist paradigm. Taking the pass, instead of the nation, as a foundational category of analysis alters the conditions of the visible, shifting the focus from a recognition of national attributes to a reading of performativity. Instead of revealing instances of Canadian theatre in the United States—for example, tallying the number of performances Brad Fraser's or Judith Thompson's work receives in US theatres— one might engage in reading (and, likely, misreading) the illusionistic apparatus of Americanness. The performativity of that very category is made available to in-group clairvoyants by the structure of the pass. In other words, one might read Canadian national passing practices in American culture as a significant *theatre* of globalization, embodying its "local/global historical encounters, co-productions, dominations, and resistances" (Clifford, "Travelling Cultures" 110). By this standard, much of US popular culture is, in fact, Canadian theatre, inflected and infected by famous Canadians living as Americans on the big and little screens. To recast John Meisel's comment on American cultural imperialism in the logic of the pass: "Inside every [American], whether he or she knows it or not, is, in fact, a [Canadian]" (qtd. in Taras 192).

(2003)

Notes

I would like to thank Adam Frank for his thoughtful comments and helpful suggestions on an earlier draft of this chapter. I would also like to express my gratitude to Jennifer Harvie, with whom I first started thinking about the cultural politics of globalization in the writing of our 1999 co-authored article, "States of Play." I am indebted to her generosity in allowing me to reformulate in this piece some of the ideas we came up with together. Her readings of drafts of this chapter are much appreciated. Phaedra Bell also generously commented on an earlier draft.

[1] Marketing national theatre brands is certainly not unique to those disseminating Canadian work. For instance, Repertorio Español, New York's premiere Spanish language theatre company, also produces festivals organized according to the nationality of the playwrights: Colombian, Puerto Rican, and Dominican in 2001 ("Latin America !En Escena! In New York"). BAM will also continue this tradition with the 2001 "Next Wave Festival" focussing on Australian performance in a mini-season called "Next Wave Down Under" ("BAM 2001 Next Wave Festival").

[1] It is imperative to note that Quebec's government, cultural institutions, and foreign policy initiatives have taken a different perspective vis-à-vis globalization and American cultural imperialism. Quebec's Liberal and Parti Quebecois governments were enthusiastic and early proponents of the FTA and NAFTA (Lachapelle; Csipak and Héroux) and have, since their implementation in the 1990s, capitalized on the extra-national economic and political networks they provide, through paradiplomatic initiatives (see Keating; Thérien, Belanger and Gosselin). Insulated to a certain extent from cultural globalization by the French language and a vibrant popular culture industry of their own (see Grescoe; Grenier), many Quebecois articulate their identity through notions of "américanité" (see Cuccioletta and Desbiens; Bernier and Bédard). The different responses to globalization by English Canada and Quebec merit extensive discussion; however, space constraints require that I limit my analysis of cultural policy to the federal sphere.

[3] At the Blue Heron Arts Center Theatre were Djanet Sears, with *Harlem Duet*; Michel Marc Bouchard, with *The Coronation Voyage*; Colleen Murphy, with *Beating Heart Cadaver*; and Jason Sherman, with *Reading Hebron*. In Washington, Montreal's

Centaur Theatre production of Michel Tremblay's *For the Pleasure of Seeing Her Again* was remounted at Washington's major regional theatre, Arena Stage; Morris Panych's *Vigil* and Daniel MacIvor's *In On It* were presented at the Studio Theatre; the American premiere of George F. Walker's *Heaven* took place at Woolly Mammoth Theatre. The Studio also hosted readings of Tremblay's Quebecois classic *Les Belles-Soeurs* and Judith Thompson's most recent work, *Perfect Pie* (Houpt R3). In 1990, BAM dedicated a portion of its "Next Wave" festival to "New Currents from Montreal," inviting Robert Lepage/Théâtre Repère, Carbone 14, Margie Gillis, and O Vertigo danse to perform. In 1984, Ubu Rep and the CEAD organized a "Festival of New Quebec Plays" at Ubu as part of the CEAD's larger "Montreal Theatre Quebec" initiative in New York City. Ubu Rep sponsored readings of Michel Garneau, René Gingras, Jovette Marchessault, Marco Micone, and Normand Chaurette (see Hurley). In 1998, Philadelphia hosted O Vertigo, Margie Gillis, Théâtre des Deux Mondes, and the play *Le Grand Hôtel des Étrangers* by Michel Lemieux and Victor Pilon (Culture et Communications, "La ministre Louise Beaudoin").

4 These include medical, technology, education, and management professionals ("TN Visas").

5 Moreover, for groups of performers touring together, as is the case in most theatrical tours, "American procedures require that an individual visa be approved for each member of the company," thereby multiplying the likelihood that the visa process will be scuttled by the number of people involved in the tour (Peel 17).

6 It is important to note that Canada is not alone in its failure to achieve fullness of signification. By current standards in the social sciences (those disciplines which normally define national entities), no nation-state can make the ontological claim to selfhood on which fullness of signification depends. The whole idea of the nation as an "entity" or "self" has been left behind in the current practices of anthropology, sociology, and political science due to the combined influences of critical theory and globalization: in anthropology see Clifford and Marcus, and Clifford; in sociology see Clough; in political science see Taylor, "Sources of the Self."

Postmodern anthropology and sociology have deconstructed the impact of their disciplinary formations and those formations' assumptions on the creation of unified wholes including the self, culture, and society. Critical theory's linguistic and cultural turns have been incorporated into recent social science discourse on the nation, altering their conception of the nation as subject with a personality to a persuasive fiction constituted through ideological and imaginative labour. Even security studies and international relations, forged during the Cold War's international balance of power era, have had to incorporate what they call the "wideners'" (Buzan 1–33) perspective on nations and their relations one to another. The wideners have been particularly successful in employing speech act theory to analyze the discourses of threat and national security on which their fields rely (see Wyn Jones; Buzan et. al.; and Campbell). Disavowing the "entitivity" (Handler 7)

and subjectivity of the nation-form, poststructuralist critics of the nation understand the nation-form as a category of practice not a category of being, a relation
not a thing. As Rogers Brubaker writes, "'Nation' is a category of 'practice,' not (in
the first instance) a category of analysis. To understand nationalism, we have to
understand the practical uses of the category 'nation,' the ways it can come to
structure perception, to inform thought and experience, to organize discourse and
political action" (qtd. in McCrone 3).

[7] Preference for American plays is borne out by recent statistics on US theatres' attendance, performance, and fiscal health, gathered by Theatre Communications
Group. *Theatre Facts 2000* indicates that US theatres are decreasing the number of
season slots dedicated to outside/touring work (in part because attendance at those
shows is down) at the same time that they are increasing the number of productions
of new American work (Voss and Voss 11). Placed within the shrinking, "touring/
non-resident," category, productions of Canadian work in US houses appear to have
been curtailed.

[8] Moreover, Elise is not alone in US popular culture in her comically paranoid sense
of the threat that misrecognized Canadians pose to the United States. The second
and third segments of "Who's Canadian" go to great lengths to jokingly prove the
Canadian biases of ABC's nightly news, "World News Tonight with Peter Jennings,"
and of the nighttime teen soap opera, "Beverly Hills 90210" starring Jason Priestley.
The central joke of "South Park: The Movie" (1999) hinges on the threat of
Canadian culture ruining young American minds. Citizens of the small Colorado
town are exhorted in song to "Blame Canada" for its predatory cultural practices.

[9] This, of course, is the famous introductory line to every episode of the television
series "Star Trek." It was spoken by William Shatner just before the theme song
began. "Star Trek" ran on NBC from 1966–1969 ("Star Trek Timeline").

[10] Exceptions to the white general rule include: jazz pianist Oscar Peterson; actor
Gloria Reuben (physician's assistant "Jeanie Boulet" on NBC's "ER"); actor Clark
Johnson (homicide detective "Meldrick Lewis" on NBC's "Homicide: Life on the
Street"); and L.A. Lakers basketball forward Rick Fox.

Works Cited

Ahmed, Sara. "'She'll Wake Up One of these Days and Find She's Turned into a
    Nigger': Passing Through Hybridity." *Theory, Culture & Society* 16.2 (1999):
    87–106.

Atwood, Margaret. "Canadian-American Relations: Surviving the Eighties." *Second
    Words: Selected Critical Prose*. Toronto: Anansi, 1982. 371–492.

Austin, J.L. *How to Do Things with Words*. Ed. J.O. Urmson and Marina Sbisà. 2nd ed. Cambridge: Harvard UP, 1975.

"BAM 2001 Next Wave Festival." Brooklyn Academy of Music Home Page. 25 June 2001. http://www. bam.org/asp/bamjrameset.asp.

Beauchamp, Helene. "Jeunes d'ici, jeunes d'ailleurs: questions de culture(s) et de theatre." *L'Annuaire théâtral* 27 (2000): 55–67.

Bélanger, Louis. "Globalization, Culture, and Foreign Policy: The Failure of 'Third Pillarization' in Canada." *International Journal of Canadian Studies/Revue internationale d'études canadiennes* 22 (2000): 163–95.

Bernier, Léon, and Guy Bédard. "Américanité-Américanisation des Québécois: quelques éclairages empiriques" *Québec Studies* 29 (2000): 15–24.

Berton, Pierre. *Hollywood's Canada: The Americanization of our National Image*. Toronto: McClelland and Stewart, 1975.

Brooklyn Academy of Music. "Financial Statements Years Ended June 30, 1997 and June 30, 1998." *Brooklyn Academy of Music Annual Report, 1996–1998*. Brooklyn: BAM, 1998. 30–33.

Budhiraja, Geeta. "A Glimpse of Canada in India." *Canadian Theatre Review* 105 (2001): 24–26.

Buell, Frederick. *National Culture and the New Global System*. Baltimore: Johns Hopkins UP, 1994.

Buzan, Barry, Ole Wæver, and Jaap de Wilde. *Security: A New Framework for Analysis*. Boulder: Lynne Rienner, 1998.

Campbell, David. *Writing Security: United States foreign policy and the politics of identity*. Manchester: Manchester UP, 1992.

Carlson, Marvin. "Professor Carlson's Tip Sheet." E-mail to the author. November 3, 2000.

Clifford, James. "Traveling Cultures." *Cultural Studies*. Ed. and Intro. Lawrence Grossberg, Cary Nelson, and Paula Treichler. New York: Routledge, 1992. 96–112.

———. *Routes: Travel and Translation in the late 20th Century*. Cambridge: Harvard UP, 1997.

———. and George E. Marcus, eds. *Writing Culture: The Poetics and Politics of Ethnography*. Berkeley: U of California P, 1986.

Clough, Patricia Ticineto. *The End(s) of Ethnography: From Realism to Social Criticism*. Newbury Park: Sage, 1992.

———. *Feminist Thought: Desire, Power, and Academic Discourse*. Oxford: Blackwell, 1994.

Csipak, James, and Lise Héroux. "NAFTA, Quebecers, and Fear (?) of Americanization: Some Empirical Evidence." *Quebec Studies* 29 (2000): 25–42.

Cuccioletta, Donald, and Albert Desbiens. 'L'Ámericanité, the Dual Nature of the Québécois Identity." *Québec Studies* 29 (2000): 3–14.

Cultural Industries Sectoral Advisory Group on International Trade. "Canadian Culture in a Global World: New Strategies for Culture and Trade." February 1999. Rpt. *Department of Foreign Affairs and International Trade/Ministère des affairs étrangères et du commerce international Home Page.* 3 July 2001. http://www.dfait-maeci.gc.ca/tna-nac/canculture-e.asp.

Culture et Communications, Quebec. "Delegation generale du Quebec—La Saison du Quebec en France: Images de la modernité." 15 May 2001. http://mcc.quebectel.qc.ca/Mcc/Communiq.nsf/8e749eflddb24b96852567e8006d400a/34cb446 8d07dO15885256936005 f3b46?OpenDocument&Highlight=0,saison.

———. "La ministre Louise Beaudoin amorce aujourd'hui une mission aux États-Unis afin d'y rencontrer les acteurs de la réussite québécoise sur la scène culturelle." 1 January 2002. http://mcc.quebectel.qc.ca/Mcc/Communiq.nsf/ 8e749efl ddb24b968 5 2 567 e8006d400a/3923c051445b68f48 5 2568cf005adc8f? OpenDocument&Highlig t=O,New.

de Lauretis, Teresa. "Film and the Visible." *How Do I Look? Queer Film and Video.* Ed. Bad Object-Choices. Seattle: Bay, 1991. 223–64.

Eagleton, Terry. "Nationalism: Irony and Commitment." *Nationalism, Colonialism, and Literature.* Ed. Seamus Deane. Minneapolis: U of Minnesota P, 1990. 23–39.

Fry, Early H. "Quebec Confronts Globalization: A Model for the Future?" *Québec Studies* 30 (2000): 57–69.

Gilroy, Paul. *The Black Atlantic: Modernity and Double Consciousness.* Cambridge: Harvard UP, 1993.

Ginsberg, Elaine K. "Introduction: The Politics of Passing." *Passing and the Fictions of Identity.* Ed. Elaine K. Ginsberg. Durham: Duke UP, 1996. 1–18.

Gould, Timothy. "The Unhappy Performative." *Performativity and Performance.* Ed. and Intro. Andrew Parker and Eve Kosofsky Sedgwick. New York: Routledge, 1995.

Grescoe, Taras. *Sacré Blues: An Unsentimental Journey Through Québec.* Toronto: Macfarlane, Walter and Ross, 2001.

Grenier, Lise. "Policing French-Language Music on Canadian Radio: The Twilight of the Popular Record Era?" *Rock and Popular Music: Politics, Policies, Institutions.* Ed. Tony Bennett, Simon Frith, Lawrence Grossberg, John Shepherd, and Graeme Turner. New York: Routledge, 1993. 119–41.

Handler, Richard. *Nationalism and the Politics of Culture in Quebec.* Madison: U of Wisconsin P, 1988.

Harvie, Jennifer and Erin Hurley. "States of Play: Locating Quebec in the Performances of Robert Lepage, Ex Machina, and the Cirque du Soleil." *Theatre Journal* 51 (1999): 299–315.

Houpt, Simon. "Enter Canada, Stage Left." *The Globe and Mail* 31 October 2000: R3.

Hurley, Erin. "Canadian Theatre on New York Stages: Ubu Repertory Theatre and the Brooklyn Academy of Music." *Canadian Theatre Review* 105 (2001): 10–15.

Joseph, May. *Nomadic Identities: The Performance of Citizenship.* Minneapolis: U of Minnesota P, 1999.

Joseph, May, and Jennifer Natalya Fink, eds. *Performing Hybridity.* Minneapolis: U of Minnesota P, 1999.

Keating, Michael. *Nations Against the State: The New Politics of Nationalism in Quebec, Catalonia and Scotland.* New York: St. Martin's, 1996.

Knowles, Richard Paul. "Voices (off): Deconstructing the Modern English-Canadian Canon." *Canadian Canons: Essays in Literary Value.* Ed. Robert Lecker. Toronto: U of Toronto P, 1991. 91–111.

Kourilsky, Françoise. Personal interview. 20 June 2000.

Lachapelle, Guy, ed. *Quebec Under Free Trade: Making Public Policy in North America.* Quebec: Presses de l'Université du Québec, 1995.

Landes, Claude des. "D'une enterprise nationale au rayonnement planétaire." *L'Annuaire théâtral* 27 (2000): 31–43.

"Latin America ¡En Escena! in New York." *Repertorio Español Home Page.* 15 June 2001. http://www.repertorio.org/festivals.htm.

McCrone, David. *The Sociology of Nationalism: Tomorrow's Ancestors.* London: Routledge, 1998.

Morin, Claude. "Le Québec dans le monde, 1. L'émergence internationale du Québec." *La Societé québécoise après 30 ans de changements.* Ed. Fernand Dumont. Québec: Institut québécois de recherche sur la culture, 1990. 231–37.

"Never heard us?" *This American Life Home Page.* 10 June 2001. www.thisamerican-life.com. Pavlovic, Diane. "Les mouvances d'une dramaturgie: au-delà du statut de curiosité." *L'Annuaire théâtral* 27 (2000): 44–54.

Peel, William. "Crossing the Canada/US Border: People, Things, and Definitions." *Canadian Theatre Review* 63 (1990): 15–19.

Phelan, Peggy. *Unmarked: the politics of performance.* London: Routledge, 1992.

"Projecting Canadian Values and Culture," In Department of Foreign Affairs and International Trade/Ministère des affairs étrangères et du commerce international. *Canada in the World*. 1999. Rpt. *Department of Foreign Affairs and International Trade/Ministère des affairs étrangères et du commerce international Home Page*. 3 July 2001. http://www.dfaitmaeci.gc.ca/ english/foreignp/end-world/chap5.htm.

Robinson, Amy. "'It Takes One to Know One': Passing and Communities of Common Interest." *Critical Inquiry* 20 (1994): 715–36.

Salter, Denis. "The Idea of a National Theatre." *Canadian Canons: Essays in Literary Value*. Ed. Robert Lecker. Toronto: U of Toronto P, 1991. 71–90.

Schwartzwald, Robert. "Introduction/Presentation." *International Journal of Canadian Studies/Revue internationale d'études canadiennes* 21 (2000): 5–16.

Simon, Sherry. "Le Québec: Une culture traduite?" *Le Trafic des langues: Traduction et culture dans la literature québécoise*. Québec: Boréal, 1994. 35–55.

Simpson, Jeffrey. *Star-Spangled Canadians: Canadians Living the American Dream*. Toronto: Harper Collins, 2000.

Smith, Allan. *Canadian Culture, the Canadian State, and the New Continentalism*. Orono: U of Maine P, 1990.

Smith, Anna Deavere. "Not So Special Vehicles." *PAJ* 17.2-3 (May/September 1995): 77–89.

"Star Trek Timeline." *Official Star Trek Homepage*. 7 January 2002. http://www.startrek.com/information/timeline.asp.

Stephens, Peter. "Tours to US." E-mail to the author. 13 July 2001.

"Summary," In Department of Foreign Affairs and International Trade/Ministère des affairs étrangères et du commerce international. *Canada in the World*. 1999. Rpt. *Department of Foreign Affairs and International Trade/Ministère des affairs étrangères et du commerce international Home Page*. 3 July 2001. http://www.dfait-maeci.gc.ca/english/foreignp/cnd-world/summary.htm.

Taras, David. "Swimming Against the Current: American Mass Entertainment and Canadian Identity." *Canada and the United States: Differences that Count*. Ed. David M. Thomas. 2nd ed. Peterborough, ON: Broadview, 2000. 192–210.

Taylor, Charles. "The Politics of Recognition." *Multiculturalism: Examining the Politics of Recognition*. Ed. and Intro. Amy Gutmann. Princeton: Princeton UP, 1994. 25–74.

———. *Sources of the Self: The Making of Modern Identity*. Cambridge: Harvard UP, 1989.

————. "Why Do Nations Have to Become States?" *Reconciling the Solitudes: Essays on Canadian Federalism and Nationalism.* Ed. Guy Laforest. Montreal and Kingston: McGill-Queens UP, 1993, 40–58.

Thérien, Jean-Philippe, Louis Belanger and Guy Gosselin. "Québec: An Expanding Foreign Policy." *Québec: State and Society.* Ed. Alain-G. Gagnon. 2nd ed. Scarborough: Nelson Canada, 1993.

"TN Visas: Professionals under NAFTA." *U.S. Department of State, Bureau of Consular Affairs Home Page.* 8 July 2001. http://travel.state.gov/tn_visas.html.

Voss, Zannie Giraud, and Glenn B. Voss, with Christopher Shuff and Dan Melia. *Theatre Facts 2000: A Report on Practices and Performance in the American Not-for-Profit Theatre Based on TCG's Annual Fiscal Survey.* New York: Theatre Communications Group, 2001. Rpt. *Theatre Communications Group Home Page.* 8 July 2001. www.tcg.org.

"Who's Canadian?" *This American Life.* Episode 65. National Public Radio. WBEZ, Chicago. May 30, 1997. www.thisamericanlife.com.

Wilson, Rob. "Goodbye Paradise: Global/Localism in the American Pacific." *Global/Local: Cultural Production and the Transnational Imaginary.* Ed. Rob Wilson and Wimal Dissanayake. Durham: Duke UP, 1996.

Wyn Jones, Richard, ed. *Critical Theory and World Politics.* Boulder: Lynne Rienner Publishers, 2001.

In the MT Space

by Guillermo Verdecchia

> *Note: The following is re-constructed, re-written, from notes for a talk given at PERFORuM, a symposium cultivating multicultural theatre practice, presented by the MT Space in Kitchener, Ontario on 13 and 14 June 2005. It contains some things I said and some things I would have liked to say. It is an accurate reflection of some of my ideas on the subject of intercultural theatre, from the point of view of a practitioner.*

I want to start by saying that I'm very pleased to be here today. It hasn't always been the case that being in or near Kitchener-Waterloo was a pleasure for me. I lived here for many years, attended elementary and high school here, and, at the time, I was less than pleased about it.

This is from my play *Fronteras Americanas*. My first day at Anne Hathaway Public School (which was actually in Stratford, but … it's close enough):

> I am seven years old. The teacher at the front of the green classroom reads names from a list.
> Jonathon Kramer?
> Jonathon puts his hand up. He is a big boy with short red hair.
> Sandy Nemeth?
> Sandy puts her hand up. She is a small girl with long hair. When she smiles we can see the gap between her front teeth.
> Michael Uffelman?
> Michael puts his hand up. He is a tall boy sitting very neatly in his chair.
> My name is next.
> Minutes, hours, a century passes as the teacher, Miss Wiseman, forces her mouth into shapes hitherto unknown to the human race as she attempts to pronounce my name.
> Gwillyou - ree - moo…. Verdeek - cheea?
> I put my hand up. I am a minuscule boy with ungovernable black hair, antennae, and gills where everyone else has a mouth.
> You can call me Willy I say. The antennae and gills disappear. (32)

Here's another bit that spells out what KW felt like to me:

> Kitchener, Ontario. There in Kitchener, where I learned to drive, where I first had sex, where there was nothing to do but eat donuts and dream of elsewhere. There in Kitchener, where I once wrote a letter to the

editor and suggested that it was not a good idea to ban books in schools and it was there in Kitchener that a stranger responded to my letter and suggested that I go back to my own country. (28)

But some things have changed. I understand there are a couple of professional or semi-professional theatres in KW, and I know that Negativland, Diamanda Galas, Hildegard Westerkamp, and Brian Eno were all here recently for the Open Ears Festival. Who'd a thunk it?

Today's symposium is all about change. The MT Space is a reflection and an agent of a very significant change in this area: the recognition and celebration of the increasing cultural diversity that most of us, in urban centres especially, experience daily. Unless … you're in the theatre.

Though the situation has improved in the last ten to fifteen years, the professional theatre for adults still appears to practise a kind of unofficial apartheid. Yes, there are—thankfully—more productions that feature Asian- or Afri-Canadian plays and casts than there used to be, but still we rarely see—I hardly ever see—onstage, the same rich mix of voices, lives, histories, cultures, ethnicities, and experiences that we find on the street. Theatres for Young Audiences, such as Green Thumb, LKTYP and Theatre Direct, are much more responsive and responsible to their diverse audiences.

And when I talk about culturally diverse theatre, this is one of the things I mean. Stages that reflect our lives, our cities today; not stages that reflect historical privilege.

Which brings us back to the MT Space. We still need companies, people, to drive the agendas of inclusiveness and diversity. The name MT Space, speaks to the need for a space, a cultural space for culturally diverse artists. The name also speaks to an absence, a space to be filled. What and who will fill the space?

When I talk about culturally diverse theatre I'm not talking about plays that try to explain a minority culture to the dominant culture. I mean a theatre where artists are writing and creating out of particular and specific experiences, contexts, and environments—environments and contexts other than the dominant Anglo-Caucasian one—in their own idioms and voices. These pieces are dialogues with our cultures, with our contemporaries; they respond to and reflect our cultures critically, with the understanding that there exists a range of opinions, of practices, of beliefs, of attitudes in any community. There is no single way of being Canadian or Muslim or working-class. A culture is not a life-script, a set of rules, or interdictions. These plays are not social justice textbooks or etiquette instruction manuals. They are pieces that place the lives and experiences of visible and ethnic minority women and men at the centre of the drama. They are personal, political, aware of the power differentials that operate in the world; they are sly and funny, musical, and provocative, and though they can be deeply idiosyncratic and individual, they sometimes touch and acknowledge a deep current of shared feeling and experience.

That's what—it seems to me—is going on here at the MT Space. Majdi Bou-Matar has insisted that the focus here is not on folkloric or static versions of culture. Instead the emphasis appears to be on innovation, discovery, hybridity; this theatre seeks to generate something new. This, it seems to me, is the real meaning and value of the multicultural project in its broadest sense. The days of singing and dancing in traditional costume for a predominantly Anglo-Caucasian audience are LONG PAST!

I'm going to try to be a little more precise about what we're up to.

Noam Chomsky has said that the responsibility of the intellectual is to try to bring the truth about matters of human significance to an audience that can do something about them (56). In his discussion, Chomsky explicitly leaves aside aesthetic dimensions of intellectual responsibility. Nonetheless, I find his definition very provocative for us as theatre-makers. I want to underline one element: matters of human significance. The texts we create are significant. They provide context, they describe the world more accurately; they help us find our way.

Or they should do so.

How many irrelevant plays do you see or read a year? It's so hard to write a play, it requires so much effort and time, why expend that effort on something trivial, on something irrelevant? Brecht felt that the bourgeois theatre, the theatre of illusion, was just a branch of the narcotics trade. I think his comments apply to the theatre today just as much as they did when he was at work. Now, I'm not advocating a theatre of such Importance and Profundity as to be Stupefyingly Boring. Brecht himself insisted the theatre had to entertain. But I am suggesting that we must take our work—for work it is—seriously. What is worth writing? What is worth staging? Because—shocking as it may sound—not everything we think of is worth staging. Just because "it really happened" to you doesn't mean it merits a production. I don't think, for example, that I need to see another play about inter-generational conflict— usually predicated on the tension between "traditional" values and mores and contemporary "Canadian" ones—in an "ethnic" family.

This is from *The Adventures of Ali and Ali and the aXes of Evil*, which I co-wrote with my friends Marcus Youssef and Camyar Chai.

> **VOICE OVER.** Ladies and Girls, Boys and Men, Ali and Ali proudly present a new Canadian play: *Grasshopper White Eyes Dreams of Home.*
> *TIM enters, wearing a coolie hat with authentic pigtail sown into it, an apron, and carrying a butcher knife. He plays DAD. ALI HAKIM plays CHARLIE.*
> **DAD.** Son, I understand you're feeling conflicted.
> **CHARLIE.** You understand? You understand??!! Did you go to school in an all-white neighbourhood when you were growing up in Dao Dong Long province? Did you have to endure bad jokes about the shape of your eyes, the colour of your skin, or your bad driving habits? Did you have kids in your cafeteria puking their guts out just because you had a chicken claw snack pack?

You understand? You understand? Do you understand what it feels like to feel like a fruit—a banana—yellow on the outside but white on the inside?

He moves to the window special.

Do you feel your soul ripping to pieces because there are two people battling inside of you. A battle that cannot be won because one side is screaming with passion: I am Charlie Chew! I like to pitch and putt. And the other side is screaming with equal passion: I am Chew Mao Dong Hung! Grasshopper Stands Firm Against Foreign Devil Oppressor!

Do you understand that I am burning in the flames of internalized racism? Fuck your understanding. I'm tired of seeing the world through white eyes! I'm a chink and I'm proud! Fuck you daddy! Fuck you! I hate you! I hate you! I hate you daddy!!

DAD. Son, I love you no matter wha'.

CHARLIE breaks down into his fathers arms, crying.

CHARLIE. I love you, Daddy. I love you. I love you. I'm Canadian dammit. I'm Canadian.

DAD. There there, we're all Canadian, Charlie. We're all Canadian.

Moving to embrace CHARLIE, DAD accidentally impales his son with the butcher knife.

CHARLIE. Daddy?

DAD. Charlie?

CHARLIE dies. DAD moves to the window special.

DAD. Damn you, Canadian Dream!

Weeping, DAD commits seppuku, carving a maple leaf into his belly.

(50–51)

I understand that young or emerging writers (and I hope there are some here today) want to deal with their families in some way. The family is after all the crucible of our identity formation, but if you're going to write a family drama, make sure you're adding something to the vast quantity of material that already exists. I suspect that the ethnic family drama is essentially an attempt to fit non-mainstream voices or histories into a form that is acceptable or familiar to mainstream (or dominant culture) producers and audiences. There are many other aspects to who we are and how we came to be who we are that are worthy of theatrical exploration; let's look at some of those and give the family drama a rest.

Whatever it is you're writing or working on ... Look around. See where your story sits in relation to the big stories being told in your city, your community, the world. I have this quotation from Salman Rushdie that I like—I have no idea where I got it, but it's stayed with me—and (my version of) it says "[L]iterature's importance derives not from its success in some sort of ratings war, but from its success in telling us things we hear from no other quarter." Do our plays repeat accepted and official truths? Are we simply making bad and expensive television? Or are we struggling for something more difficult, more vital?

Chicana playwright Cherríe Moraga says she has

> always written as a self-acknowledged Chicana lesbian. With little to lose
> in the way of privilege in the theatre world I believe this has helped me
> get to the heart of the matter in my work. I feel less afraid of breaking
> taboo, so my characters feel less afraid to tell me what's really on their
> mind." (291–92)

What do we have to lose? What is keeping us from getting to the heart of the matter?
Who are we trying to please? Which internal critic is jabbering away in our head?
What are we afraid of? What do we have to lose? Or win?

If and when we manage to get to the heart of the matter, then what? Are we going
to jam our particular perspective on the world, on the moment, into dominant ways
of writing? Why should our plays look and sound like the latest Pulitzer Prize winner?
We need to find the forms that will express, will communicate most effectively. That
means that we may borrow what we can use from dominant (and familiar) ways
of writing and make them work for us, instead of trying to force-fit our singular
experiences into ready-made forms. If we're going to "reflect" our hybridized,
mongrel, evolving, complex lives and relationships accurately then we'll need
hybridized, mongrel, evolving, and complex forms to do so. We'll write from our lives,
from our perspectives, in our tongues and voices, telling the truth about matters of
significance by whatever means necessary.

That said, let's not indulge the romantic notion that all that matters is the pure
and unfettered expression of our feelings, please. Meyerhold said something like
"[P]assion without technique is like a letter without a stamp—it doesn't go
anywhere." We need to work, to practice, to study, to understand what has come
before, what our colleagues are up to now, and to carefully consider what is required
now.

I want to briefly consider the last part of Chomsky's dictum about the writer's
responsibility. Writers should tell the truth (we didn't touch that one—some other
time) about matters of human significance *to an audience that can do something about
them.* The audience. Whom do we speak to and with? How do we find, cultivate,
construct an audience we can speak to and with? An audience in a position to "do
something" about the matter under discussion? It's neither simple nor obvious. It's
not just a matter of matching the ethnicity of the playwright, for example, with an
audience targeted through advertising in "ethnic" publications. (I've tried that—it has
only been intermittently successful). Rahul Varma again has an interesting spin to
offer on the subject of audiences. He says that at Teesri Duniya (the company he runs
in Montreal) it's not a question of who speaks for whom, but rather, who will listen
to what.

It has repeatedly been my experience that diversity in programming yields a
diverse audience. But what is going on in the audience? (Wouldn't we love to know!)
One of the things that I think can happen in an audience is a renegotiation of one's

sense of self. Charles Taylor argues that we don't discover our own identity in isolation, rather we "negotiate it through dialogue, partly overt, partly internal, with others" (34). We can work out who we are in the theatre, through our encounters with others onstage and in the public.

This dialogic process of negotiating our identities and place in the world may (should? must?) continue after the performance. (This is one of way of interpreting Chomsky's idea about the audience being in a position to do something about the significant matter under discussion). But this conversation, this process, is not automatic. Nor is it easy to achieve. Diana Taylor warns us, "It is not so easy to achieve communication. Intercultural dialogue ... is even more difficult, and often treacherous. It turns, too often, into power's megalomaniacal monologue with itself" (235). The process of negotiation and dialogue has to be elicited or engendered by the form and *attitude* of the production. I mean many things by a production's attitude— too many things to address thoroughly here but I can give an incomplete list.

A production that is trying to elicit a negotiation of identity and not simply repeat tired assumptions or produce a "megalomaniacal monologue" will have given serious consideration to the factors that influence an audience before the play begins. The publicity for the show, the physical environment of the theatre, even the design of the programme have been understood as contributing to the meanings the audience will make. A production that strives to "challenge conventions" and, perhaps, even "reform" (inter)cultural boundaries (Bennett 180) must actively acknowledge and engage the audience. The audience must be something other than a passive consumer of spectacle. Theatrical opportunities will be found to challenge assumptions and "colonial" spectatorship. (Singing and dancing in folkloric costumes for an Anglo-Caucasian audience reproduces a colonial model of spectatorship. So do plays that try to "explain" the culturally "marginal" to an audience positioned as dominant or central). At the same time we must honour the audience's intelligence (to borrow a phrase from Howard Barker 43). One way to do this is to refuse to tidy up the performance.

A production, a play, that reassures, that resolves neatly, that offers easy "closure," will probably not give us in the audience anything to "do." Such a play will have purged us of difficult, potentially productive ideas and feelings. But if, as theatre-makers, we can write our way towards something that we didn't already know, if we manage to make our rehearsal, and our production a process of uncovering and understanding (rather than the repetition of rhetorical, theatrical, and institutional habits), if we implicate ourselves, if we acknowledge that we are as lost, as culpable, as brilliant as the audience, then we might join together into that necessary conversation and re-evaluation.

Then we might become part of a larger struggle: a process being carried out in private and public ways, at policy meetings and dance clubs, in bedrooms and restaurants, on community radio, in the *K-W Record*, in poems and on street corners. We become part of the ongoing, necessary process of identifying and defining, of understanding and discovering, the process of creating meaning, the process of creating meaningful, equitable, beautiful communities, cities, and lives.

(2006)

Works Cited

Barker, Howard. *Arguments for a Theatre*. London: Calder; New York: Riverrun, 1989.

Bennett, Susan. *Theatre Audiences: a Theory of Production and Reception*. London: Routledge, 1997.

Chomsky, Noam. *Powers and Prospects*. Boston: South End, 1996.

Moraga, Cheríe. "The Writer Speaks." *Out of the Fringe*. Ed. Caridad Svich and Maria Teresa Marrero. New York: Theatre Communications Group, 2000.

Taylor, Charles. *Multiculturalism: Examining the Politics of Recognition*. Ed. Amy Gutman, with additional commentary by Jurgen Habermas and K. Anthony Appiah. Princeton: Princeton UP, 1994.

Taylor, Diana. *The Archive and the Repertoire: Performing Cultural Memory in the Americas*. Durham: Duke UP, 2003.

Verdecchia, Guillermo. *Fronteras Americanas*. Vancouver: Talonbooks, 1997.

Youssef, Marcus et al. *The Adventures of Ali and Ali and the aXes of Evil*. Vancouver: Talonbooks, 2004.

TO Live With Culture:
Torontopia and the
Urban Creativity Script

by Laura Levin

It is midnight on October 1, 2006. For many Torontonians, this is a night *unlike* all other nights. From sunset to sunrise, the city is transformed into an art wonderland, with entire districts in the downtown core given over to performances, art installations, poetry readings, film screenings, and walking tours. Modeled after Paris's annual *Nuit Blanche* event begun in 2002, Toronto's curated all-nighter invites its inhabitants to re-experience the city through many hours and city blocks of artistic expression. And there are so many events to choose from! There is "Ballroom Dancing," a party where adults and kids gleefully dance the night away in a room filled with thousands of rubber balls. There is "Night Swim," where a Community Pool-turned-Roman-Bath is opened up to the public for a midnight dip. You can hop on the artist-run Toronto Performance Transit System to bond with a "non-passive moving public," or get up close and personal with Toronto's fabulous front lawns, one of many walking tours on offer of "Hidden Toronto" (*Nuit*). There are marble tournaments and sit-ins and house calling and all-night knits. There are car washes and clothes swaps and poetry slams and bedtime readings.

It is estimated that 425,000 spectators turn out for Toronto's "free all-night contemporary art thing" (*Nuit*), officially named *Scotiabank Nuit Blanche* after its very visible corporate sponsor. For many Torontonians, this night feels like a culmination of sorts for a city that is in the midst of a cultural renaissance. Rita Davies, the Executive Director of Toronto's Culture Division describes *Nuit Blanche* as "a superb finale to a spectacle [sic] year of culture in Toronto." "The city's Poet Laureate, Pier Giorgio Di Cicco, often says that Toronto needs to fall in love with itself," Davies explains. "With Nuit Blanche I think that's exactly what happened ... the joy, the wonder, the reverie ... it was magical" (*Nuit*). Davies' account, which simultaneously gestures towards the "magic" of the city and an all-too-apparent sense of lack ("Toronto *needs* to fall in love with itself"), echoes the language of the burgeoning "Torontopia" movement, a loose-knit group of urban activists and artists who are working to re-imagine Toronto's urban identity from within and transform its residents' daily interactions with public space. This utopian movement, propelled by a profound social optimism about what *Toronto is not but could one day be*, has been introduced to city-dwellers through a set of signature performative practices. These range from staged interventions like those found in *Nuit Blanche* (i.e. here, ballroom dancing is posed as a challenge to social atomization) to performances of urban self within its assorted manifestos and indie publications. In their poignant rehearsals of and for civic engagement, this guerrilla group aims to produce what Jill Dolan has called "utopian performatives," those moments where performance becomes a "doing," thereby producing "an affective vision of how the world might be better" (6).

While a number of performance theorists have taken a keen interest in Torontopia, celebrating it as evidence both of urban vitality and the productive marriage of performance and urban geography (see, e.g., Stonyk, Zaointz, and Nanni), some of the important critiques of this kind of civic cheerleading, advanced in the field of cultural geography, have not made their way into performance studies accounts of the movement. [1] Urban performance artists are celebrated as counter-cultural heroes either for having been "brave" enough to stage theatre outside of a theatre, bringing the spheres of theatre and the everyday into collision, or for asking spectators to engage with public space in a new, different, or unexpected way. In the former, we often fail to consider how the city streets, now remade as a site of performance, can mirror and/or reinforce the very social arrangements that we might have found in a "traditional" theatre venue. In the latter, we can forget to ask about the larger social, political, or economic forces that sanction this "magical" urban re-orientation.

In what follows, I hope to tease out a few areas of Torontopian performance that demand this kind of cultural critique and, in doing so, open up another form of civic engagement that is vital to the development of this important urban genre. In particular I will look at the seemingly unusual symmetry between the movement's anti-commercial self-fashioning strategies and the global marketing of Toronto by the city's tourist and culture industries. Strange bedfellows, perhaps, but this union has much to do with the mutual adoption of an increasingly popular urban creativity script, a set of cultural guidelines that promises to remake formerly uninspiring cities—or cities with low self-esteem—into culturally diverse hipster havens. Why are the utopian performatives of Toronto's creative "underground" so easily recuperated within corporate (i.e. Scotiabank) and gentrifying urban initiatives? Whose utopia is being rehearsed in the prevailing urban creativity script? If, as Dolan argues, a utopia is always partial and hence potentially exclusionary, what are the possibilities and limits of Torontopia's alternative social fantasies?

Toronto's Creative Utopias

We are creating culture. We are reclaiming public space. We are transforming neighbourhoods. We are rediscovering or recovering history.
We are trying to make home feel more like home. We are telling people
that we live in Toronto with a proud smile instead of an embarrassed
titter.

—Jason McBride and Alana Wilcox,
uTOpia: Towards a New Toronto (11)

In order to track the central preoccupations of the Torontopia movement, one need look no further than Coach House Books' recent publication, *uTOpia: Towards a New Toronto*, edited by Jason McBride and Alana Wilcox. A collection of texts by most of Torontopia's key players, the book reads as a compelling manifesto for this alternative urban scene. When reading across these articles, produced by artists and activists from very different fields (music, journalism, urban planning, theatre, etc.), a surprisingly coherent and unified history of the movement comes into view. It is a history told in a journalistic tone that lists toward the soundbite, showing the authors' hyper-awareness of their role in making cultural history and hinting at just how newsworthy their civic interventions have become. It is no secret that many of the figures featured in this book (David Meslin, Shawn Micallef, Sheila Heti, and Darren O'Donnell) have become important Toronto personalities, regularly asked to consult on public space issues in the popular press and, much more unusually, on policy matters arising at city hall.

Just as Torontopia straddles the realms of art and politics, so too do the origin stories of the movement. Most of the anthology's authors situate the beginnings of the movement at the turn of the millennium when "a bunch of youngish indie rockers, political activists and small press literati" (Keenan 22) began to see Toronto's apparently unremarkable civic identity as a major impediment to the growth of its artistic and cultural communities. Almost every article in *uTOpia* diagnoses Toronto as suffering from some kind of inferiority complex, as evidenced by titles like "Psssst. Modern Toronto Just Wants Some Respect" (Micallef 36), though few agree on the etiology of this identity-related disease. For some, this crisis comes out Toronto's excessive domesticity. Reinforcing familiar and formerly masculinist oppositions between public/private, active/passive, Bert Archer argues that Toronto has been perceived as "a place [where] people live, not a place where things happen, or, at least, not where the sorts of things happen that forge a place for the city in the imagination" (220). Others interpret Toronto's failures in the self-assertion department as a sign of teen angst: "it is a young city in a young country, famously grappling with its identity" (Keenan 24). A further explanation, which betrays a low-level liberal guilt or class ambivalence shared by several uTOpians, describes Toronto's urban persona as the product of years of altruism, with Torontonians guiltily trying to downplay the concentration of fiscal and cultural resources in their boomtown. The familiar, and for some, grating image of Toronto as Canada's centre of gravity comes to mind here. As musician Steve Kado puts it, the image of Toronto has been conflated with the moral bankruptcy of big business: "Yes, this is where the bank is that made the decision to close all of your farms. We're from the place where some guy in a blue suit fucked up your fishery and then closed it. It's got nothing to do with us" (qtd. in Barclay).

The response to this malaise is something called Torontopia. Although the term Torontopia is not uniformly embraced by figures in the movement—after all, naming the underground is the surest way to make it mainstream—it is the one most commonly applied to this eclectic group of agitators that seem to be working towards a similar set of goals. The word Torontopia, to begin with, has its roots in the local indie music community. Musicians Steve Kado and Jonathan "Jonny Dovercourt" Bunce[2] are usually credited for having popularized the term, with Kado specifically having first made it public on a show poster. Kado first heard the word when playing Fototag, a form of indoor tag with cameras. Fototag is one of many urban games for adults that have been devised by Torontopians as a means of activating the public sphere.[3] Manhunt, a variation on hide and seek played in areas like the Financial District, is another example of this live gaming fad that links together the subculture groups that I listed above. According to Kado, one Fototagger "had this idea for a hilarious magazine called Torontopia. It would be about how awesome Toronto was, but it would be about really boring stuff. It would be based on Japanese magazines that freak out about 'stuff,' about the corner of Grace and Dundas or something, which has a church and a convenience store and nothing else" (qtd. in Barclay).

The term Torontopia quickly caught on in a local music scene that was, in the late 90s, still divided into "little cliques and enclaves" (Keenan 26). This was a place where artists for the most part "did their own thing" and spent much of their time competing with each other for the little media attention that was available for experimental work. Most musicians saw themselves as eventually moving to major music centres like Los Angeles and New York where there was a well-established and thriving alternative music scene. The prospect of promoting a vibrant, homegrown music scene in Toronto, one that would acknowledge, support, and create links among local artists, made the concept of Torontopia especially urgent and seductive.

As *The Globe and Mail* reporter Carl Wilson wrote, Torontopia was a decidedly immediate and collective call to action; it "had to do with doing it here, doing it now, and doing it with whoever else felt the same way" (qtd. in Ravensbergen). This utopian impulse produced Wavelength, a pay-what-you-can weekly live music series founded in late 1999 by Jonny Dovercourt, Duncan MacDonnell and Derek Westerholm. The Wavelength series, named after Canadian artist Michael Snow's legendary avant-garde film, aimed to create a context for experimental or "oddball" work that was routinely overlooked by the media, and to build a support network for independent musicians. Wavelength has grown into an artistic meeting place for the city's now thriving indie scene. It is defined not only by its live shows, which have served to launch internationally renowned bands like the Hidden Cameras, the Constantines and Broken Social Scene, but also by a monthly zine, lightshows, art installations, and an indie rock drop-in centre.

Meanwhile similar Happenings were popping up in other cultural arenas, sharing with Wavelength an excitement about Toronto's future, a participatory aesthetic, and a DIY spirit. As Michael Barclay points out: "What began as a sly wink in the indie music scene soon evolved into a genuine philosophy applied to larger civic engage-ment. Torontopia was/is about re-imagining your city, creating new models, forging new communities, building sustainable institutions, celebrating diversity." Among the many very visible groups worshipping at the temple of Torontopia, we find the Toronto Public Space Committee (TPSC), a grassroots non-profit organization that has become the most outspoken defender of public space within this movement.

Under the leadership of founder David Meslin, TPSC has led several successful campaigns to protect common spaces in Toronto against the twinned influences of privatization and corporatization. These campaigns are routinely carried out through imaginative performative interventions: Guerrilla Gardening, in which activists plant flowers in neglected or banal areas of the city; the De-fence Project, where participants remove fences around residents' private property at their request; and Art Attacks, an evening of public art creation in the Gladstone Hotel followed by its installation over top of commercial advertising spaces. More recently, in 2005, Meslin launched City Idol, a competition among would-be city councillors that provides a forum for expressing new ideas about the city's future. Asking candidates to make speeches, improvise in debates, engage in press conferences and react to emergencies, City Idol provides a fresh new kind of actor training: rehearsals for political office. More crucially, City Idol offers to support the winners of the contest in their "real" campaigns for municipal election.

These and other Torontopian performances are documented in *Spacing*, a magazine loosely affiliated with TPSC that is devoted to bringing to life "the joys and obstacles surrounding Toronto's public spaces" ("Spacing"). In the pages of *Spacing*, published three times a year, and in its online blog, *Spacing Wire*, Torontonians can get a sense of just how many of the city's subcultural events have been given over in recent years to civic boosterism and community building. These include happenings like the Trampoline Lectures, a lecture series where Torontonians speak "on topics of personal rather than professional interest" (Keenan, "The Space") and 101 Games, evenings of Scrabble and Charade staged at the Drake Hotel which explore unexpected social interactions. Perhaps more prominent within Toronto's theatre community are [murmur], an audio annotation project that records residents' stories about Toronto and makes them accessible via cell phone at physical locations in the city, and The Talking Creature, social experiments conducted by playwright Darren O'Donnell and his group Mammalian Diving Reflex, which examine the art of conversing with strangers out in public. While few of these performative interventions are as overtly political as the TPSC's advocacy actions, they share a belief in the socially liberating potential of creative play and its ability to transform the city from a place of alienation to a place of meaningful connection.

There has been a lot of talk about "creativity" in Toronto lately, and much of it has been generated by one of the heroes of the Torontopia movement, Mayor David Miller. Not so coincidentally, Miller has written the forward to *uTOpia* and he is mentioned fawningly by many of the authors in the book. "In a way, with the election of Miller," Keenan muses, "the Torontopia movement already has one of its own in office" (35). A disciple of urban planning guru Jane Jacobs—and her vision of distinctive neighborhoods, common public spaces, and resident-scaled environments— Miller has, since his election in 2003, routinely turned to arts and culture as the primary ground for urban renewal. "Creativity should play a role in every part of our daily lives," Miller has said, "When it comes to city building, it is vital that we constantly challenge our own limitations, and force ourselves to re-imagine everything about our city" ("Creativity").

This statement sits well with the Torontopian ethic of civic engagement, and this group has been unflagging in its support of Miller's "creative" initiatives, from increasing funding to the arts, to providing creative outlets for young artists, to beautifying and preserving public spaces. Yet it is important to remember that this language of creativity, so appealing to the urban avant-garde, is also the central feature of the "Creative City Model," a capitalist "urban-development script" (Peck 740) that has become central to regeneration projects and the branding of cities within the global marketplace. The Creative City is the brainchild of Richard Florida, who has put a forward a proposition that will sound somewhat counterintuitive to the starving artist, that "human creativity is the ultimate economic resource" (xiii). In his book, *The Rise of the Creative Class: And How It's Transforming Work, Leisure, Community, and Everyday Life*, Florida argues that we are moving from a corporate-based economy to a creative economy, one driven in other words by people who "do creative work for a living" (xiii). "These are the scientists, engineers, artists, musicians, designers and knowledge based professionals," Florida explains, "whom collectively I call the 'Creative Class'" (xiii). In order for cities to thrive in this new climate, they must lure this coveted class of creative types and the best way to do this is by producing those hip environments to which they are, it seems, inexorably attracted. In a practical sense, this means reversing the traditional corporate priorities of urban construction:

> The physical attractions that most cities focus on building—sports stadiums, freeways, urban malls and tourism-and-entertainment districts that resemble theme parks—are irrelevant, insufficient or actually unattractive to many Creative Class people. What they look for in communities are abundant high-quality amenities and experiences, an openness to diversity of all kinds, and above all else the opportunity to validate their identities as creative people. (Florida 218)

This form of validation, Florida asserts, is a must for the creative class, as the institutions that have in the past conferred a sense of personal identity, such as family or religion, are no longer the dominant influences on these nonconformists' lives. Instead, "creatives" are more likely to gain a sense of identity from their "knowledge work," lifestyle choices, leisure and recreation, and acts of consumption. Not only does Florida put forward a set of narrow performance guidelines to help the drab city transform itself into the vivacious "creative city," but he also includes a whole section of urban rankings at the back of his book that grades cities based on how well they "perform" this extreme makeover. Quantifying what many of us would consider to be ephemeral, qualitative social phenomena, Florida creates such categories as the "Composite Diversity Index," which measures the number of gays and lesbians, bohemians, and "foreign-born people" there are in a particular region, an urban mélange that he tells us is sure to attract the coolest of the creatives.

If, as Jamie Peck has intimated, Florida has essentially composed a "creative city" script, with privileged "actors" being called upon to take on "significant new roles" within a rapidly changing urban economy, it is clear that Toronto has rushed in along with other cities like Memphis, Cincinnati and Detroit to mount its own spectacular production. In Toronto, this script takes the form of the "Culture Plan for the Creative City," a 10-year program adopted in 2003 by City Council to foster Toronto's economic growth. In Toronto's official "Culture Plan" documents, which carefully adhere to Florida's diversity imperative by for example including photos of multicultural theatre productions (e.g. Cahoots Theatre's *Coups and Calypsos*),[4] the Council tells us that "arts, culture and heritage are the vital centre of Toronto's expanding economy" ("Culture" 4). They are the prime vehicles through which Toronto should be "selling" itself, both to its own citizens and to the world.

Peck reminds us that this new type of marketing relies on "the earnest efforts of creative strivers, since these experiences suggestively place the goal of creative transformation within reach, even for 'ordinary' places" (749). Following the creativity script to a T, then, Toronto's Culture Plan might be seen to call upon individual artists to "concretize the creativity script through [their] performative enactment in the domain of everyday urban policy" (Peck 749). It is "not enough to generate new ideas or even new offerings" ("The Creative" 16), Toronto's Culture Plan tells artists, they must also consider how these ideas will sell, how they can simultaneously be turned into "amenities that everyone wants to see" (18). "We have two tough audiences to entice," the Culture Plan states, "Torontonians, and those who might want to come and visit if they knew about what we have to show. How can we talk to both groups best?" (16).

While Toronto is thus being transformed to cater specifically to the needs of artists and knowledge-workers, these members of the creative class are in turn asked to produce marketable projects that will "wow" (16) an international audience.

Few Torontopians would want to see themselves as the stars of this creative show, working to bring a new form of capitalist spectacle into being. After all, a huge part of this subcultural identity rests on its resistance to the alienating structures of capitalism, which have replaced "real" community values with commercial or retail values. One of its central avant-garde influences in this respect has been the practices of the Situationists, a group of French leftist intellectuals who, in the 1960s and 70s, sought to revive the Marxist potential of their surrealist ancestors. One of the ur-texts of the Situationists, often cited as a genealogical precedent by Torontopians, is Guy Debord's *Society of the Spectacle* (1967), a book that suggests that the marketing of commodities has supplanted authentic human relations, thereby hastening the colonization of social life by capital. Reproducing a familiar Platonic schism between the original and the copy, between reality and artifice, Debord argues that this commodity fetishism produces an "immense accumulation of spectacles. Everything that was directly lived has moved away into a representation" ("The Society").[5] Mass media images like billboard advertisements have robbed us of a "lived reality," a preexisting utopian plenitude.

Many of the culture-jamming actions staged by the Torontopians are explicitly designed along Debordian lines, reproducing the binary of authentic life versus inauthentic spectacle. Day Milman, for example, recently organized a "Civic Holiday" in Trinity Bellwoods Park on August 7, 2006, to offer participants release from "our pressing duty to consume." "It's an acknowledgement that public space and shopping are virtually synonymous," Milman explains, "and a quiet appreciation of the existence of the park as a place we can enjoy together without the mediating presence of product and mass media." Day Milman is perhaps best known for Free Dance Lessons, where strangers are invited out of the blue "to dance, take a lesson, or give one" ("July"). In this collaboration with Paige Gratland, alienated citizens are given the opportunity to reconnect with each other and with their own bodies. In this respect, the lessons challenge members of the public to engage "in non-commodified exchange."

Another version of the neo-Situationist critique can be seen in the performative actions of the Toronto Psychogeography Society, a "loose collection of relentless *flâneurs*, explorers and walkers," co-founded by Shawn Micallef, an editor at *Spacing* and curator of [murmur]. This form of civic engagement is directly taken from the Situationists, who believed that the key to resisting the banality of urban life was to reinterpret the city from below and experiment with the spatial conventions of everyday experience. To achieve this end, they invented the practice of "psychogeography," defined as "study of the specific effects of the geographical environment, consciously organized or not, on the emotions and behavior of individuals" (Debord, "Introduction"). The chief form of psychogeographical research was the dérive or "the drift," which involved a kind of aimless urban wandering; the drifter must lose himself in the city, surrendering to "the attractions of the terrain and the encounters they find there" (Debord, "Theory"). According to Sadie Plant, this practice of willed self-disorientation, inherited from the surrealists, was "intended to cultivate an awareness of the ways in which everyday life is presently conditioned and controlled, the ways in which this manipulation can be exposed and subverted, and the possibilities for chosen forms of constructed situations in the post-spectacular world" (58). Following in the footsteps of their Situationist predecessors, the Toronto Psychogeographers meet every Thursday to go on a dérive through a different part of the city. As their website states, this practice allows participants to "step out of their daily routine and explore the city's overlooked corners to imagine the dynamics of a better future urban environment." Like the ad-busting interventions of affiliate groups like TPSC, these walks are devised to undermine and recontextualize the constructed urban spectacle, using public space for reasons other than the capitalist ones for which they were planned or designed.

Yet while this anti-commercial stance has been regularly described in accounts of the Torontopia movement, few have registered the interesting contradictions that attend this position when it is expressed in Toronto's present cultural context. It is important to note, in particular, that the subversive Torontopian actors and Florida's urban creative capitalists often find themselves sharing the same creative script. Most obviously, these two groups share a strong anxiety around self-differentiation and a related willingness to engage in the kind of global competition that drives the creative city model. As cultural geographers like David Harvey have pointed out, cities have increasingly been forced to take up a competitive entrepreneurial stance within the postmodern global economy:

> Cities and places now, it seems, take much more care to create a positive and high quality image of place, and have sought an architecture and forms of urban design that respond to such need. That they should be so pressed, and the result should be a serial repetition of successful models (such as Baltimore's Harbor Place) is understandable, given the grim history of deindustrialization and restructuring that left most major cities in the advanced capitalist world with few options except to compete with each other, mainly as financial, consumption, and entertainment centres. Imaging a city through the organization of spectacular urban spaces became a means to attract capital and people (of the right sort) in a period (since 1973) of intensified inter-urban competition and urban entrepreneurialism." (92)

Within this process, global cities must construct a unique and alluring urban image in order to attract investors and tourists. Toronto's choice to don the mantle of creativity is thus part of its global branding activities and its desire to beat out competitor cities in the struggle for talent and capital. This strategy is clearly outlined in Toronto's Culture Plan: "We can be very proud of what we have achieved, but we must be very smart if we are going to keep growing. Our competitors are snapping at our heels. They outspend and outmarket us. [...] In order to keep our best at home and entice their counterparts from around the world to visit or move right in, we must become more intensely Toronto and less like everywhere else" ("Culture" 9–10). Although the Culture Plan articulates a sincere commitment to redressing social inequalities—for example, by providing low-cost admission to cultural events for youth under 20 and supporting community arts programs for disadvantaged groups—it reproduces what Peck sees as the creative city's unacknowledged neoliberal framework. Florida's strategies, he points out, "work quietly with the grain of extant 'neoliberal' development agendas, framed around interurban competition, gentrification, middle-class consumption and place-marketing—quietly in the sense that the banal nature of urban creativity strategies in *practice* is drowned out by the hyperbolic and overstated character of Florida's sales pitch, in which the arrival of the Creative Age takes the form of an unstoppable social revolution" (741). The rhetoric of social revolution is of course vital to securing Torontopian buy-in, as few members of this enlightened class would want to see themselves as promoting liberal capitalist policies.

"How can we transform ourselves into a productive, creative, attractive global city with a sharply delineated, vital identity?" Toronto's Culture Plan asks ("The Creative 19). Although Torontopians might be reticent to jump in with a solution, especially given their allergy to commodity branding and the imperialist forces of globalization, they implicitly answer this call in their devoted civic boosterism. This is evident in the editorial letter published in the inaugural issue of *Wavelength*: "We all feel that Toronto is on the cusp of something, something exciting and potentially big. The music being made here—in all genres—is unparalleled on an international scale. We want to let people here, and in the rest of the world, know about it" (qtd. in Keenan 27).

This ebullient performance of civic pride is accompanied in Torontopian litera-ture with attempts to explain, with dutiful specificity, what is so unique about Toronto. In this sense, a new answer to the Culture Division's question is articulated in almost every article in *uTOpia*, where contributors help to construct a "sharply delineated, vital identity" for their city, calling our attention to its lack of founding mythologies (18), its mix of architectural styles (36), its radical playfulness (63), its progressive values (172), or its "live-and-let-live/all-in-the-same-canoe ethos" (275). Mirroring what Peck sees as a central ambiguity in the creative city thesis—its oscilla-tion between "cosmopolitan elitism and pop universalism" (741)—Torontopians frequently reassure us that they are only playing at global competition and not investing in it in any real sense. As Jonny Dovercourt argues, "Torontopia is not about fomenting civic rivalries; *it's about making your town the best*, no matter where you live. Improving the place you call home, rather than just complaining about how *boring* it is" (232). Whatever the intention, this form of urban cheerleading plays an important role in the global inter-urban war for talent by transforming Toronto into a hipster or bohemian magnet and by sending a message to the world about the rich cultural products than can be found there.

That this should be the case makes perfect sense if one follows the logic of Florida's creative class argument. "Capitalism," he tells us, "has also expanded its reach to capture the talents of the heretofore excluded groups of eccentrics and noncon-formists. In doing so, it has pulled off yet another astonishing mutation: taking people who would have been viewed as bizarre mavericks operating at the bohemian fringe and setting them at the very heart of the process of innovation and economic growth" (6). To see this kind of incorporation at work, it is also instructive to look at the treatment of tourism within the Torontopia and Creative City camps. Torontopians often set up their art interventions in opposition to the "touristy" urban image marketed by Toronto's Culture Division. The "Curious Walking Tours" of the city, for example, which were guided by Torontopian celebrities throughout *Nuit Blanche*, were billed as anti-tourist, offering the uninitiated a more authentic experience of Toronto: "Have you ever wondered what happens in the nooks, crannies and alleyways of Toronto? Are you curious about what lies beneath the typical tourist façade? Uncover Toronto's secrets through specialized walking tours that will enrich both locals and visitors" (*Nuit*). In a similar fashion, the [murmur] project positions itself over and against Toronto's official tourist mapping, which in the past has been restricted to large-scale attractions or sites transparently linked to big business. "[murmur] believes interesting things don't just happen at the Rogers Centre and Nathan Phillips Square," the project's curators explain, "the city is full of stories, and some of them happen in parking lots and bungalows, diners and front lawns. The smallest, greyest or most nondescript building can be transformed by the stories that live in it" ("About"). Reproducing what Lucy Lippard calls "the underlying contradic-tion of tourism ... the need to see beneath the surface when only the surface is available," [murmur] offers spectators a chance to see "behind the [tourist] stage set, or the wizard's curtain" (8).

While Torontopian walking tours present themselves as off-the-beaten-track alternatives to official tourist culture, they end up acting out the new repertoire of urban renewal strategies mapped out in Toronto's new tourism agenda. As Florida has noted, creative city strategies always privilege the local; a city becomes "world-class" by capitalizing on its local authenticity, something that can only be experienced by individuals on the neighborhood and interpersonal scale. The Torontopian genre of "the walk" nicely fulfills this requirement, much like the street-level cultural events that Florida prescribes for creative cities—for example, festivals in the park or weekly farmers markets. More specifically, these walks respond to the Culture Division's appeal to ordinary citizens to retell "Toronto's story" and to make it sound like an "invitation to the world" ("Toronto on"). As if describing project [murmur], Toronto's Culture Plan seeks out local narratives that can be performed as part of the tourist spectacle: "Toronto has ghostly layers of history and prehistory beneath its streets waiting to be rediscovered, and stories to tell that are utterly unique: it also has the means to make them known. Taken all together, Toronto has remarkable powers to bring the Creative City into glittering focus" (10).

It only makes sense then that these strategies of recovering authentic local histories have been placed at the centre of the Toronto's Live With Culture campaign, a 16-month celebration of Toronto's arts scene programmed by the Culture Division. Their signature events include the Secret City program in *Nuit Blanche* which allows citizens to "participate in uncovering secrets concealed by or revealed in the 20 artworks by Toronto artists, many of them the driving force behind the younger cultural movement in the city" (*Nuit*), and the Humanitas Festival, a month-long celebration of the histories found in Toronto's diverse communities. For the latter event, Toronto enlisted [murmur] to drive around in an Airstream trailer/recording studio, gathering the unheard stories of people on the street. Connecting these creative projects to the larger Culture Plan, which aims to discover the story that Toronto will market to the world, the Humanitas website tells participants: "Your stories *are* The Toronto story" ("Introducing").

Given these telling meetings between Torontopia's urban interventions and Toronto's self-branding, we might ask what it is about Torontopia's performances that are so easily recuperated within the creative city paradigm. Although there are many possible answers to this question I would suggest that it has something to do with the particular kind of creativity celebrated by both parties. In both *uTOpia* and Florida's *Rise of the Creative Class*, we witness what Peck describes as "the mobilization of creativity as a distinctly positive, nebulous-yet-attractive, apple-pie-like phenomenon: like its stepcousin flexibility, creativity preemptively disarms critics and opponents, whose resistance implicitly mobilizes creativity's antonymic others—rigidity, philistinism, narrow mindedness, intolerance, insensitivity, conservativism, *not getting it*" (765). Embracing the image of Toronto that I began with, a city of magic and of endless creative play, obviously makes these performances much easier to market.

"The streets of Toronto become a playground," the Psychogeography Website states, "and each route presents a new urban adventure." Yet committing to these exciting new forms of *flâneurie* demands that you have a lot of free time on your hands, or at least a boss that lets you come in to work late the next day. Like their Benjaminian forebears, these urban actors have enough leisure time to get lost in the city, to play Manhunt every week, and to stay up all night at *Nuit Blanche*.

The most publicly admired of the Torontopians have fit the profile of the creative type celebrated both by Florida and by Toronto's Live With Culture campaign: a young, optimistic, fit, and able-bodied artist. This ideal type is present in the TO Live With Culture ads, which feature attractive artists of different races, each displaying their physical agility as they go about their creative work. A dancer stretches over to touch her toe. A filmmaker does the splits as she prepares to slate a scene. Jared Mitchell and R.M. Vaughan recently staged an alternate campaign in response called *Live Without Culture*, a series of less than flattering portraits of an artist with his gut hanging out, in an effort to remind Torontonians that this playful image is ultimately an oversimplification of an artist's life. Vaughan writes, "Making art is sometimes lots of fun—but most of the time it is just a job. ... Sometimes, art makes you feel ugly and disillusioned, mean and slow, fat and tired. This reality needs to be presented to the public alongside the more peppy vision offered by the official campaign." To put this argument in a different way, while the creativity script presents an art that seems to transcend its work function, it is also disturbingly selective about what constitutes art. If, as Toronto's Culture Plan suggests "creative individuals" are "the heart of Toronto's cultural experience" (10), what place is there for the rest of the city's workers who make up the seemingly uncreative service industry, or for those stuck working the late shift while the creatives roll by revelling in the nightscape at *Nuit Blanche*?

This raises larger questions that will need to be answered in future years about how "diversity" is being embraced by and reflected in the Torontopia movement. Most of the key players who I have described are white and the chief spokespersons are young men (Sheila Heti is a notable exception). Certainly this helps to explain some of the gendered urban metaphors found in histories of the movement. Take for example Erik Rutherford's analogy in the very first essay of *uTOpia*, which likens Toronto to "a young man, just out of university. He's done a degree in commerce with a minor in the humanities, where he's showing surprising talent. He's always been an A student and done what was expected of him. When you praise him, he doesn't believe you; when you criticize him, his pride is wounded" (21). This masculine civic persona is contrasted with the city of Paris who is likened to a "brilliant and beautiful woman" who is "past her finest hour" (20). It is telling that Rutherford chooses to align Torontopia with the male point of view instead of "*une jolie jeune femme*" (21), especially given that women's issues are so rarely addressed in the movement's interventions into public space. In this sense, the Torontopians have yet to explore the role that gender difference plays in the experience of *flâneurie*, a practice that has traditionally been dominated by men. Can women *flâneurs*, we might ask, safely drift around Toronto at night?

There are few descriptions in *uTOpia*, moreover, of the tensions surrounding ethnicity and race, something that would complicate the image of multicultural harmony promoted by the creative city script. The photo in the far left on the Live With Culture website sums up the dominant approach found here as well; here we see a white man, his face painted in a design that mimics an implicitly racialized tribal pattern. This visually mirrors the salad bar approach to multiculturalism that is found on Toronto's Tourism website, a multiculturalism of aesthetically pleasing surfaces. "You know the feeling you get when you come across an amazing menu and want to order every dish?" the website states, "That's what it's like to be here." This orientation is echoed in Archer's *uTOpia* contribution where he describes those parts of the city that he'd like to get to know better; here, ethnic neighborhoods are reduced to "halal pizza places (with names like Mecca and Madina) in the Muslim section of the Danforth that you're always intending to get a slice from, just to see" (223). Within this framework, ironically, ethnic neighborhoods are defined more by tourist consumption than by the experiences of those people who might live there.

Perhaps the biggest shortcoming of Torontopia and the creativity script to which it is linked is its reification of existing city mappings and reproduction of familiar centres and peripheries.⁶ This is apparent not only in the overwhelming focus on the downtown core in *uTOpia* but also in the performances of civic engagement that I have described. [murmur], for example, has recorded its stories primarily in the trendy downtown areas of Spadina, Kensington Market, and the Annex. When Torontopian actions are staged in the northern parts of the city, it is usually in places like Scarborough, which are seemingly chosen because they allow artists to explore the other side of the tracks. Flipping through the pages of *uTOpia* we get the sense that this group's civic pride extends only to those chosen people who live downtown, with the other parts of Toronto routinely dismissed as "relentless housing farms" (Evans 96). According to Archer, these outlying developments are places "where people move when their domestic lives become more important than their social ones" (223).

Unfortunately this idea is reinscribed in the two maps that are included with *uTOpia*, each depicting an imagined Toronto or what they call "Toronto the Could." These whimsical cartographies, which include napping stations in public parks, outdoor alleyway movies, scenic canals, and giant sandboxes, are cut off just north of Dupont as if sailing towards St. Clair (or the rest of Toronto for that matter) would lead you off the edge of the world. Here be dragons. Scarborough, North York, and Etobicoke make appearances in small insets on one of the two maps, presumably to remind us that the margins, or at least their traditional stand-ins, have not been forgotten. Confirming the movement's obsession with becoming part of the urban in-crowd, this map includes a hyperbullet train to "all good cities" and a special underwater tunnel to Manhattan. Strangely, within this brave new world, which promises to deliver new social mappings, all of Toronto's neighborhoods stay in the same place, maintaining the city's ethnic enclaves and its central tourist destinations. Perversely, as these cartographers succeed in making Toronto's downtown core a more desirable place to live, housing costs will rise and the city's vaunted diversity—one of its central creative ingredients—will undergo a powerful homogenizing shift. In this respect, the resistant mappings of Torontopia can obscure their complicity with gentrification and the overarching capitalist system.

Towards a New Torontopia

Clearly the Torontopia movement, born in the then-smoky halls of Toronto's indie music venues, formerly shabby hotels and almost famous social scenes, has gained a lot of momentum in recent years. As I have suggested, this has much to do with the convergence of creativity and capital, which always offers a mix of pitfalls and rewards. As the Torontopian and creativity scripts continue to collide, some urban actors have begun to notice and to question this seemingly symbiotic union. "It's been fun to experience the last few years," Darren O'Donnell writes in his new book, *Social Acupuncture*, "as art production has begun to incorporate increasingly sophisticated approaches to fostering dialogue and we've seen the proliferation of events designed to create networks, friendships and communities. But this, too, now seems about to unravel with its co-optation by a manic and hollow civic boosterism" (22).

Transforming this awareness into a productive steering mechanism for the movement will require more widespread acknowledgement of this co-optation, and more importantly, of the artist's tacit investment in being co-opted. Artists are in the enviable and unusual position of being consulted by the governing apparatus about how to conduct its business. Knowing the role that one is expected to play, and actively deciding whether, when, and how to play it, will allow the Torontopia movement to go beyond the creativity script. There, beyond the formulae for determining the optimal number of bohemians per square kilometre, is a more socially responsive city where an expansive understanding of creativity is sought out, where cartographies of centre and margin are thoughtfully remapped, and where artmaking is no longer commissioned by lack.

(2007)

Notes

[1] This, in part, is symptomatic of a larger blind spot in performance studies around the politics of environmental and site-specific performance. As Una Chaudhuri argues, the genre's "political implications remain largely unexamined" (24).

[2] To express his civic pride, Jonathan Bunce adopted the name of one of Toronto's main streets, Dovercourt.

[3] This can also be viewed as part of the massively multiplayer urban gaming movement which is gaining momentum in North America in general, which includes practices such as parkour, flash mobs, and alternate reality gaming.

⁴ These images can be found in "The Creative City: A Workprint," a brochure put out by the Toronto Culture Division. The document also includes photos of Ballet Creole, Caribana, a First Nations man, and Cahoots Theatre's *Mom, Dad, I'm Living With a White Girl.*

⁵ See Kaja Silverman's chapter "The Screen," in *Threshold of the Visible World* for a critique of Debord. "There can never have been a moment when specularity was not at least in part constitutive of human subjectivity," she argues, "ever since the inception of cave drawing, it has been via images that we see and are seen" (195).

⁶ For an insightful discussion of this problem, see McLean and Laidley.

Works Cited

"About [murmur]." *Murmurtoronto.ca.* 30 October 2006. http://murmurtoronto.ca/about.php.

Archer, Bert. "Making a Toronto of the Imagination." *uTOpia: Towards a New Toronto.* Ed. Jason McBride and Alana Wilcox. Toronto: Coach House, 2005. 220–29.

Barclay, Michael. "This is Torontopia." *Exclaim!: Canada's Music Authority.* 23 August 2006. 26 October 2006. http://www.exclaim.ca/index.asp?layid=22&csid1=5527.

Chaudhuri, Una. *Staging Place: The Geography of Modern Drama.* Ann Arbor: U of Michigan P, 1995.

"Creativity is Key to Modern City Building, International Expert Tells Toronto." *Official Website of the City of Toronto.* 7 December 2004: News Releases. 26 October 2006. http://wx.toronto.ca/inter/it/newsrel.nsf/0/5bbb934ac91969728 5256f64007783e1?OpenDocument.

"Culture Plan for the Creative City." *Official Website of the City of Toronto.* 2003. Toronto Culture Division. 26 October 2006. http://www.toronto.ca/culture-brochures/2003_cultureplan.pdf.

Debord, Guy-Ernest. "Introduction to a Critique of Urban Geography." *Nothingness.org: The Situationist International Text Library.* 1955. Originally published in *Les Lèvres Nues #6.* 31 October 2006. http://library.nothingness.org/articles/SI/en/display/2.

Dovercourt, Jonny. "Making a Green Scene." *uTOpia: Towards a New Toronto.* Ed. Jason McBride and Alana Wilcox. Toronto: Coach House, 2005. 230–37.

Dolan, Jill. *Utopia in Performance: Finding Hope at the Theater.* Ann Arbor: U of Michigan P, 2005.

Evans, Philip. "Paved Impressions." *uTOpia: Towards a New Toronto.* Ed. Jason McBride and Alana Wilcox. Toronto: Coach House P, 2005. 96–103.

Florida, Richard. *The Rise of the Creative Class: And How It's Transforming Work, Leisure, Community, and Everyday Life.* New York: Basic Books, 2002.

Harvey, David. *The Condition of Postmodernity.* Oxford: Blackwell, 1990.

"Introducing the Humanitas Festival." *TO Live With Culture: The Ultimate Guide to Toronto's Culture Scene.* 2005. City of Toronto. 26 October 2006. http://www.live-withculture.ca/.

Keenan, Edward. "Making a Scene: A Bunch of Youngish Indie Rockers, Political Activists and Small-Press Literati are Creating the Cultural History of Toronto." *uTOpia: Towards a New Toronto.* Ed. Jason McBride and Alana Wilcox. Toronto: Coach House, 2005. 22–35.

————. "The Space Between Party and a Show: Offbeat Salon Packs Them In." *Eye Weekly.* 24 October 2002: Arts Section. 30 October 2006. http://www.eye.net/eye/issue/issue_10.24.02/arts/trampolinehall.html.

Lippard, Lucy. *On the Beaten Track: Tourism, Art, and Place.* New York: New Press, 1999.

McBride, Jason and Alana Wilcox. "Introduction," *uTOpia: Towards a New Toronto: Towards a New Toronto.* Ed. Jason McBride and Alana Wilcox. Toronto: Coach House, 2005. 10–13.

McLean, Heather and Jennifer Laidley, *"Utopia for whom?: Cautionary thoughts on celebrating the neoliberal city, uTOpia: Towards a New Toronto,"* *Fuse Magazine* 29.4 (2006): 45–47.

Milman, Day. "Civic Holiday, Trinity Bellwoods Park." *Act 27: Shop. Public Acts 1–29.* 7 August 2006. 27 October 2006. http://www.publicacts.ca/act27/.

————. "July 18 Dance Lessons." *Lttr.org.* Events Page. 20 October 2006. http://www.lttr.org/events/july18.html.

Mitchell, Jared and R. M. Vaughan. "Live Without Culture." *Paulpetro.com.* April 2006. Paul Petro Contemporary Art. 30 October 2006. http://www.paulpetro.com/vaughan/2006.shtml.

Nanni, Laura. "Anecdotes Off the Map: Sites Archived, Revisited and Replayed in Toronto and Montreal." *Canadian Theatre Review* 126 (2006): 71–77.

Nuit Blanche. 2006. Live With Culture. 30 October 2006. http://nuitblanche.livewithculture.ca.

O'Donnell, Darren. *Social Acupuncture: A Guide to Suicide, Performance and Utopia.* Toronto: Coach House P, 2006.

Peck, Jamie. "Struggling with the Creative Class." *International Journal of Urban and Regional Research.* Vol 29.4 (December 2005): 740–70.

Plant, Sadie. *The Most Radical Gesture: The Situationist International in a Postmodern Age.* London: Routledge, 1992.

Ravensbergen, David. "No Band is an Island: Aaargh! Records and Self Righteous Records Guide Victoria's Musical Utopia." *Discorder Magazine.* November 2006. 30 October 2006. http://discorder.ca/2006/04/no-band-is-an-island/.

Rutherford, Erik. "Toronto: A City in Our Image." *uTOpia: Towards a New Toronto.* Ed. Jason McBride and Alana Wilcox. Toronto: Coach House, 2005. 16–21.

Silverman, Kaja. *The Threshold of the Visible World.* New York: Routledge, 1996.

"Spacing." *Spacing: Understanding Toronto's Urban Landscapes.* 2006. Spacing Publications. 30 October 2006. http://spacing.ca/contact.htm.

Stonyk, Zoë. "Monolith Makeover: The Art of Subversive Urban Enhancement." *Canadian Theatre Review* 126 (2006): 68–70.

"The Creative City: A Workprint." *Official Website of the City of* Toronto. April 2001. Toronto Culture Division. 26 October 2006. http://www.toronto.ca/culture/brochures/brochureculture_workprint.pdf.

The Society of the Spectacle. Nothingness.org: The Situationist International Text Library. 1967. Translated by Black and Red. 31 October 2006. http://library.nothingness.org/articles/SI/en/display/16

"Toronto on Target as Creative City," *Official Website of the City of Toronto.* Toronto Culture Division. 26 October 2006. http://www.toronto.ca/culture/cultureplan.htm.

Toronto Psychogeography Society. "Who." *Toronto Psychogeography Society Website.* 26 October 2006. http://psychogeography.ca/who.htm.

Zaiontz, Keren. "Urban Research, Collective Report, Audience Encounter: Darren O'Donnell Discusses the Benefits of Talking to Strangers in Diplomatic Immunities." *Canadian Theatre Review* 127 (2006): 87–92.

Suggested Further Reading

Canadian Theatre Criticism

Alcorn, Emmy. "The Economy versus God (Everything Comes with Fries)." *Canadian Theatre Review* 108 (2001): 43–47.

Arnott, Brian. "Performing Arts Buildings in Canada." *Contemporary Canadian Theatre: New World Visions.* Ed. Anton Wagner. Toronto: Simon and Pierre, 1985.

Bessai, Diane. "Centres on the Margin: Contemporary Prairie Drama." *Contemporary Issues in Canadian Drama.* Ed. Per Brask. Winnipeg: Blizzard, 1995.

Canadian Theatre Review 93 (1997). "Regions, Regionals and Regionalism." Ed. Ann Wilson.

Chadder, Jane. "The Canada of Sinclair's *The Blood is Strong*: 'A Country Without a Mythology?'" *Canadian Drama/L'Art dramatique canadien* 3.2 (1977): 100–04.

Czarnecki, Mark. "To Serve the Art." *Canadian Theatre Review* 45 (1985): 6–11.

Dickinson, Peter. "Duets, Duologues, and Black Diasporic Theatre: Djanet Sears, William Shakespeare, and Others." *Modern Drama* 45.2 (2002): 188–208.

Downton, Dawn Rae. "Soap on a Rope." *Canadian Theatre Review* 62 (1990): 24–29.

Filewod, Alan. "Community and Development in Canadian Popular Theatre." *Canadian Drama/L'Art dramatique canadien* 16.2 (1990): 173–83.

———. "'One Big Ontario': Nation-Building in The Village of the Small Huts." *Contemporary Issues in Canadian Drama.* Ed. Per Brask. Winnipeg: Blizzard, 1995. 208–20.

———. "The Political Dramaturgy of the Mummers Troupe." *Canadian Drama/L'Art dramatique canadien* 13.1 (1987): 60–72.

Gómez, Mayte. "'Coming Together' in Lift Off! '93: Intercultural Theatre in Toronto and Canadian Multiculturalism." *Essays in Theatre/Études Théâtrales* 13.1 (1994): 45–59.

Grace, Sherrill. "A Northern Quality: Herman Voaden's Canadian Expressionism." *Canadian Drama/L'Art dramatique canadien* 8.1 (1982): 1–14.

———. "Putting the North on Stage." *Canada and the Idea of North.* Montreal and Kingston: McGill-Queen's UP, 2001: 140–55.

Hauck, Gerhard. "Redrawing *The Drawer Boy.*" *Canadian Theatre Review* 108 (2001): 29–34.

Hinchcliffe, Judith. "*Still Stands the House:* the Failure of the Pastoral Dream." *Canadian Drama/L'Art dramatique canadien* 3.2 (1977): 183–91.

Johnston, Denis. "Drama in British Columbia: A Special Place." *Contemporary Issues in Canadian Drama.* Ed. Per Brask. Winnipeg: Blizzard, 1995. 171–83.

Kerr, Rosalind. "Borderline Crossings in Sharon Pollock's Out-Law Genres: *Blood Relations* and *Doc.*" *Theatre Research in Canada/Recherches théâtrales au Canada* 17.2 (1996): 200–15.

Knowles, Richard Paul. "Responding to the Region: Co-operative Theatre on Mulgrave Road." *Canadian Theatre Review* 37 (1983): 51–54.

———. "Survival Spaces: Space and the Politics of Dislocation." *Canadian Theatre Review* 88 (1996): 31–34.

Lane, Richard J. "Passing the Province, or, the Tyrannical Prehension: Theoretical Readings of BC Theatre." *Canadian Theatre Review* 101 (2000): 7–10.

Levin, Laura. "Environmental Affinities: Naturalism and the Porous Body." *Theatre Research in Canada/Recherches théâtrales au Canada* 24.1–2 (2003): 171–86.

Little, Edward. "Aesthetic Morality in the Blyth and District Community Play: A Festival Hosts a Celebration." *Canadian Theatre Review* 90 (1997): 20–27.

McKinnie, Michael. *City Stages: Theatre and Urban Space in a Global City.* Toronto: U of Toronto P, 2007.

Moser, Marlene. "Reconfiguring Home: Geopathology and Heterotopia in Margaret Hollingsworth's *The House that Jack Built* and *It's Only Hot for Two Months in Kapuskasing.*" *Theatre Research in Canada/Recherches théâtrales au Canada* 23:1–2 (2002): 1–18.

Nunn, Robert. "Spatial Metaphor in the Plays of Judith Thompson." *Theatre Research in Canada/Recherches théâtrales au Canada* 10.1 (1989): 3–29.

O'Donnell, Darren. *Social Acupuncture: A Guide to Suicide, Performance and Utopia.* Toronto: Coach House P, 2006.

Page, Malcolm. "Canadian Plays in Britain: 1972–85." *Canadian Drama* 12.1 (1986): 64–73.

Parker, Brian. "Is There a Canadian Drama?" *The Canadian Imagination: Dimensions of a Literary Culture.* Ed. David Staines. Cambridge, Mass: Harvard UP, 1977. 152–87.

Peel, Bill. "Models for the Future: The Space Crisis in Toronto." *Canadian Theatre Review* 60 (1989): 81–89.

Reimer, Margaret Loewen. "Regionalism as a Definitive Characteristic in Four Canadian Dramas." *Canadian Drama/L'Art dramatique canadien* 2.2 (1976): 144–53.

Stuart, Ross. "A Circle Without a Centre: The Predicament of Toronto's Theatre Space." *Canadian Theatre Review* 38 (1983): 18–24.

Walcott, Rinaldo. "Dramatic Instabilities: Diasporic Aesthetics as a Question for and about Nation." *Canadian Theatre Review* 118 (2004): 99–118.

Wallace, Robert. "Growing Pains: Toronto Theatre in the 1970's." *Canadian Literature* 85 (1980): 71–85.

———. "Survival Tactics: Size, Space and Subjectivity in Recent Toronto Theatre." *Essays in Theatre/Études théâtrales* 10.1 (1991): 5–15.

———. "Writing the Land Alive: The Playwrights' Vision in English Canada." *Contemporary Canadian Theatre: New World Visions.* Ed. Anton Wagner. Toronto: Simon and Pierre, 1985: 69–81.

Whittaker, Robin. "Feeling Around the Repressed: Performing Uncanny Space in Sally Clark's *Jehanne of the Witches.*" *Canadian Theatre Review* 120 (2004): 5–11.

Wilson, Ann. "Border Crossing: The Technologies of Identity in *Fronteras Americanas.*" *Australasian Drama Studies* 29 (1996): 7–15.

Spatial Criticism

Bachelard, Gaston. *The Poetics of Space.* Boston: Beacon, 1994.

Baker, Alan R.H. and Derek Gregory, eds. *Explorations in Historical Geography.* Cambridge: Cambridge UP, 1984.

Barnes, Trevor and James Duncan, eds. *Writing Worlds.* London: Routledge, 1992.

Bell, David and Gill Valentine, eds. *Mapping Desire: Geographies of Sexualities.* London: Routledge, 1995.

Blunt, Alison and Gillian Rose. *Writing Women and Space: Colonial and Postcolonial Geographies.* New York: Guilford P, 1994.

Carlson, Marvin A. *Places of Performance: The Semiotics of Theatre Architecture.* Ithaca, N.Y.: Cornell UP, 1989.

Caulfield, Jon. *City Form and Everyday Life: Toronto's Gentrification and Critical Social Practice.* Toronto: U of Toronto P, 1996.

Chaudhuri, Una. *Staging Place: The Geography of Modern Drama.* Ann Arbor: U of Michigan P, 1995.

Cosgrove, Denis and Stephen Daniels, eds. *The Iconography of Landscape: Essays on the Symbolic Representation, Design and Use of Past Environments.* Cambridge: Cambridge UP, 1988.

De Certeau, Michel. "Spatial Practices." *The Practice of Everyday Life.* Vol. 1. Berkeley: U of California P, 1984. 91–130.

Duncan, James and David Ley. *Place/Culture/Representation.* London: Routledge, 1993.

Florida, Richard. *The Rise of the Creative Class: And How It's Transforming Work, Leisure, Community, and Everyday Life.* New York: Basic Books, 2002.

Foote, Kenneth et al., eds. *Re-Reading Cultural Geography.* Austin: U of Texas P, 1994.

Fuchs, Elinor, and Una Chaudhuri, ed. *Land/Scape/Theater.* Ann Arbor: U of Michigan P, 2002.

Harvey, David. *The Condition of Postmodernity.* Oxford: Blackwell, 1989.

———. *Spaces of Capital: Towards a Critical Geography.* New York: Routledge, 2001.

Johnston, R.J. *A Question of Place: Exploring the Practice of Human Geography.* Oxford: Blackwell, 1991.

Knowles, Ric. "Space and Place." *Reading the Material Theatre.* Cambridge: Cambridge UP, 2004. 62–91.

Landy, Charles. *The Creative City: A Toolkit for Urban Innovators.* London: Earthscan, 2000.

Lash, Scott and John Urry. *Economies of Signs and Space.* London: Sage, 1994.

Lefebvre, Henri. *The Production of Space.* Oxford: Blackwell, 1991.

Livingstone, David. *The Geographical Tradition: Episodes in the History of a Contested Enterprise.* Oxford: Blackwell, 1992.

Logan, John, and Harvey Molotch. *Urban Fortunes: The Political Economy of Place.* Berkeley: U of California P, 1987.

Massey, Doreen B. *Spatial Divisions of Labour: Social Structures and the Geography of Production.* 2nd ed. Basingstoke: Macmillan, 1995.

McAuley, Gay. *Space in Performance: Making Meaning in the Theatre.* Ann Arbor: U of Michigan P, 1999.

Modern Drama. "Space and the Geographies of the Theatre." Special Issue. 46.4 (2003).

Pile, Steve and Nigel Thrift. *Mapping the Subject: Geographies of Cultural Transformation.* London: Routledge, 1995.

Price, M. and M. Lewis. "The Reinvention of Cultural Geography." *Annals of the Association of American Geographers* 83.1 (1993): 1–17.

Read, Alan, ed. *Architecturally Speaking: Practices of Art, Architecture and the Everyday.* London: Routledge, 2000.

Sassen, Saskia. *Cities in a World Economy.* 2nd ed, *Sociology for a New Century.* Thousand Oaks, Calif.: Pine Forge, 2000.

Schechner, Richard. "6 Axioms for Environmental Theatre." *TDR* 12.3 (1968): 41–64.

Sennett, Richard. *The Fall of Public Man.* New York: W.W. Norton, 1976.

Sewell, John. *The Shape of the City: Toronto Struggles with Modern Planning.* Toronto: U of Toronto P, 1993.

Smith, Neil. *The New Urban Frontier: Gentrification and the Revanchist City.* London: Routledge, 1996.

Soja, Edward W. *Postmodern Geographies: The Reassertion of Space in Critical Social Theory.* London: Verso, 1989.

Theatre Journal. "Theatre and the City." Special Issue. 53.2 (2001).

Tompkins, Joanne. *Unsettling Space: Contestations in Contemporary Australian Theatre.* Basingstoke: Palgrave Macmillan, 2006.

Urry, John. *Consuming Places.* London: Routledge, 1995.

Wiles, David. *A Short History of Western Performance Space.* Cambridge: Cambridge UP, 2003.

Wolf, Stacy. "Civilizing and Selling Spectators: Audiences at the Madison Civic Center." *Theatre Survey* 39.2 (1998): 7–23.

Notes on Contributors

Rob Appleford is Associate Professor in the English and Film Studies Department at the University of Alberta. He teaches and researches in the areas of Canadian Aboriginal/First Nations Literatures and Native American Literatures, with an emphasis on contemporary and emergent writing and critical theory. His articles have appeared in the *American Indian Culture and Research Journal, Canadian Theatre Review, Modern Drama, Theatre Research in Canada/Recherches théâtrales au Canada, Canadian Literature, Social Text* [forthcoming], and in the book collections *Native America: Portrait of the Peoples, Siting the Other: Marginal Identities in Australian and Canadian Drama, Crucible of Cultures: Anglophone Drama at the Dawn of a New Millennium, Canadian Author Series: Drew Hayden Taylor.* He has edited a collection of essays on Canadian *Aboriginal Drama and Theatre* for Playwrights Canada Press (2005). Currently, he is at work on a book-length study of Aboriginal literatures and critical theory entitled *The Ghost/Dance of North American Aboriginal Literature.*

Diane Bessai is Professor Emeritus of English at the University of Alberta. She is the author of *Playwrights of Collective Creation* (1992) and numerous essays, articles, and reviews on Canadian theatre and drama in journals and book collections. She has been the editor of the Prairie Play Series at NeWest Press since 1980 and from 1976–1988 served as theatre editor of *NeWest Review.*

Alan Filewod is Professor of Theatre Studies at the University of Guelph. His research fields are Canadian theatre cultures, political intervention theatre, and subjunctive authenticity roleplay. He is the author of *Collective Encounters: Documentary Theatre in English Canada* (1987), *Performing Canada: The Nation Enacted in the Imagined Theatre* (2002) and, with David Watt, *Workers' Playtime: Theatre and Labour since 1970* (2001).

Mayte Gómez's research on *Fronteras Americanas* was part of the MA thesis she wrote for the University of Guelph in 1993. After a PhD on Cultural Studies at McGill University, she moved to the University of London (England) as a SSHRCC postdoctoral fellow. She is now a Lecturer in Hispanic Studies at the University of Nottingham. After publishing a book on communist cultural politics in Spain in the 1930s, her current research is on Spain as an intercultural society.

Sherrill Grace teaches Canadian literature and culture in the English Department at the University of British Columbia. She has published widely on Canadian subjects with special emphasis on the North, theatre, and twentieth century writers. Her most recent books include *Canada and the Idea of North* (2001), *Inventing Tom Thomson* (2004), and *Theatre and AutoBiography* (2006), co-edited with Jerry Wasserman. She is currently writing *Making Theatre: A Life of Sharon Pollock*.

Erin Hurley is Assistant Professor of English at McGill University. Work in her speciality areas of Québécois performance and national performatives has been published in *Theatre Journal, Theatre Research in Canada /Recherches théâtrales au Canada, Canadian Theatre Review,* and in the edited volume, *Performing National Identities: International Perspectives on Contemporary Canadian Theatre.* She is guest-editor of a forthcoming special issue of *Globe: Revue internationale d'études québécoises* on "les arts de la scène".

Ric Knowles is Professor of Drama at the University of Guelph. He is editor of *Canadian Theatre Review* and former editor (1999–2005) of *Modern Drama,* author of *The Theatre of Form and the Production of Meaning* (1999), *Shakespeare and Canada* (2004), *Reading the Material Theatre* (2004), and *Remembering Women Murdered by Men* (2006, with the Cultural Memory Group), and editor of *Theatre in Atlantic Canada* (1988), *Staging Coyote's Dream* (2003, with Monique Mojica), *Modern Drama: Defining the Field* (2003, with Joanne Tompkins and W.B. Worthen), *Judith Thompson* (2005) and *The Masks of Judith Thompson* (2006). He is general editor of Critical Perspectives on Canadian Theatre in English.

Alexander Leggatt is Professor Emeritus of English at University College, University of Toronto, and a Fellow of the Royal Society of Canada. His publications include *English Stage Comedy 1480–1990: Five Centuries of a Genre* (1998) and *Shakespeare's Tragedies: Violation and Identity* (2005). He is editor of *The Cambridge Companion to Shakespearean Comedy* (2002).

Laura Levin is Assistant Professor of Theatre at York University. Her research focuses on contemporary theatre and performance art, performing gender and sexuality, site-specific and intermedia performance. Laura has worked as a director and dramaturge on a number of productions in North America and is currently participating in two transnational research projects, *Common Plants* and *Blur Street,* which investigate intersections of performance, geography, and digital technologies. Laura is on the Executive Board of the Association for Canadian Theatre Research and chaired its 2007 conference on the theme of "Performing the City." She is co-editor of the *Canadian Theatre Review*'s "Views and Reviews" section and is also co-editing an issue of *Theatre Research in Canada/Recherches théâtrales au Canada* on space and subjectivity in performance.

Michael McKinnie is Senior Lecturer in Drama at Queen Mary, University of London (United Kingdom). He is the author of *City Stages: Theatre and Urban Space in a Global City* (2007), and his work has appeared, among other places, in *Theatre Journal, Modern Drama, Theatre Research in Canada/Recherches théâtrales au Canada, Contemporary Theatre Review, Essays on Canadian Writing,* and *Canadian Theatre Review.* He has also served as reviews editor for *Modern Drama.*

Guillermo Verdecchia is a playwright, director, and actor. He is the author or co-author of, among other plays, *Fronteras Americanas, The Adventures of Ali and Ali and the aXes of Evil,* and *bloom.*

Anton Wagner is Adjunct Professor in the Dance Department at York University. He is the editor of ten books on Canadian theatre and drama including *Contemporary Canadian Theatre: New World Visions* and *Establishing Our Boundaries: English Canadian Theatre Criticism.*

Robert Wallace is Professor Emeritus of English and Drama Studies at Glendon College, York University, in Toronto. He is author of *Staging a Nation: Evolutions in Contemporary Canadian Theatre* (2003), *Theatre and Transformation in Contemporary Canada* (1999), and *Producing Marginality: Theatre and Criticism in Canada* (1990); co-author of *The Work: Conversations with English-Canadian Playwrights* (1981); editor of *Quebec Voices* (1986) and *Making, Out: Plays by Gay Men* (1992). In addition to writing and lecturing widely about theatre and cultural policy, he has produced 10 radio documentaries and edited more than 20 volumes of Canadian plays.